D1258423

WRITER: JONATHAN HICKMAN
ARTISTS: ALESSANDRO VITTI & GIANLUCA GUGLIOTTA [ISSUE #16]

COLOR ARTIST: SUNNY GHO OF IFS
LETTERER: ARTMONKEYS' DAVE LANPHEAR
COVER ARTISTS: JIM CHEUNG, MARK MORALES & JUSTIN PONSOR
ASSOCIATE EDITOR: LAUREN SANKOVITCH
EDITOR: TOM BREVOORT

COLLECTION EDITOR: JENNIFER GRÜNWALD
EDITORIAL ASSISTANT: JAMES EMMETT & JOE HOCHSTEIN
ASSISTANT EDITOR: ALEX STARBUCK
ASSOCIATE EDITOR: JOHN DENNING
EDITOR, SPECIAL PROJECTS: MARK D. BEAZLEY
SENIOR EDITOR, SPECIAL PROJECTS: JEFF YOUNGQUIST
SENIOR VICE PRESIDENT OF SALES: DAVID GABRIEL

EDITOR IN CHIEF: JOE QUESADA
PUBLISHER: DAN BUCKLEY
EXECUTIVE PRODUCER: ALAN FINE

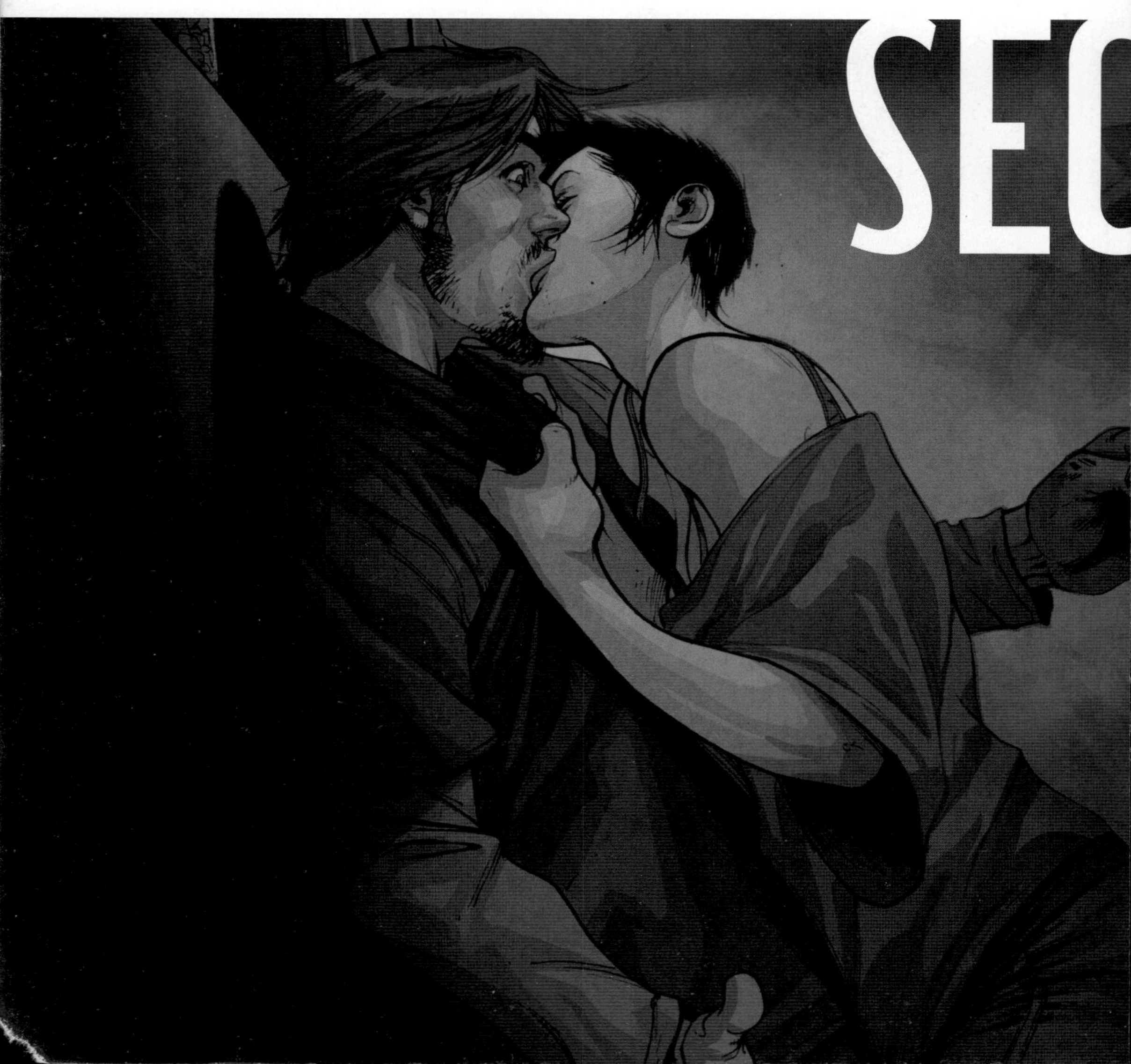
SEC

RET WARRIORS

CREATED BY: BRIAN MICHAEL BENDIS & ALEX MALEEV

SECRET WARRIORS VOL. 3: WAKE THE BEAST. Contains material originally published in magazine form as SECRET WARRIORS #11-16. First printing 2010. Hardcover ISBN# 978-0-7851-4757-2. Softcover ISBN# 978-0-7851-4758-9. Published by MARVEL WORLDWIDE, INC., a subsidiary of MARVEL ENTERTAINMENT, LLC. OFFICE OF PUBLICATION: 417 5th Avenue, New York, NY 10016. Copyright © 2009, 2010 and 2010 Marvel Characters, Inc. All rights reserved. Hardcover: $19.99 per copy in the U.S. and $22.50 in Canada (GST #R127032852). Softcover: $15.99 per copy in the U.S. and $17.99 in Canada (GST #R127032852). Canadian Agreement #40668537. All characters featured in this issue and the distinctive names and likenesses thereof, and all related indicia are trademarks of Marvel Characters, Inc. No similarity between any of the names, characters, persons, and/or institutions in this magazine with those of any living or dead person or institution is intended, and any such similarity which may exist is purely coincidental. **Printed in the U.S.A.** ALAN FINE, EVP - Office of the President, Marvel Worldwide, Inc. and EVP & CMO Marvel Characters B.V.; DAN BUCKLEY, Chief Executive Officer and Publisher - Print, Animation & Digital Media; JIM SOKOLOWSKI, Chief Operating Officer; DAVID GABRIEL, SVP of Publishing Sales & Circulation; DAVID BOGART, SVP of Business Affairs & Talent Management; MICHAEL PASCIULLO, VP Merchandising & Communications; JIM O'KEEFE, VP of Operations & Logistics; DAN CARR, Executive Director of Publishing Technology; JUSTIN F. GABRIE, Director of Publishing & Editorial Operations; SUSAN CRESPI, Editorial Operations Manager; ALEX MORALES, Publishing Operations Manager; STAN LEE, Chairman Emeritus. For information regarding advertising in Marvel Comics or on Marvel.com, please contact Ron Stern, VP of Business Development, at rstern@marvel.com. For Marvel subscription inquiries, please call 800-217-9158. Manufactured between 6/14/10 and 7/14/10 (hardcover), and 6/14/10 and 12/15/10 (softcover) by

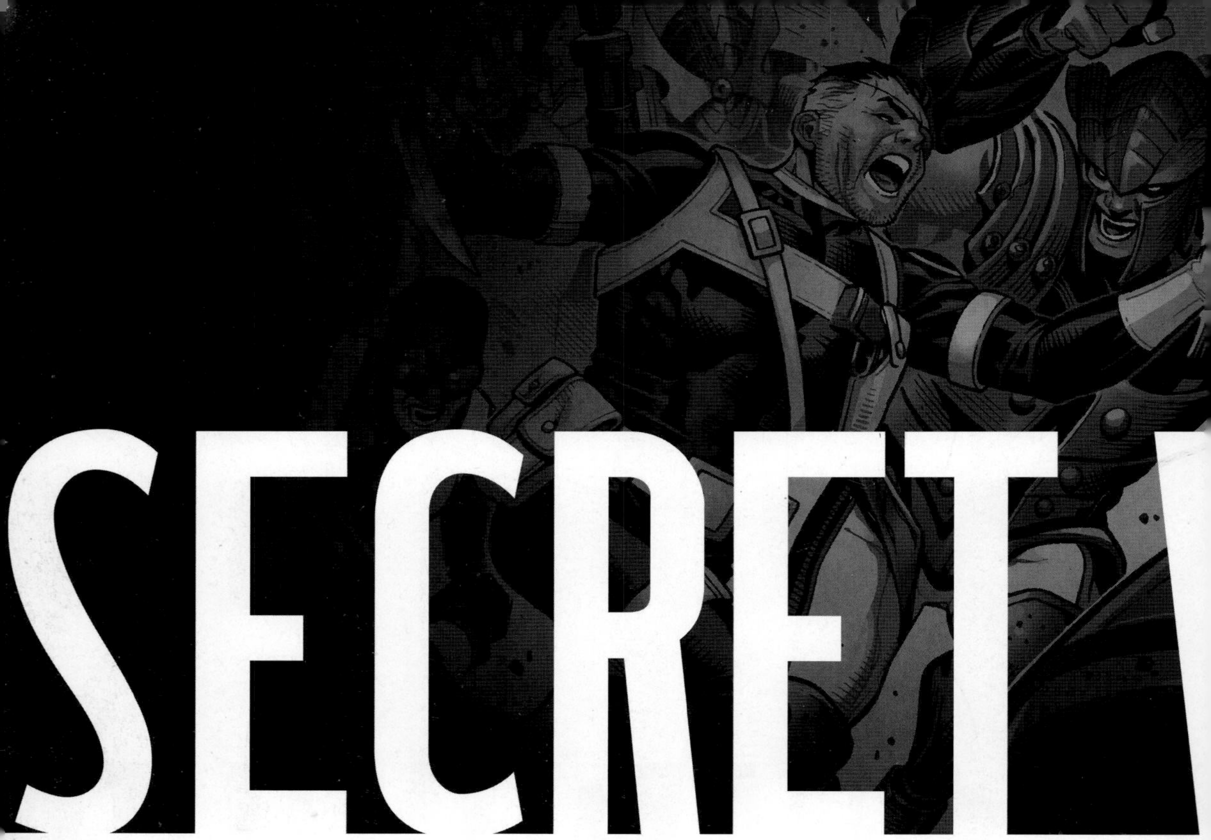
SECRET

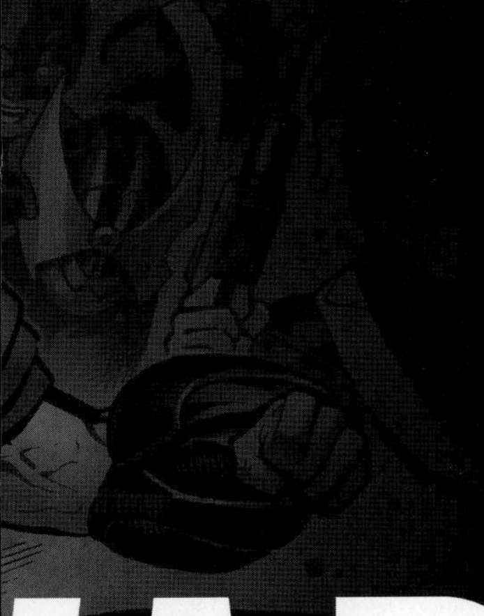

ARRIORS

VOL THREE WAKE THE BEAST

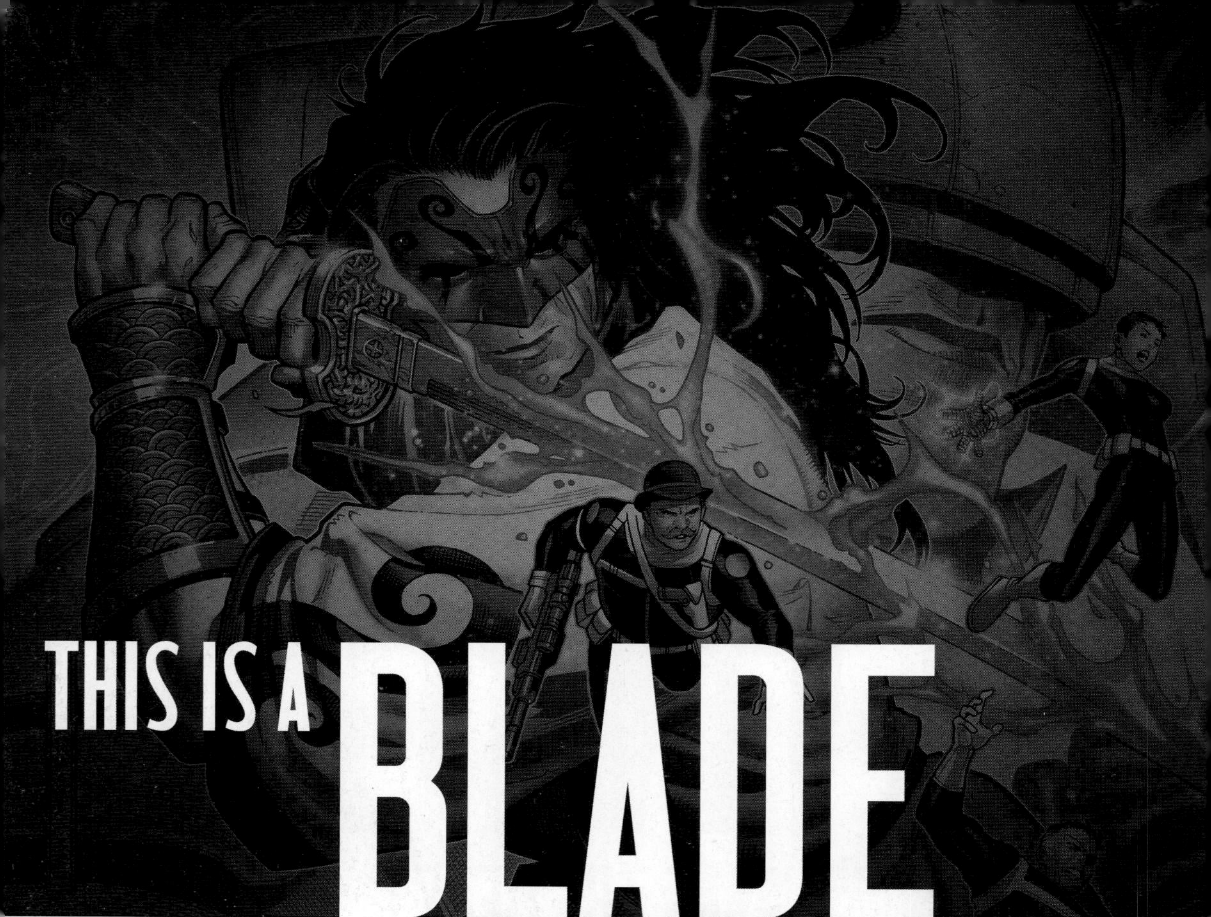

THIS IS A BLADE

WITH A PURPOSE

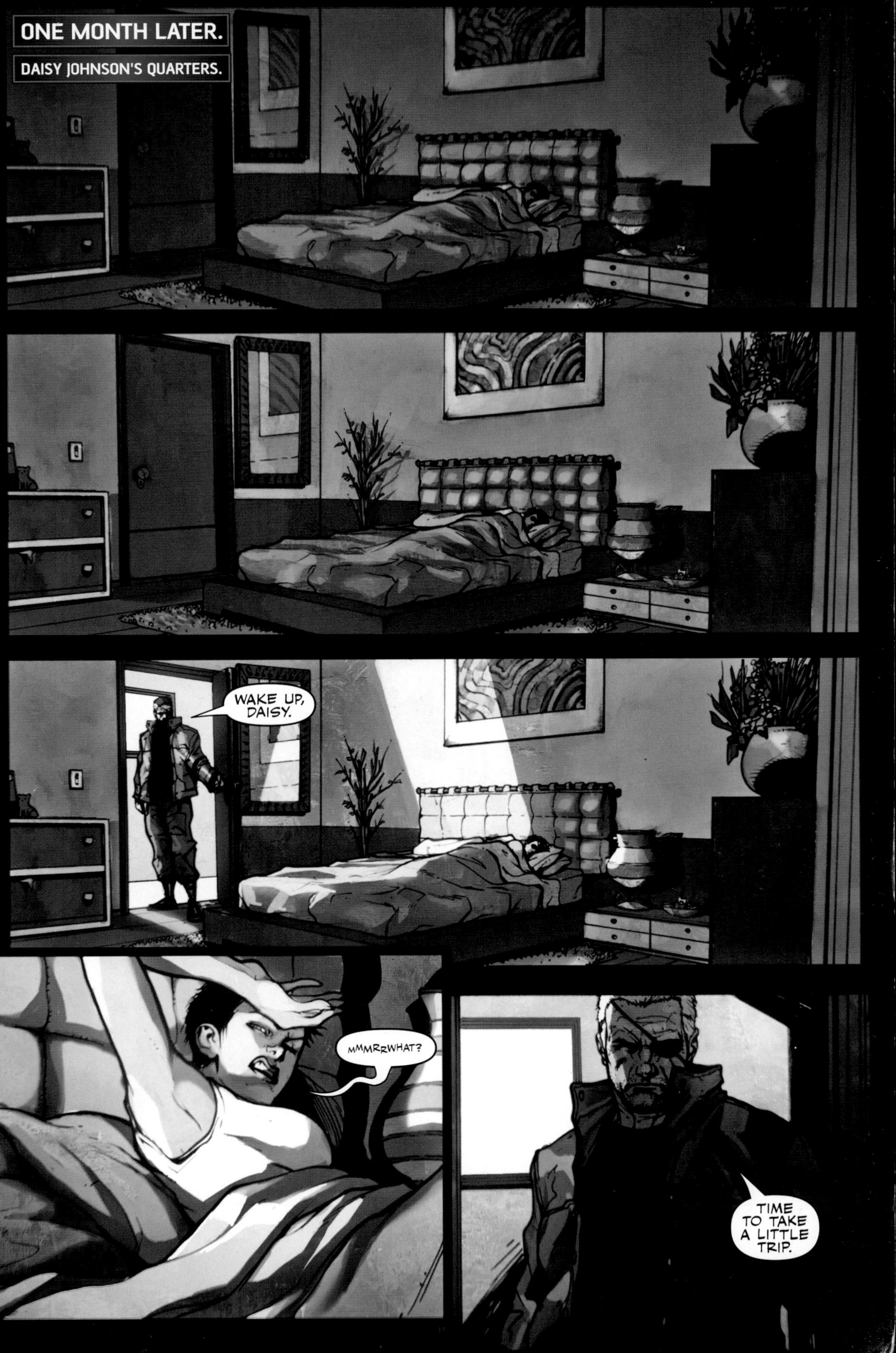
ONE MONTH LATER.
DAISY JOHNSON'S QUARTERS.
WAKE UP, DAISY.
MMMRRWHAT?
TIME TO TAKE A LITTLE TRIP.

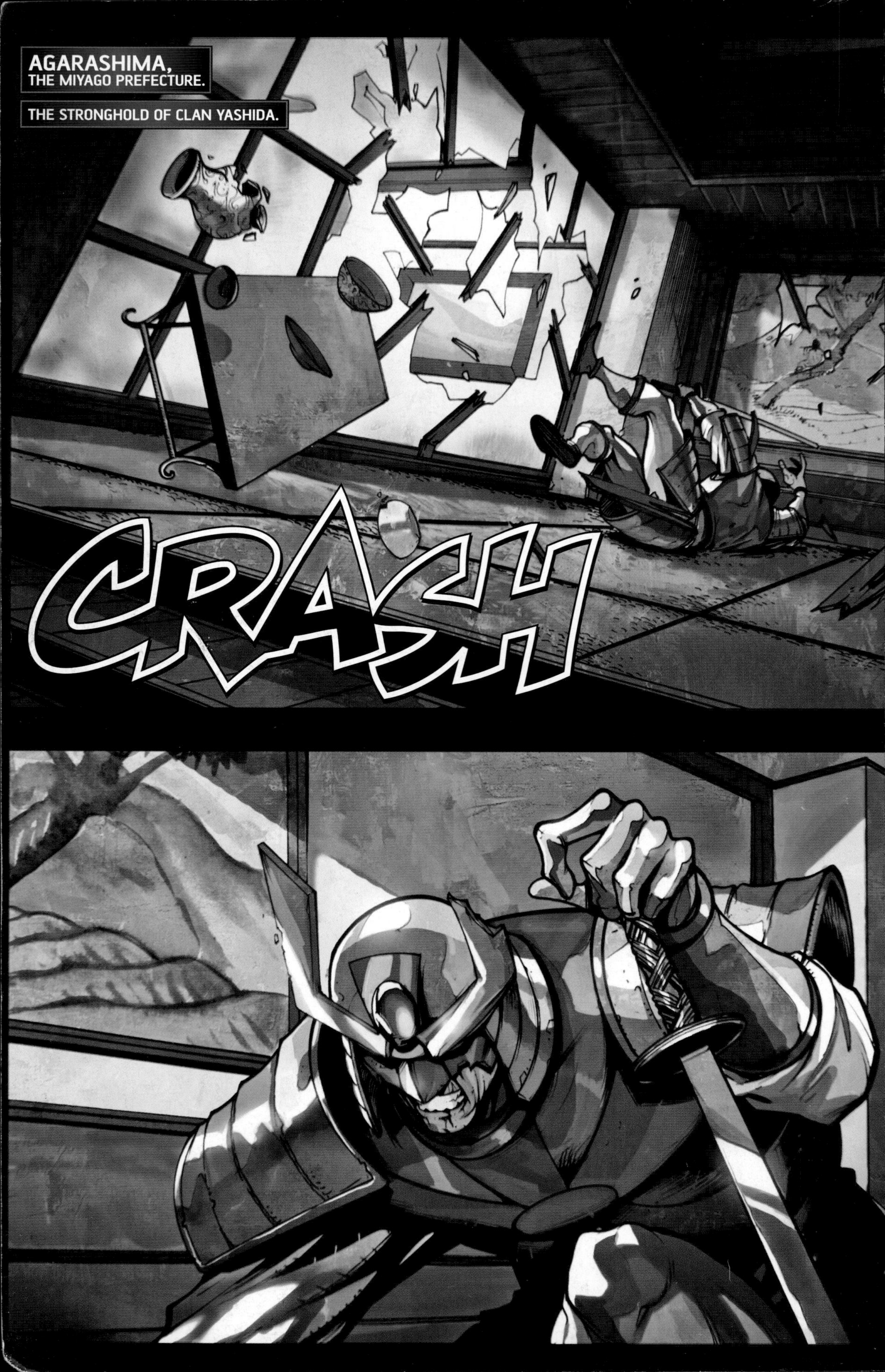
AGARASHIMA,
THE MIYAGO PREFECTURE.
THE STRONGHOLD OF CLAN YASHIDA.
CRASH

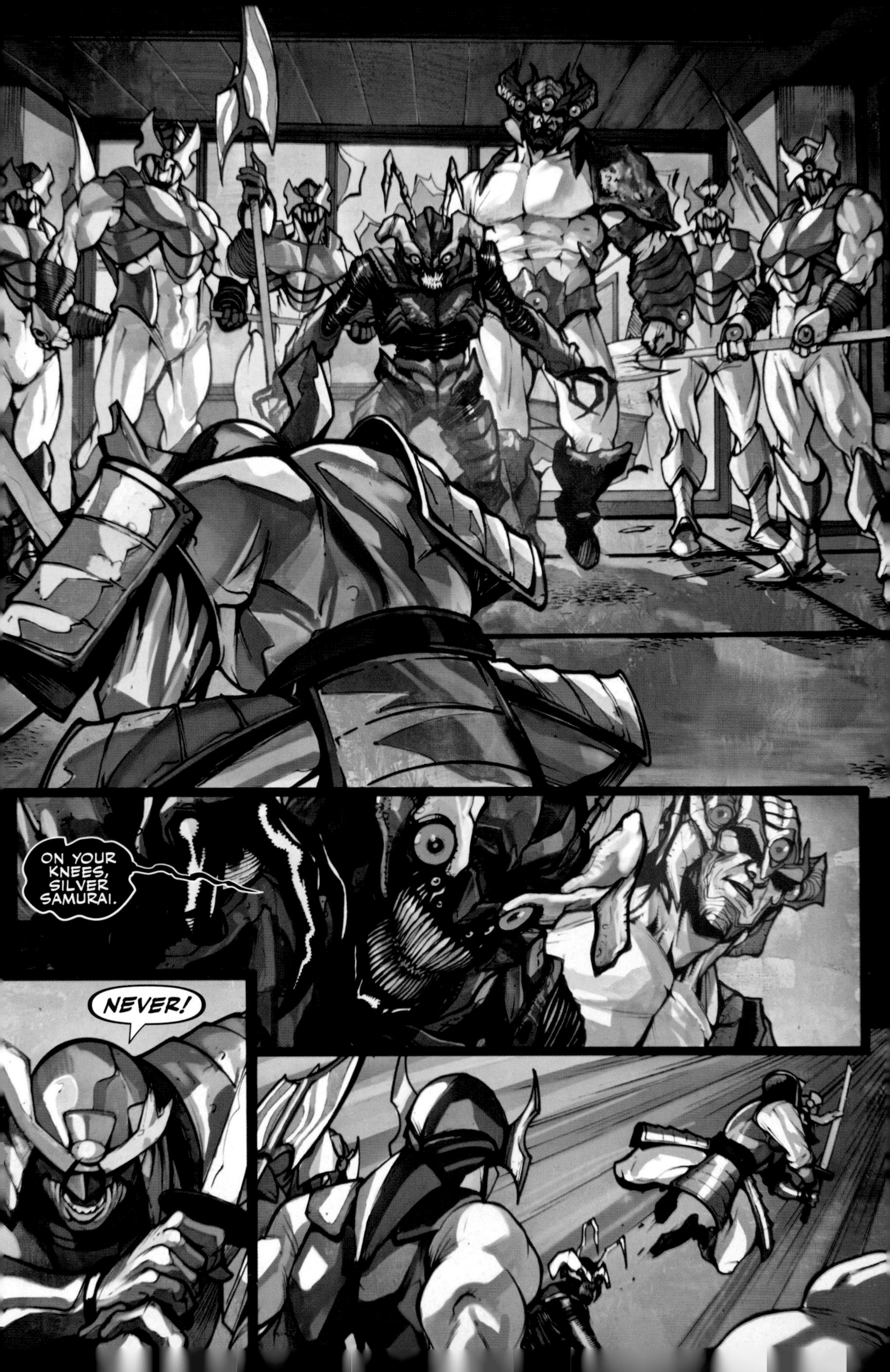
ON YOUR KNEES, SILVER SAMURAI.
NEVER!

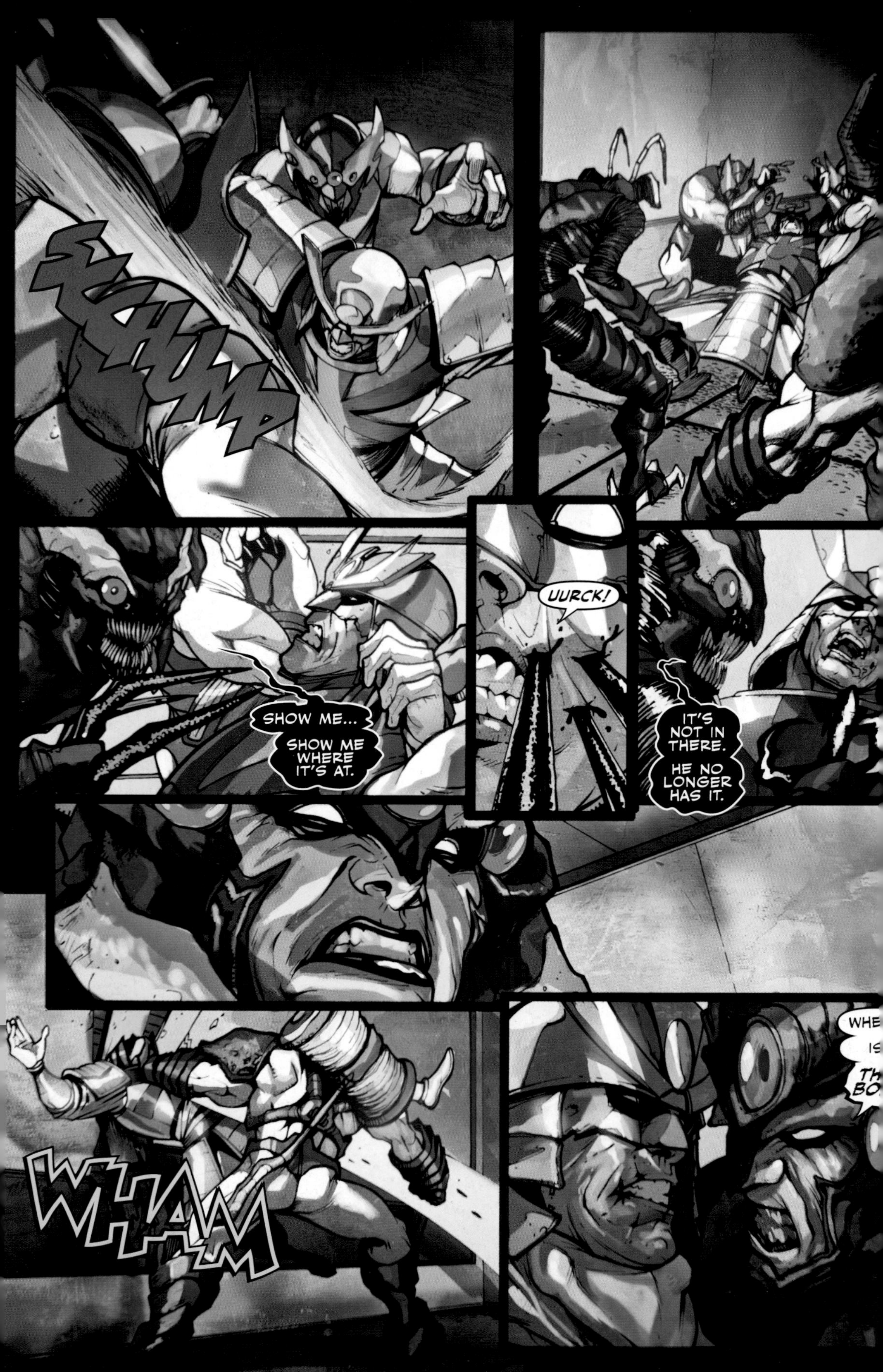
SCHUMP
SHOW ME... SHOW ME WHERE IT'S AT.
UURCK!
IT'S NOT IN THERE.
HE NO LONGER HAS IT.
WHAM

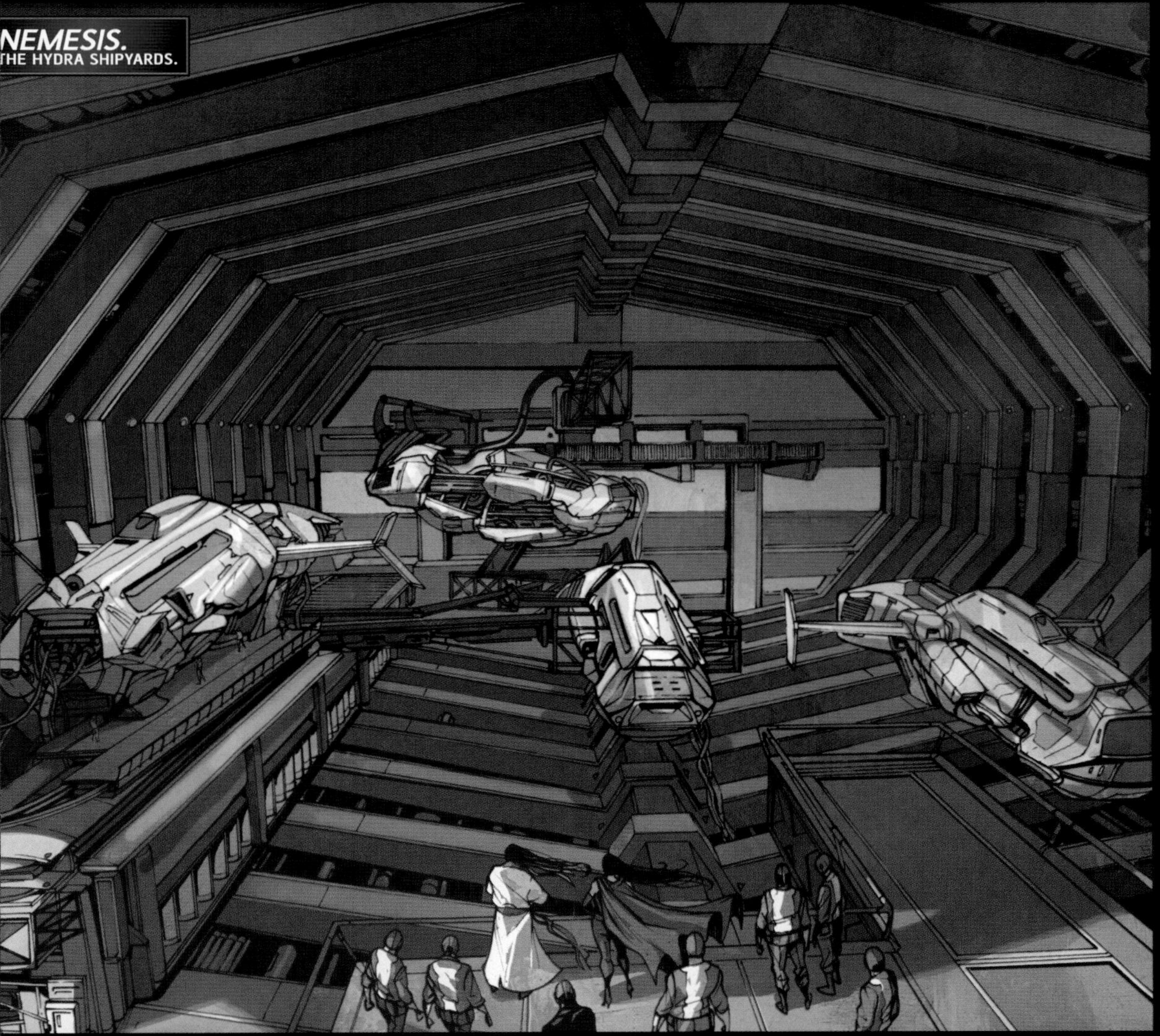
NEMESIS.
THE HYDRA SHIPYARDS.

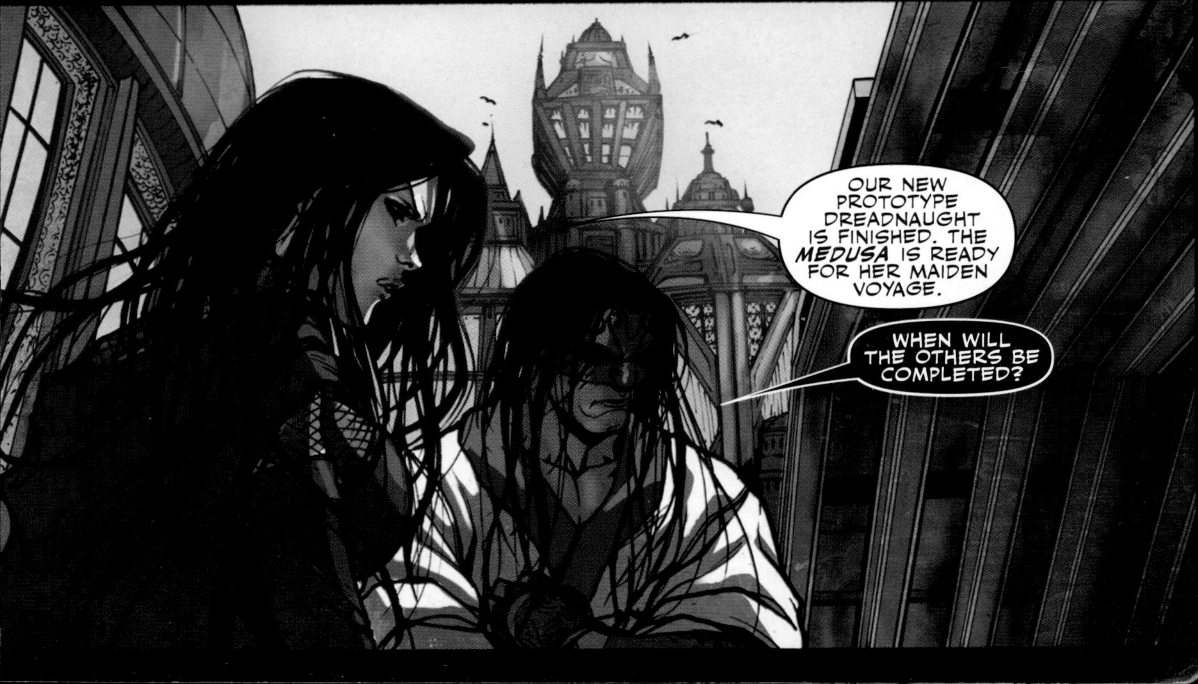
OUR NEW PROTOTYPE DREADNAUGHT IS FINISHED. THE *MEDUSA* IS READY FOR HER MAIDEN VOYAGE.
WHEN WILL THE OTHERS BE COMPLETED?

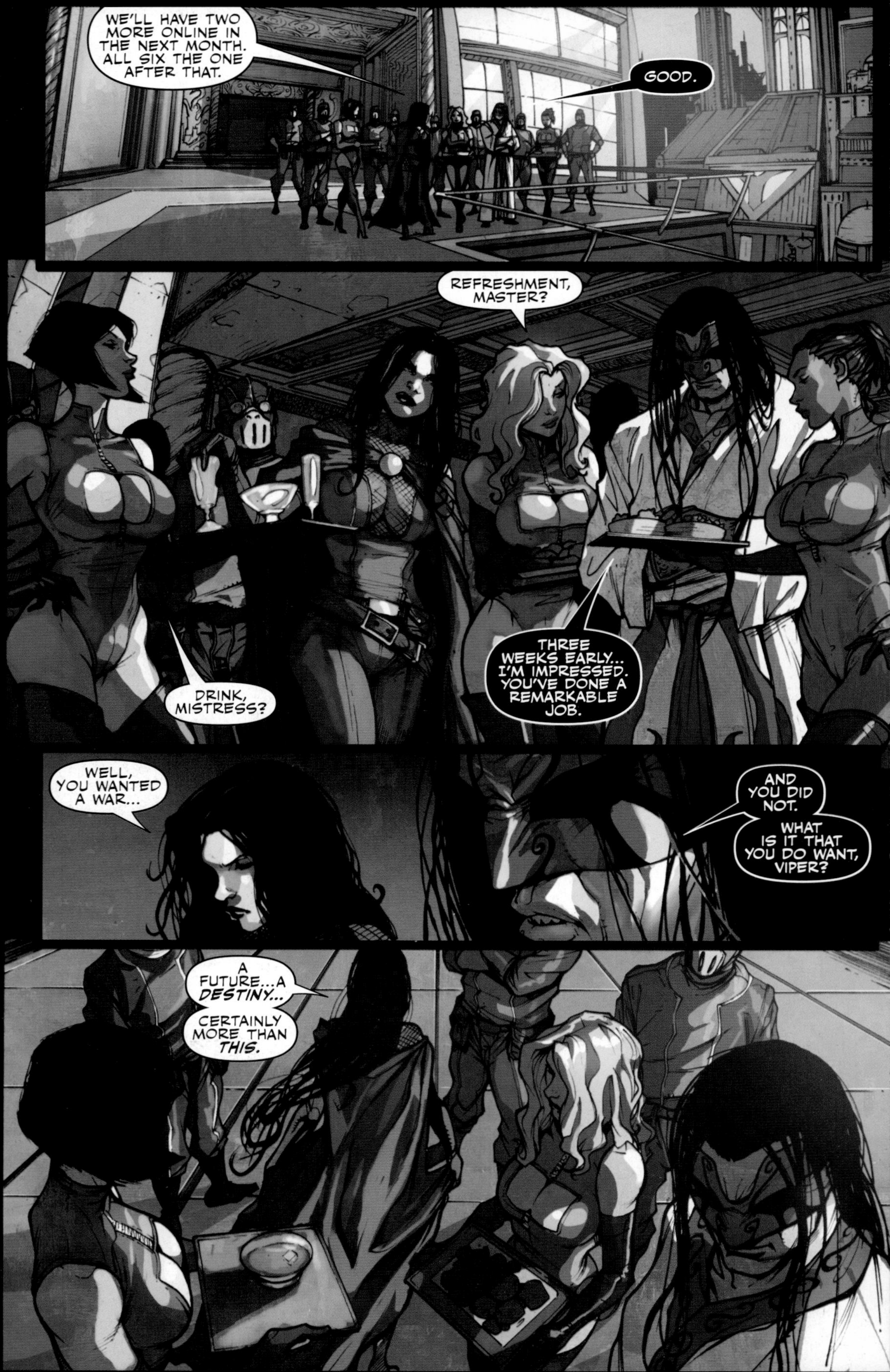
WE'LL HAVE TWO MORE ONLINE IN THE NEXT MONTH. ALL SIX THE ONE AFTER THAT.
GOOD.
REFRESHMENT, MASTER?
DRINK, MISTRESS?
THREE WEEKS EARLY... I'M IMPRESSED. YOU'VE DONE A REMARKABLE JOB.
WELL, YOU WANTED A WAR...
AND YOU DID NOT.
WHAT IS IT THAT YOU DO WANT, VIPER?
A FUTURE...A DESTINY...
CERTAINLY MORE THAN THIS.

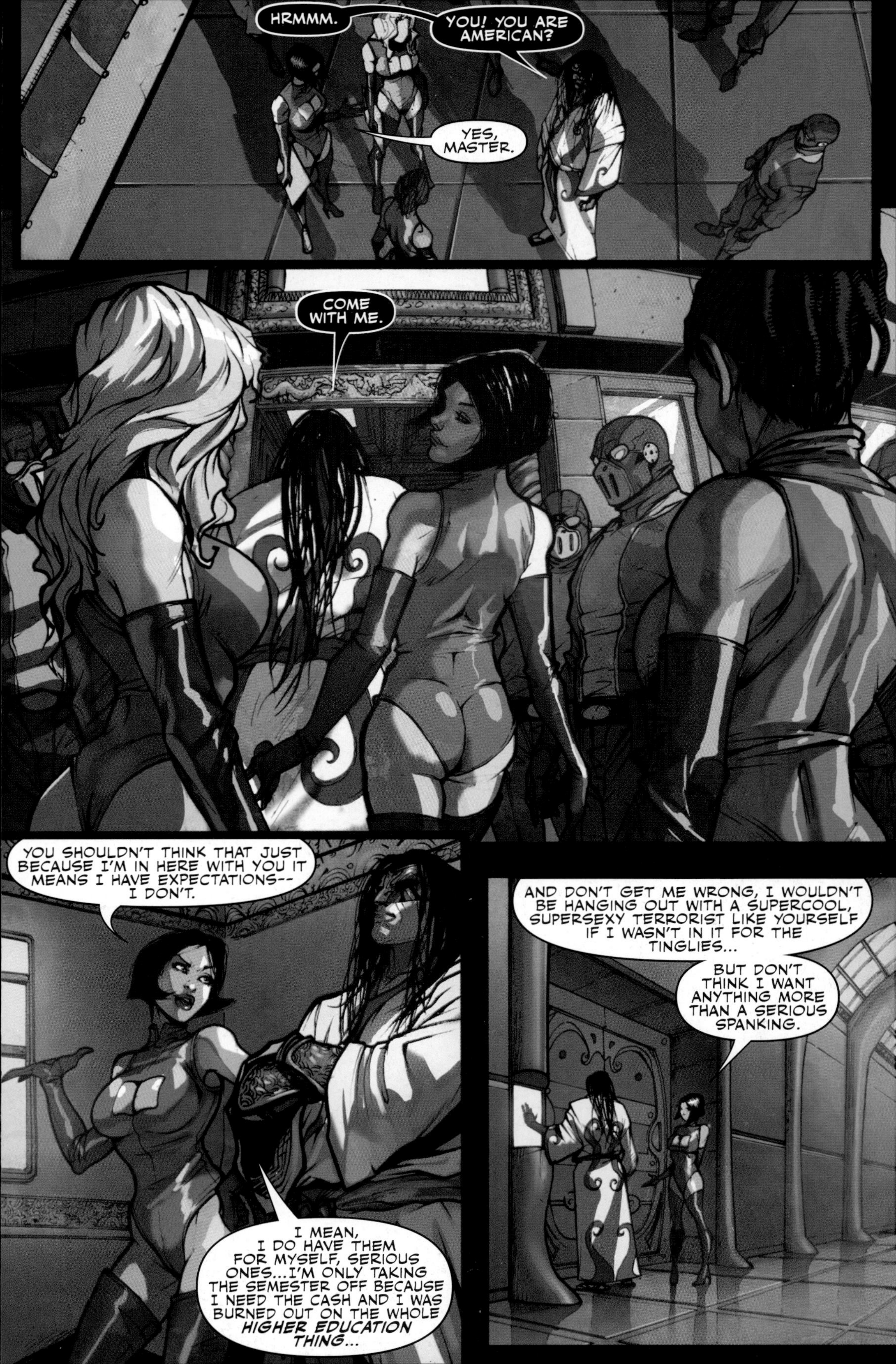
HRMMM.
YOU! YOU ARE AMERICAN?
YES, MASTER.
COME WITH ME.
YOU SHOULDN'T THINK THAT JUST BECAUSE I'M IN HERE WITH YOU IT MEANS I HAVE EXPECTATIONS-- I DON'T.
I MEAN, I DO HAVE THEM FOR MYSELF, SERIOUS ONES...I'M ONLY TAKING THE SEMESTER OFF BECAUSE I NEED THE CASH AND I WAS BURNED OUT ON THE WHOLE *HIGHER EDUCATION THING*...
AND DON'T GET ME WRONG, I WOULDN'T BE HANGING OUT WITH A SUPERCOOL, SUPERSEXY TERRORIST LIKE YOURSELF IF I WASN'T IN IT FOR THE TINGLIES...
BUT DON'T THINK I WANT ANYTHING MORE THAN A SERIOUS SPANKING.

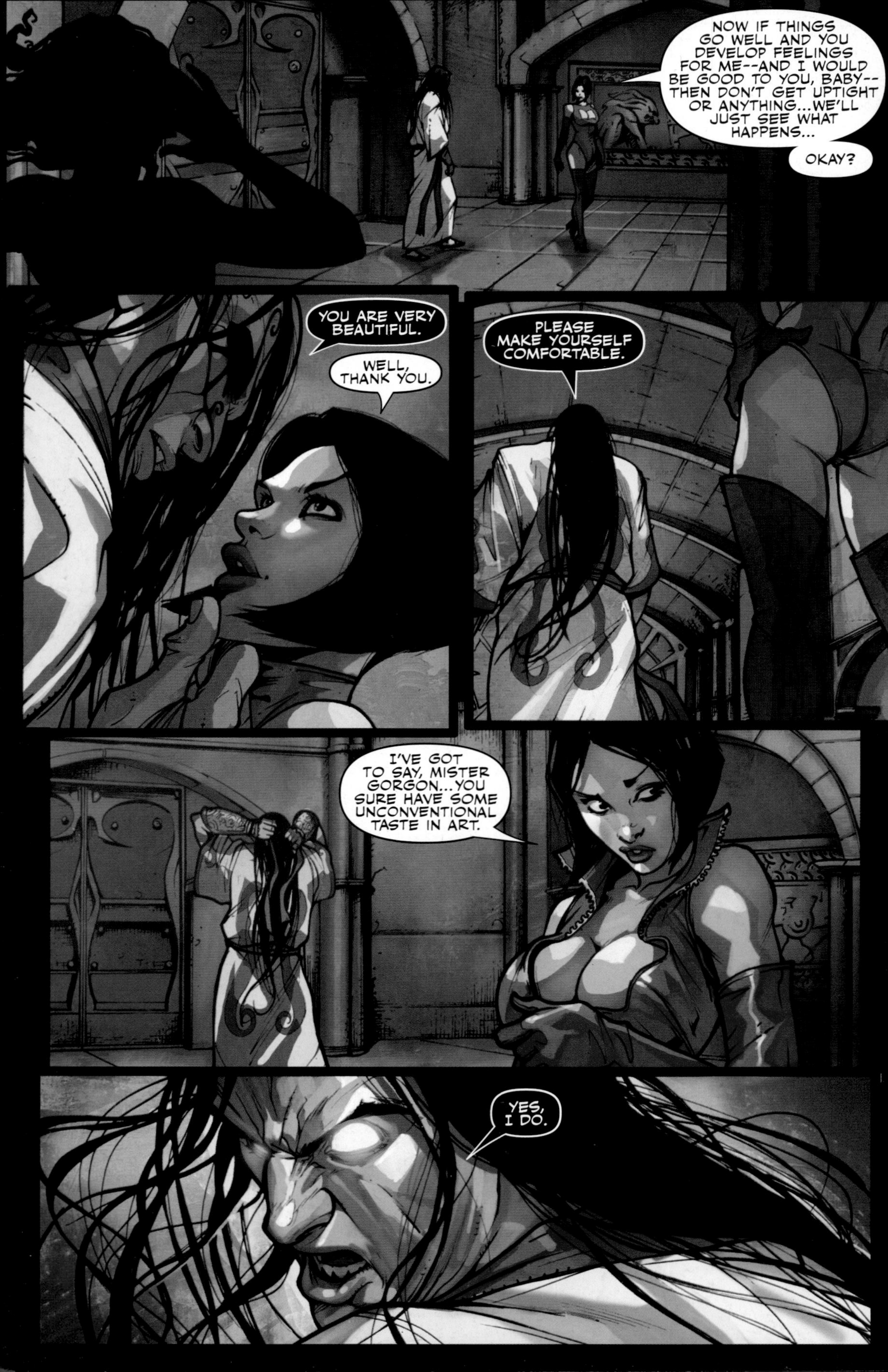
NOW IF THINGS GO WELL AND YOU DEVELOP FEELINGS FOR ME--AND I WOULD BE GOOD TO YOU, BABY--THEN DON'T GET UPTIGHT OR ANYTHING...WE'LL JUST SEE WHAT HAPPENS...
OKAY?
YOU ARE VERY BEAUTIFUL.
WELL, THANK YOU.
PLEASE MAKE YOURSELF COMFORTABLE.
I'VE GOT TO SAY, MISTER GORGON...YOU SURE HAVE SOME UNCONVENTIONAL TASTE IN ART.
YES, I DO.

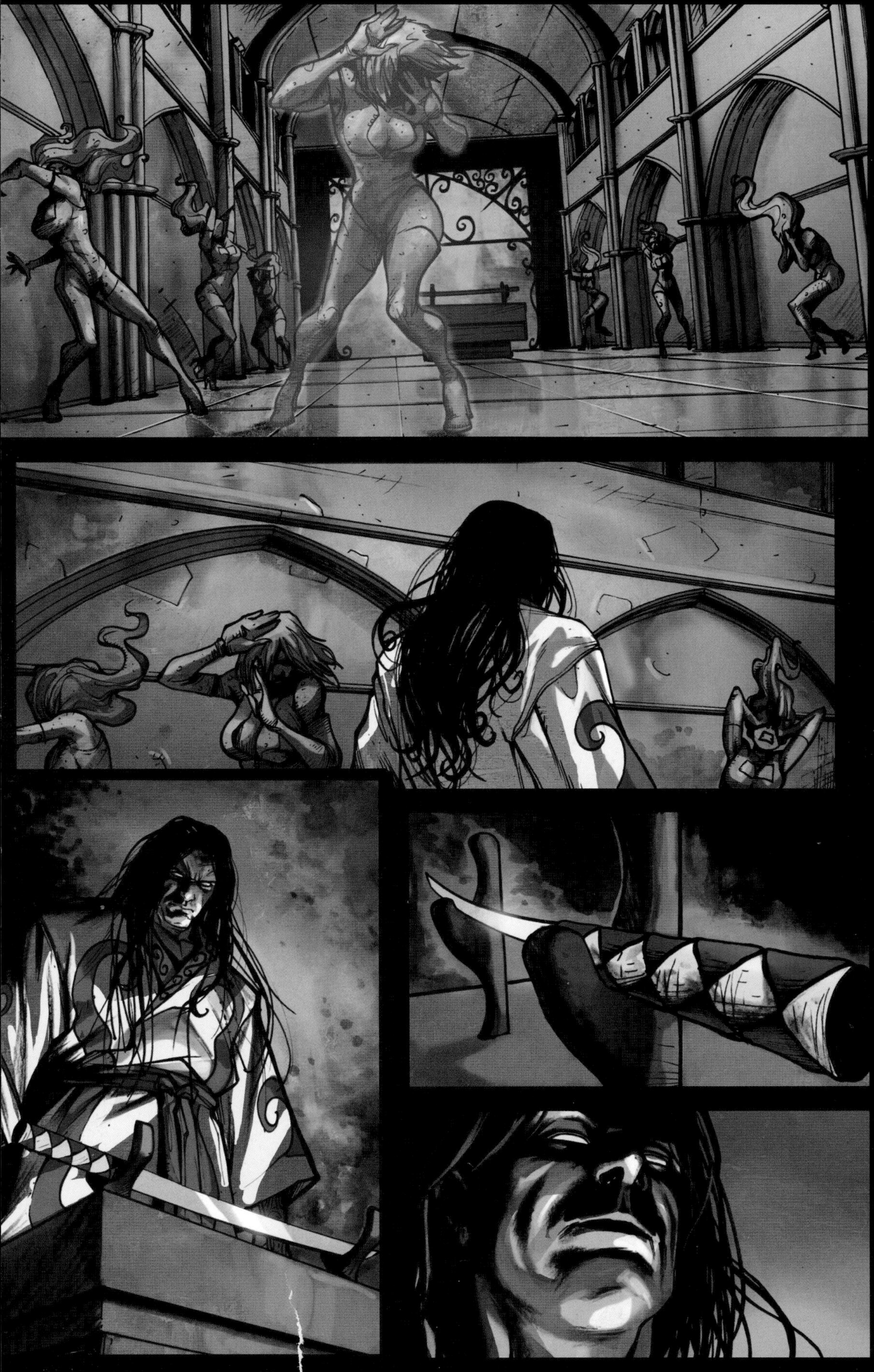

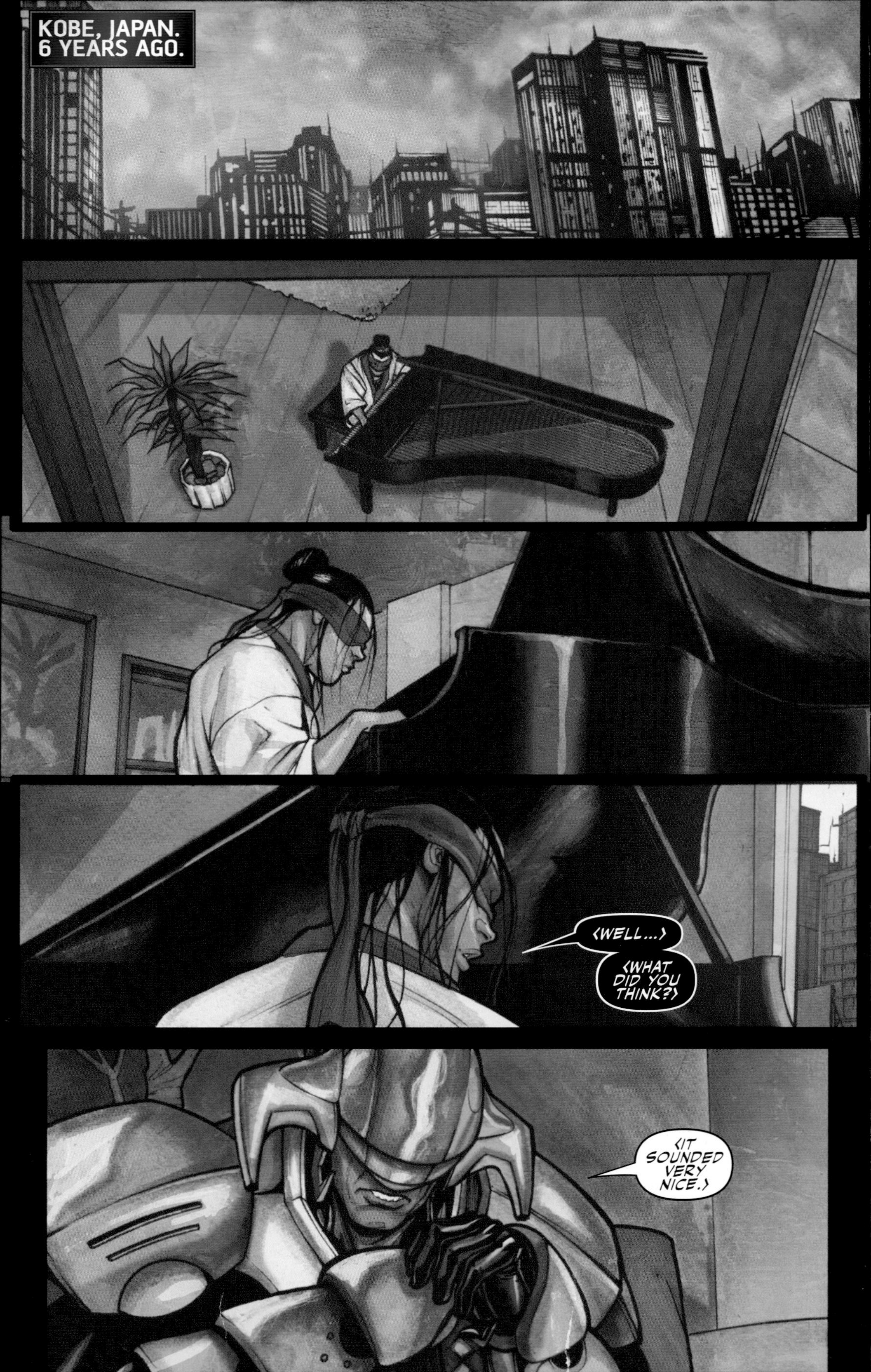
KOBE, JAPAN.
6 YEARS AGO.
‹WELL...›
‹WHAT DID YOU THINK?›
‹IT SOUNDED VERY NICE.›

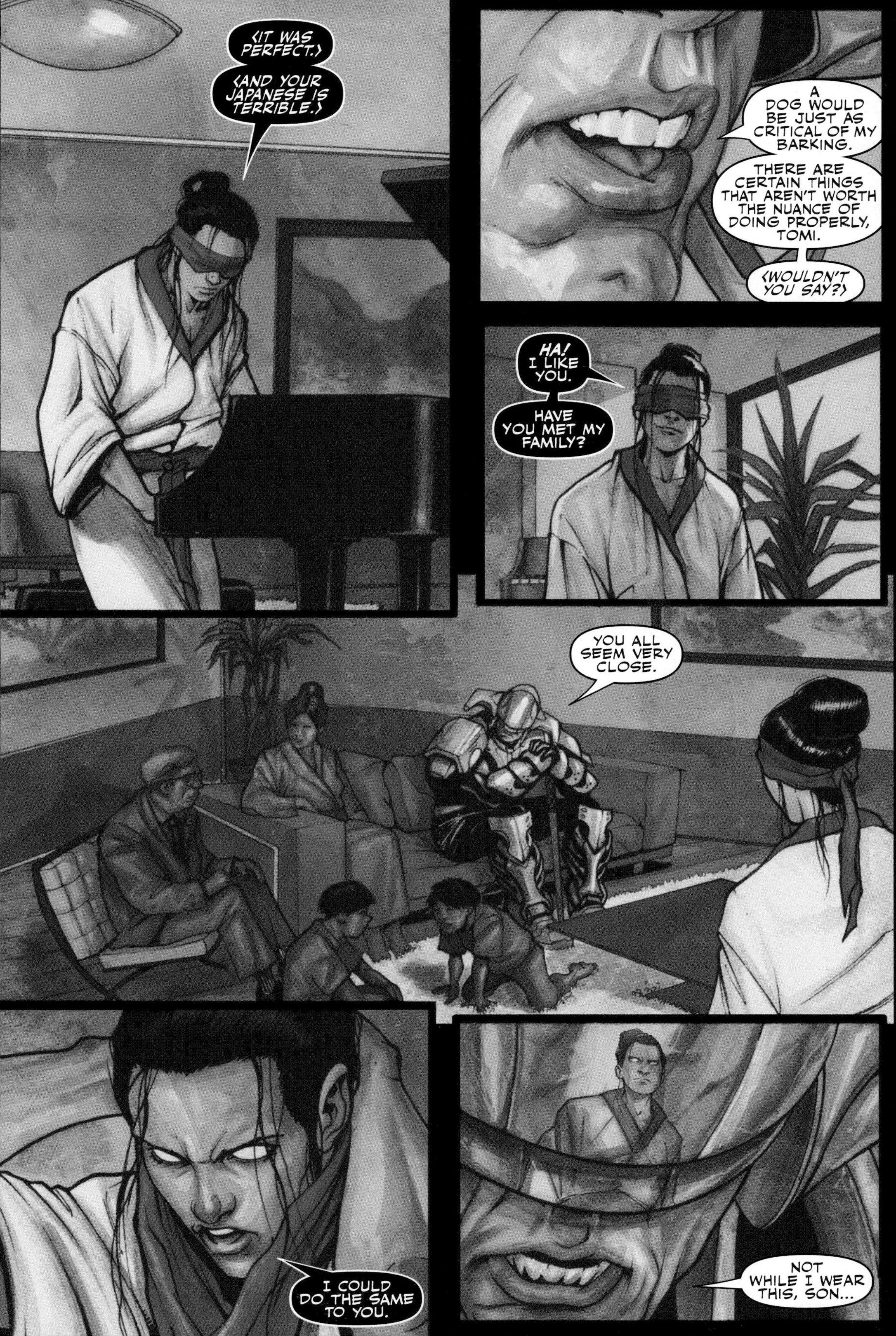
<IT WAS PERFECT.>
<AND YOUR JAPANESE IS TERRIBLE.>
A DOG WOULD BE JUST AS CRITICAL OF MY BARKING.
THERE ARE CERTAIN THINGS THAT AREN'T WORTH THE NUANCE OF DOING PROPERLY, TOMI.
<WOULDN'T YOU SAY?>
HA! I LIKE YOU.
HAVE YOU MET MY FAMILY?
YOU ALL SEEM VERY CLOSE.
I COULD DO THE SAME TO YOU.
NOT WHILE I WEAR THIS, SON...

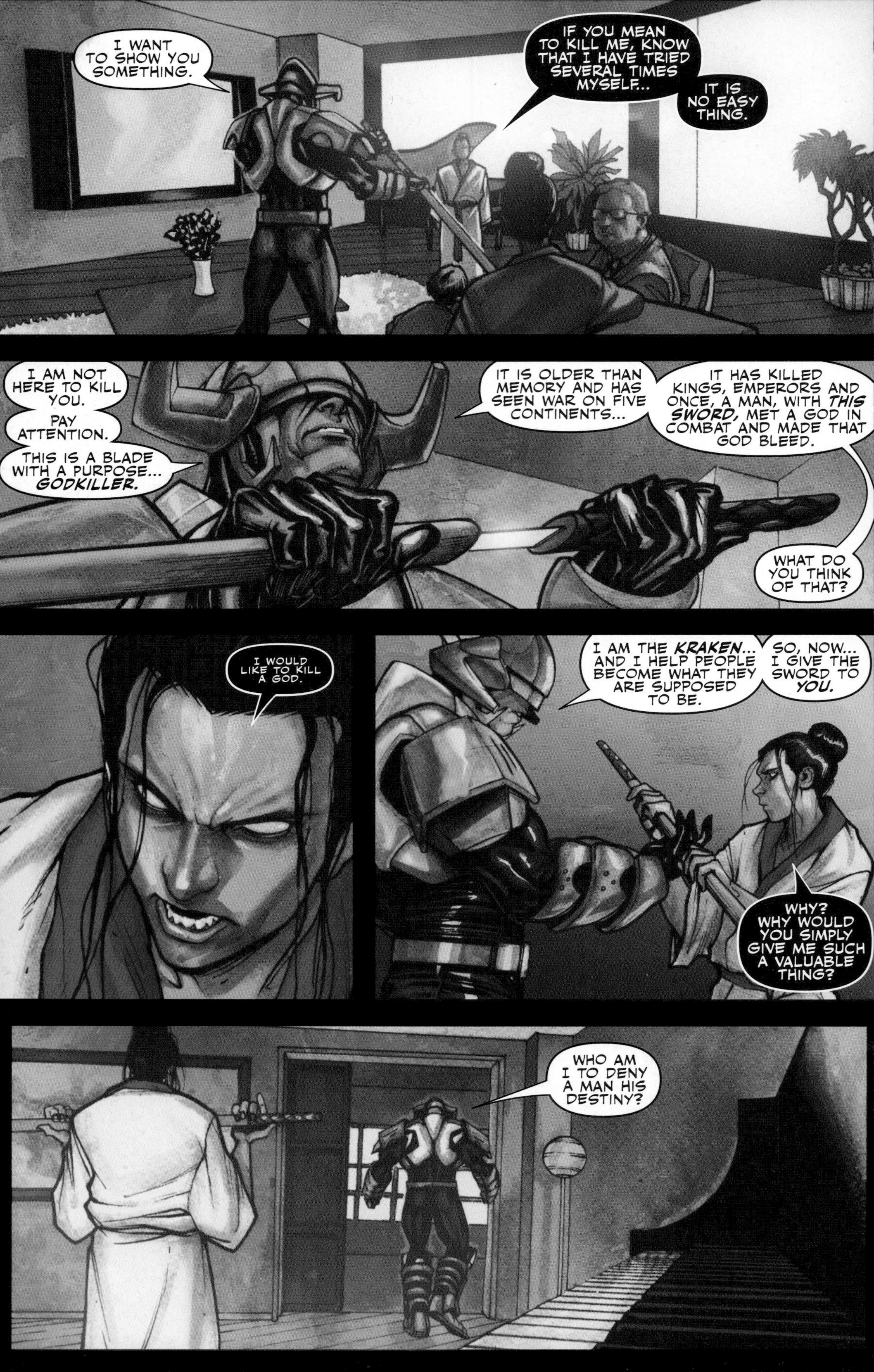
I WANT TO SHOW YOU SOMETHING.
IF YOU MEAN TO KILL ME, KNOW THAT I HAVE TRIED SEVERAL TIMES MYSELF...
IT IS NO EASY THING.
I AM NOT HERE TO KILL YOU.
PAY ATTENTION.
THIS IS A BLADE WITH A PURPOSE... GODKILLER.
IT IS OLDER THAN MEMORY AND HAS SEEN WAR ON FIVE CONTINENTS...
IT HAS KILLED KINGS, EMPERORS AND ONCE, A MAN, WITH THIS SWORD, MET A GOD IN COMBAT AND MADE THAT GOD BLEED.
WHAT DO YOU THINK OF THAT?
I WOULD LIKE TO KILL A GOD.
I AM THE KRAKEN... AND I HELP PEOPLE BECOME WHAT THEY ARE SUPPOSED TO BE.
SO, NOW... I GIVE THE SWORD TO YOU.
WHY? WHY WOULD YOU SIMPLY GIVE ME SUCH A VALUABLE THING?
WHO AM I TO DENY A MAN HIS DESTINY?

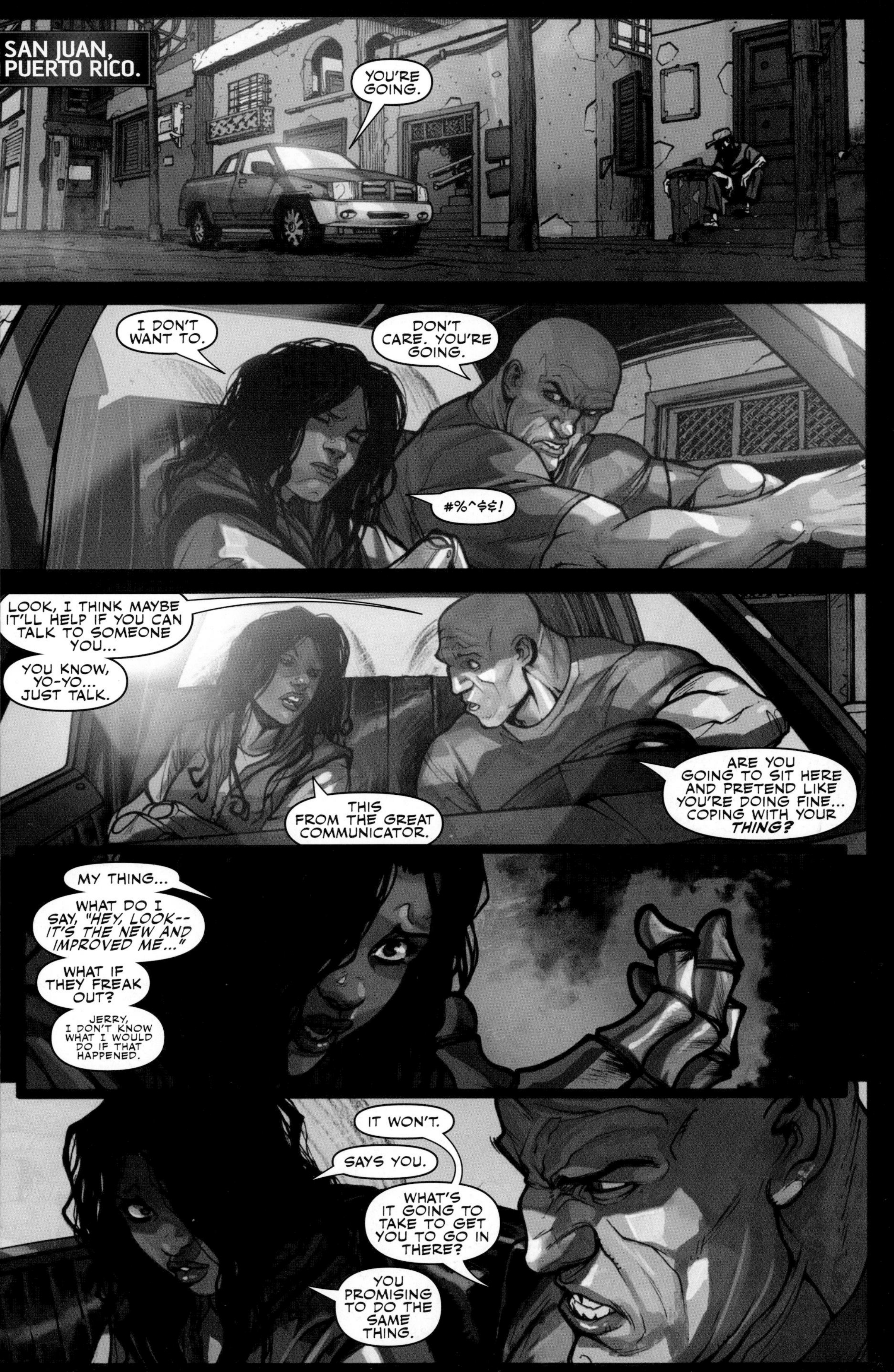
SAN JUAN, PUERTO RICO.
YOU'RE GOING.
I DON'T WANT TO.
DON'T CARE. YOU'RE GOING.
#%^$¢!
LOOK, I THINK MAYBE IT'LL HELP IF YOU CAN TALK TO SOMEONE YOU...
YOU KNOW, YO-YO... JUST TALK.
THIS FROM THE GREAT COMMUNICATOR.
ARE YOU GOING TO SIT HERE AND PRETEND LIKE YOU'RE DOING FINE... COPING WITH YOUR THING?
MY THING...
WHAT DO I SAY, "HEY, LOOK-- IT'S THE NEW AND IMPROVED ME..."
WHAT IF THEY FREAK OUT?
JERRY, I DON'T KNOW WHAT I WOULD DO IF THAT HAPPENED.
IT WON'T.
SAYS YOU.
WHAT'S IT GOING TO TAKE TO GET YOU TO GO IN THERE?
YOU PROMISING TO DO THE SAME THING.

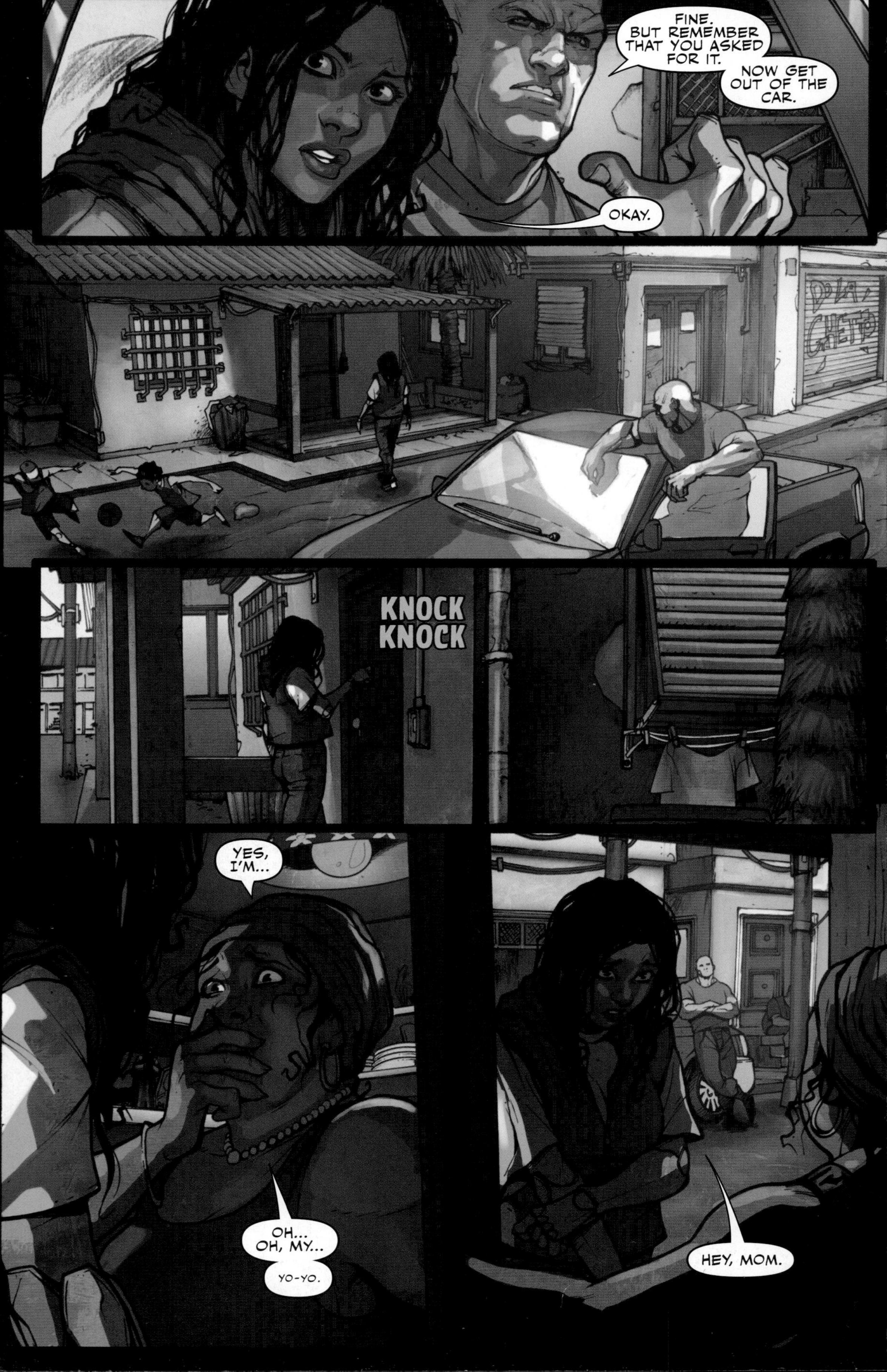
FINE. BUT REMEMBER THAT YOU ASKED FOR IT.
NOW GET OUT OF THE CAR.
OKAY.
DO LA GHETTO
KNOCK KNOCK
YES, I'M...
OH... OH, MY...
YO-YO.
HEY, MOM.

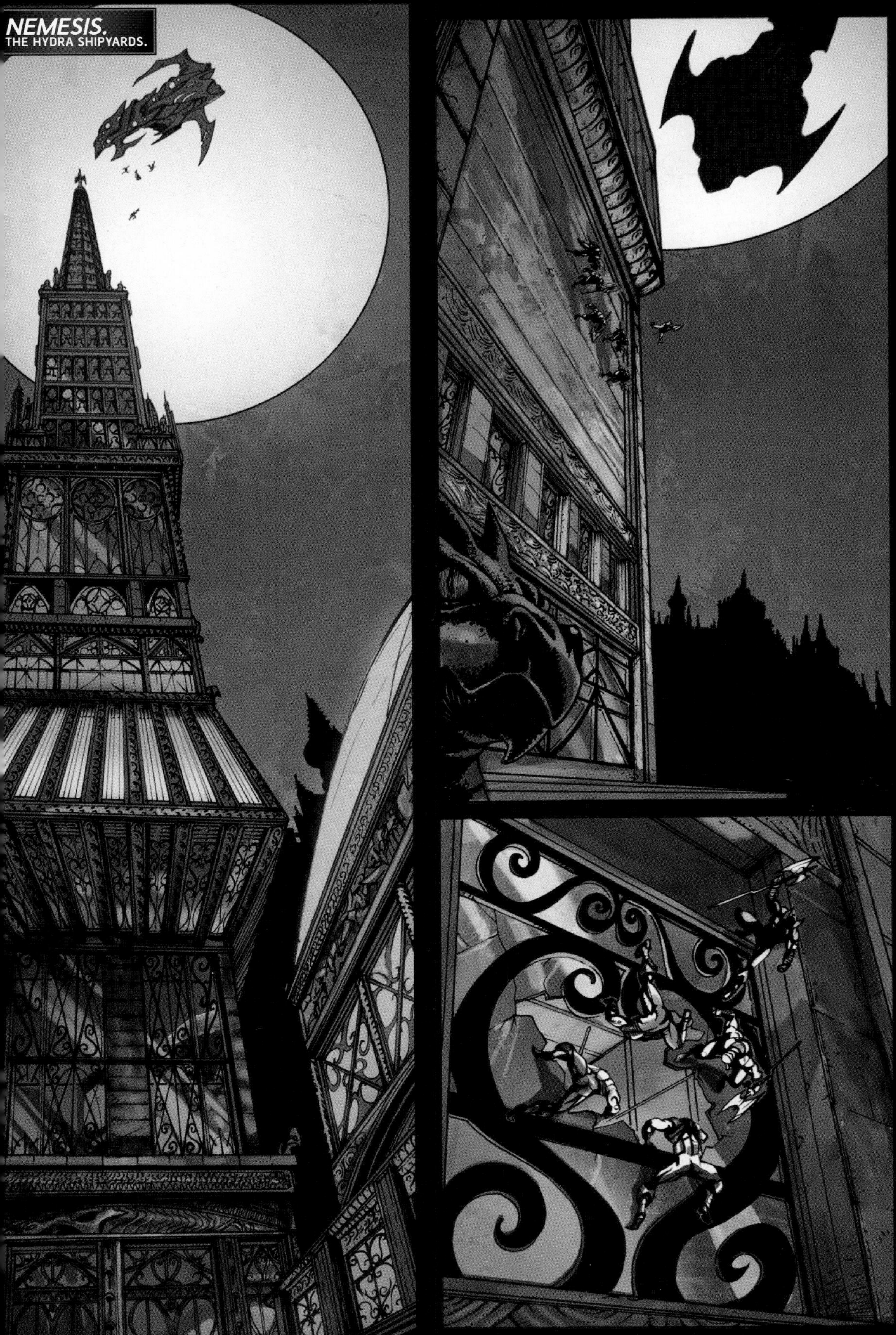
NEMESIS.
THE HYDRA SHIPYARDS.

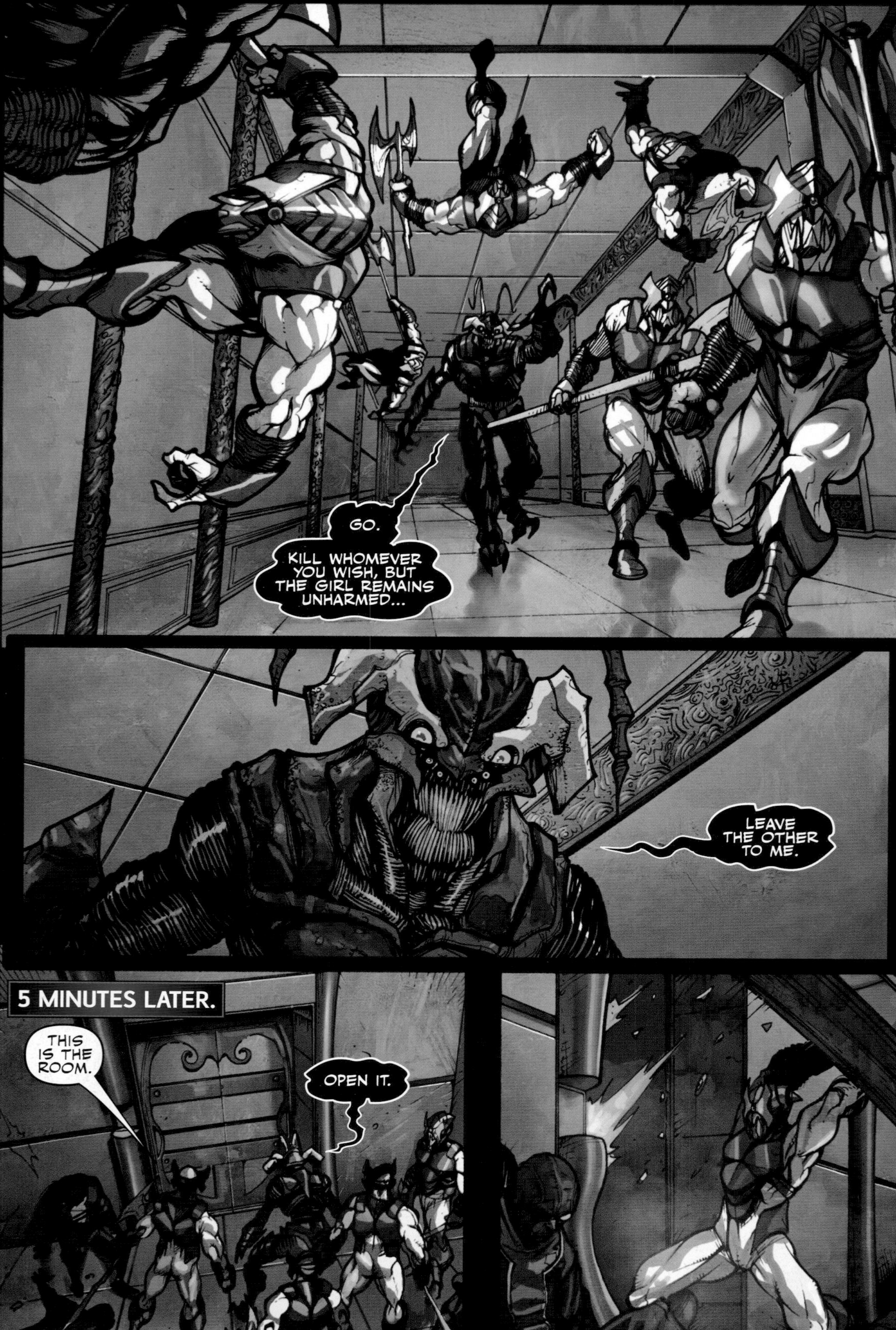
GO.
KILL WHOMEVER YOU WISH, BUT THE GIRL REMAINS UNHARMED...
LEAVE THE OTHER TO ME.
5 MINUTES LATER.
THIS IS THE ROOM.
OPEN IT.

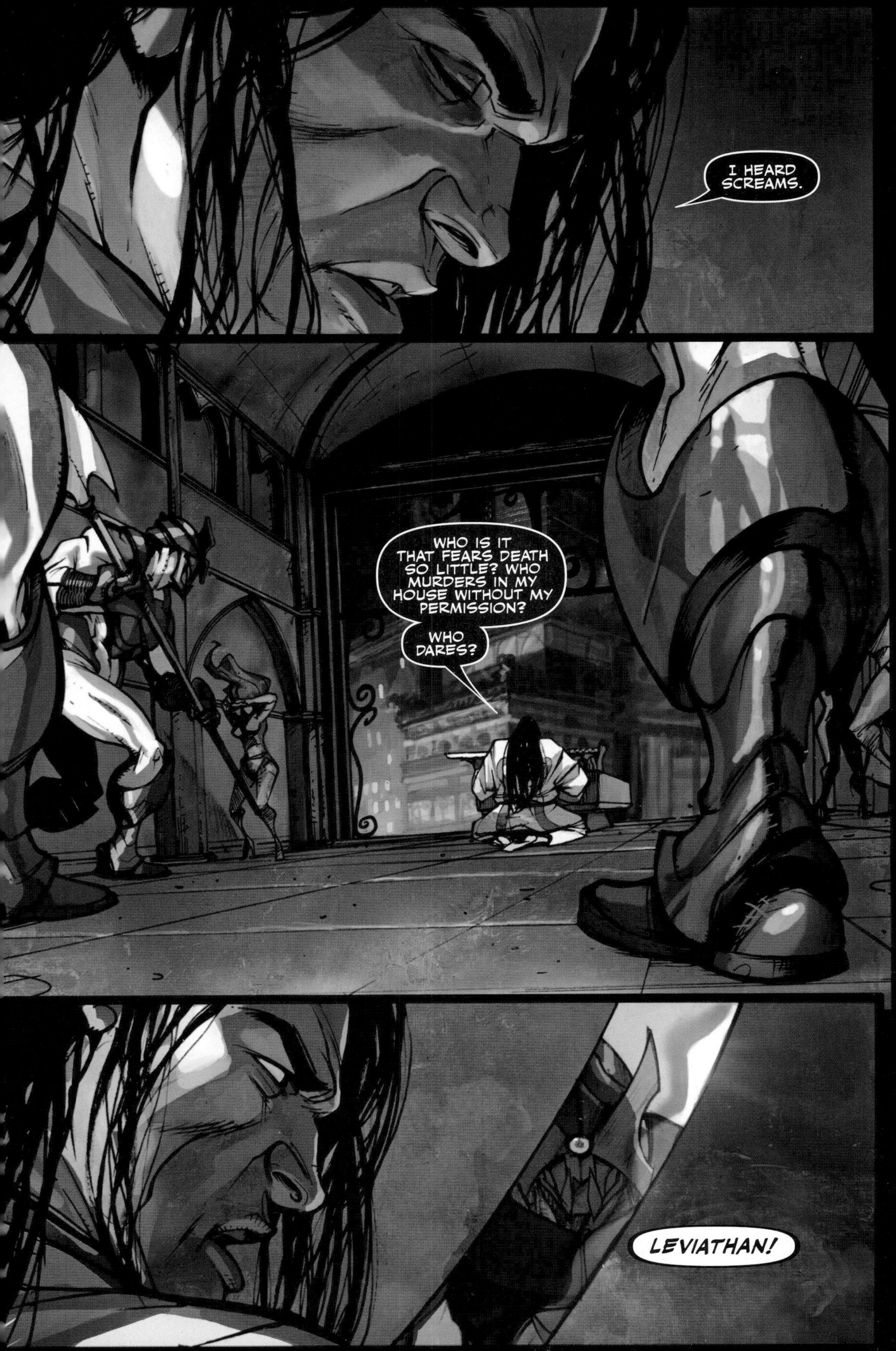
I HEARD SCREAMS.
WHO IS IT THAT FEARS DEATH SO LITTLE? WHO MURDERS IN MY HOUSE WITHOUT MY PERMISSION?
WHO DARES?
LEVIATHAN!

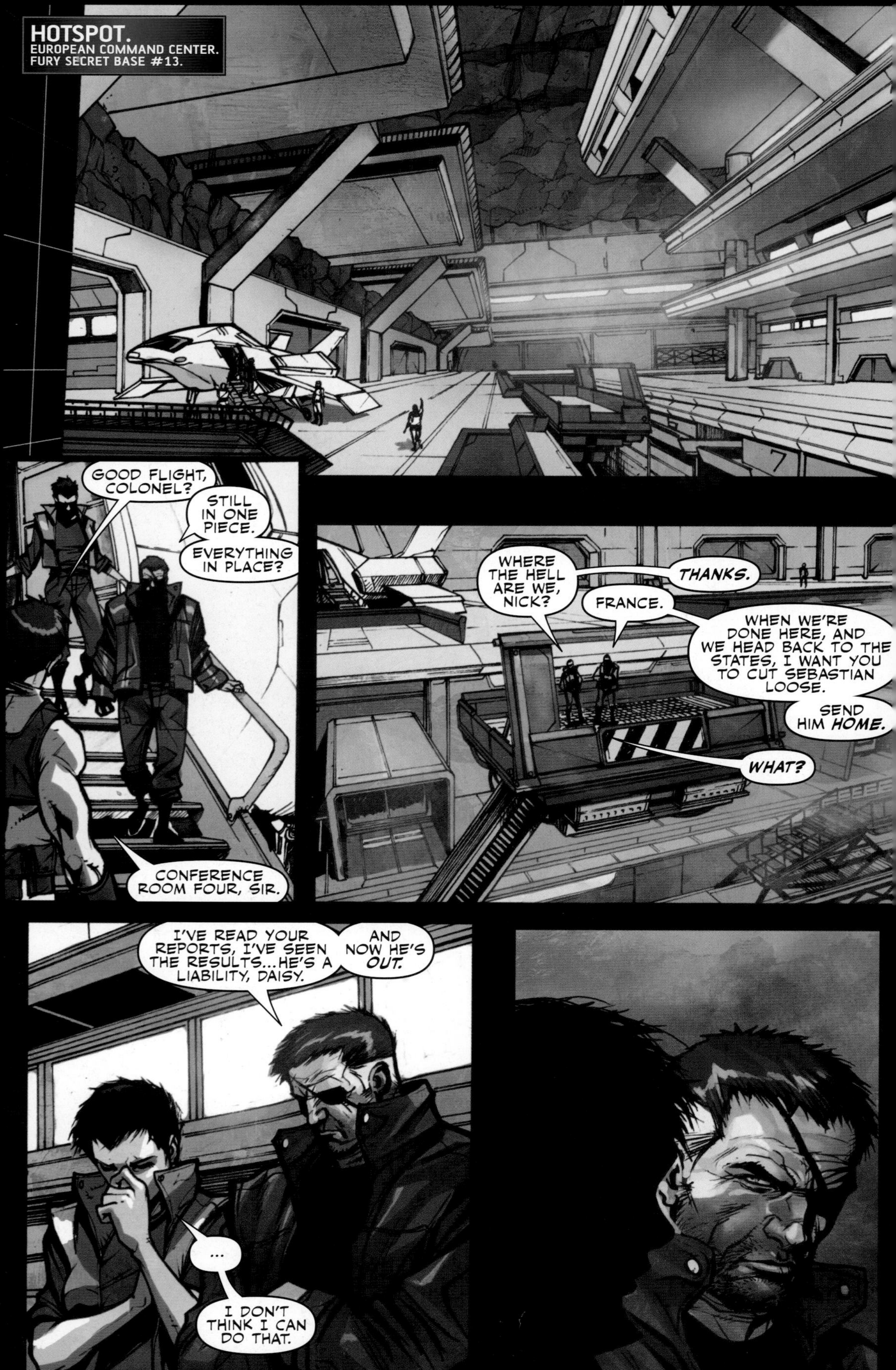
HOTSPOT.
EUROPEAN COMMAND CENTER.
FURY SECRET BASE #13.
GOOD FLIGHT, COLONEL?
STILL IN ONE PIECE.
EVERYTHING IN PLACE?
CONFERENCE ROOM FOUR, SIR.
WHERE THE HELL ARE WE, NICK?
THANKS.
FRANCE.
WHEN WE'RE DONE HERE, AND WE HEAD BACK TO THE STATES, I WANT YOU TO CUT SEBASTIAN LOOSE.
SEND HIM HOME.
WHAT?
I'VE READ YOUR REPORTS, I'VE SEEN THE RESULTS...HE'S A LIABILITY, DAISY.
AND NOW HE'S OUT.
...
I DON'T THINK I CAN DO THAT.

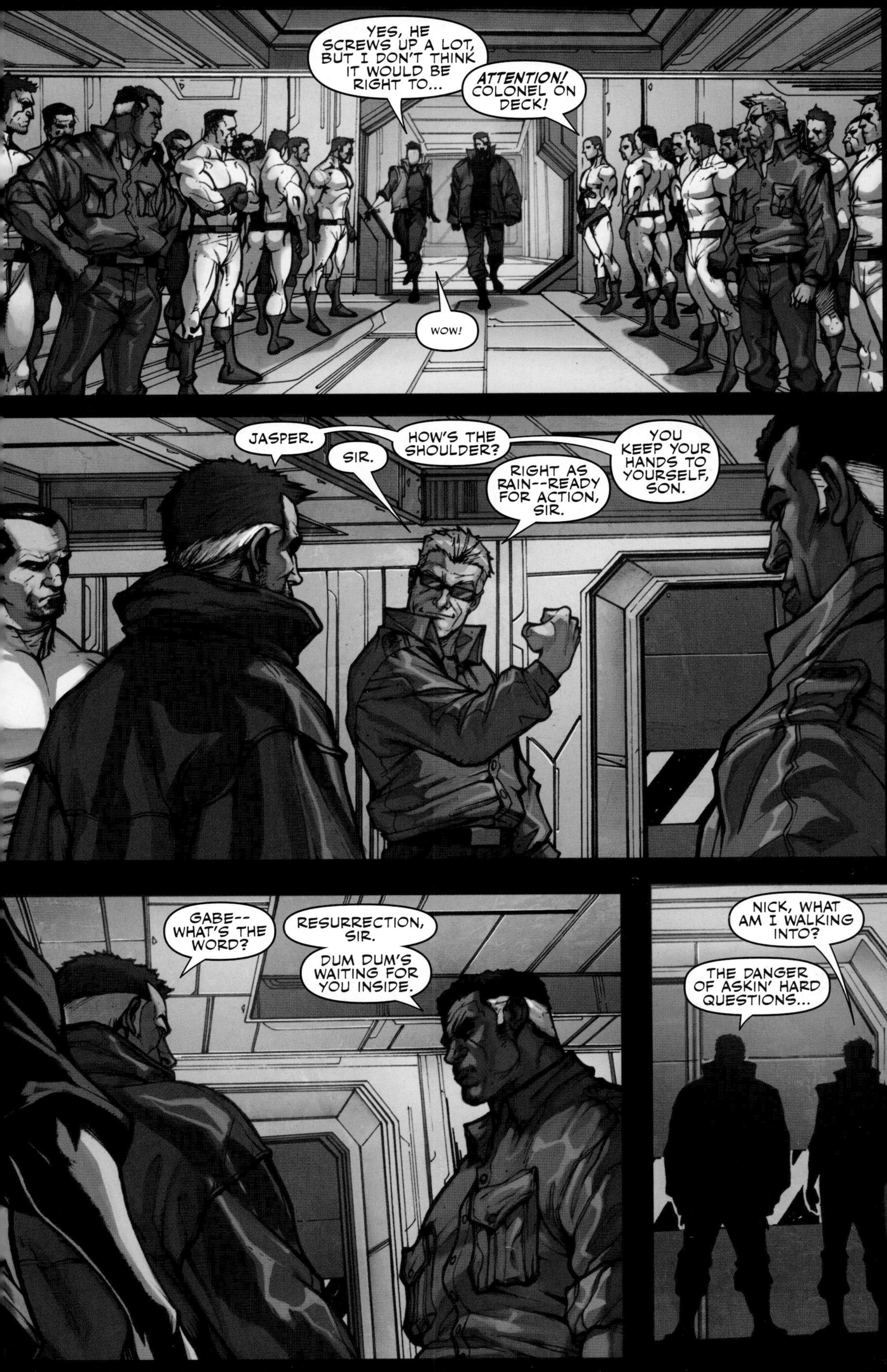
YES, HE SCREWS UP A LOT, BUT I DON'T THINK IT WOULD BE RIGHT TO...
ATTENTION! COLONEL ON DECK!
WOW!
JASPER.
SIR.
HOW'S THE SHOULDER?
RIGHT AS RAIN--READY FOR ACTION, SIR.
YOU KEEP YOUR HANDS TO YOURSELF, SON.
GABE--WHAT'S THE WORD?
RESURRECTION, SIR.
DUM DUM'S WAITING FOR YOU INSIDE.
NICK, WHAT AM I WALKING INTO?
THE DANGER OF ASKIN' HARD QUESTIONS...

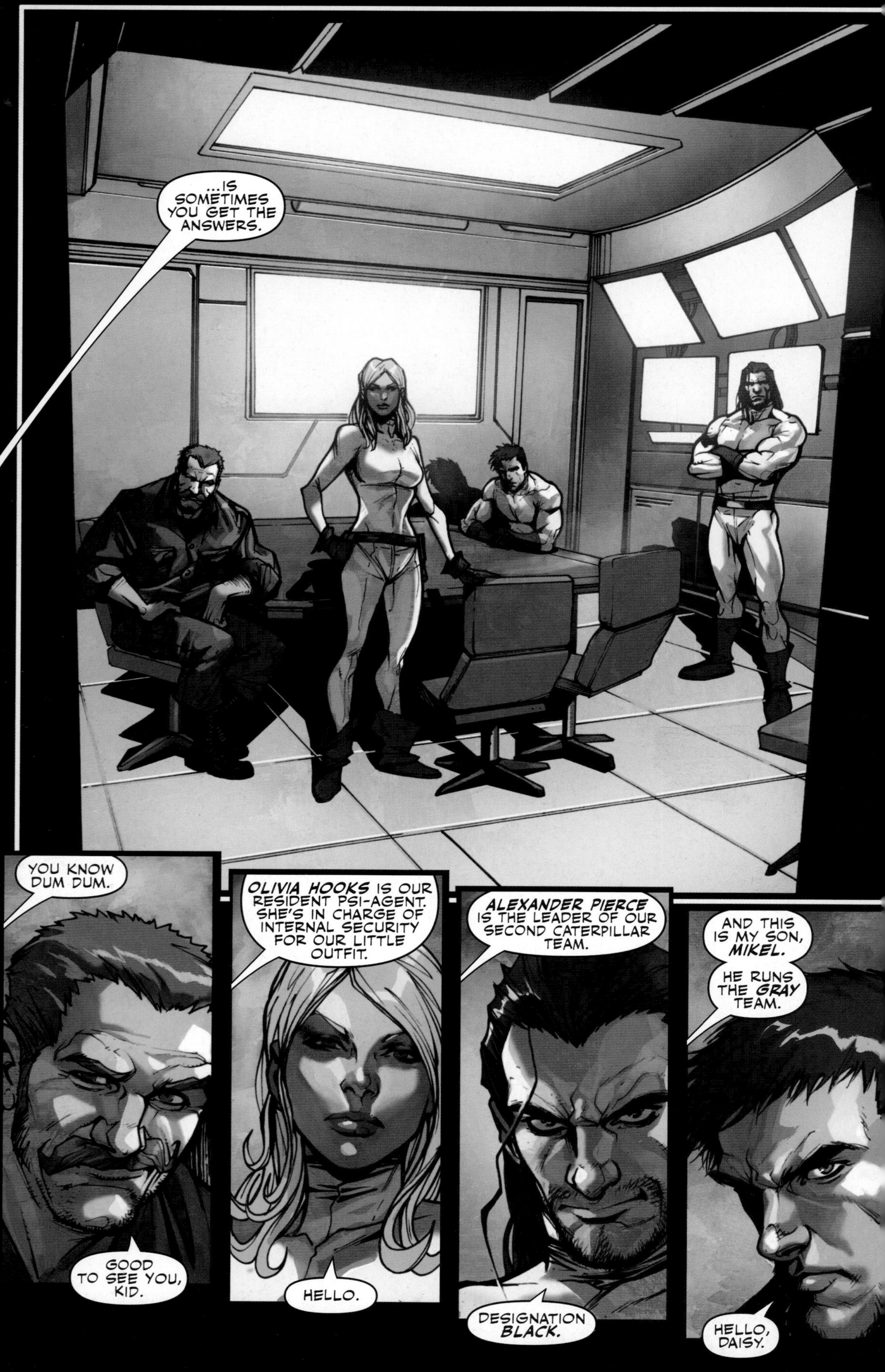

...IS SOMETIMES YOU GET THE ANSWERS.
YOU KNOW DUM DUM.
GOOD TO SEE YOU, KID.
OLIVIA HOOKS IS OUR RESIDENT PSI-AGENT. SHE'S IN CHARGE OF INTERNAL SECURITY FOR OUR LITTLE OUTFIT.
HELLO.
ALEXANDER PIERCE IS THE LEADER OF OUR SECOND CATERPILLAR TEAM.
DESIGNATION BLACK.
AND THIS IS MY SON, MIKEL.
HE RUNS THE GRAY TEAM.
HELLO, DAISY.

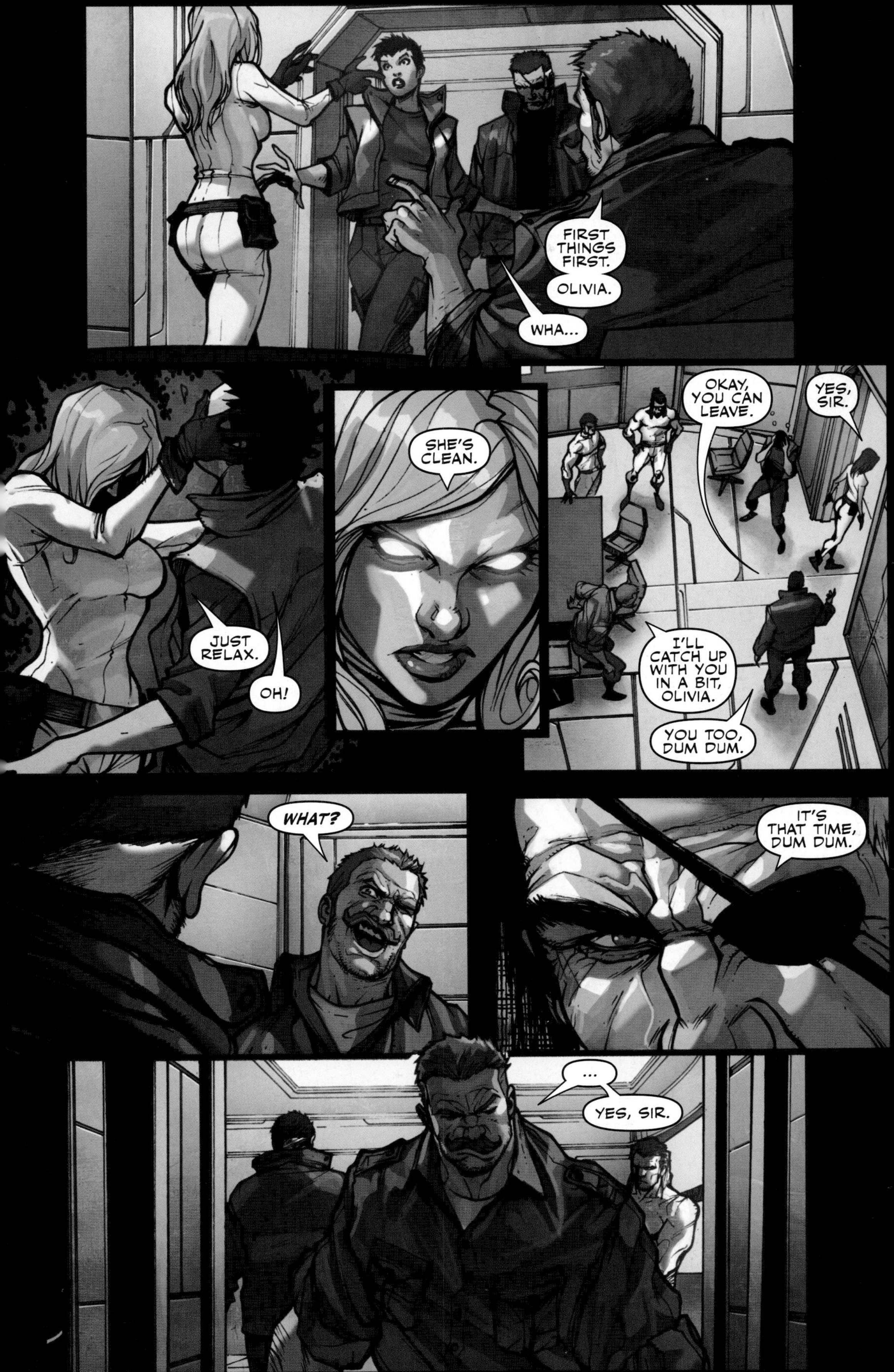
FIRST THINGS FIRST.
OLIVIA.
WHA...
JUST RELAX.
OH!
SHE'S CLEAN.
OKAY, YOU CAN LEAVE.
YES, SIR.
I'LL CATCH UP WITH YOU IN A BIT, OLIVIA.
YOU TOO, DUM DUM.
WHAT?
IT'S THAT TIME, DUM DUM.
...
YES, SIR.

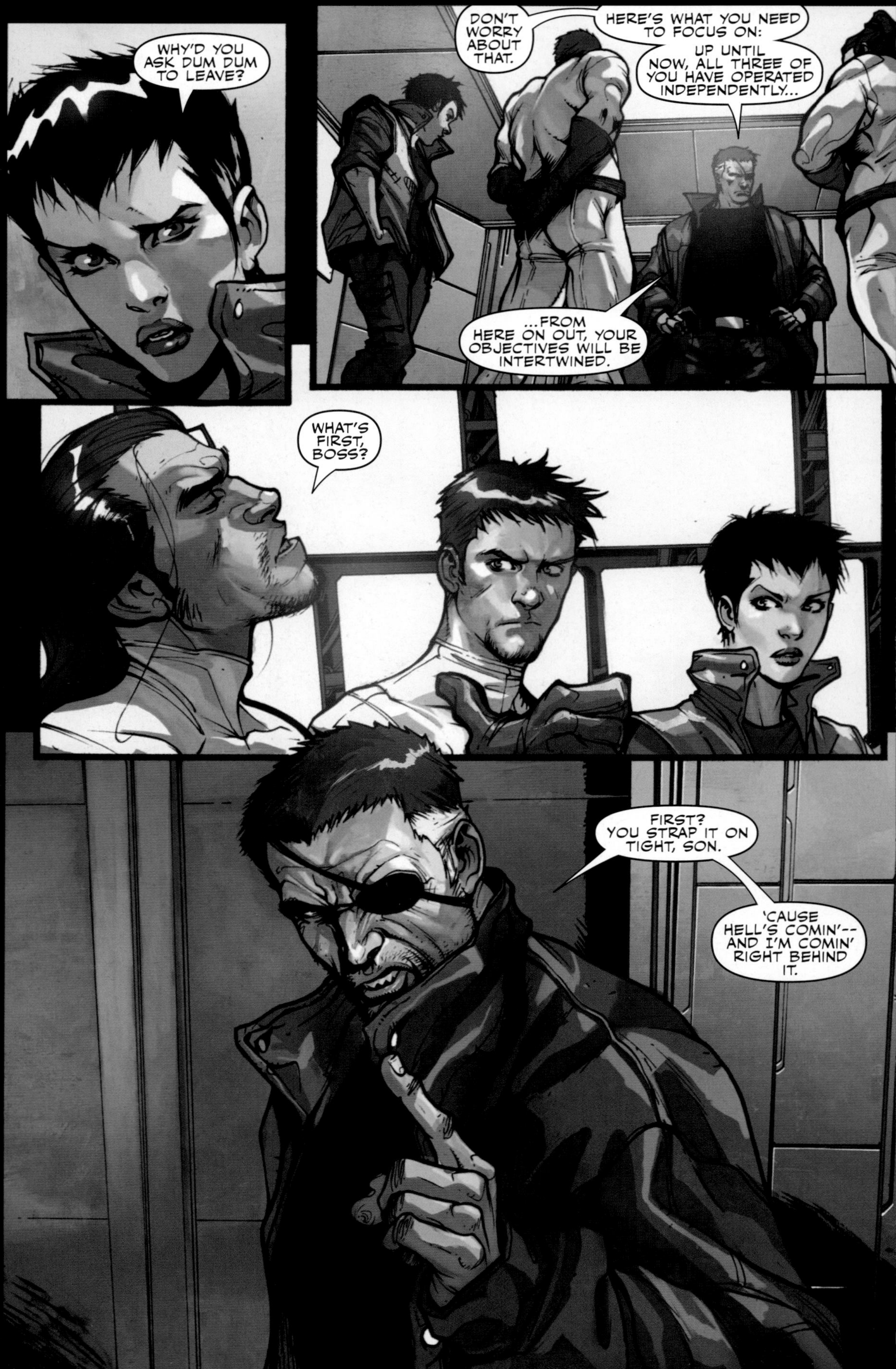

WHY'D YOU ASK DUM DUM TO LEAVE?
DON'T WORRY ABOUT THAT.
HERE'S WHAT YOU NEED TO FOCUS ON:
UP UNTIL NOW, ALL THREE OF YOU HAVE OPERATED INDEPENDENTLY...
...FROM HERE ON OUT, YOUR OBJECTIVES WILL BE INTERTWINED.
WHAT'S FIRST, BOSS?
FIRST? YOU STRAP IT ON TIGHT, SON.
'CAUSE HELL'S COMIN'-- AND I'M COMIN' RIGHT BEHIND IT.

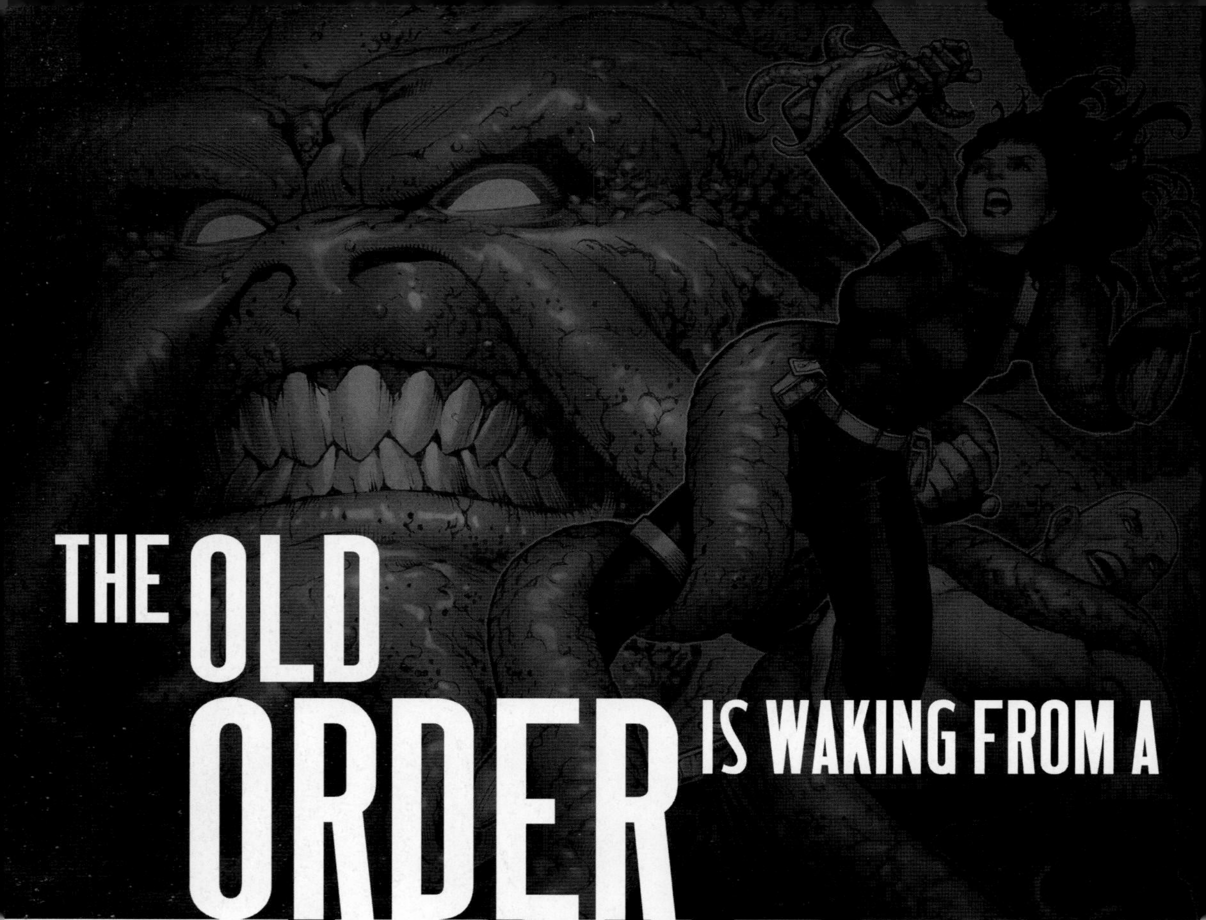

THE OLD ORDER IS WAKING FROM A LONG SLEEP

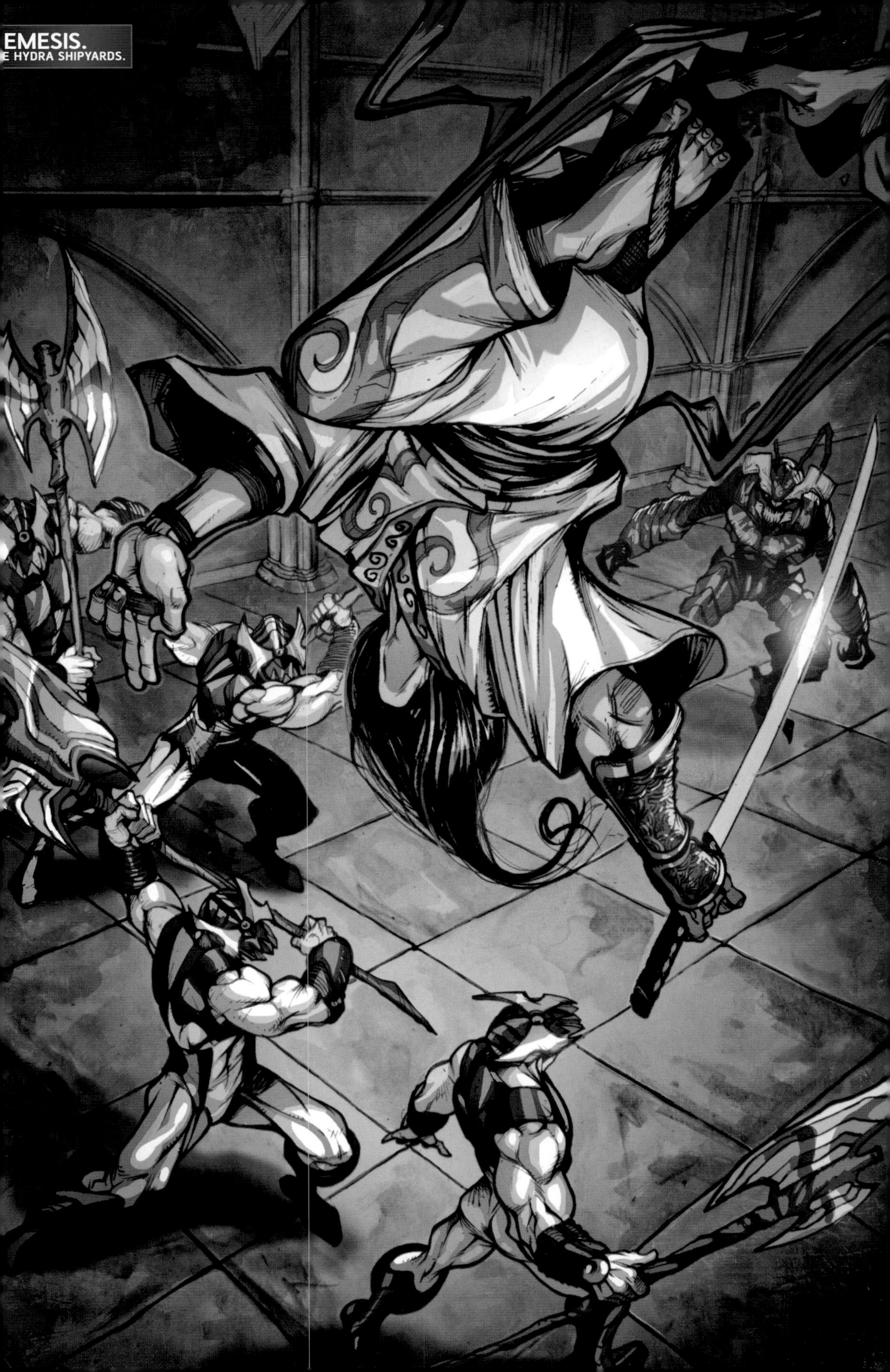
EMESIS.
E HYDRA SHIPYARDS.

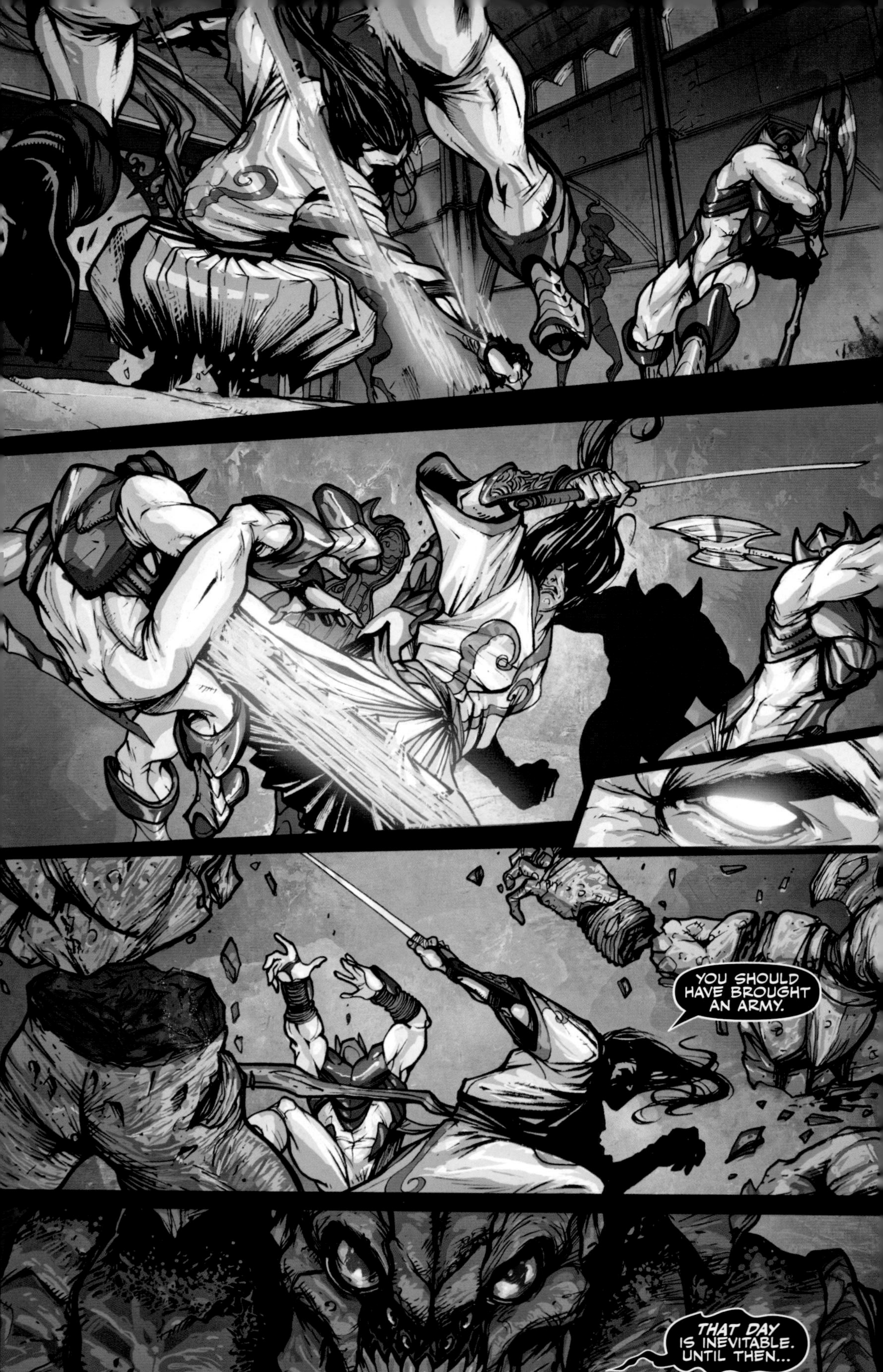
YOU SHOULD HAVE BROUGHT AN ARMY.
THAT DAY IS INEVITABLE. UNTIL THEN...

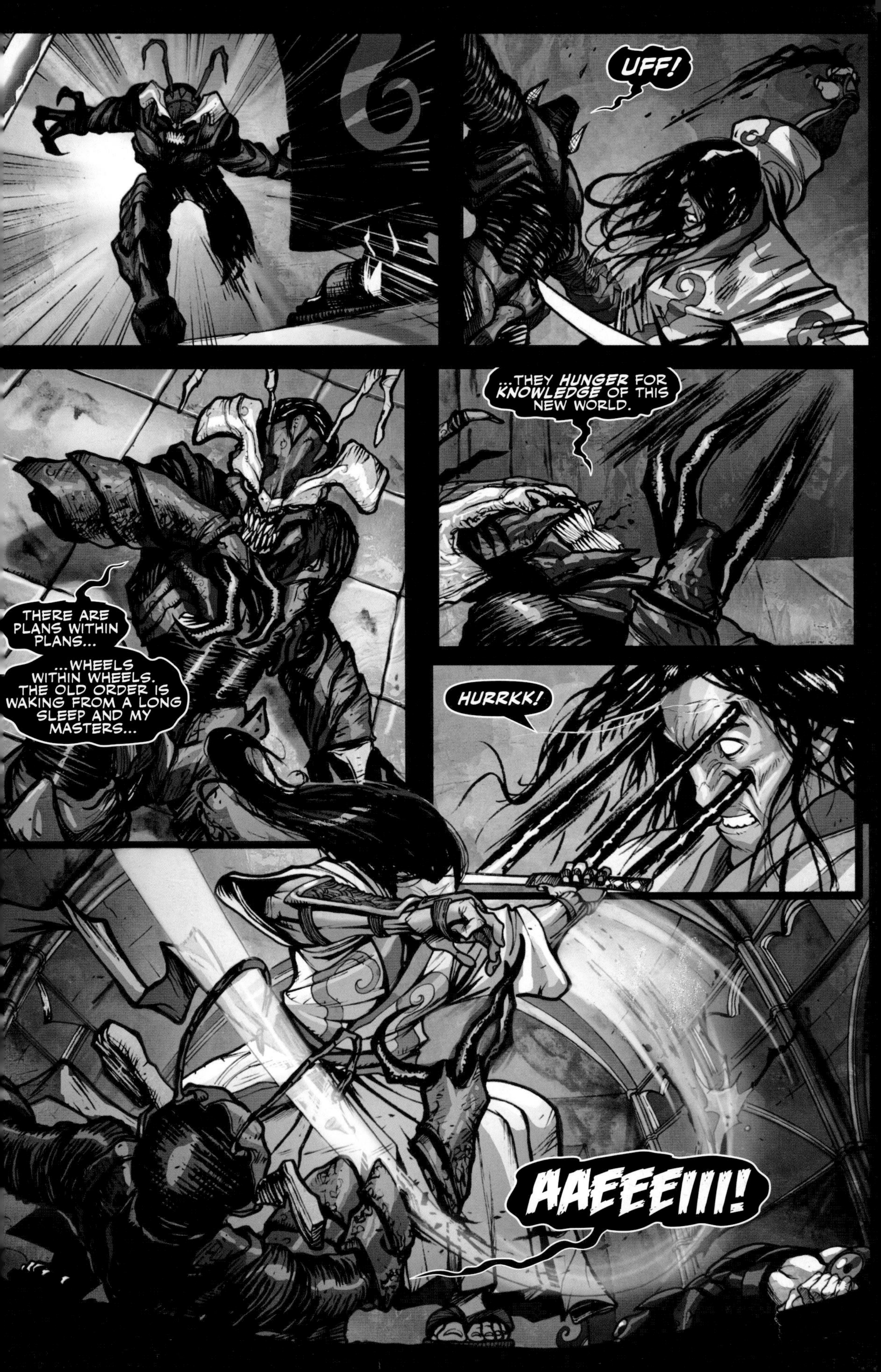
UFF!
THERE ARE PLANS WITHIN PLANS...
...WHEELS WITHIN WHEELS. THE OLD ORDER IS WAKING FROM A LONG SLEEP AND MY MASTERS...
...THEY HUNGER FOR KNOWLEDGE OF THIS NEW WORLD.
HURRKK!
AAEEEIII!

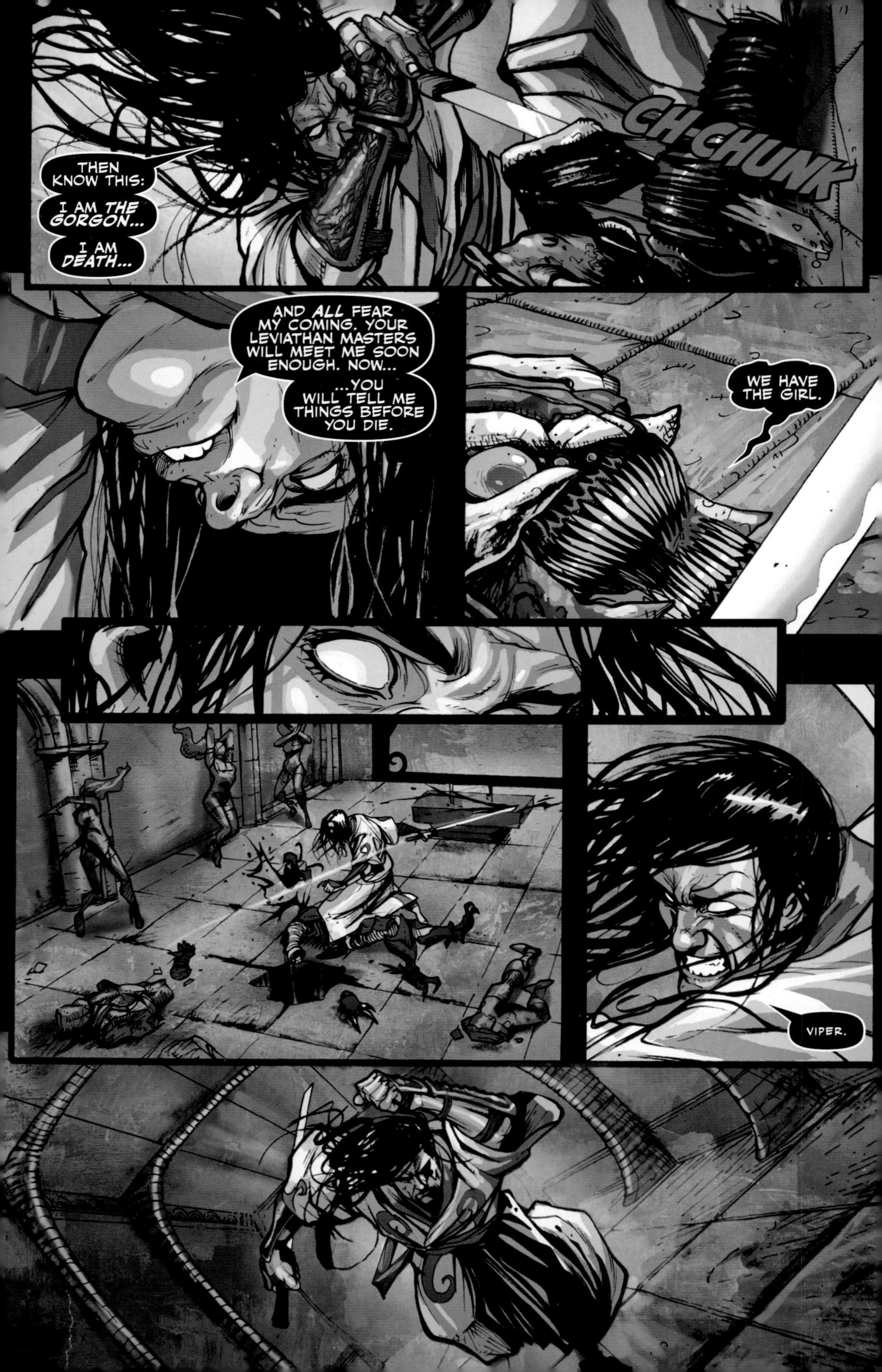
THEN KNOW THIS:
I AM THE GORGON...
I AM DEATH...
CH-CHUNK
AND ALL FEAR MY COMING. YOUR LEVIATHAN MASTERS WILL MEET ME SOON ENOUGH. NOW...
...YOU WILL TELL ME THINGS BEFORE YOU DIE.
WE HAVE THE GIRL.
VIPER.

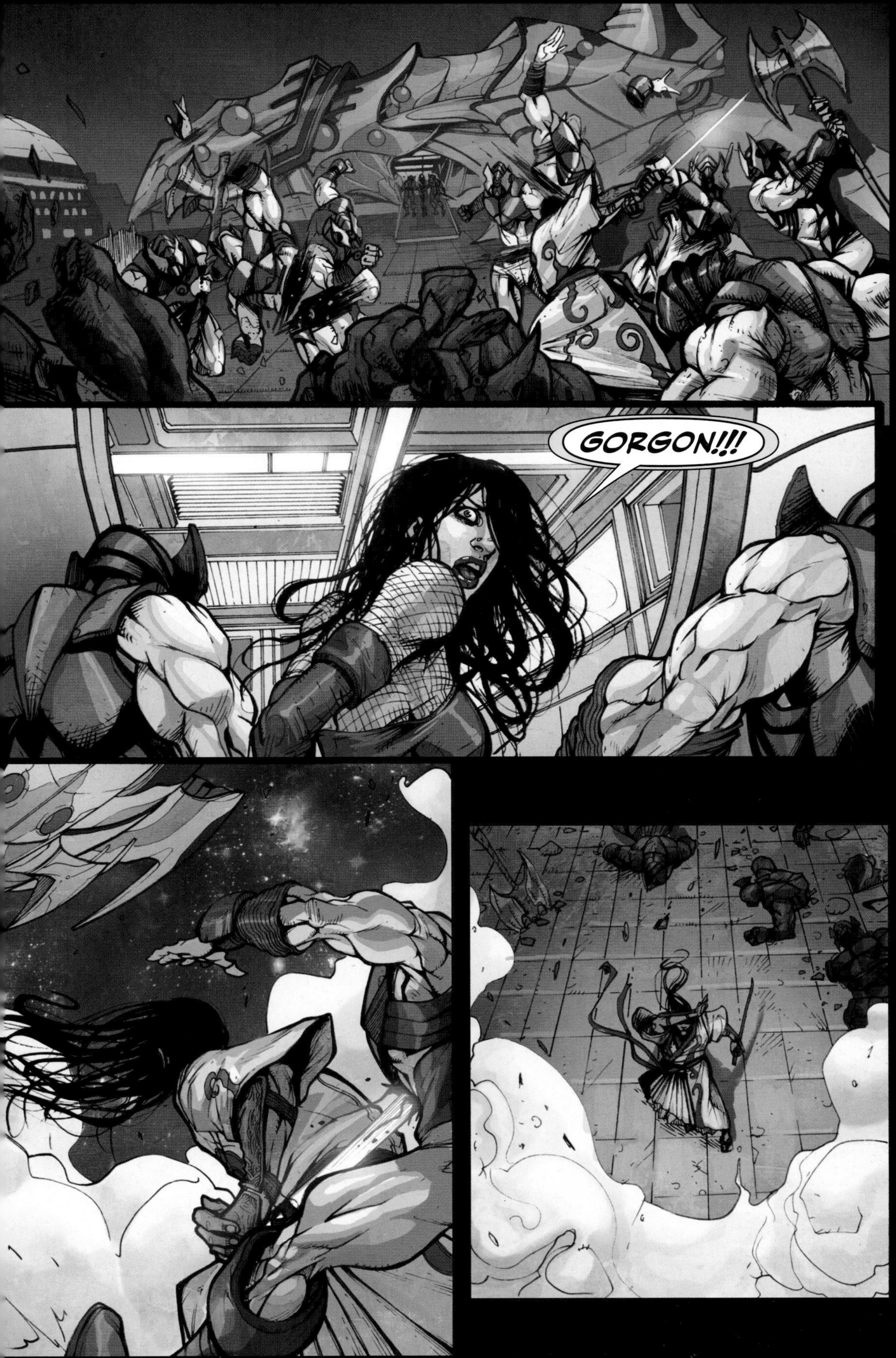
GORGON!!!

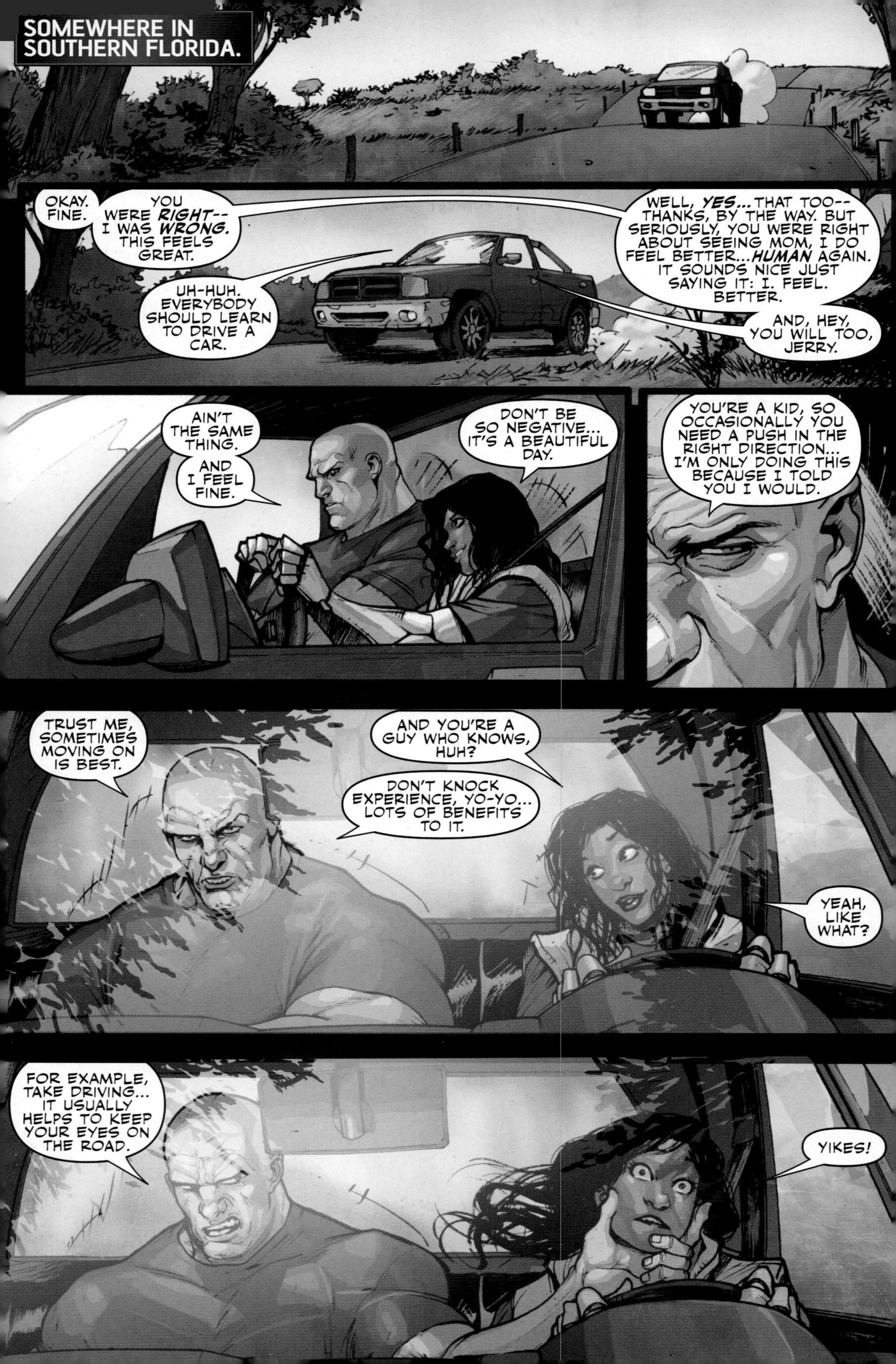
SOMEWHERE IN SOUTHERN FLORIDA.
OKAY. FINE.
YOU WERE RIGHT-- I WAS WRONG. THIS FEELS GREAT.
UH-HUH. EVERYBODY SHOULD LEARN TO DRIVE A CAR.
WELL, YES... THAT TOO-- THANKS, BY THE WAY. BUT SERIOUSLY, YOU WERE RIGHT ABOUT SEEING MOM, I DO FEEL BETTER... HUMAN AGAIN. IT SOUNDS NICE JUST SAYING IT: I. FEEL. BETTER.
AND, HEY, YOU WILL TOO, JERRY.
AIN'T THE SAME THING.
AND I FEEL FINE.
DON'T BE SO NEGATIVE... IT'S A BEAUTIFUL DAY.
YOU'RE A KID, SO OCCASIONALLY YOU NEED A PUSH IN THE RIGHT DIRECTION... I'M ONLY DOING THIS BECAUSE I TOLD YOU I WOULD.
TRUST ME, SOMETIMES MOVING ON IS BEST.
AND YOU'RE A GUY WHO KNOWS, HUH?
DON'T KNOCK EXPERIENCE, YO-YO... LOTS OF BENEFITS TO IT.
YEAH, LIKE WHAT?
FOR EXAMPLE, TAKE DRIVING... IT USUALLY HELPS TO KEEP YOUR EYES ON THE ROAD.
YIKES!

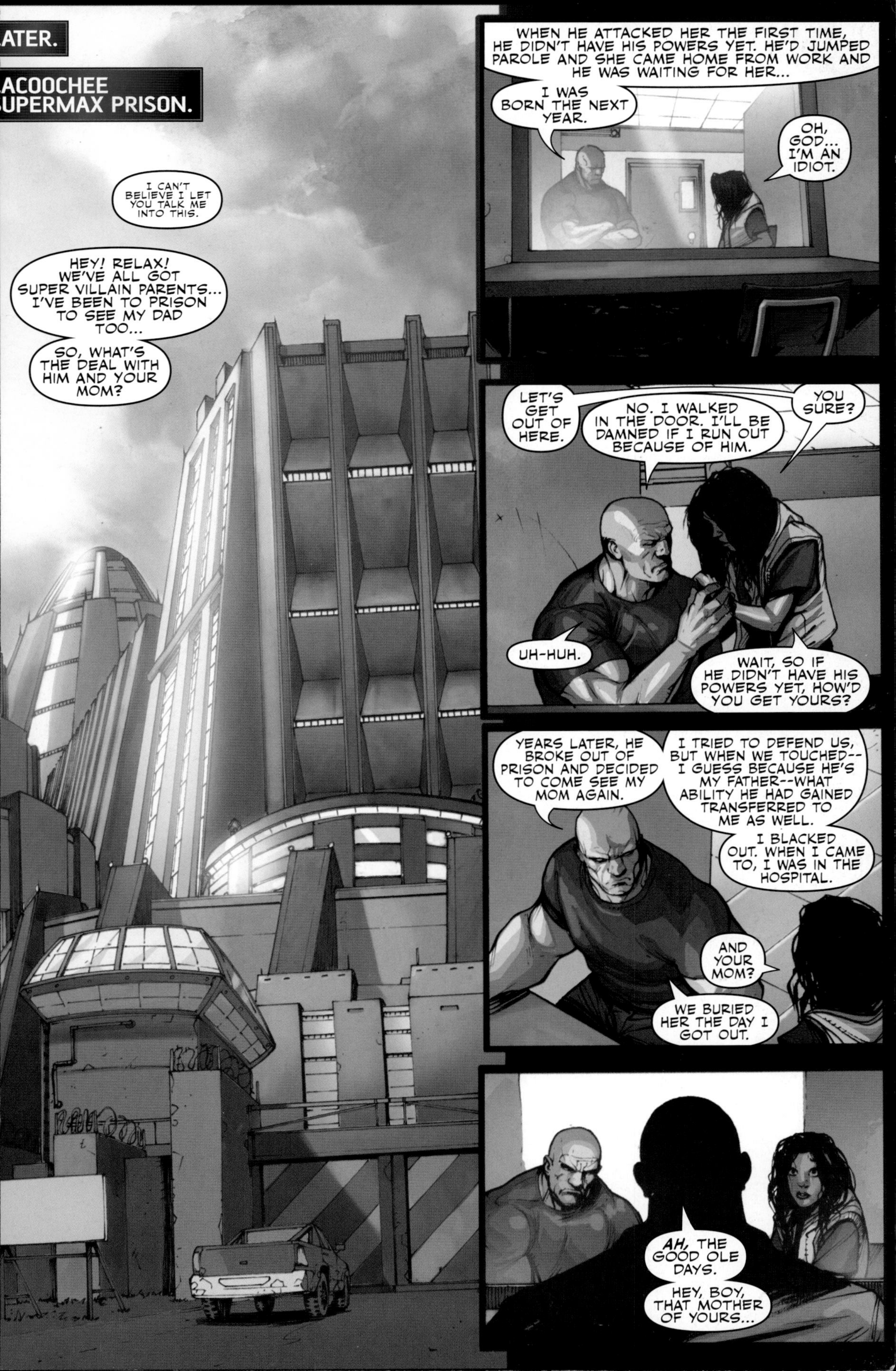

LATER.
ACOOCHEE SUPERMAX PRISON.
I CAN'T BELIEVE I LET YOU TALK ME INTO THIS.
HEY! RELAX! WE'VE ALL GOT SUPER VILLAIN PARENTS... I'VE BEEN TO PRISON TO SEE MY DAD TOO...
SO, WHAT'S THE DEAL WITH HIM AND YOUR MOM?
WHEN HE ATTACKED HER THE FIRST TIME, HE DIDN'T HAVE HIS POWERS YET. HE'D JUMPED PAROLE AND SHE CAME HOME FROM WORK AND HE WAS WAITING FOR HER...
I WAS BORN THE NEXT YEAR.
OH, GOD... I'M AN IDIOT.
LET'S GET OUT OF HERE.
NO. I WALKED IN THE DOOR. I'LL BE DAMNED IF I RUN OUT BECAUSE OF HIM.
YOU SURE?
UH-HUH.
WAIT, SO IF HE DIDN'T HAVE HIS POWERS YET, HOW'D YOU GET YOURS?
YEARS LATER, HE BROKE OUT OF PRISON AND DECIDED TO COME SEE MY MOM AGAIN.
I TRIED TO DEFEND US, BUT WHEN WE TOUCHED-- I GUESS BECAUSE HE'S MY FATHER--WHAT ABILITY HE HAD GAINED TRANSFERRED TO ME AS WELL.
I BLACKED OUT. WHEN I CAME TO, I WAS IN THE HOSPITAL.
AND YOUR MOM?
WE BURIED HER THE DAY I GOT OUT.
AH, THE GOOD OLE DAYS.
HEY, BOY, THAT MOTHER OF YOURS...

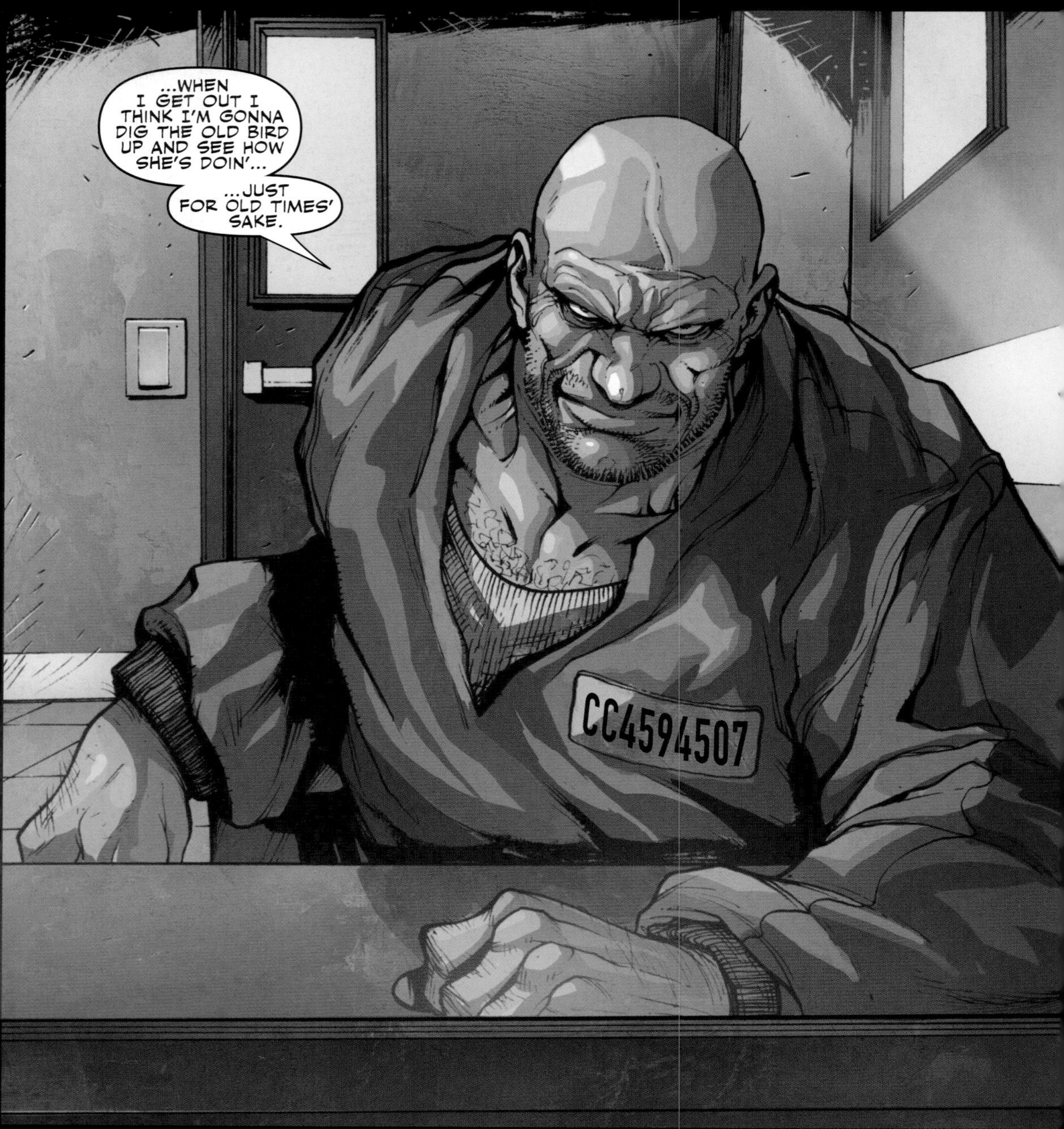
...WHEN I GET OUT I THINK I'M GONNA DIG THE OLD BIRD UP AND SEE HOW SHE'S DOIN'...
...JUST FOR OLD TIMES' SAKE.
CC4594507
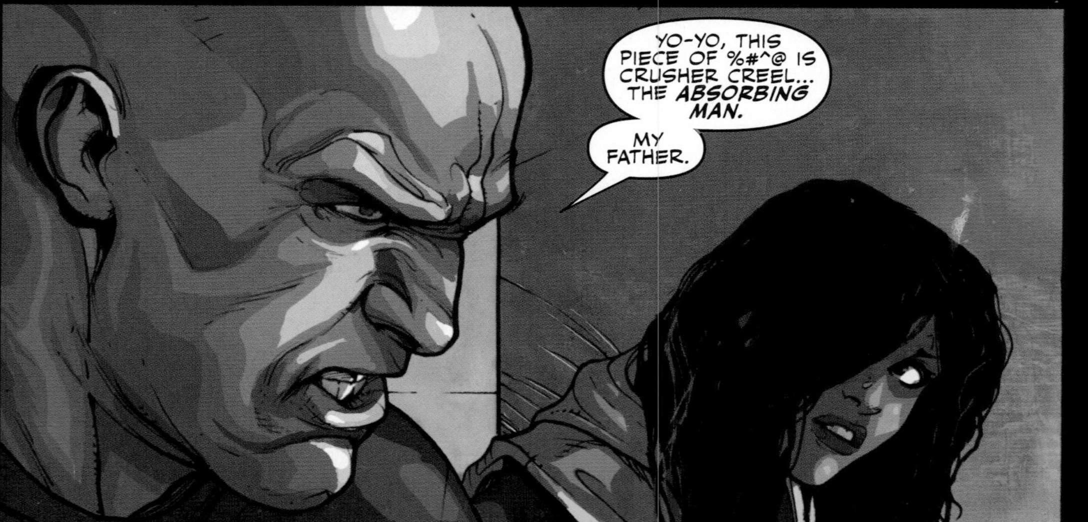
YO-YO, THIS PIECE OF %#^@ IS CRUSHER CREEL... THE ABSORBING MAN.
MY FATHER.

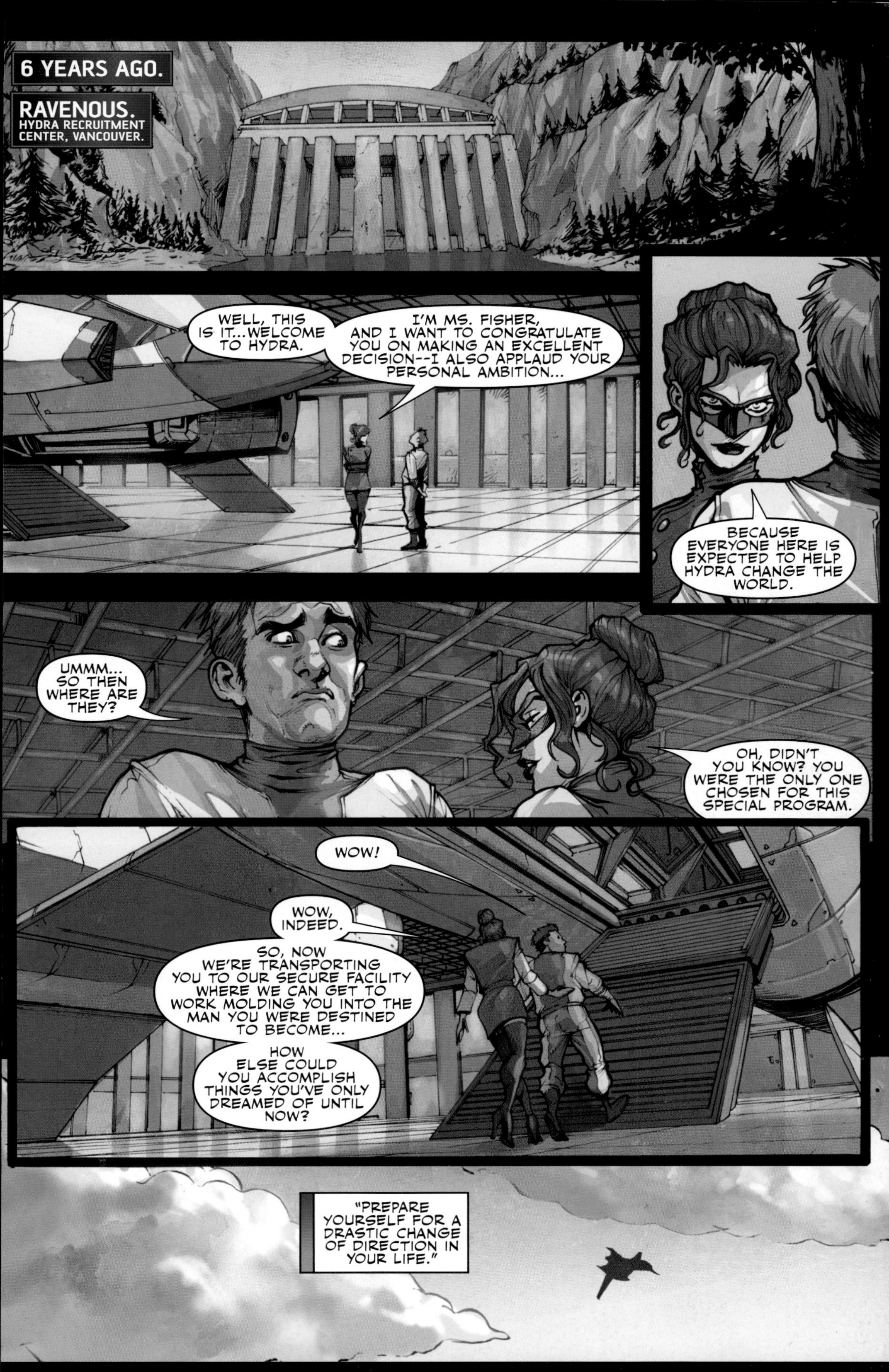
6 YEARS AGO.
RAVENOUS. HYDRA RECRUITMENT CENTER, VANCOUVER.
WELL, THIS IS IT...WELCOME TO HYDRA.
I'M MS. FISHER, AND I WANT TO CONGRATULATE YOU ON MAKING AN EXCELLENT DECISION--I ALSO APPLAUD YOUR PERSONAL AMBITION...
BECAUSE EVERYONE HERE IS EXPECTED TO HELP HYDRA CHANGE THE WORLD.
UMMM... SO THEN WHERE ARE THEY?
OH, DIDN'T YOU KNOW? YOU WERE THE ONLY ONE CHOSEN FOR THIS SPECIAL PROGRAM.
WOW!
WOW, INDEED.
SO, NOW WE'RE TRANSPORTING YOU TO OUR SECURE FACILITY WHERE WE CAN GET TO WORK MOLDING YOU INTO THE MAN YOU WERE DESTINED TO BECOME...
HOW ELSE COULD YOU ACCOMPLISH THINGS YOU'VE ONLY DREAMED OF UNTIL NOW?
"PREPARE YOURSELF FOR A DRASTIC CHANGE OF DIRECTION IN YOUR LIFE."

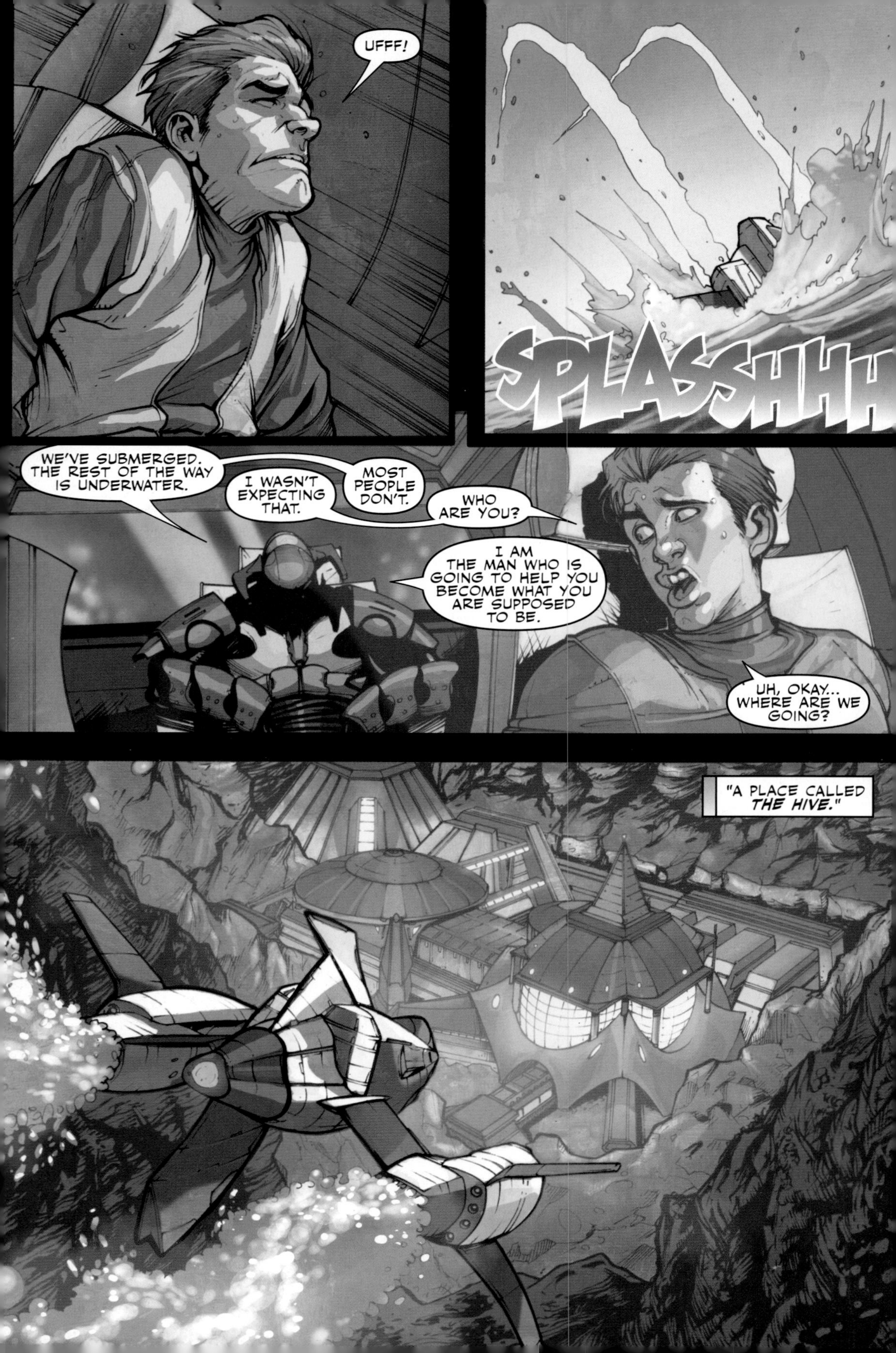
UFFF!
SPLASSHHH
WE'VE SUBMERGED. THE REST OF THE WAY IS UNDERWATER.
I WASN'T EXPECTING THAT.
MOST PEOPLE DON'T.
WHO ARE YOU?
I AM THE MAN WHO IS GOING TO HELP YOU BECOME WHAT YOU ARE SUPPOSED TO BE.
UH, OKAY... WHERE ARE WE GOING?
"A PLACE CALLED *THE HIVE*."

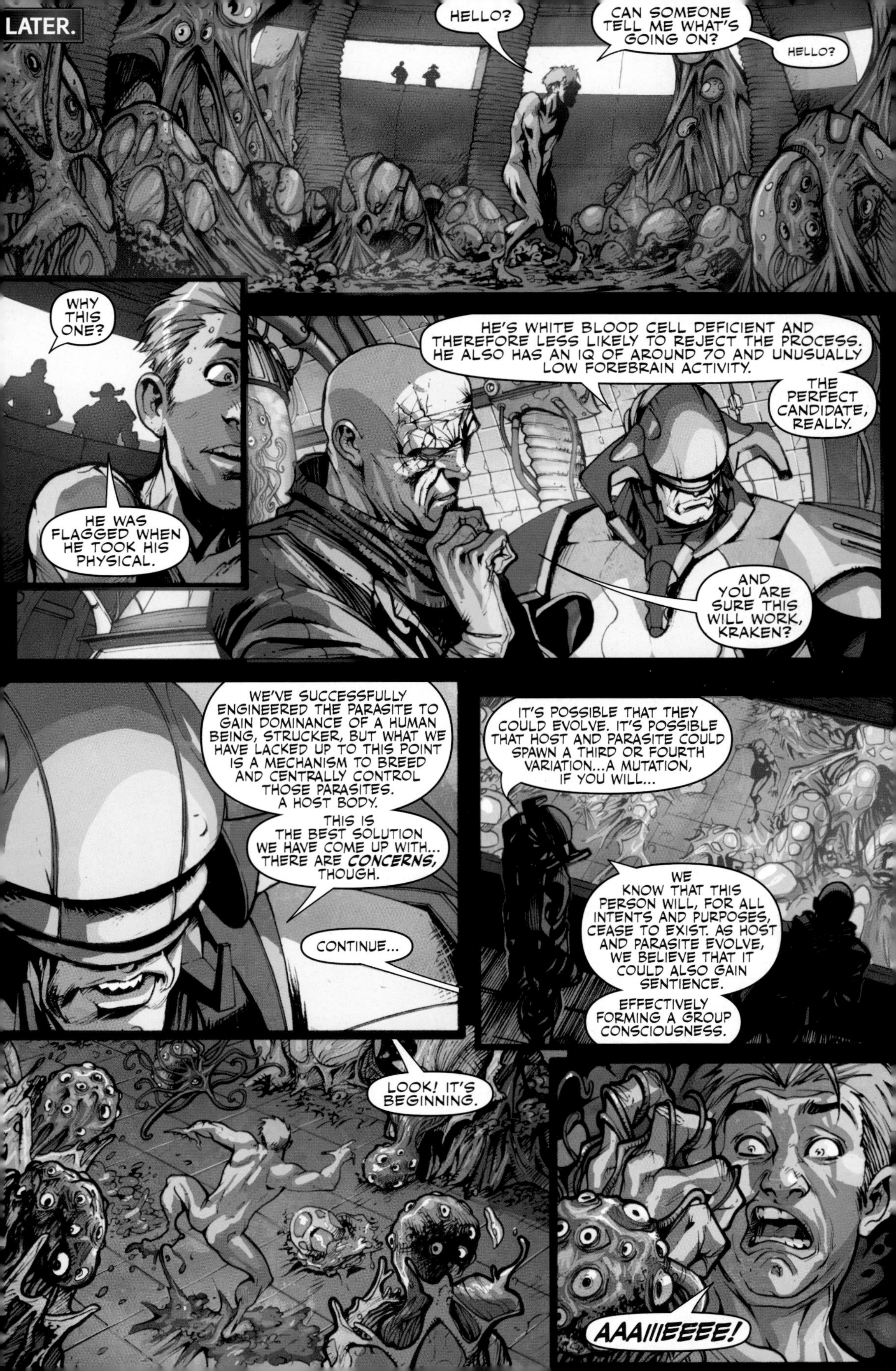
LATER.
HELLO?
CAN SOMEONE TELL ME WHAT'S GOING ON?
HELLO?
WHY THIS ONE?
HE WAS FLAGGED WHEN HE TOOK HIS PHYSICAL.
HE'S WHITE BLOOD CELL DEFICIENT AND THEREFORE LESS LIKELY TO REJECT THE PROCESS. HE ALSO HAS AN IQ OF AROUND 70 AND UNUSUALLY LOW FOREBRAIN ACTIVITY.
THE PERFECT CANDIDATE, REALLY.
AND YOU ARE SURE THIS WILL WORK, KRAKEN?
WE'VE SUCCESSFULLY ENGINEERED THE PARASITE TO GAIN DOMINANCE OF A HUMAN BEING, STRUCKER, BUT WHAT WE HAVE LACKED UP TO THIS POINT IS A MECHANISM TO BREED AND CENTRALLY CONTROL THOSE PARASITES. A HOST BODY.
THIS IS THE BEST SOLUTION WE HAVE COME UP WITH... THERE ARE *CONCERNS,* THOUGH.
CONTINUE...
IT'S POSSIBLE THAT THEY COULD EVOLVE. IT'S POSSIBLE THAT HOST AND PARASITE COULD SPAWN A THIRD OR FOURTH VARIATION...A MUTATION, IF YOU WILL...
WE KNOW THAT THIS PERSON WILL, FOR ALL INTENTS AND PURPOSES, CEASE TO EXIST. AS HOST AND PARASITE EVOLVE, WE BELIEVE THAT IT COULD ALSO GAIN SENTIENCE.
EFFECTIVELY FORMING A GROUP CONSCIOUSNESS.
LOOK! IT'S BEGINNING.
AAAIIIEEEE!

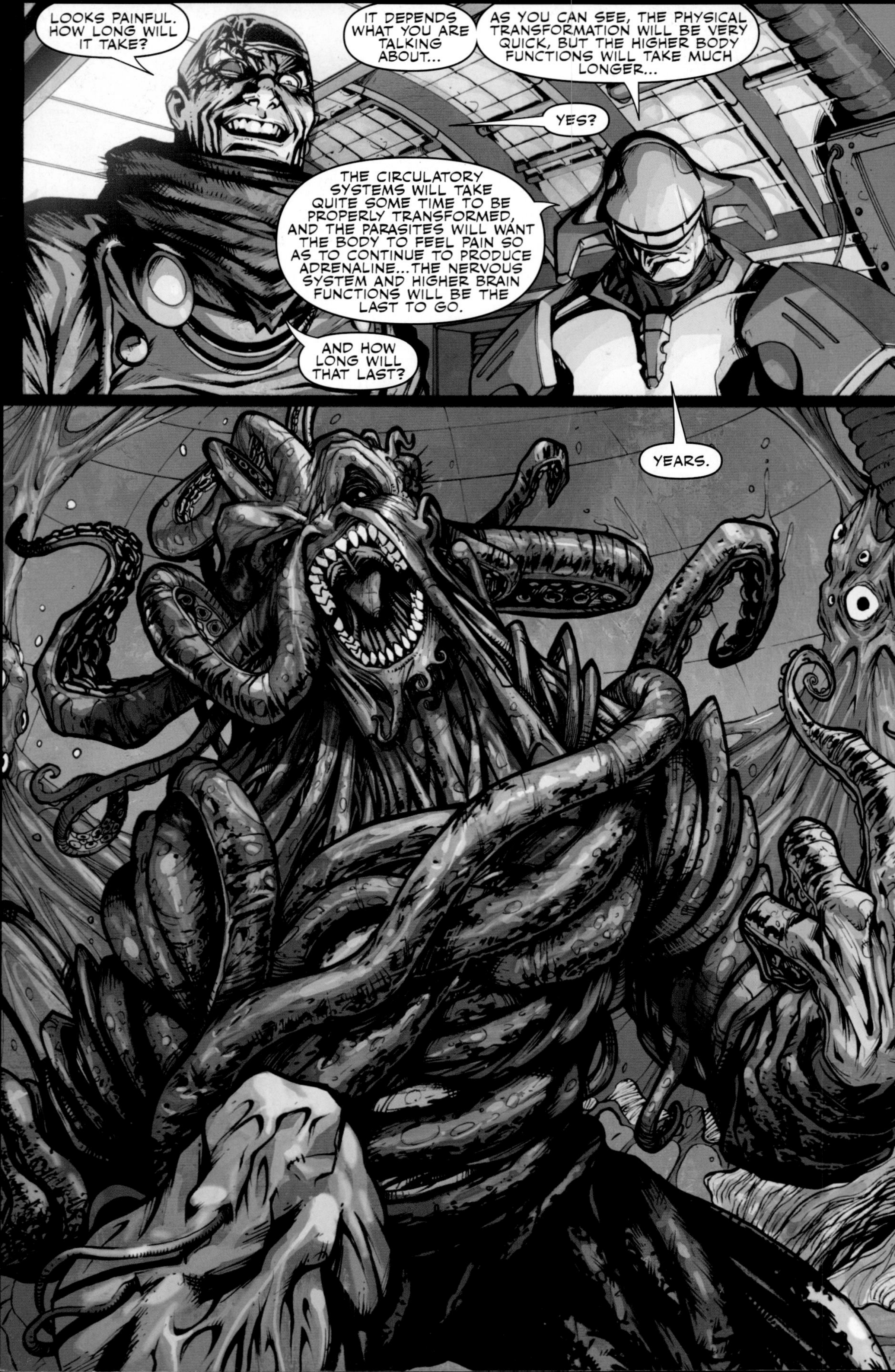
LOOKS PAINFUL. HOW LONG WILL IT TAKE?
IT DEPENDS WHAT YOU ARE TALKING ABOUT...
AS YOU CAN SEE, THE PHYSICAL TRANSFORMATION WILL BE VERY QUICK, BUT THE HIGHER BODY FUNCTIONS WILL TAKE MUCH LONGER...
YES?
THE CIRCULATORY SYSTEMS WILL TAKE QUITE SOME TIME TO BE PROPERLY TRANSFORMED, AND THE PARASITES WILL WANT THE BODY TO FEEL PAIN SO AS TO CONTINUE TO PRODUCE ADRENALINE...THE NERVOUS SYSTEM AND HIGHER BRAIN FUNCTIONS WILL BE THE LAST TO GO.
AND HOW LONG WILL THAT LAST?
YEARS.

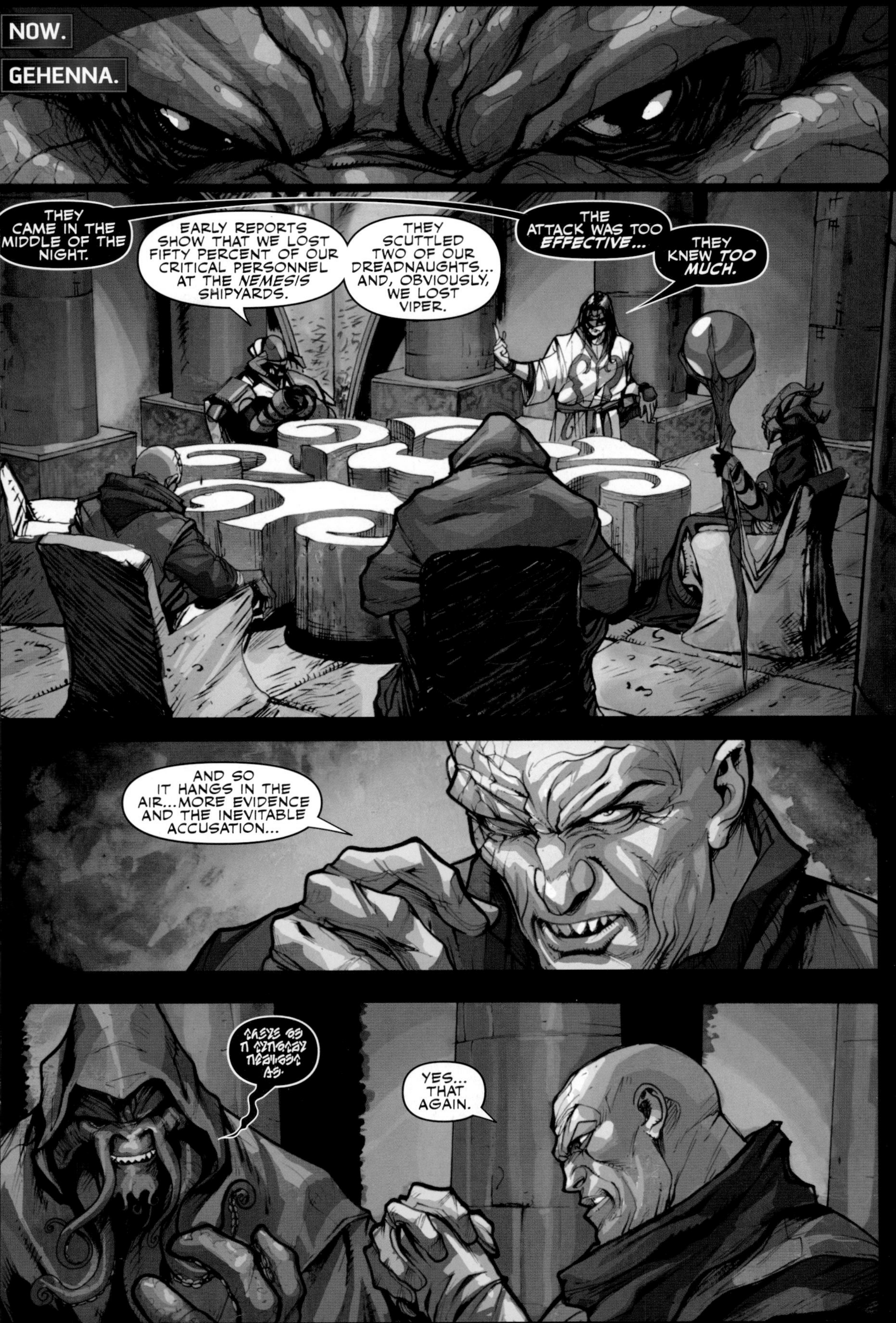
NOW.
GEHENNA.
THEY CAME IN THE MIDDLE OF THE NIGHT.
EARLY REPORTS SHOW THAT WE LOST FIFTY PERCENT OF OUR CRITICAL PERSONNEL AT THE *NEMESIS* SHIPYARDS.
THEY SCUTTLED TWO OF OUR DREADNAUGHTS... AND, OBVIOUSLY, WE LOST VIPER.
THE ATTACK WAS TOO *EFFECTIVE...*
THEY KNEW *TOO MUCH.*
AND SO IT HANGS IN THE AIR...MORE EVIDENCE AND THE INEVITABLE ACCUSATION...
YES... THAT AGAIN.

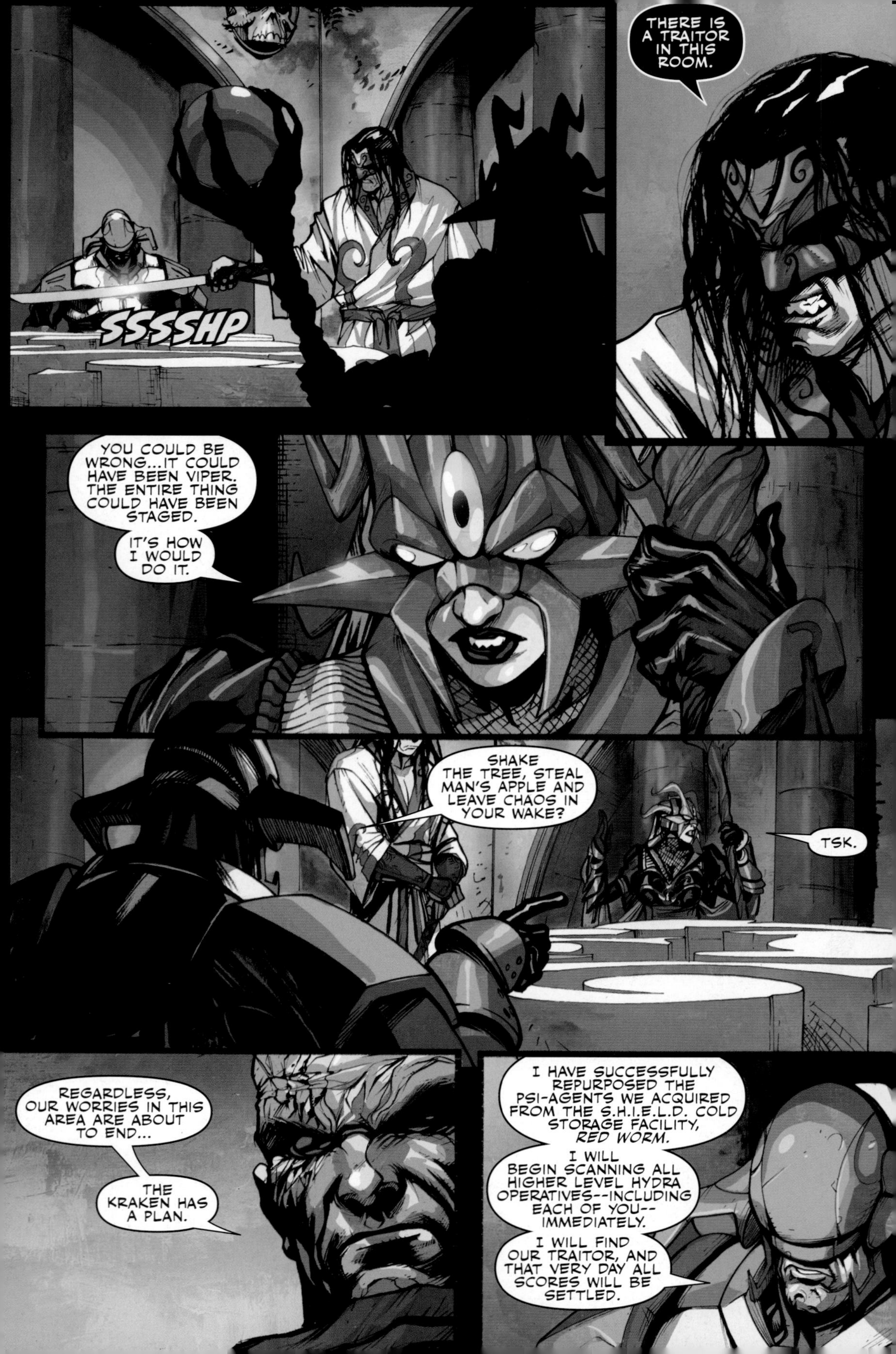
SSSSHP
THERE IS A TRAITOR IN THIS ROOM.
YOU COULD BE WRONG...IT COULD HAVE BEEN VIPER. THE ENTIRE THING COULD HAVE BEEN STAGED.
IT'S HOW I WOULD DO IT.
SHAKE THE TREE, STEAL MAN'S APPLE AND LEAVE CHAOS IN YOUR WAKE?
TSK.
REGARDLESS, OUR WORRIES IN THIS AREA ARE ABOUT TO END...
THE KRAKEN HAS A PLAN.
I HAVE SUCCESSFULLY REPURPOSED THE PSI-AGENTS WE ACQUIRED FROM THE S.H.I.E.L.D. COLD STORAGE FACILITY, *RED WORM.*
I WILL BEGIN SCANNING ALL HIGHER LEVEL HYDRA OPERATIVES--INCLUDING EACH OF YOU--IMMEDIATELY.
I WILL FIND OUR TRAITOR, AND THAT VERY DAY ALL SCORES WILL BE SETTLED.

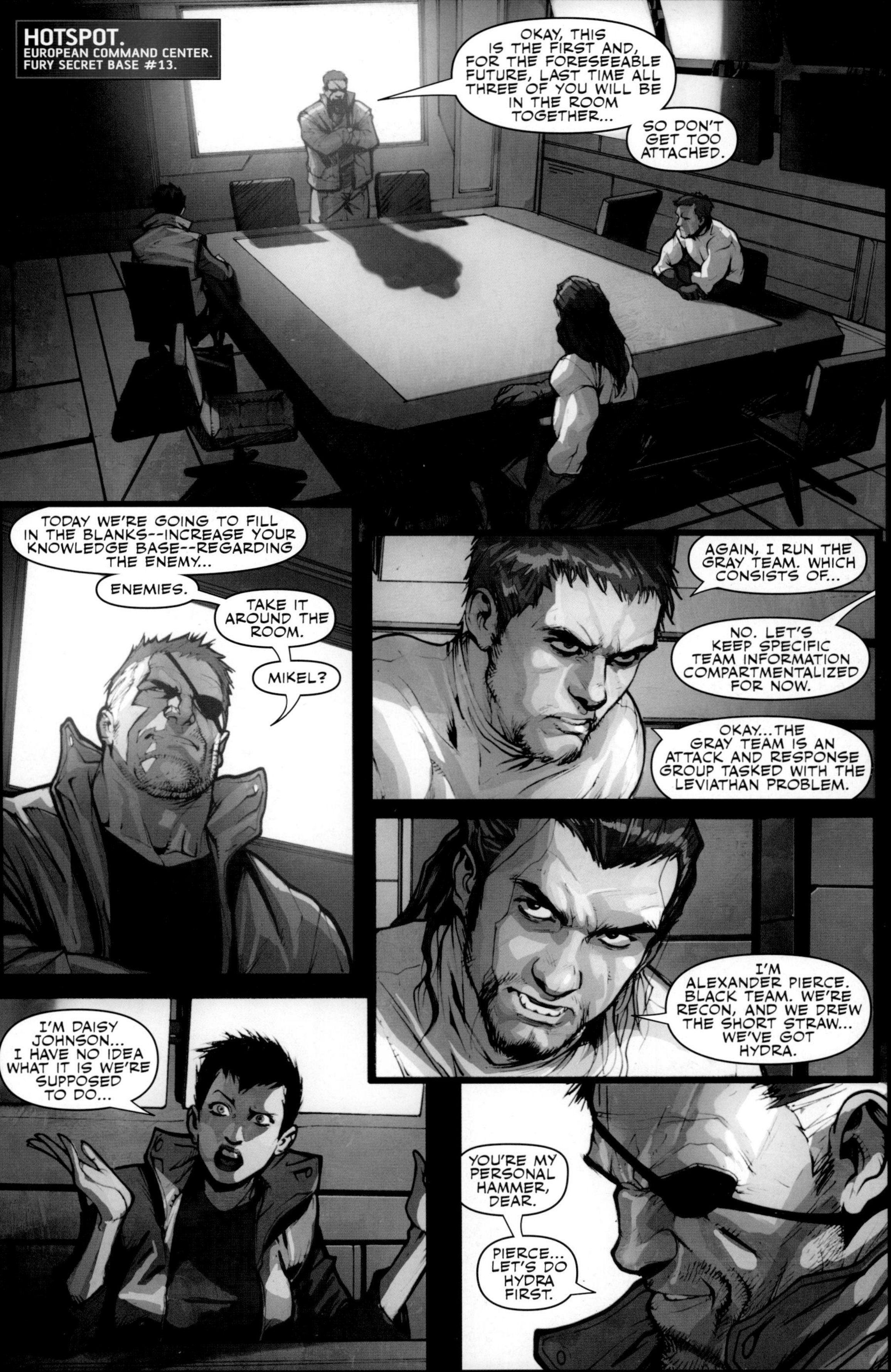
HOTSPOT.
EUROPEAN COMMAND CENTER. FURY SECRET BASE #13.
OKAY, THIS IS THE FIRST AND, FOR THE FORESEEABLE FUTURE, LAST TIME ALL THREE OF YOU WILL BE IN THE ROOM TOGETHER...
SO DON'T GET TOO ATTACHED.
TODAY WE'RE GOING TO FILL IN THE BLANKS--INCREASE YOUR KNOWLEDGE BASE--REGARDING THE ENEMY...
ENEMIES.
TAKE IT AROUND THE ROOM.
MIKEL?
AGAIN, I RUN THE GRAY TEAM. WHICH CONSISTS OF...
NO. LET'S KEEP SPECIFIC TEAM INFORMATION COMPARTMENTALIZED FOR NOW.
OKAY...THE GRAY TEAM IS AN ATTACK AND RESPONSE GROUP TASKED WITH THE LEVIATHAN PROBLEM.
I'M ALEXANDER PIERCE. BLACK TEAM. WE'RE RECON, AND WE DREW THE SHORT STRAW... WE'VE GOT HYDRA.
I'M DAISY JOHNSON... I HAVE NO IDEA WHAT IT IS WE'RE SUPPOSED TO DO...
YOU'RE MY PERSONAL HAMMER, DEAR.
PIERCE... LET'S DO HYDRA FIRST.

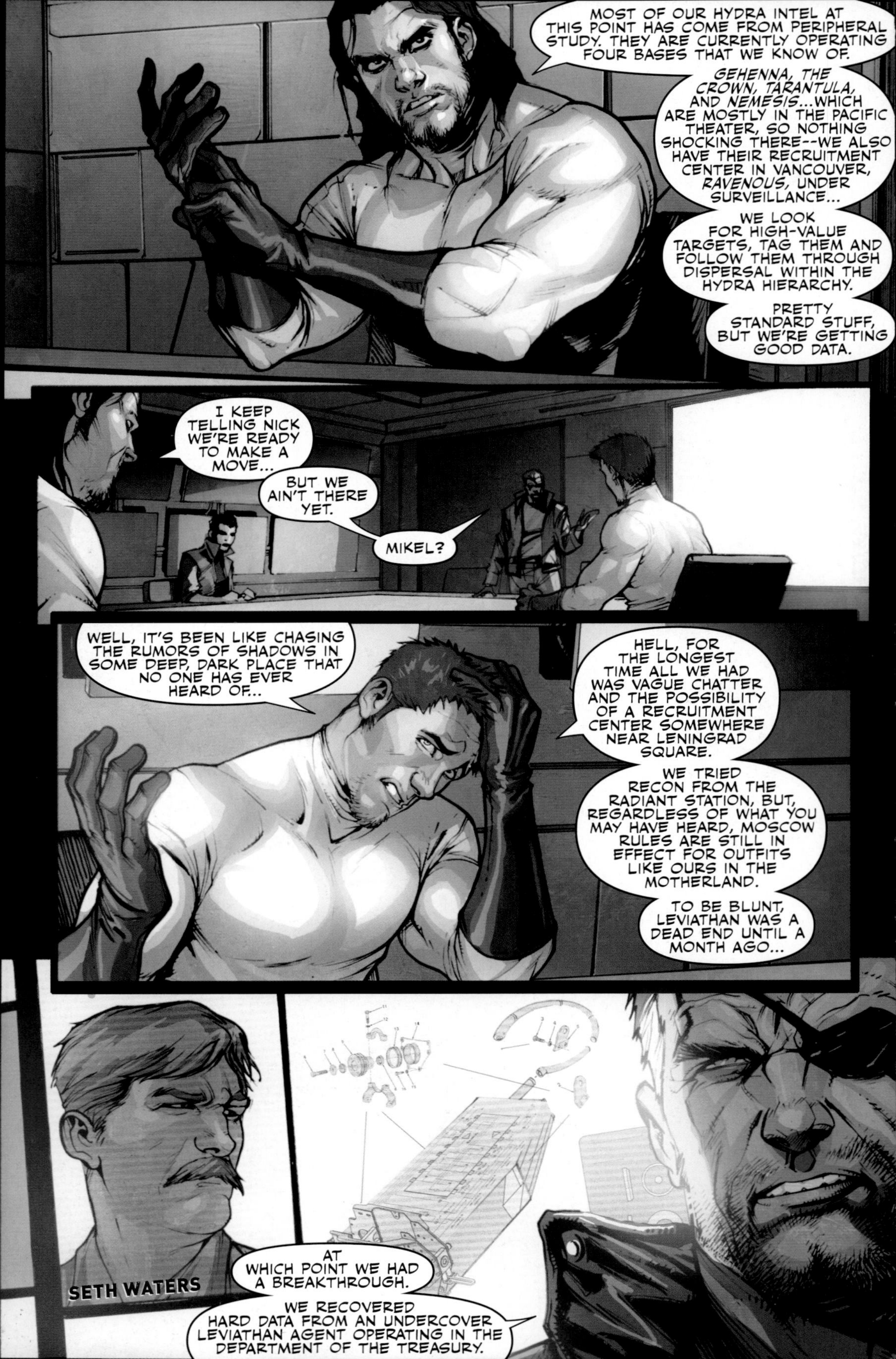
MOST OF OUR HYDRA INTEL AT THIS POINT HAS COME FROM PERIPHERAL STUDY. THEY ARE CURRENTLY OPERATING FOUR BASES THAT WE KNOW OF.
GEHENNA, THE CROWN, TARANTULA, AND *NEMESIS*...WHICH ARE MOSTLY IN THE PACIFIC THEATER, SO NOTHING SHOCKING THERE--WE ALSO HAVE THEIR RECRUITMENT CENTER IN VANCOUVER, *RAVENOUS,* UNDER SURVEILLANCE...
WE LOOK FOR HIGH-VALUE TARGETS, TAG THEM AND FOLLOW THEM THROUGH DISPERSAL WITHIN THE HYDRA HIERARCHY.
PRETTY STANDARD STUFF, BUT WE'RE GETTING GOOD DATA.
I KEEP TELLING NICK WE'RE READY TO MAKE A MOVE...
BUT WE AIN'T THERE YET.
MIKEL?
WELL, IT'S BEEN LIKE CHASING THE RUMORS OF SHADOWS IN SOME DEEP, DARK PLACE THAT NO ONE HAS EVER HEARD OF...
HELL, FOR THE LONGEST TIME ALL WE HAD WAS VAGUE CHATTER AND THE POSSIBILITY OF A RECRUITMENT CENTER SOMEWHERE NEAR LENINGRAD SQUARE.
WE TRIED RECON FROM THE RADIANT STATION, BUT, REGARDLESS OF WHAT YOU MAY HAVE HEARD, MOSCOW RULES ARE STILL IN EFFECT FOR OUTFITS LIKE OURS IN THE MOTHERLAND.
TO BE BLUNT, LEVIATHAN WAS A DEAD END UNTIL A MONTH AGO...
SETH WATERS
AT WHICH POINT WE HAD A BREAKTHROUGH.
WE RECOVERED HARD DATA FROM AN UNDERCOVER LEVIATHAN AGENT OPERATING IN THE DEPARTMENT OF THE TREASURY.

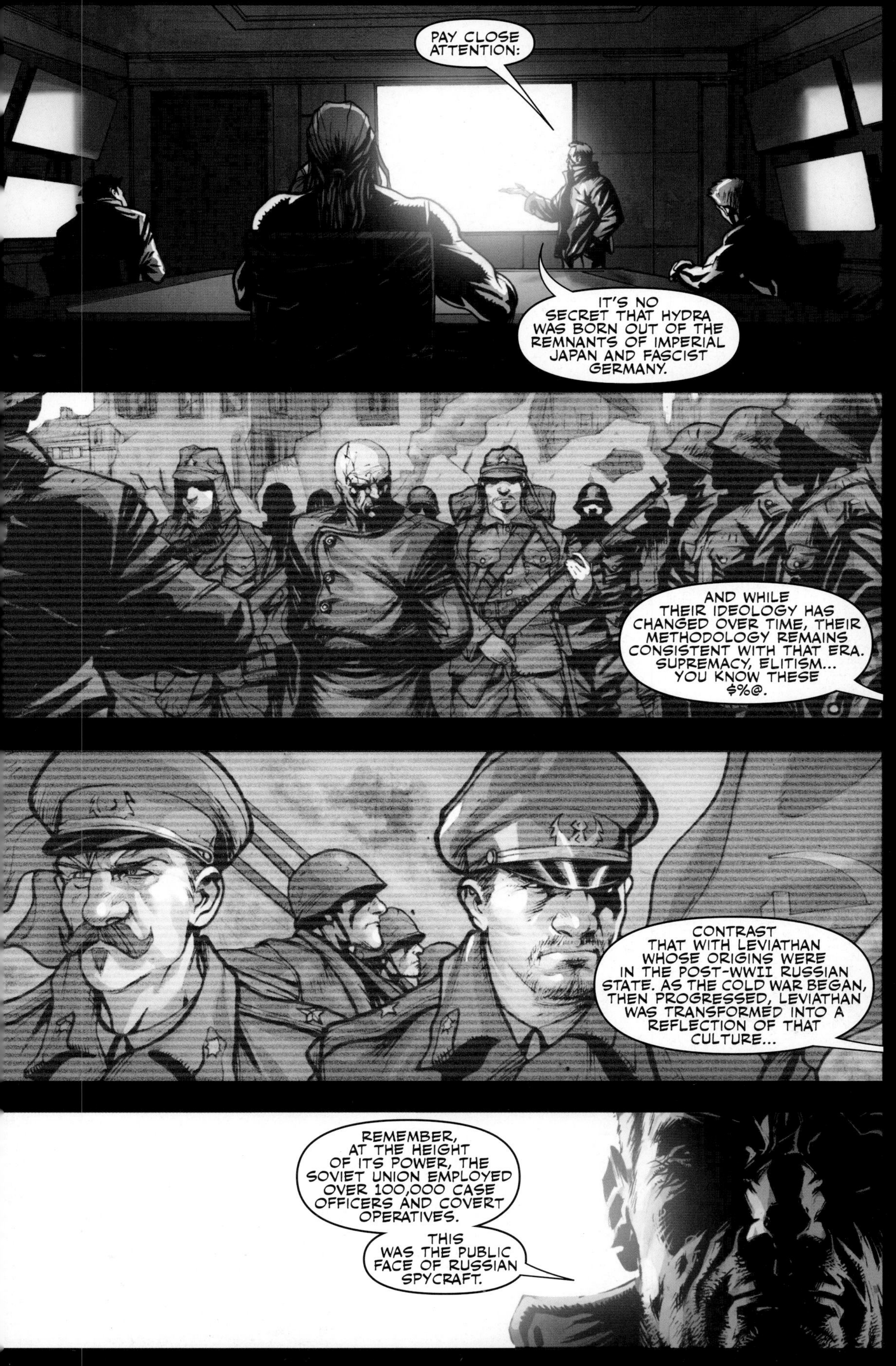
PAY CLOSE ATTENTION:
IT'S NO SECRET THAT HYDRA WAS BORN OUT OF THE REMNANTS OF IMPERIAL JAPAN AND FASCIST GERMANY.
AND WHILE THEIR IDEOLOGY HAS CHANGED OVER TIME, THEIR METHODOLOGY REMAINS CONSISTENT WITH THAT ERA. SUPREMACY, ELITISM... YOU KNOW THESE $%@.
CONTRAST THAT WITH LEVIATHAN WHOSE ORIGINS WERE IN THE POST-WWII RUSSIAN STATE. AS THE COLD WAR BEGAN, THEN PROGRESSED, LEVIATHAN WAS TRANSFORMED INTO A REFLECTION OF THAT CULTURE...
REMEMBER, AT THE HEIGHT OF ITS POWER, THE SOVIET UNION EMPLOYED OVER 100,000 CASE OFFICERS AND COVERT OPERATIVES.
THIS WAS THE PUBLIC FACE OF RUSSIAN SPYCRAFT.

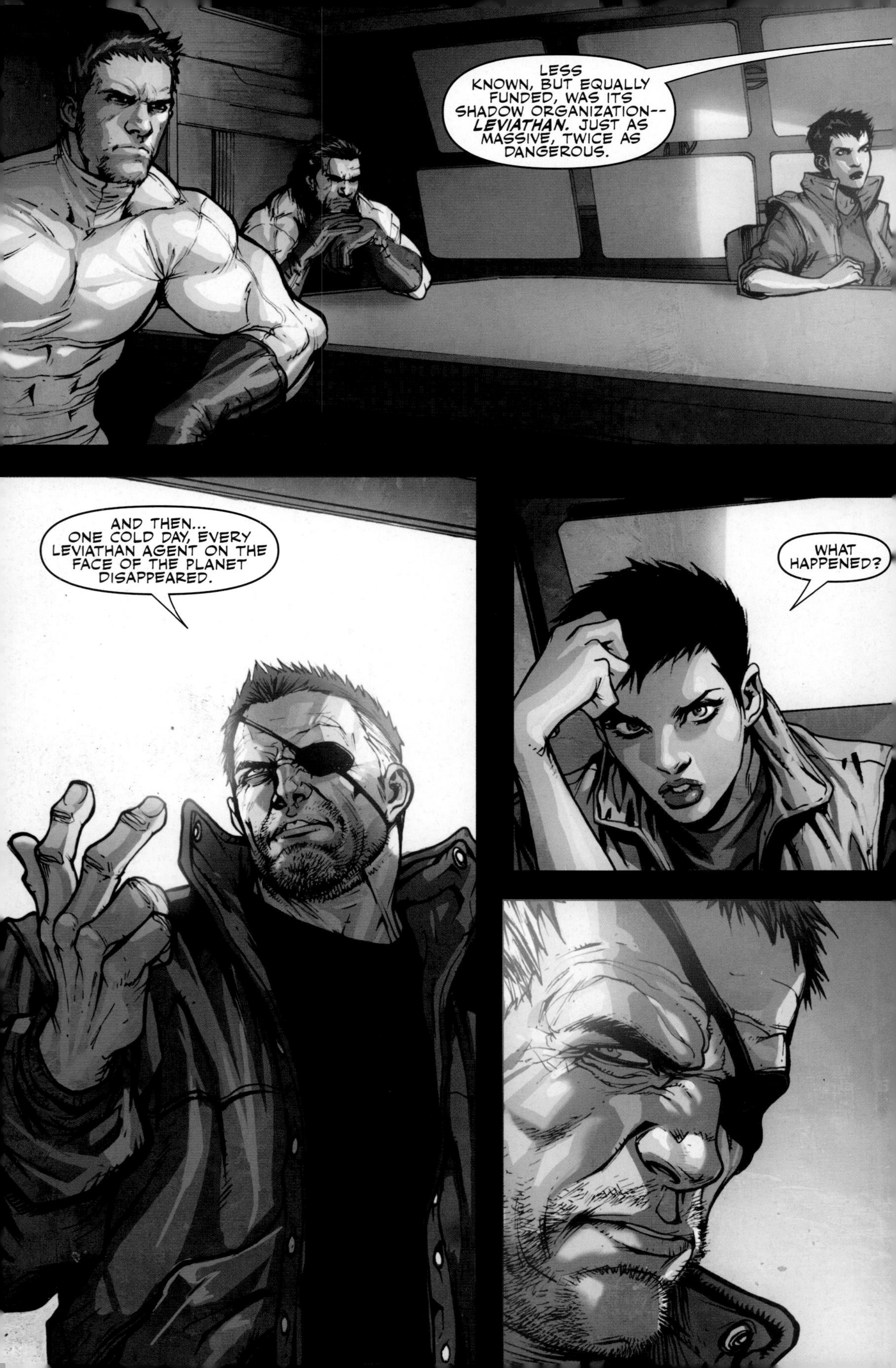
LESS KNOWN, BUT EQUALLY FUNDED, WAS ITS SHADOW ORGANIZATION-- *LEVIATHAN.* JUST AS MASSIVE, TWICE AS DANGEROUS.
AND THEN... ONE COLD DAY, EVERY LEVIATHAN AGENT ON THE FACE OF THE PLANET DISAPPEARED.
WHAT HAPPENED?

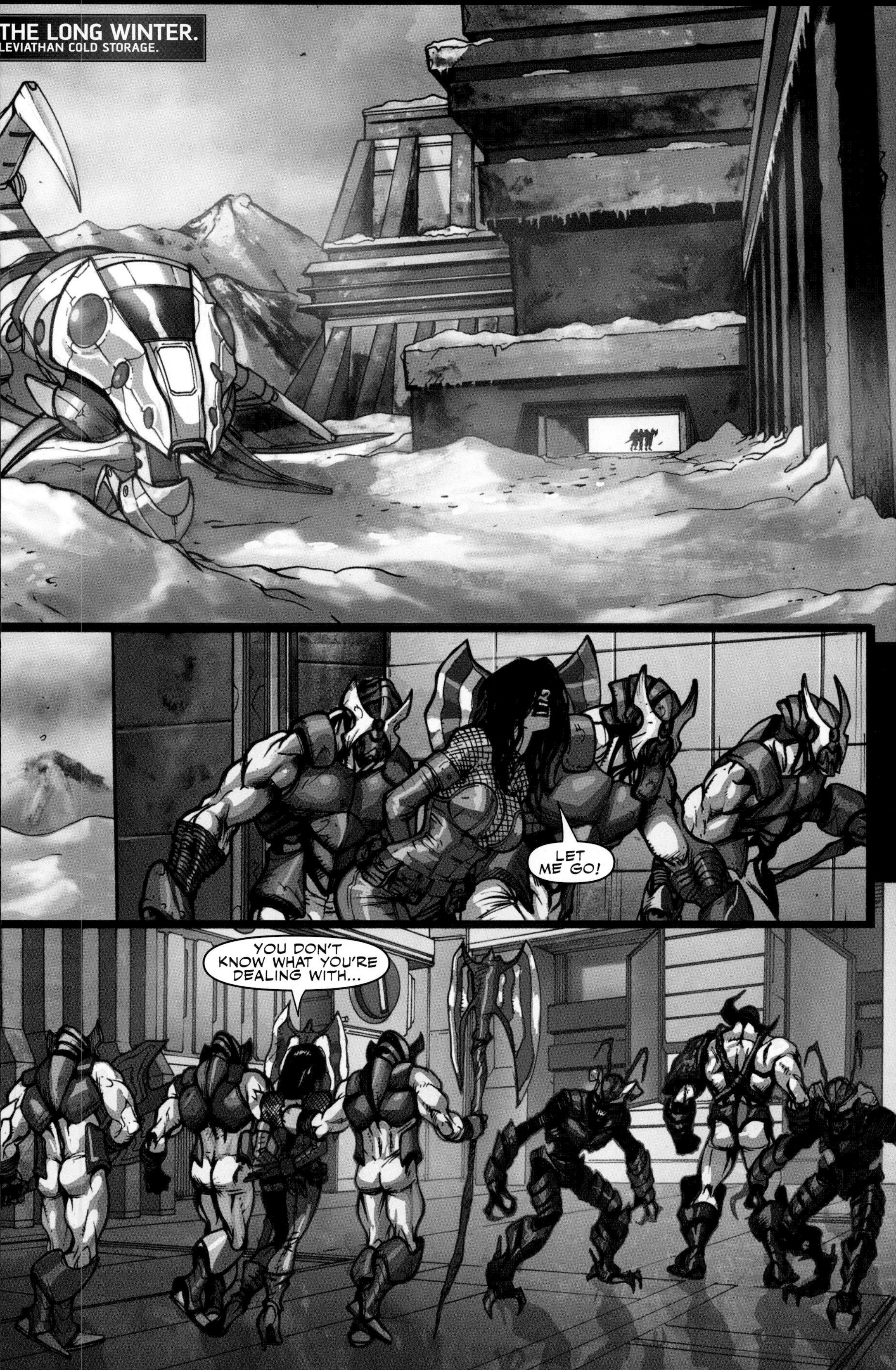
THE LONG WINTER.
LEVIATHAN COLD STORAGE.
LET ME GO!
YOU DON'T KNOW WHAT YOU'RE DEALING WITH...

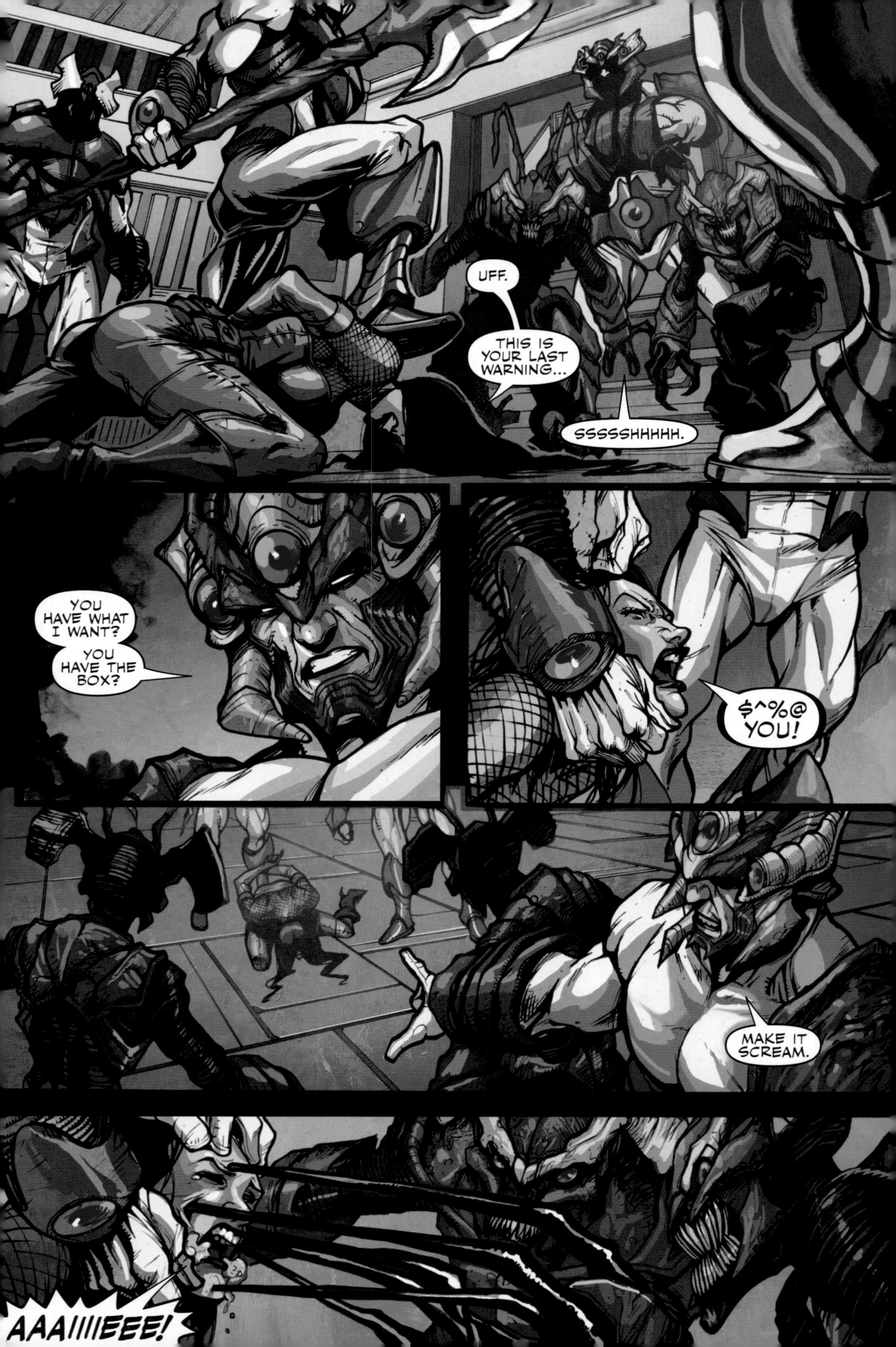
UFF.
THIS IS YOUR LAST WARNING...
SSSSSHHHHH.
YOU HAVE WHAT I WANT?
YOU HAVE THE BOX?
$^%@ YOU!
MAKE IT SCREAM.
AAAIIIIIEEE!

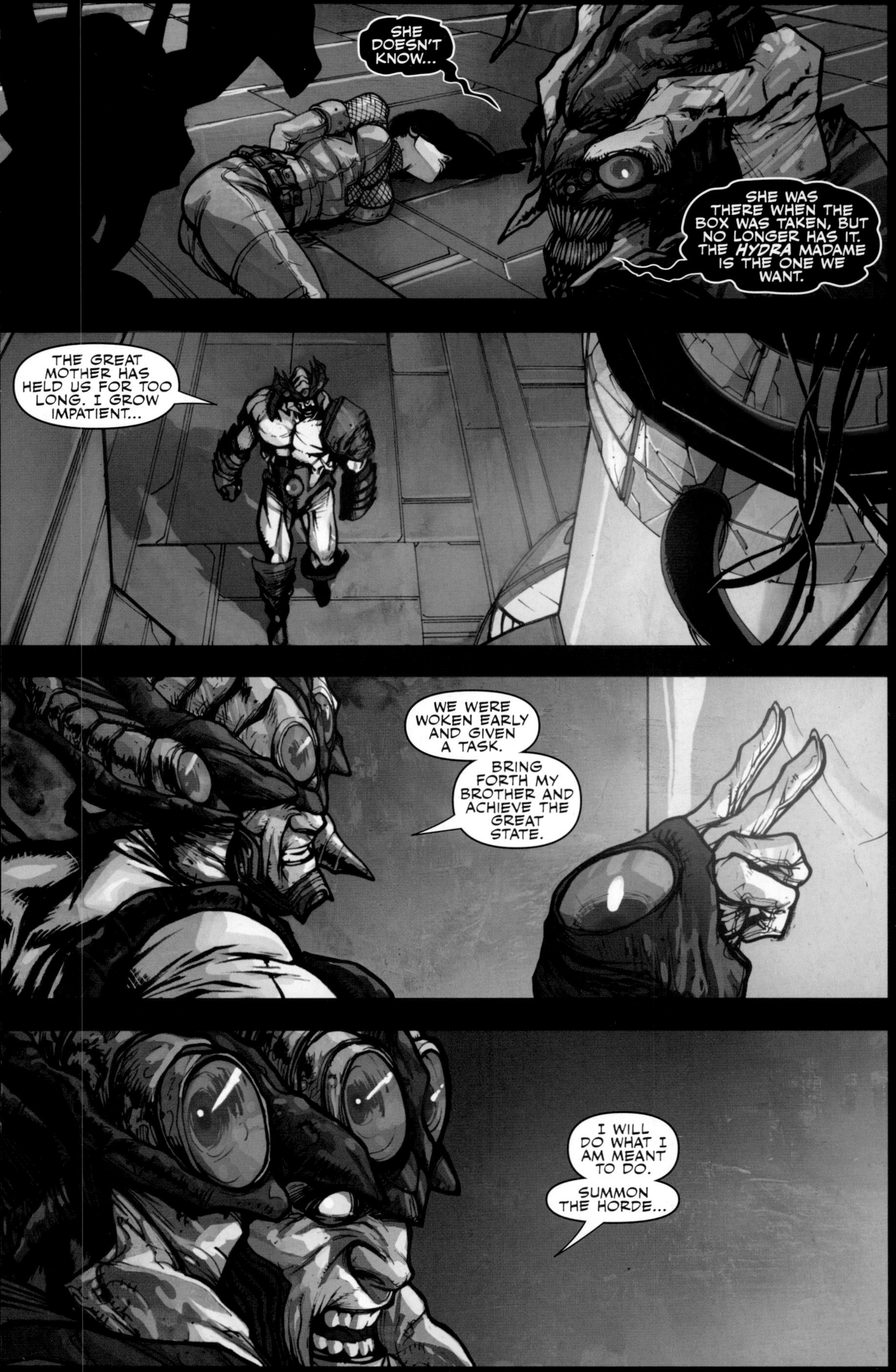
SHE DOESN'T KNOW...
SHE WAS THERE WHEN THE BOX WAS TAKEN, BUT NO LONGER HAS IT. THE *HYDRA* MADAME IS THE ONE WE WANT.
THE GREAT MOTHER HAS HELD US FOR TOO LONG. I GROW IMPATIENT...
WE WERE WOKEN EARLY AND GIVEN A TASK.
BRING FORTH MY BROTHER AND ACHIEVE THE GREAT STATE.
I WILL DO WHAT I AM MEANT TO DO.
SUMMON THE HORDE...

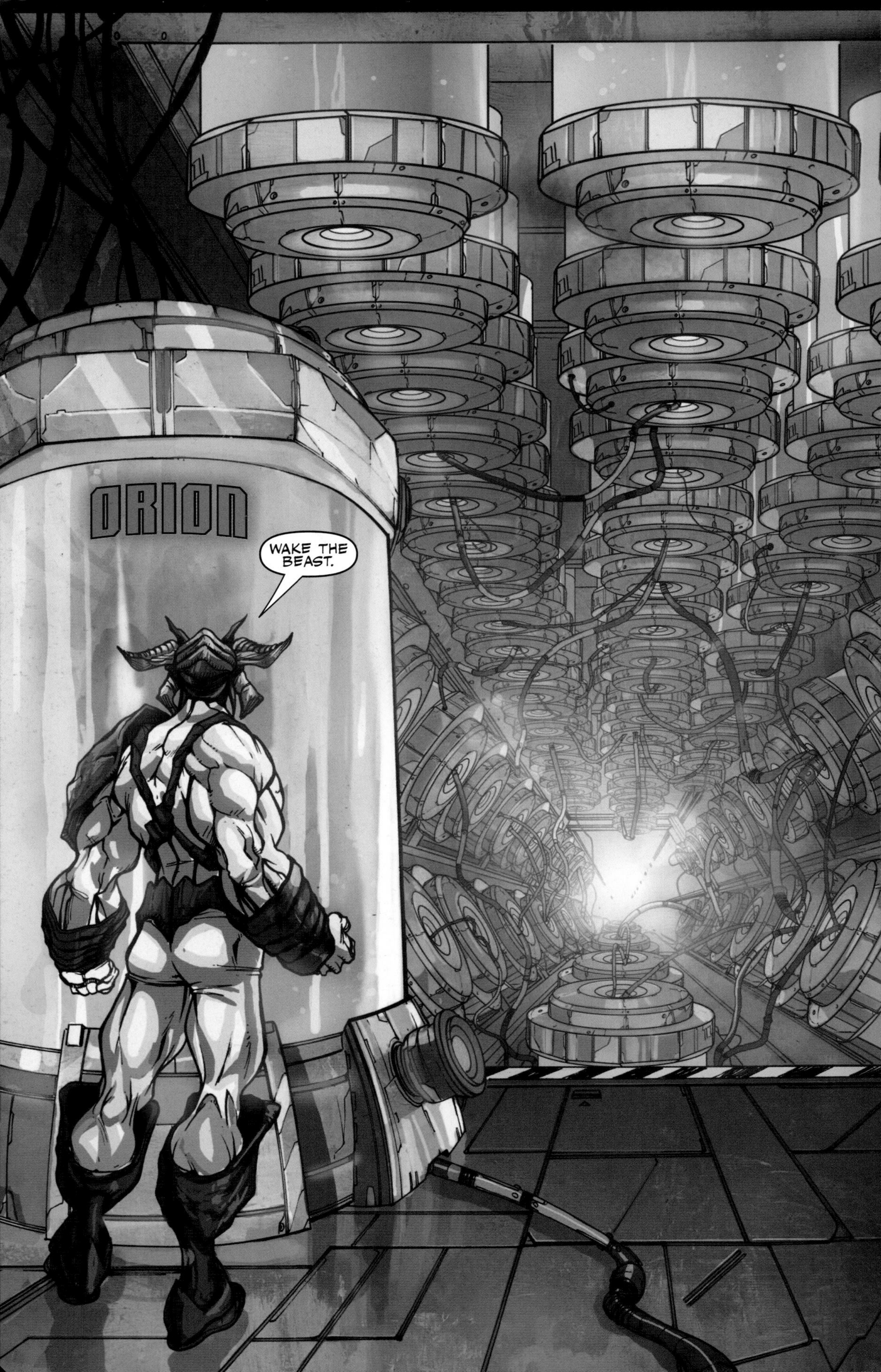
ORION
WAKE THE BEAST.

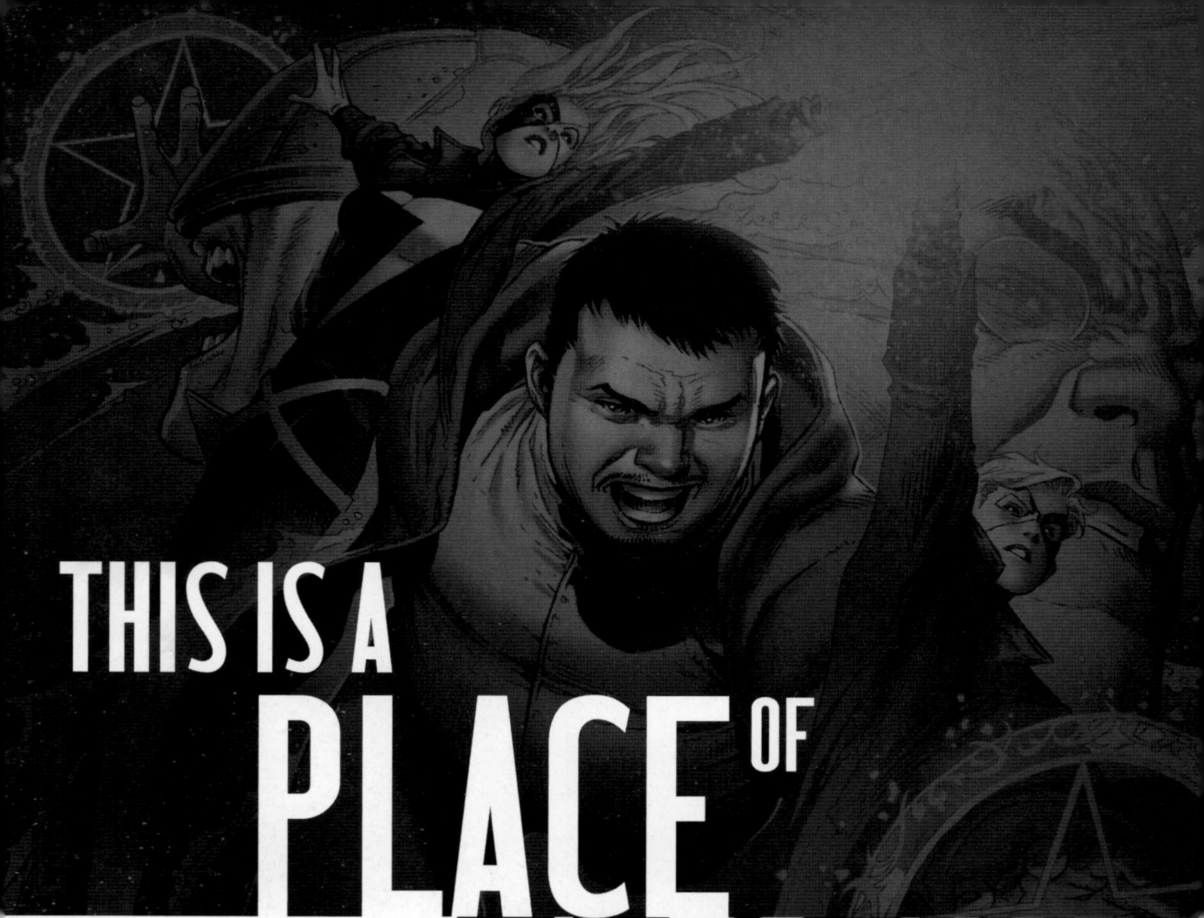

THIS IS A PLACE OF TESTING

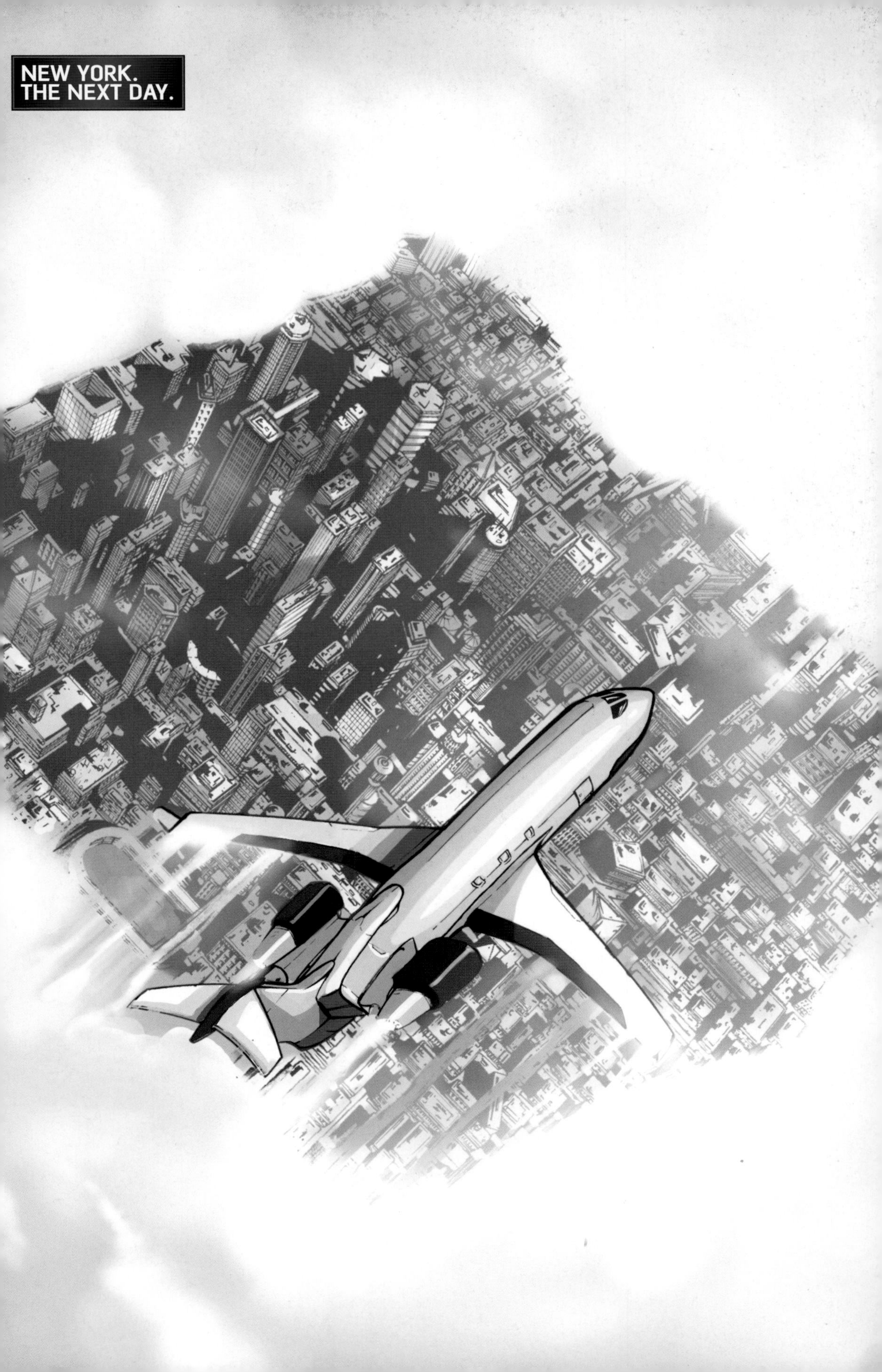
NEW YORK.
THE NEXT DAY.

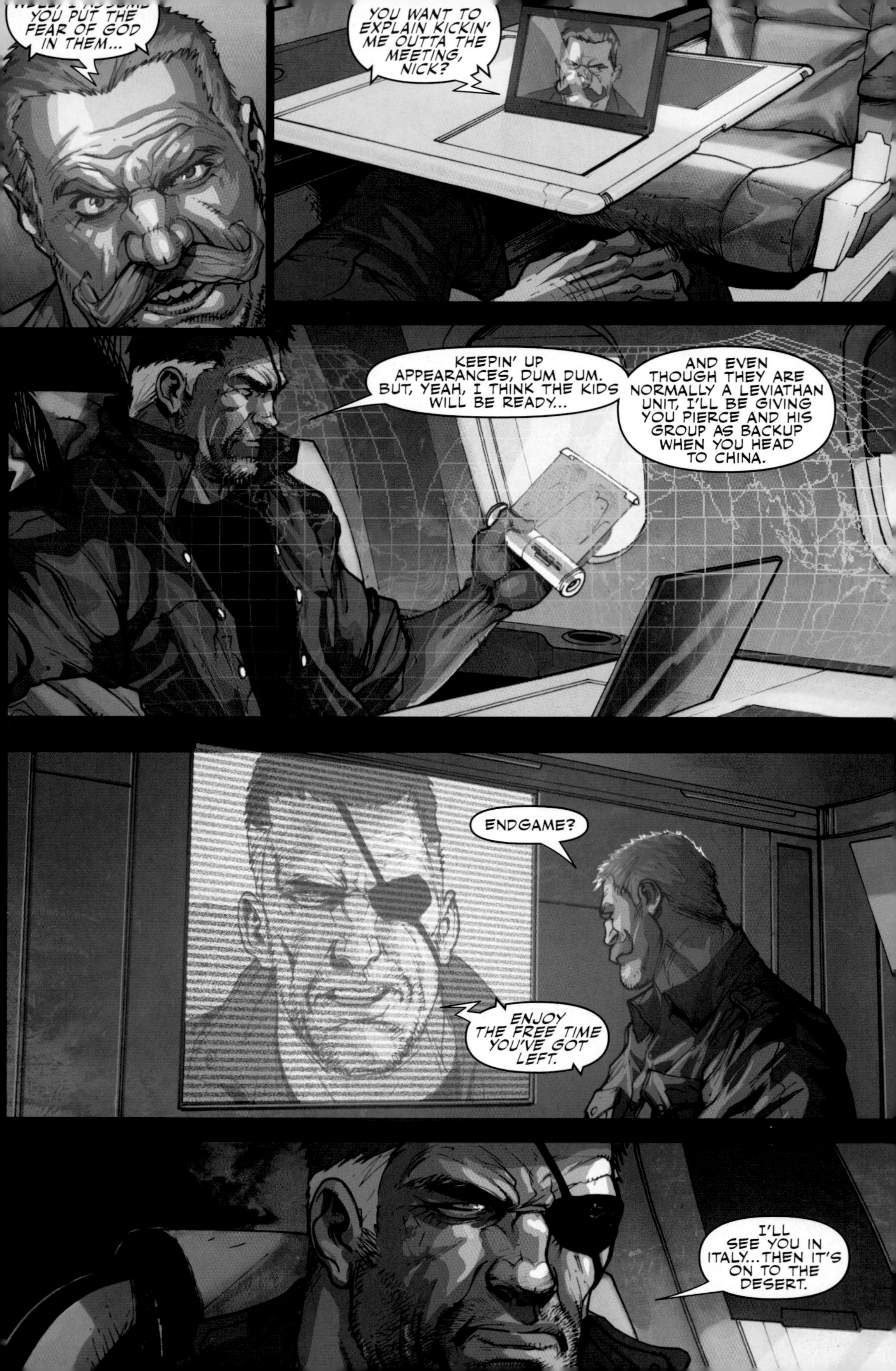
YOU PUT THE FEAR OF GOD IN THEM...
YOU WANT TO EXPLAIN KICKIN' ME OUTTA THE MEETING, NICK?
KEEPIN' UP APPEARANCES, DUM DUM. BUT, YEAH, I THINK THE KIDS WILL BE READY...
AND EVEN THOUGH THEY ARE NORMALLY A LEVIATHAN UNIT, I'LL BE GIVING YOU PIERCE AND HIS GROUP AS BACKUP WHEN YOU HEAD TO CHINA.
ENDGAME?
ENJOY THE FREE TIME YOU'VE GOT LEFT.
I'LL SEE YOU IN ITALY...THEN IT'S ON TO THE DESERT.

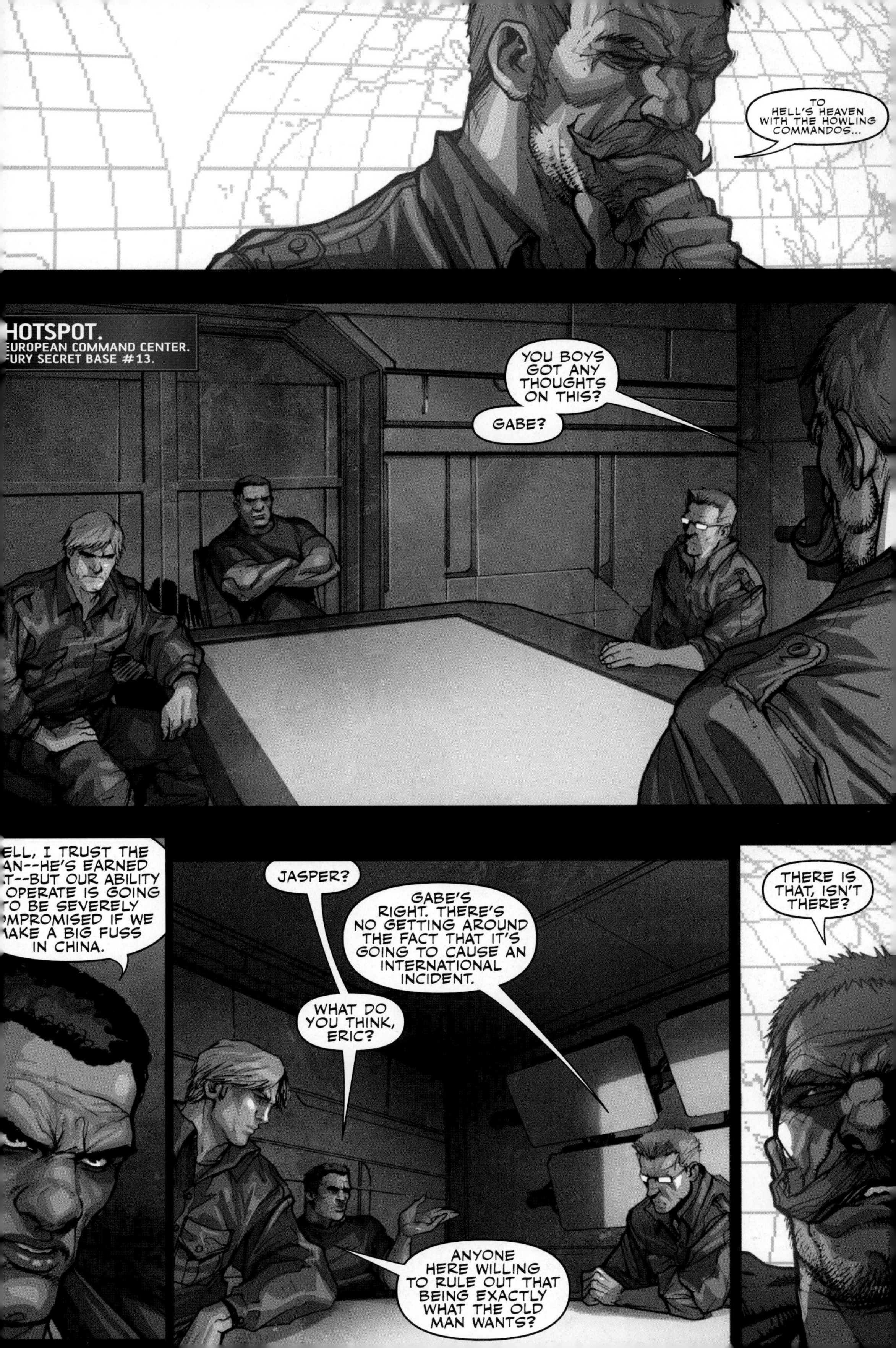
TO HELL'S HEAVEN WITH THE HOWLING COMMANDOS...
HOTSPOT.
EUROPEAN COMMAND CENTER.
FURY SECRET BASE #13.
YOU BOYS GOT ANY THOUGHTS ON THIS?
GABE?
ELL, I TRUST THE AN--HE'S EARNED T--BUT OUR ABILITY O OPERATE IS GOING TO BE SEVERELY OMPROMISED IF WE MAKE A BIG FUSS IN CHINA.
JASPER?
GABE'S RIGHT. THERE'S NO GETTING AROUND THE FACT THAT IT'S GOING TO CAUSE AN INTERNATIONAL INCIDENT.
WHAT DO YOU THINK, ERIC?
ANYONE HERE WILLING TO RULE OUT THAT BEING EXACTLY WHAT THE OLD MAN WANTS?
THERE IS THAT, ISN'T THERE?

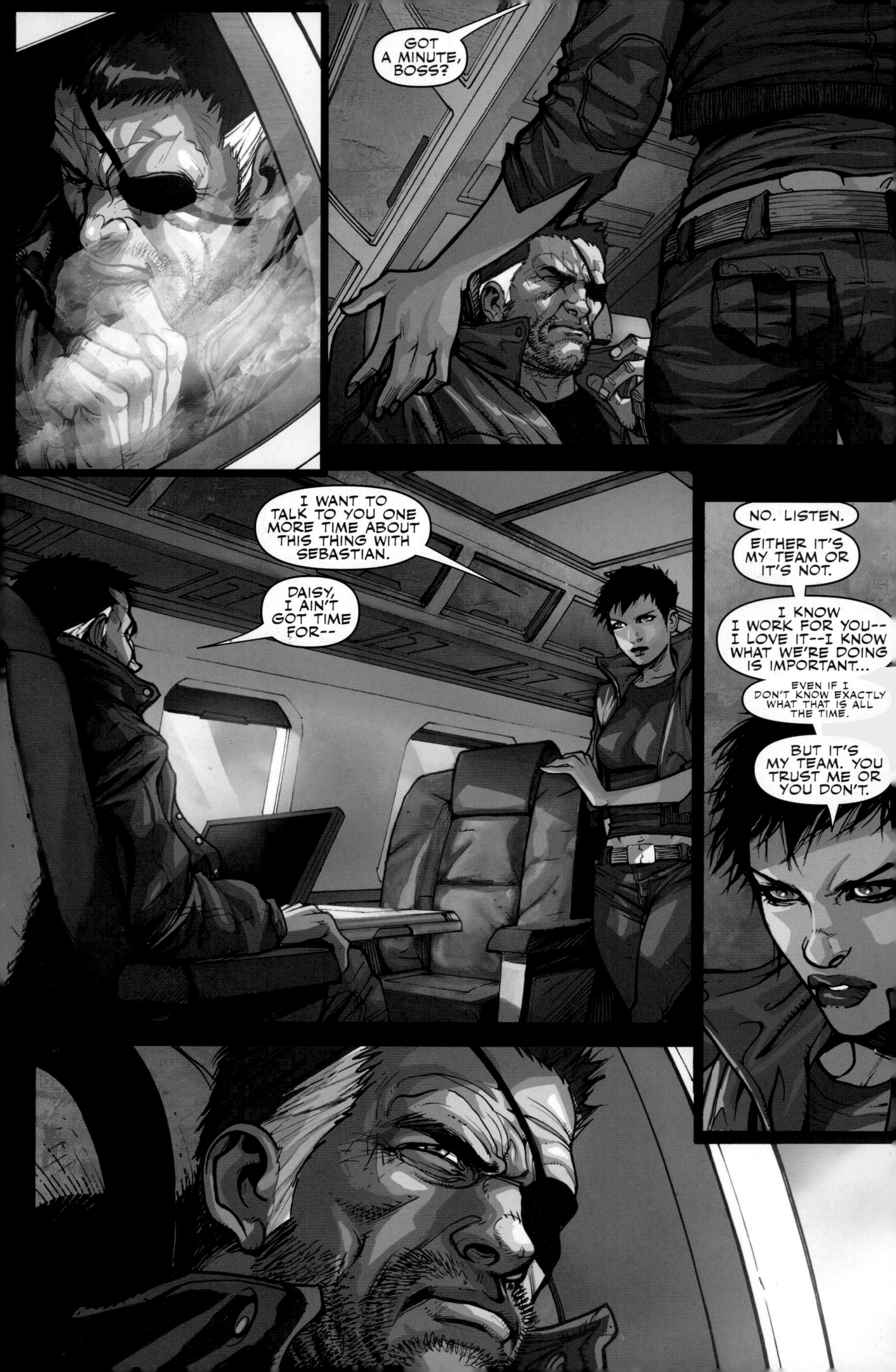
GOT A MINUTE, BOSS?
I WANT TO TALK TO YOU ONE MORE TIME ABOUT THIS THING WITH SEBASTIAN.
DAISY, I AIN'T GOT TIME FOR--
NO. LISTEN.
EITHER IT'S MY TEAM OR IT'S NOT.
I KNOW I WORK FOR YOU-- I LOVE IT--I KNOW WHAT WE'RE DOING IS IMPORTANT...
EVEN IF I DON'T KNOW EXACTLY WHAT THAT IS ALL THE TIME.
BUT IT'S MY TEAM. YOU TRUST ME OR YOU DON'T.

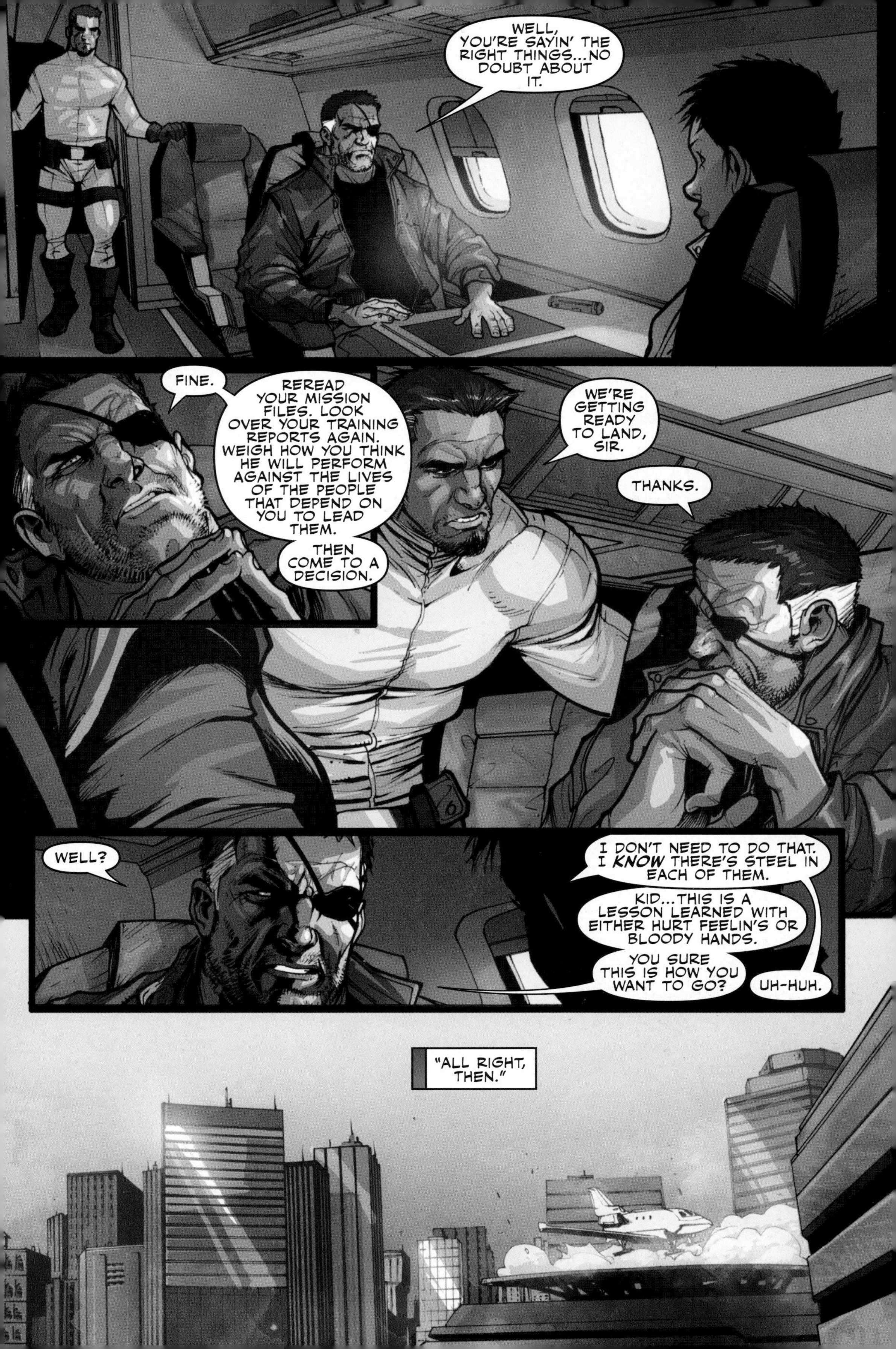
WELL, YOU'RE SAYIN' THE RIGHT THINGS...NO DOUBT ABOUT IT.
FINE.
REREAD YOUR MISSION FILES. LOOK OVER YOUR TRAINING REPORTS AGAIN. WEIGH HOW YOU THINK HE WILL PERFORM AGAINST THE LIVES OF THE PEOPLE THAT DEPEND ON YOU TO LEAD THEM.
THEN COME TO A DECISION.
WE'RE GETTING READY TO LAND, SIR.
THANKS.
WELL?
I DON'T NEED TO DO THAT. I *KNOW* THERE'S STEEL IN EACH OF THEM.
KID...THIS IS A LESSON LEARNED WITH EITHER HURT FEELIN'S OR BLOODY HANDS.
YOU SURE THIS IS HOW YOU WANT TO GO?
UH-HUH.
"ALL RIGHT, THEN."

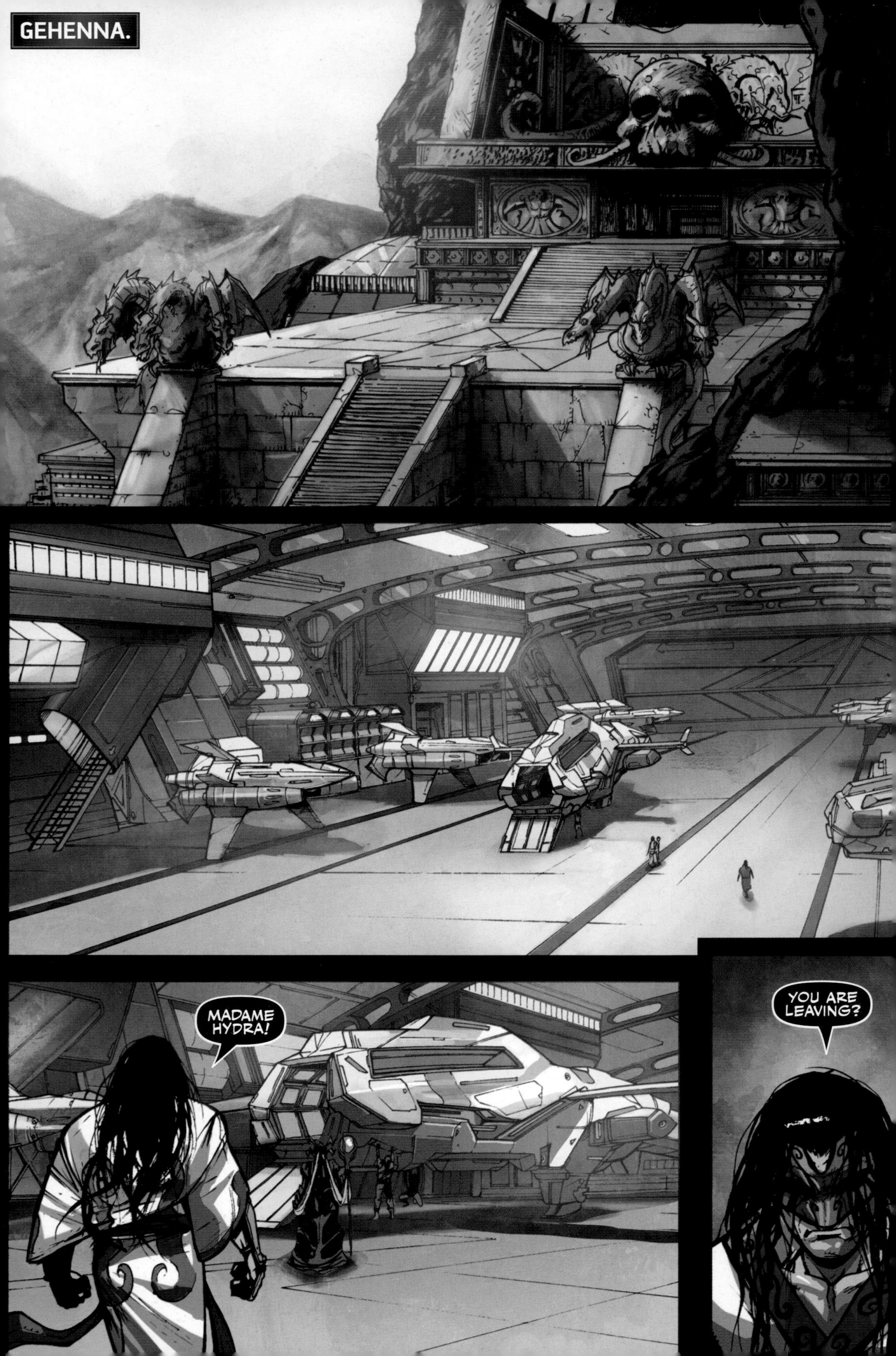

GEHENNA.
MADAME HYDRA!
YOU ARE LEAVING?

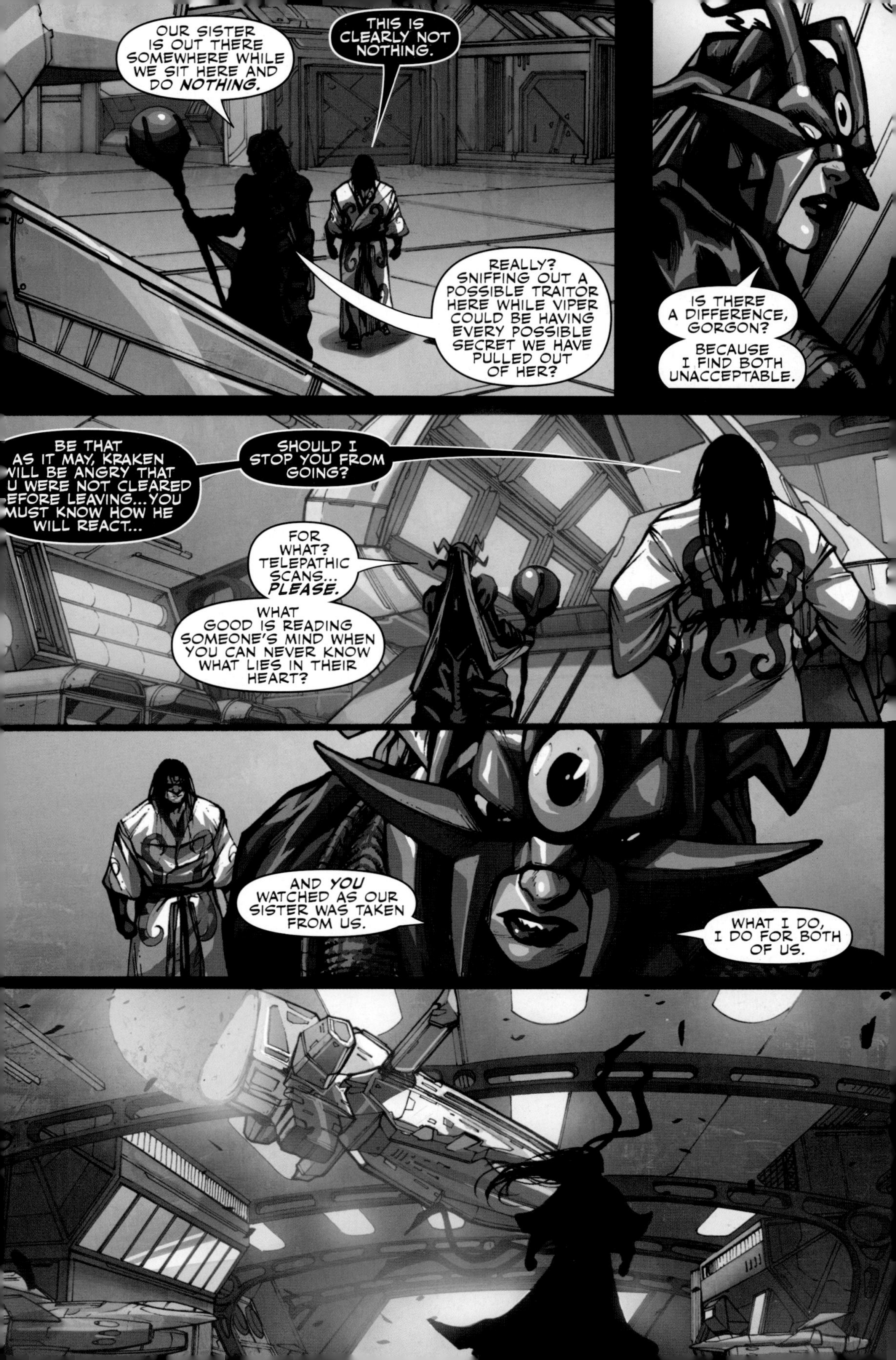

OUR SISTER IS OUT THERE SOMEWHERE WHILE WE SIT HERE AND DO NOTHING.
THIS IS CLEARLY NOT NOTHING.
REALLY? SNIFFING OUT A POSSIBLE TRAITOR HERE WHILE VIPER COULD BE HAVING EVERY POSSIBLE SECRET WE HAVE PULLED OUT OF HER?
IS THERE A DIFFERENCE, GORGON?
BECAUSE I FIND BOTH UNACCEPTABLE.
BE THAT AS IT MAY, KRAKEN WILL BE ANGRY THAT U WERE NOT CLEARED EFORE LEAVING...YOU MUST KNOW HOW HE WILL REACT...
SHOULD I STOP YOU FROM GOING?
FOR WHAT? TELEPATHIC SCANS... PLEASE.
WHAT GOOD IS READING SOMEONE'S MIND WHEN YOU CAN NEVER KNOW WHAT LIES IN THEIR HEART?
AND YOU WATCHED AS OUR SISTER WAS TAKEN FROM US.
WHAT I DO, I DO FOR BOTH OF US.

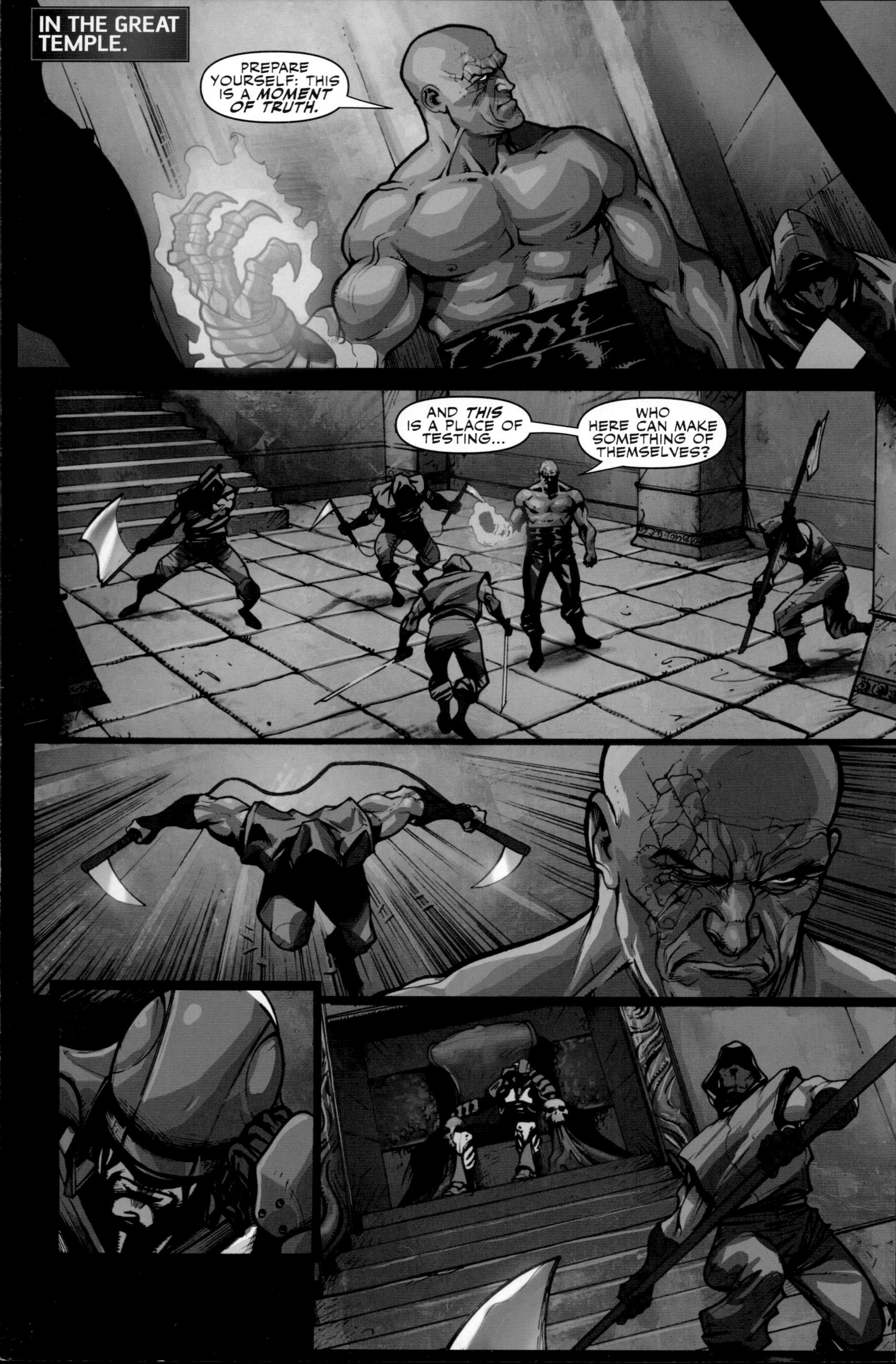
IN THE GREAT TEMPLE.
PREPARE YOURSELF: THIS IS A *MOMENT OF TRUTH.*
AND *THIS* IS A PLACE OF TESTING...
WHO HERE CAN MAKE SOMETHING OF THEMSELVES?

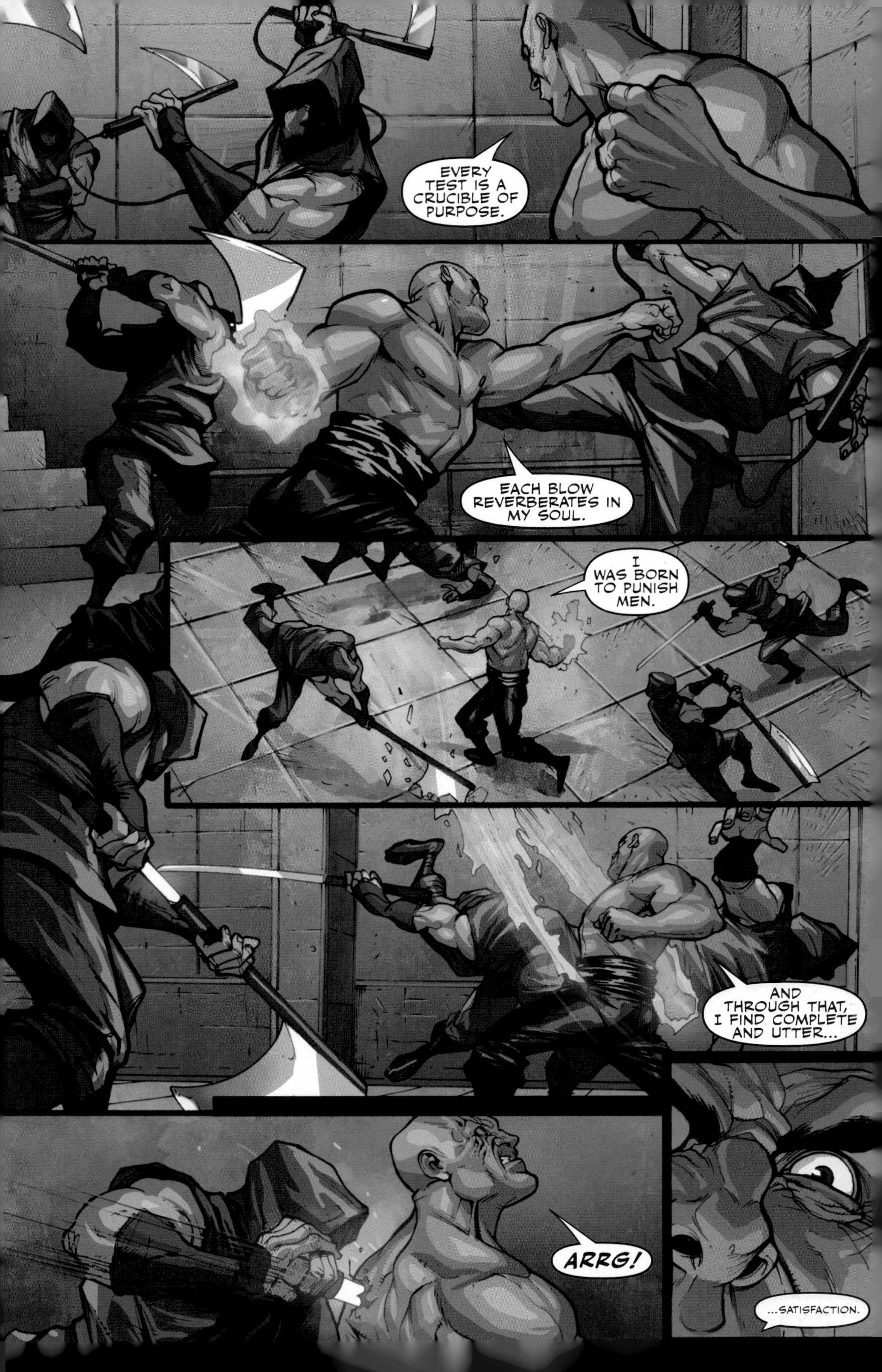
EVERY TEST IS A CRUCIBLE OF PURPOSE.
EACH BLOW REVERBERATES IN MY SOUL.
I WAS BORN TO PUNISH MEN.
AND THROUGH THAT, I FIND COMPLETE AND UTTER...
ARRG!
...SATISFACTION.

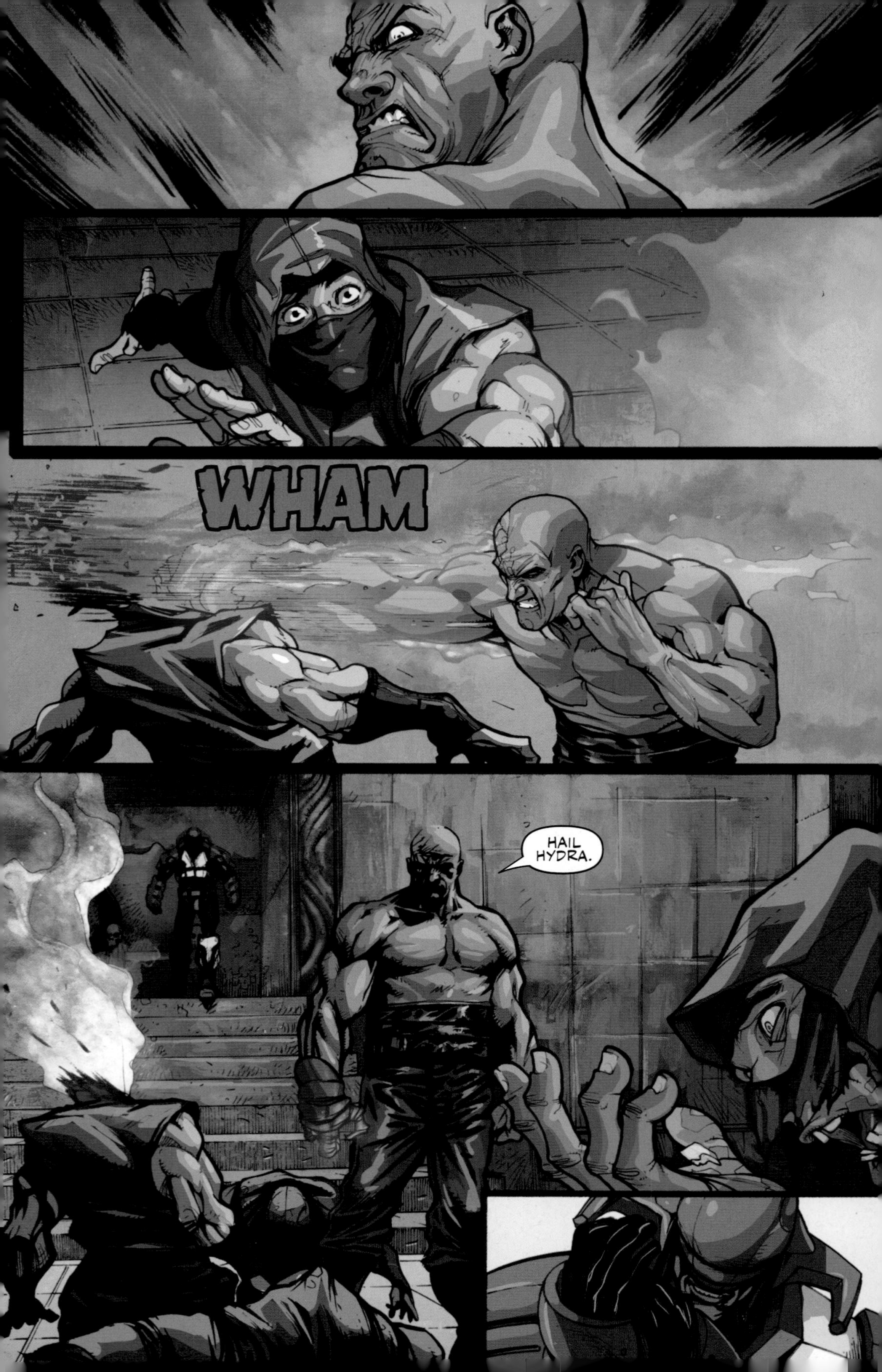
WHAM
HAIL HYDRA.

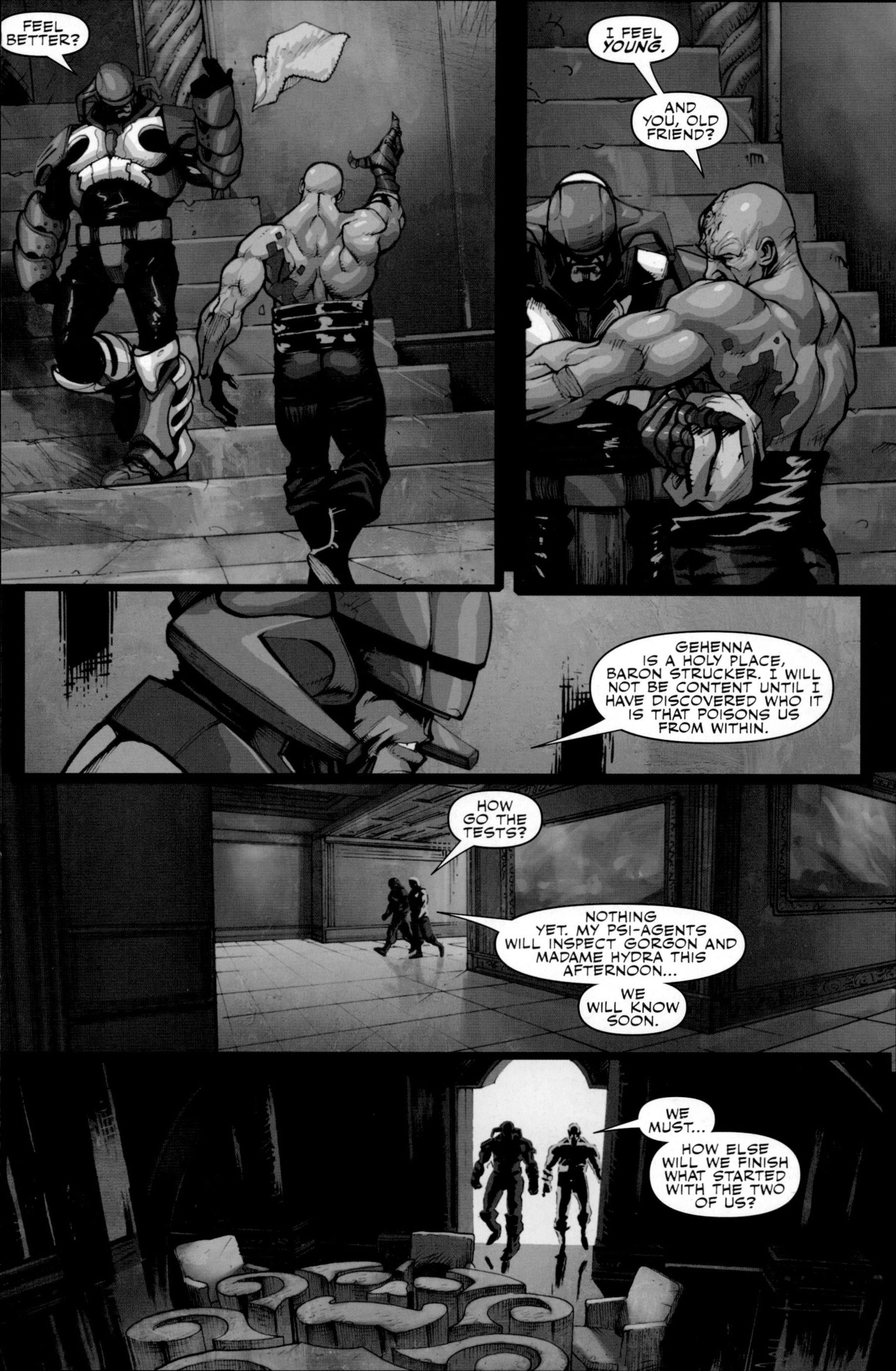
FEEL BETTER?
I FEEL YOUNG.
AND YOU, OLD FRIEND?
GEHENNA IS A HOLY PLACE, BARON STRUCKER. I WILL NOT BE CONTENT UNTIL I HAVE DISCOVERED WHO IT IS THAT POISONS US FROM WITHIN.
HOW GO THE TESTS?
NOTHING YET. MY PSI-AGENTS WILL INSPECT GORGON AND MADAME HYDRA THIS AFTERNOON...
WE WILL KNOW SOON.
WE MUST...
HOW ELSE WILL WE FINISH WHAT STARTED WITH THE TWO OF US?

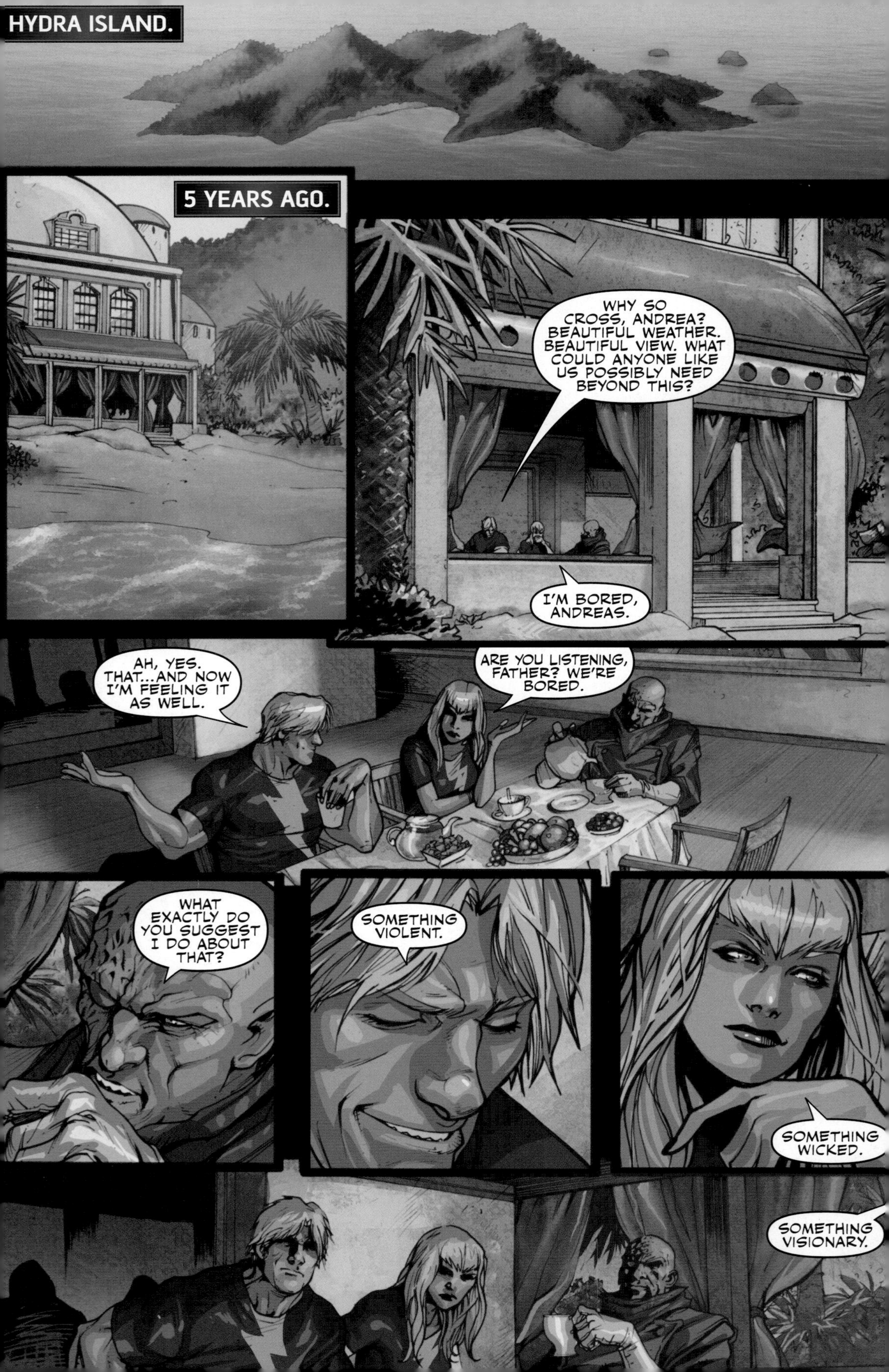
HYDRA ISLAND.
5 YEARS AGO.
WHY SO CROSS, ANDREA? BEAUTIFUL WEATHER. BEAUTIFUL VIEW. WHAT COULD ANYONE LIKE US POSSIBLY NEED BEYOND THIS?
I'M BORED, ANDREAS.
AH, YES. THAT...AND NOW I'M FEELING IT AS WELL.
ARE YOU LISTENING, FATHER? WE'RE BORED.
WHAT EXACTLY DO YOU SUGGEST I DO ABOUT THAT?
SOMETHING VIOLENT.
SOMETHING WICKED.
SOMETHING VISIONARY.

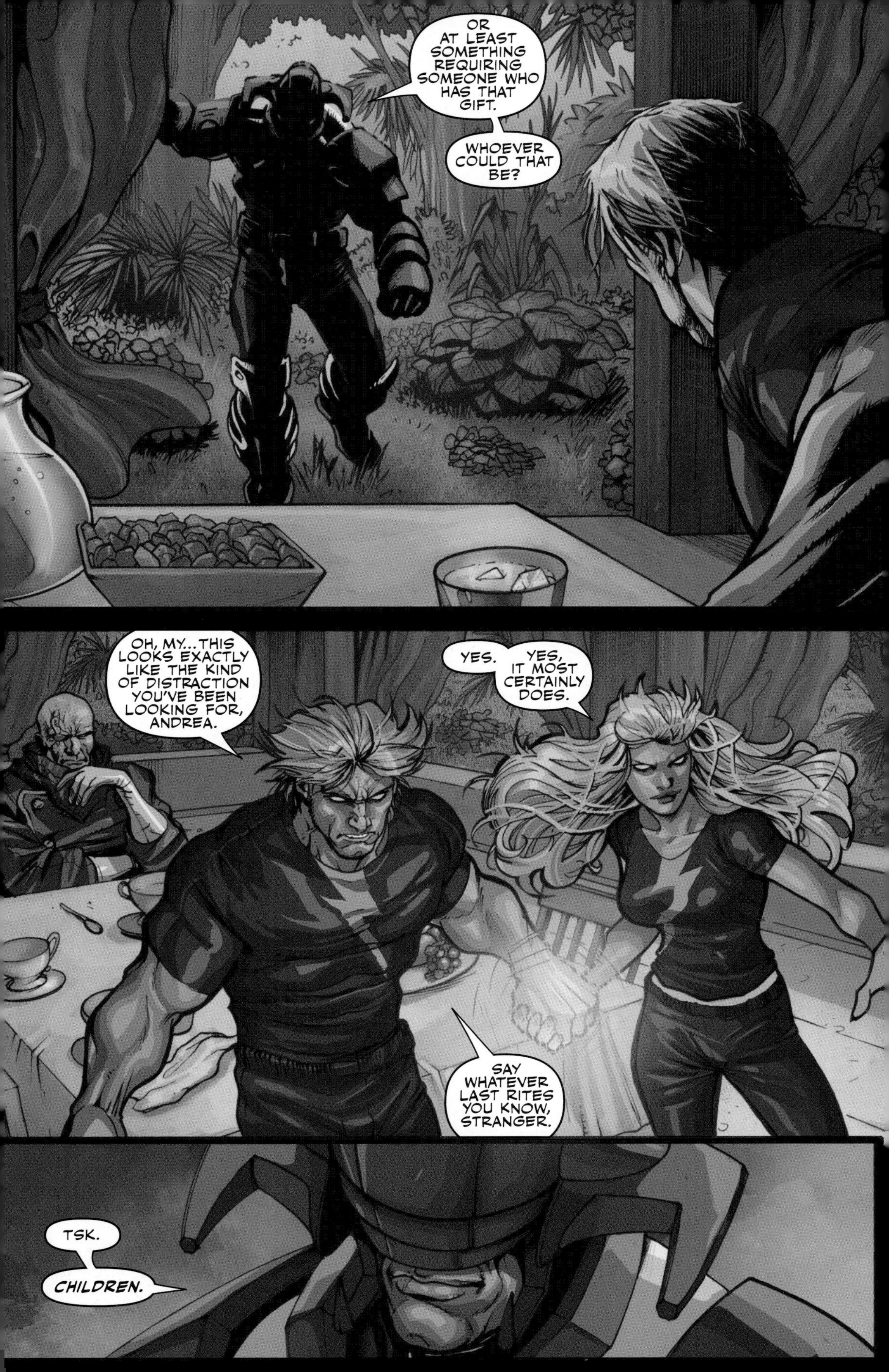
OR AT LEAST SOMETHING REQUIRING SOMEONE WHO HAS THAT GIFT.
WHOEVER COULD THAT BE?
OH, MY...THIS LOOKS EXACTLY LIKE THE KIND OF DISTRACTION YOU'VE BEEN LOOKING FOR, ANDREA.
YES.
YES, IT MOST CERTAINLY DOES.
SAY WHATEVER LAST RITES YOU KNOW, STRANGER.
TSK.
CHILDREN.

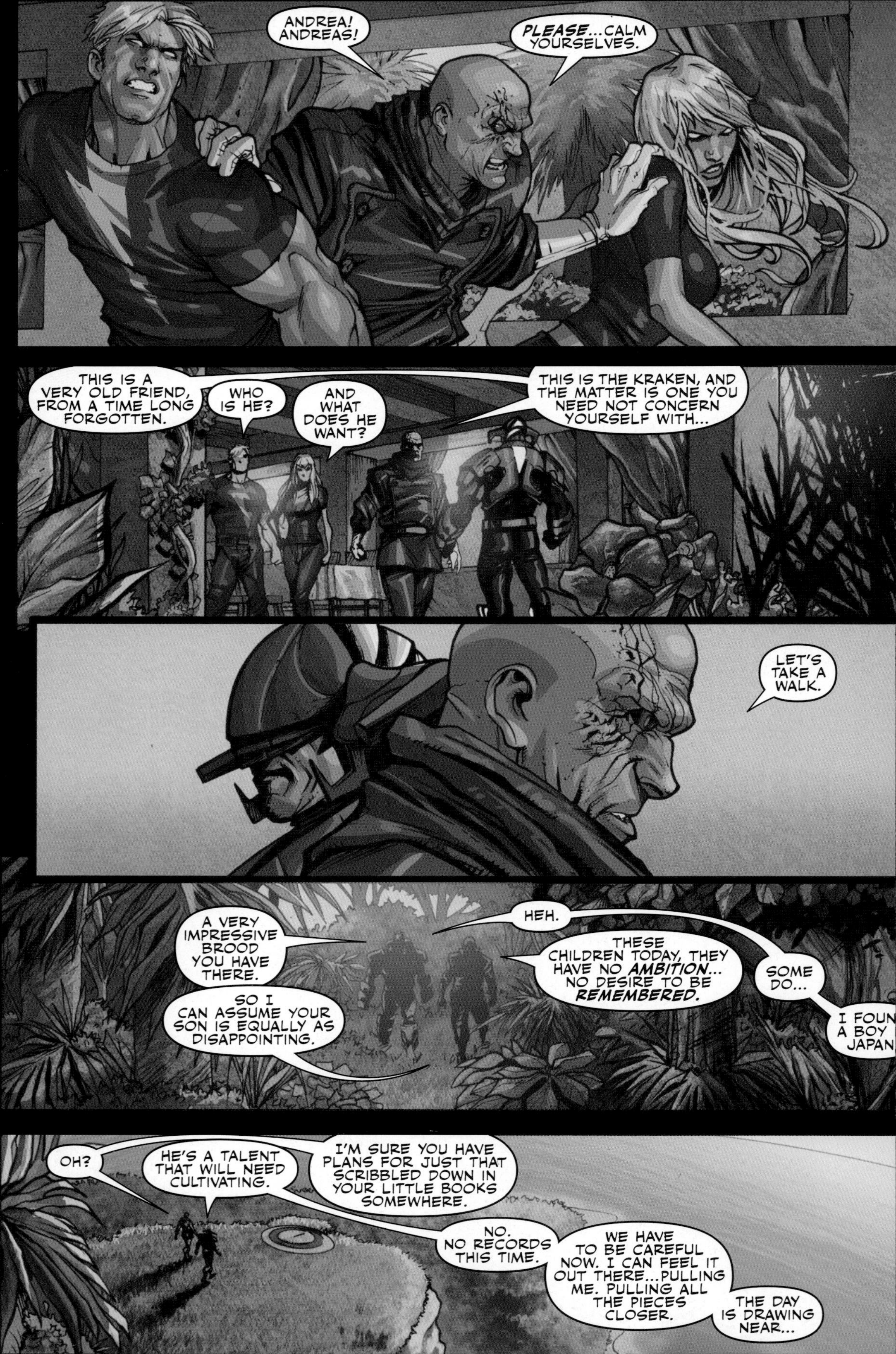

ANDREA! ANDREAS!
PLEASE...CALM YOURSELVES.
THIS IS A VERY OLD FRIEND, FROM A TIME LONG FORGOTTEN.
WHO IS HE?
AND WHAT DOES HE WANT?
THIS IS THE KRAKEN, AND THE MATTER IS ONE YOU NEED NOT CONCERN YOURSELF WITH...
LET'S TAKE A WALK.
A VERY IMPRESSIVE BROOD YOU HAVE THERE.
HEH.
THESE CHILDREN TODAY, THEY HAVE NO *AMBITION*... NO DESIRE TO BE *REMEMBERED.*
SO I CAN ASSUME YOUR SON IS EQUALLY AS DISAPPOINTING.
SOME DO...
I FOUN A BOY JAPAN
OH?
HE'S A TALENT THAT WILL NEED CULTIVATING.
I'M SURE YOU HAVE PLANS FOR JUST THAT SCRIBBLED DOWN IN YOUR LITTLE BOOKS SOMEWHERE.
NO. NO RECORDS THIS TIME.
WE HAVE TO BE CAREFUL NOW. I CAN FEEL IT OUT THERE...PULLING ME. PULLING ALL THE PIECES CLOSER.
THE DAY IS DRAWING NEAR...

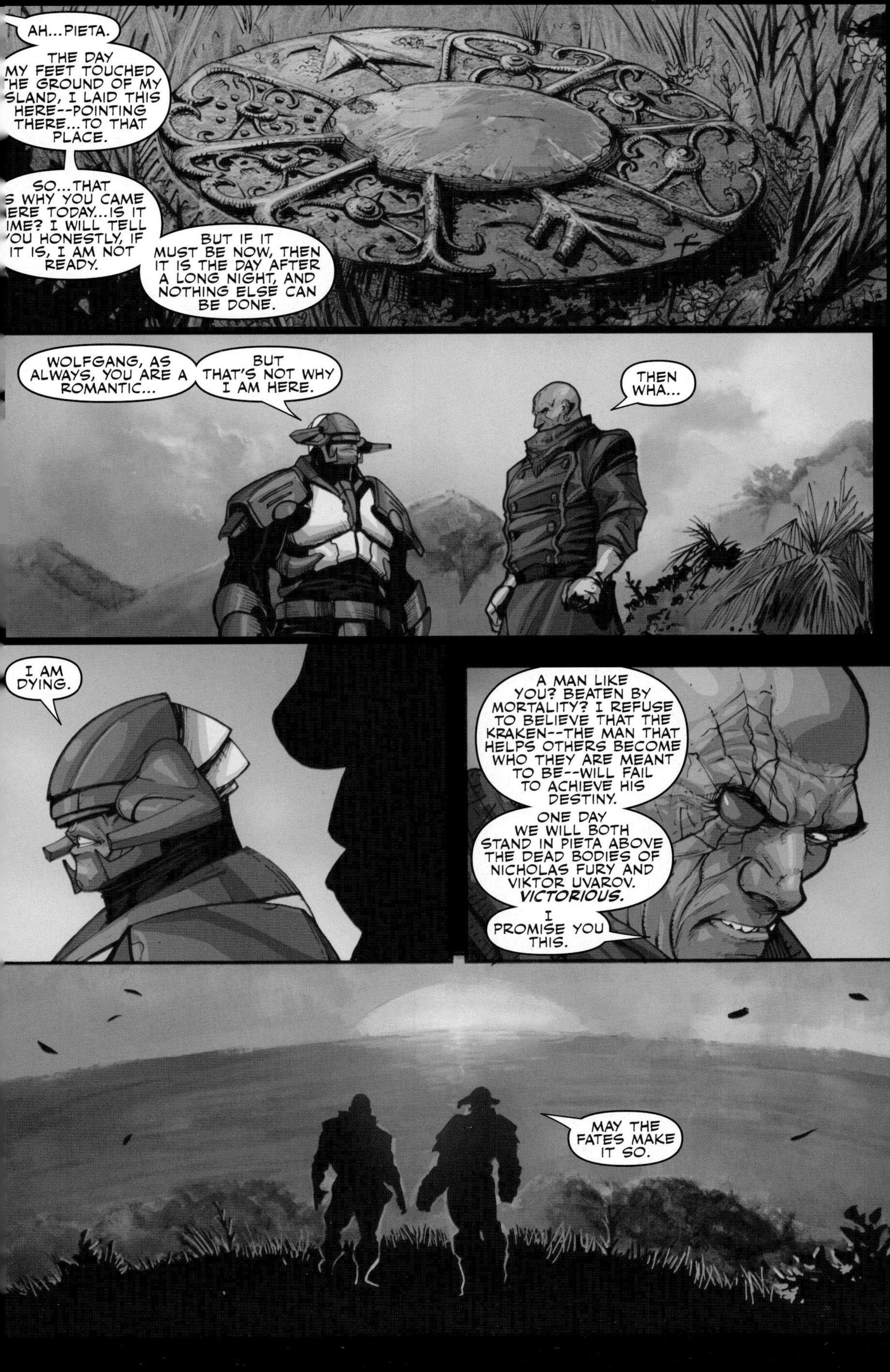
AH...PIETA.
THE DAY MY FEET TOUCHED THE GROUND OF MY ISLAND, I LAID THIS HERE--POINTING THERE...TO THAT PLACE.
SO...THAT IS WHY YOU CAME HERE TODAY...IS IT TIME? I WILL TELL YOU HONESTLY, IF IT IS, I AM NOT READY.
BUT IF IT MUST BE NOW, THEN IT IS THE DAY AFTER A LONG NIGHT, AND NOTHING ELSE CAN BE DONE.
WOLFGANG, AS ALWAYS, YOU ARE A ROMANTIC...
BUT THAT'S NOT WHY I AM HERE.
THEN WHA...
I AM DYING.
A MAN LIKE YOU? BEATEN BY MORTALITY? I REFUSE TO BELIEVE THAT THE KRAKEN--THE MAN THAT HELPS OTHERS BECOME WHO THEY ARE MEANT TO BE--WILL FAIL TO ACHIEVE HIS DESTINY.
ONE DAY WE WILL BOTH STAND IN PIETA ABOVE THE DEAD BODIES OF NICHOLAS FURY AND VIKTOR UVAROV. *VICTORIOUS.*
I PROMISE YOU THIS.
MAY THE FATES MAKE IT SO.

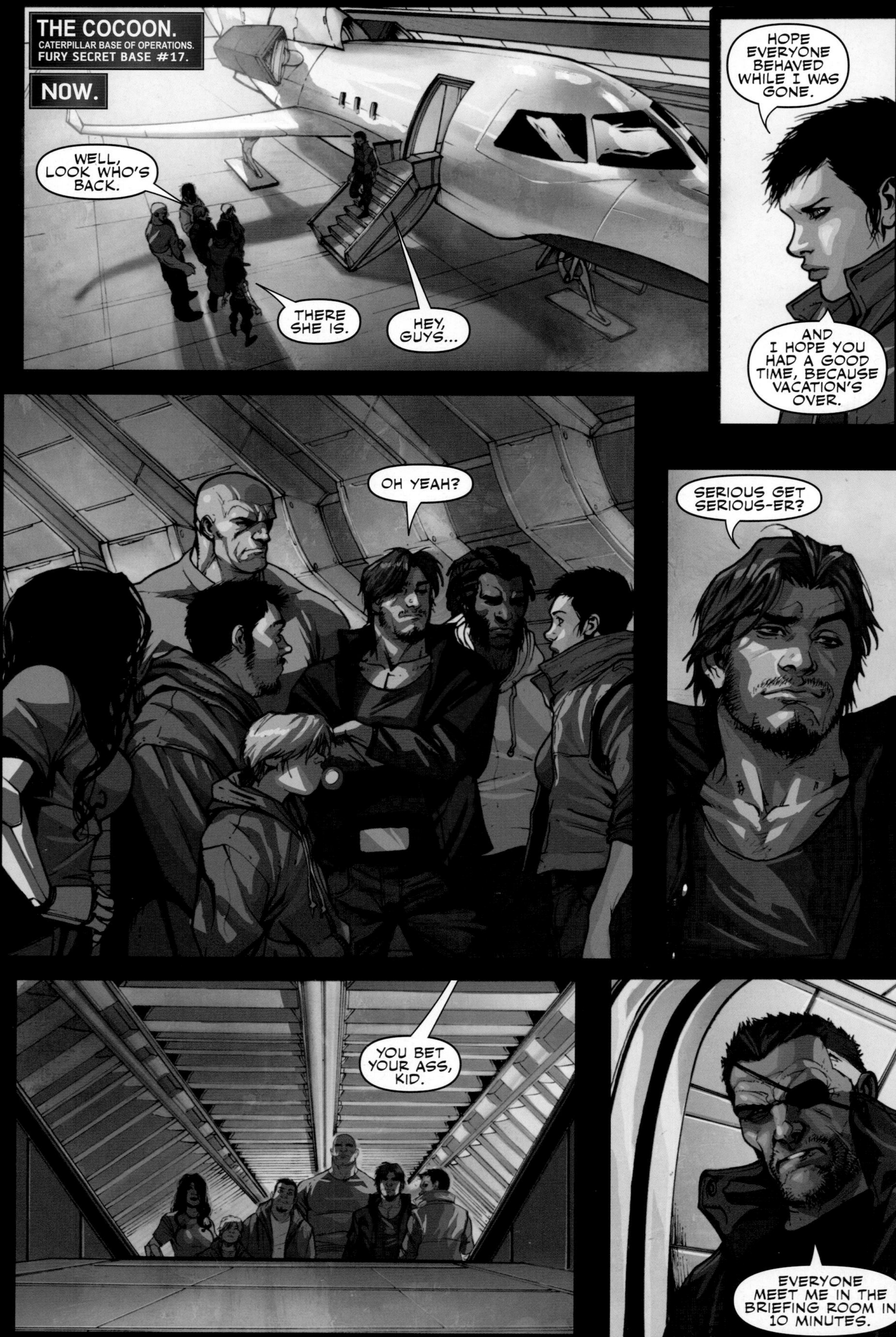
THE COCOON.
CATERPILLAR BASE OF OPERATIONS.
FURY SECRET BASE #17.
NOW.
WELL, LOOK WHO'S BACK.
THERE SHE IS.
HEY, GUYS...
HOPE EVERYONE BEHAVED WHILE I WAS GONE.
AND I HOPE YOU HAD A GOOD TIME, BECAUSE VACATION'S OVER.
OH YEAH?
SERIOUS GET SERIOUS-ER?
YOU BET YOUR ASS, KID.
EVERYONE MEET ME IN THE BRIEFING ROOM IN 10 MINUTES.

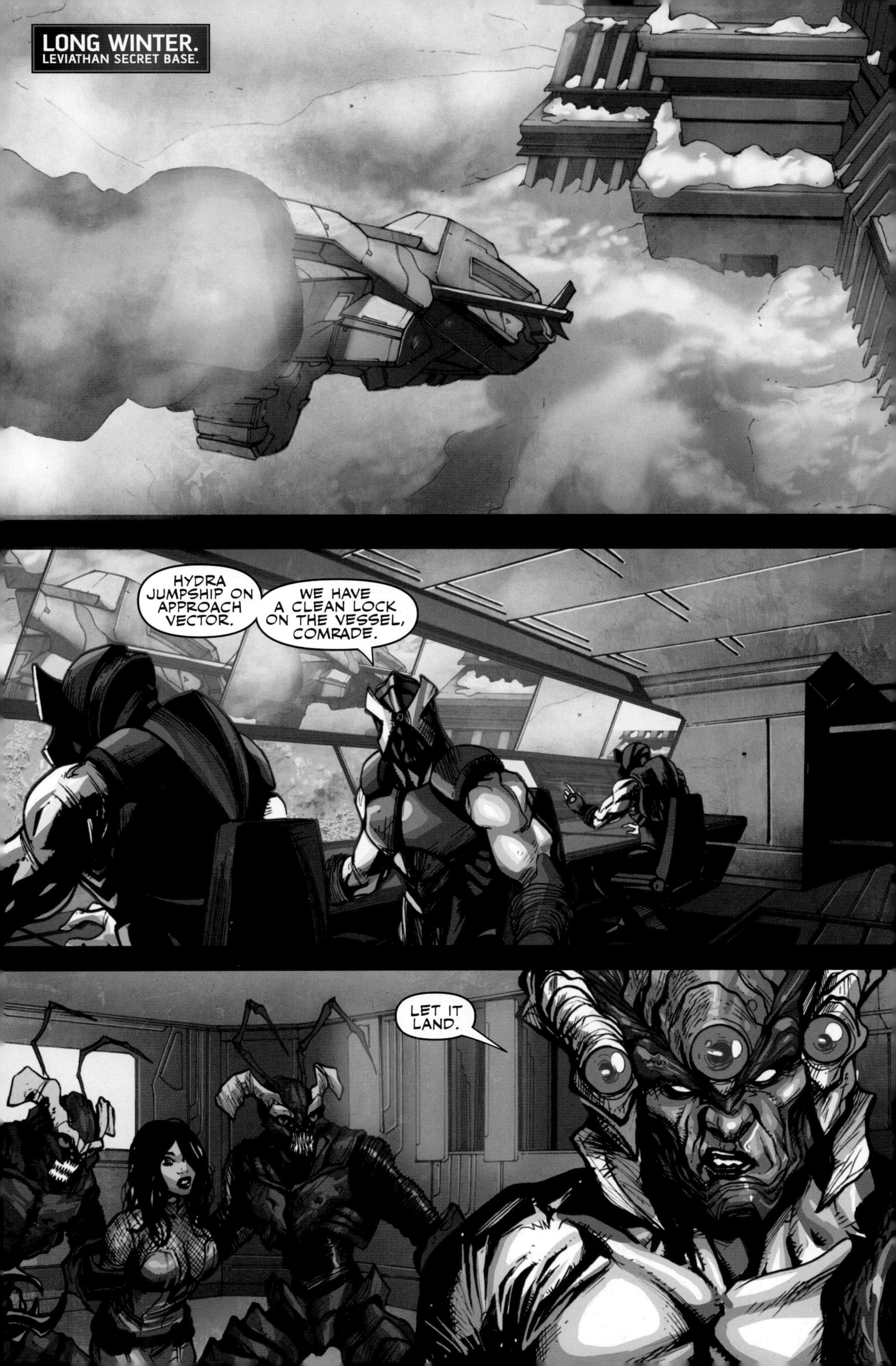
LONG WINTER.
LEVIATHAN SECRET BASE.
HYDRA JUMPSHIP ON APPROACH VECTOR.
WE HAVE A CLEAN LOCK ON THE VESSEL, COMRADE.
LET IT LAND.

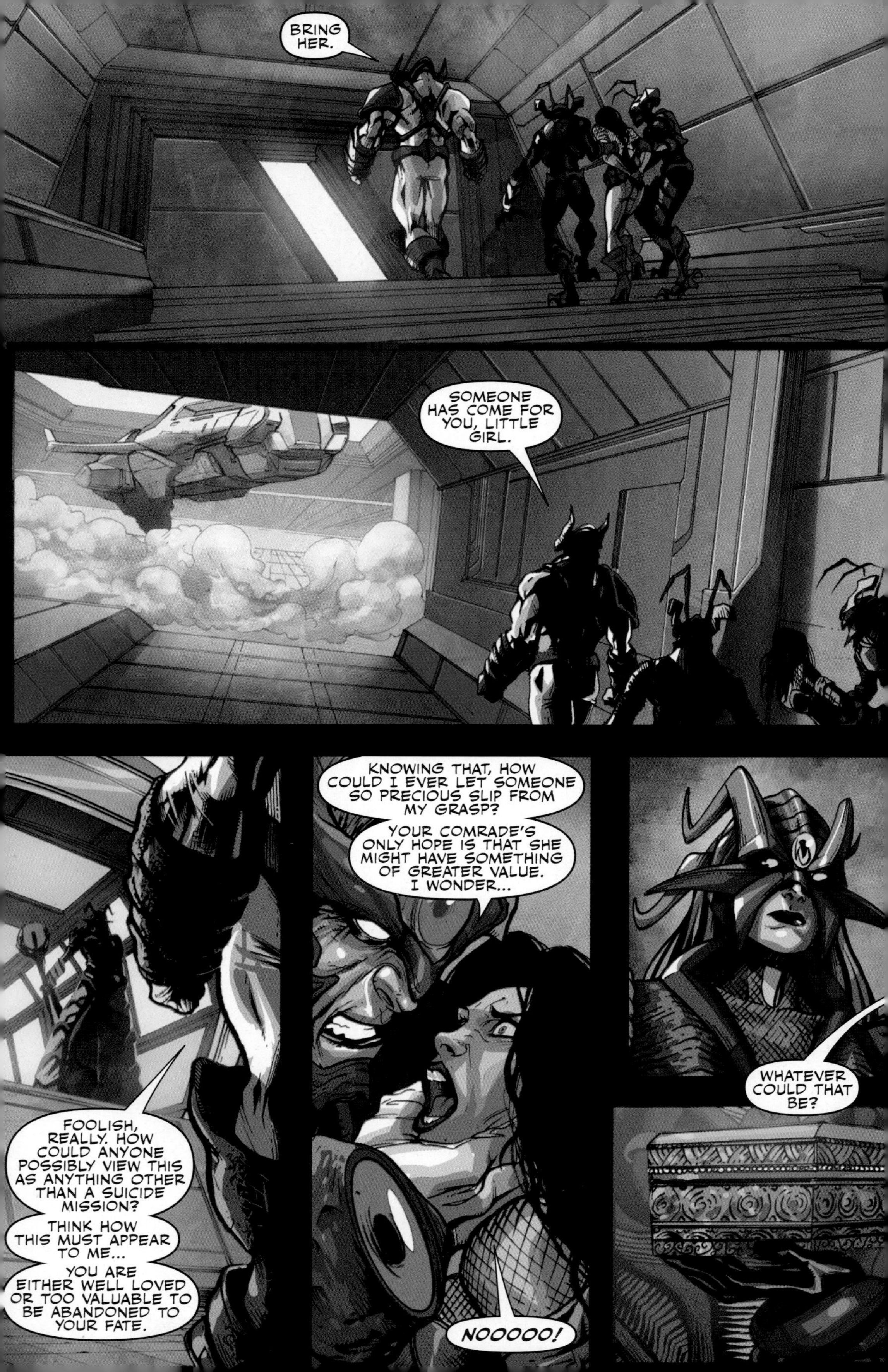
BRING HER.
SOMEONE HAS COME FOR YOU, LITTLE GIRL.
FOOLISH, REALLY. HOW COULD ANYONE POSSIBLY VIEW THIS AS ANYTHING OTHER THAN A SUICIDE MISSION?
THINK HOW THIS MUST APPEAR TO ME...
YOU ARE EITHER WELL LOVED OR TOO VALUABLE TO BE ABANDONED TO YOUR FATE.
KNOWING THAT, HOW COULD I EVER LET SOMEONE SO PRECIOUS SLIP FROM MY GRASP?
YOUR COMRADE'S ONLY HOPE IS THAT SHE MIGHT HAVE SOMETHING OF GREATER VALUE. I WONDER...
NOOOOO!
WHATEVER COULD THAT BE?

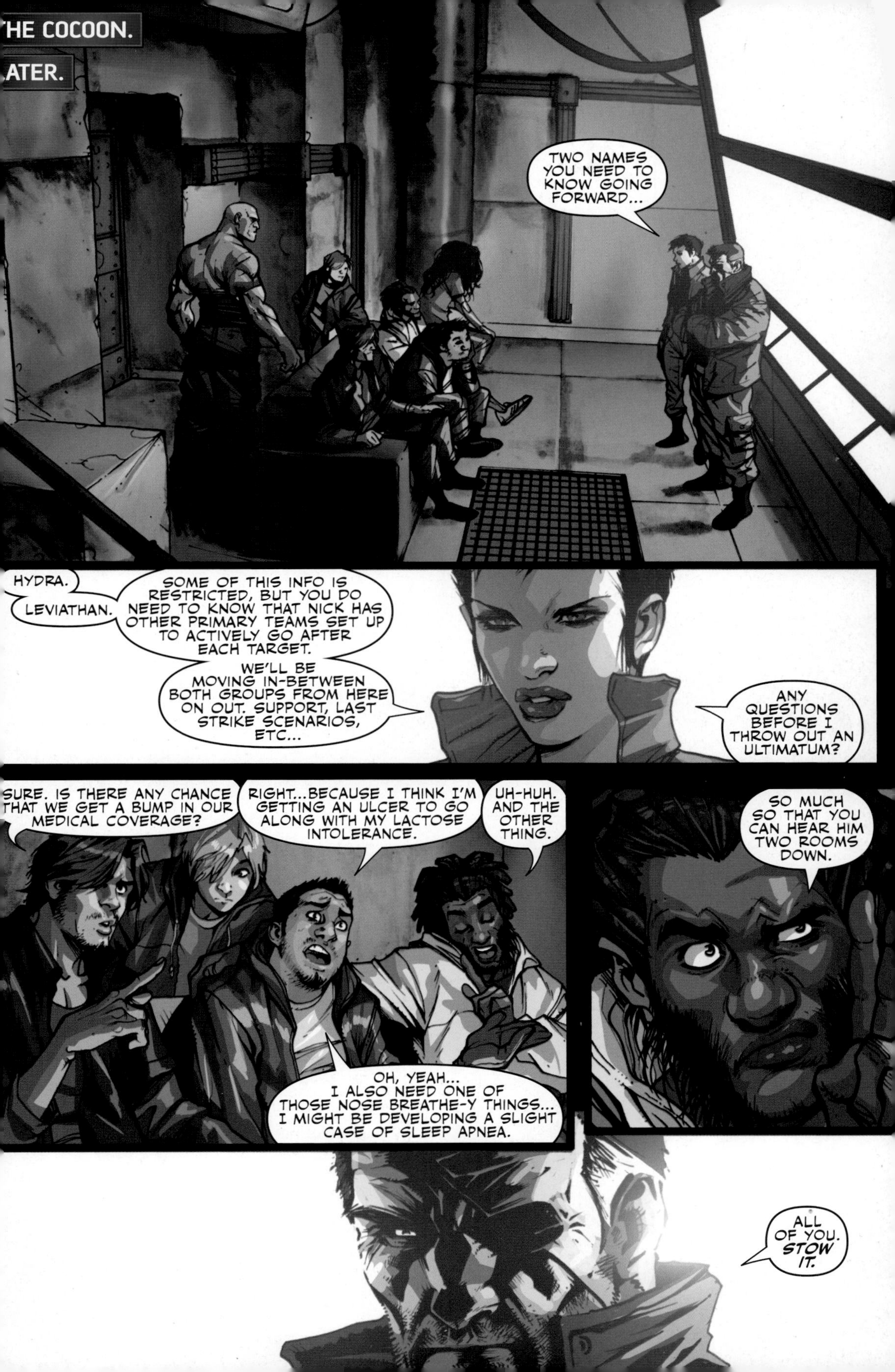

THE COCOON.
LATER.
TWO NAMES YOU NEED TO KNOW GOING FORWARD...
HYDRA.
LEVIATHAN.
SOME OF THIS INFO IS RESTRICTED, BUT YOU DO NEED TO KNOW THAT NICK HAS OTHER PRIMARY TEAMS SET UP TO ACTIVELY GO AFTER EACH TARGET.
WE'LL BE MOVING IN-BETWEEN BOTH GROUPS FROM HERE ON OUT. SUPPORT, LAST STRIKE SCENARIOS, ETC...
ANY QUESTIONS BEFORE I THROW OUT AN ULTIMATUM?
SURE. IS THERE ANY CHANCE THAT WE GET A BUMP IN OUR MEDICAL COVERAGE?
RIGHT...BECAUSE I THINK I'M GETTING AN ULCER TO GO ALONG WITH MY LACTOSE INTOLERANCE.
UH-HUH. AND THE OTHER THING.
OH, YEAH... I ALSO NEED ONE OF THOSE NOSE BREATHE-Y THINGS... I MIGHT BE DEVELOPING A SLIGHT CASE OF SLEEP APNEA.
SO MUCH SO THAT YOU CAN HEAR HIM TWO ROOMS DOWN.
ALL OF YOU. *STOW IT.*

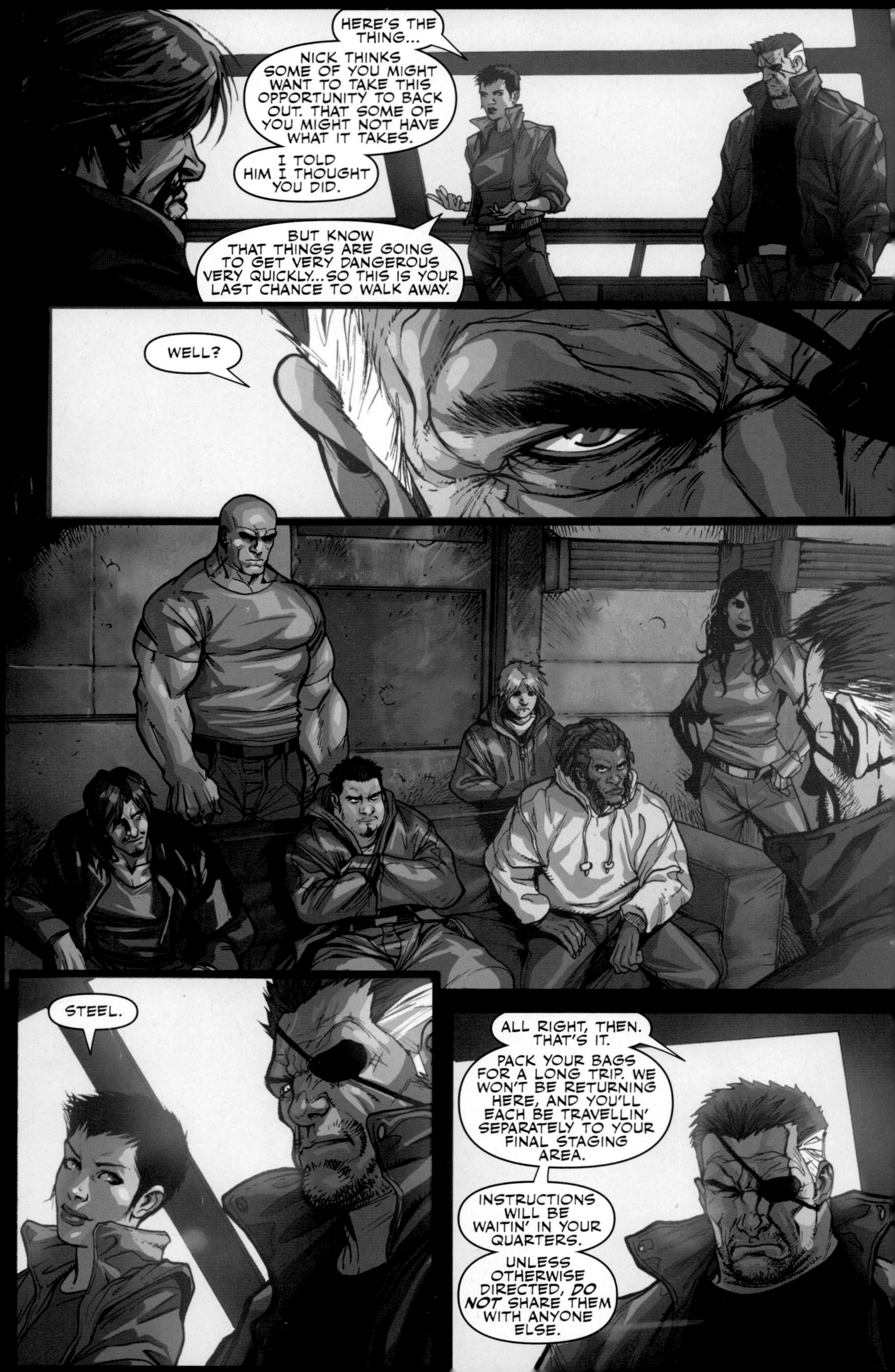

HERE'S THE THING...
NICK THINKS SOME OF YOU MIGHT WANT TO TAKE THIS OPPORTUNITY TO BACK OUT. THAT SOME OF YOU MIGHT NOT HAVE WHAT IT TAKES.
I TOLD HIM I THOUGHT YOU DID.
BUT KNOW THAT THINGS ARE GOING TO GET VERY DANGEROUS VERY QUICKLY...SO THIS IS YOUR LAST CHANCE TO WALK AWAY.
WELL?
STEEL.
ALL RIGHT, THEN. THAT'S IT.
PACK YOUR BAGS FOR A LONG TRIP. WE WON'T BE RETURNING HERE, AND YOU'LL EACH BE TRAVELLIN' SEPARATELY TO YOUR FINAL STAGING AREA.
INSTRUCTIONS WILL BE WAITIN' IN YOUR QUARTERS.
UNLESS OTHERWISE DIRECTED, *DO NOT* SHARE THEM WITH ANYONE ELSE.

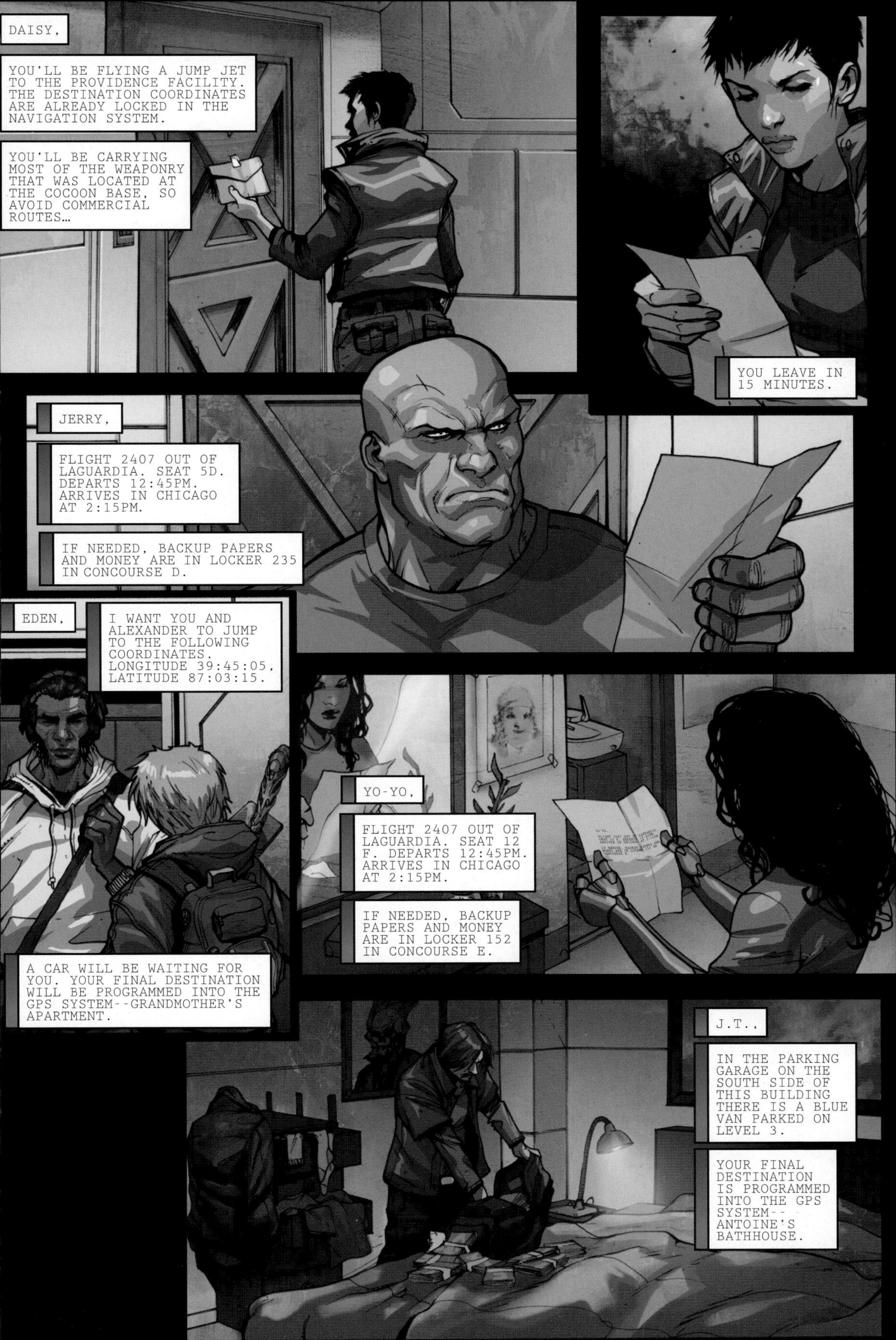
DAISY,
YOU'LL BE FLYING A JUMP JET TO THE PROVIDENCE FACILITY. THE DESTINATION COORDINATES ARE ALREADY LOCKED IN THE NAVIGATION SYSTEM.
YOU'LL BE CARRYING MOST OF THE WEAPONRY THAT WAS LOCATED AT THE COCOON BASE, SO AVOID COMMERCIAL ROUTES...
YOU LEAVE IN 15 MINUTES.
JERRY,
FLIGHT 2407 OUT OF LAGUARDIA. SEAT 5D. DEPARTS 12:45PM. ARRIVES IN CHICAGO AT 2:15PM.
IF NEEDED, BACKUP PAPERS AND MONEY ARE IN LOCKER 235 IN CONCOURSE D.
EDEN,
I WANT YOU AND ALEXANDER TO JUMP TO THE FOLLOWING COORDINATES. LONGITUDE 39:45:05, LATITUDE 87:03:15.
A CAR WILL BE WAITING FOR YOU. YOUR FINAL DESTINATION WILL BE PROGRAMMED INTO THE GPS SYSTEM--GRANDMOTHER'S APARTMENT.
YO-YO,
FLIGHT 2407 OUT OF LAGUARDIA. SEAT 12 F. DEPARTS 12:45PM. ARRIVES IN CHICAGO AT 2:15PM.
IF NEEDED, BACKUP PAPERS AND MONEY ARE IN LOCKER 152 IN CONCOURSE E.
J.T.,
IN THE PARKING GARAGE ON THE SOUTH SIDE OF THIS BUILDING THERE IS A BLUE VAN PARKED ON LEVEL 3.
YOUR FINAL DESTINATION IS PROGRAMMED INTO THE GPS SYSTEM--ANTOINE'S BATHHOUSE.

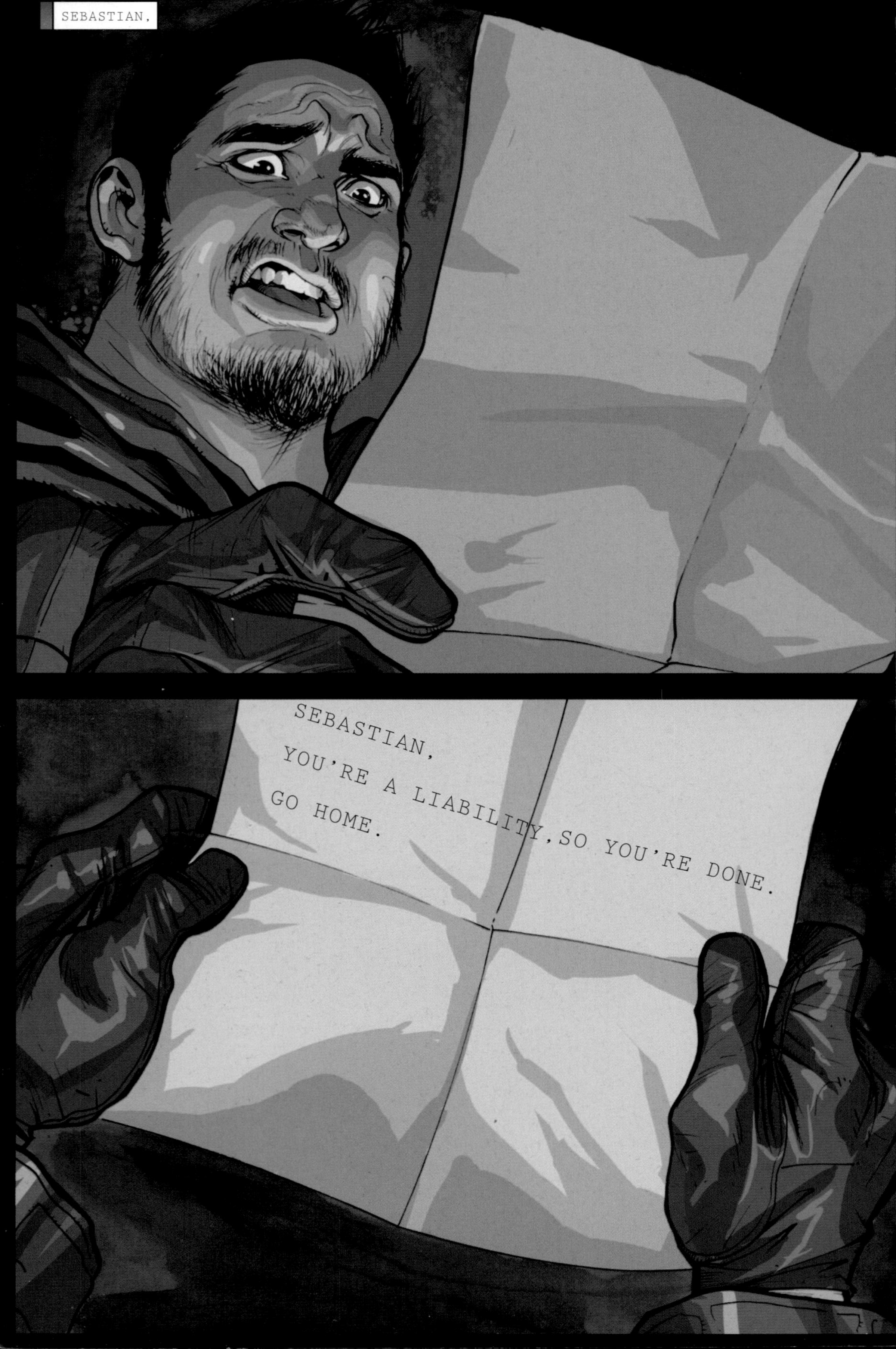
SEBASTIAN,
SEBASTIAN,
YOU'RE A LIABILITY, SO YOU'RE DONE.
GO HOME.

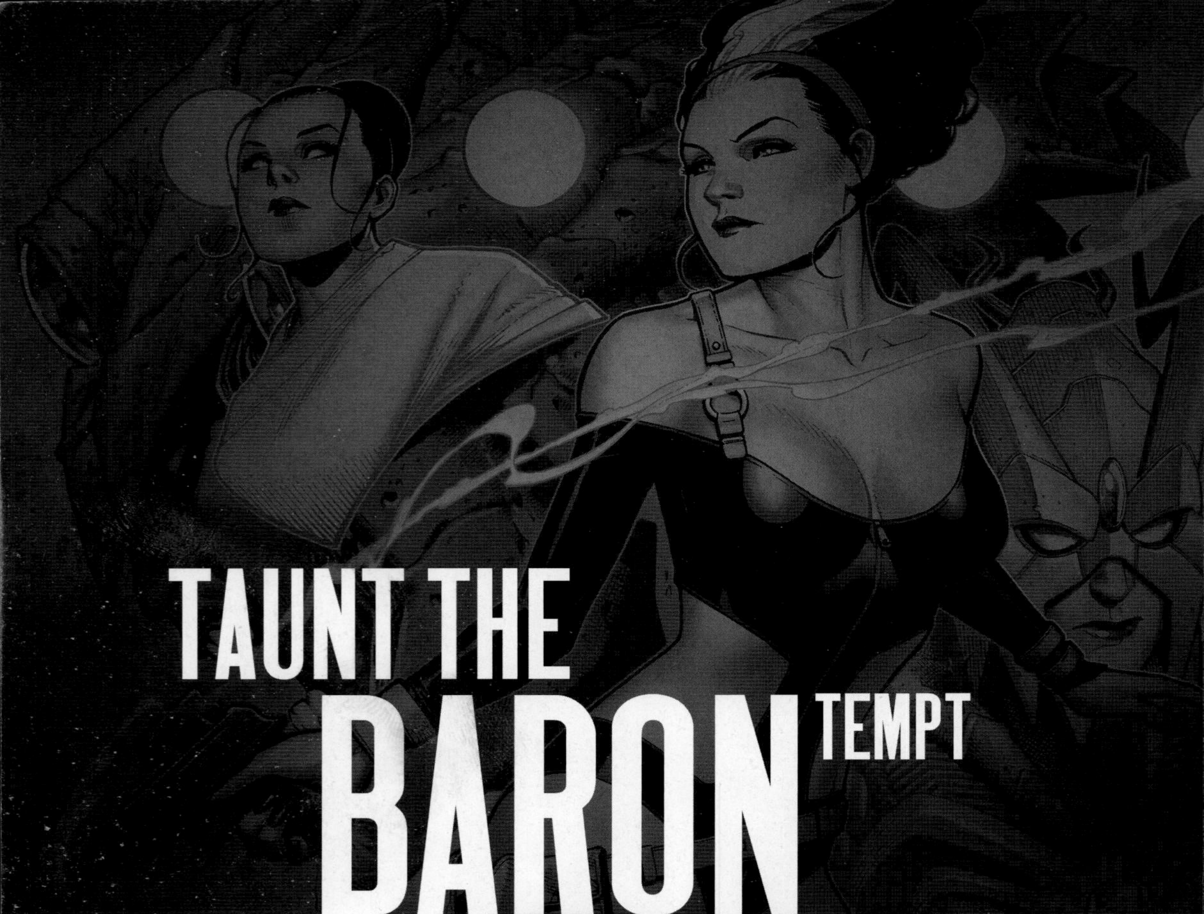

TAUNT THE BARON TEMPT THE FURY

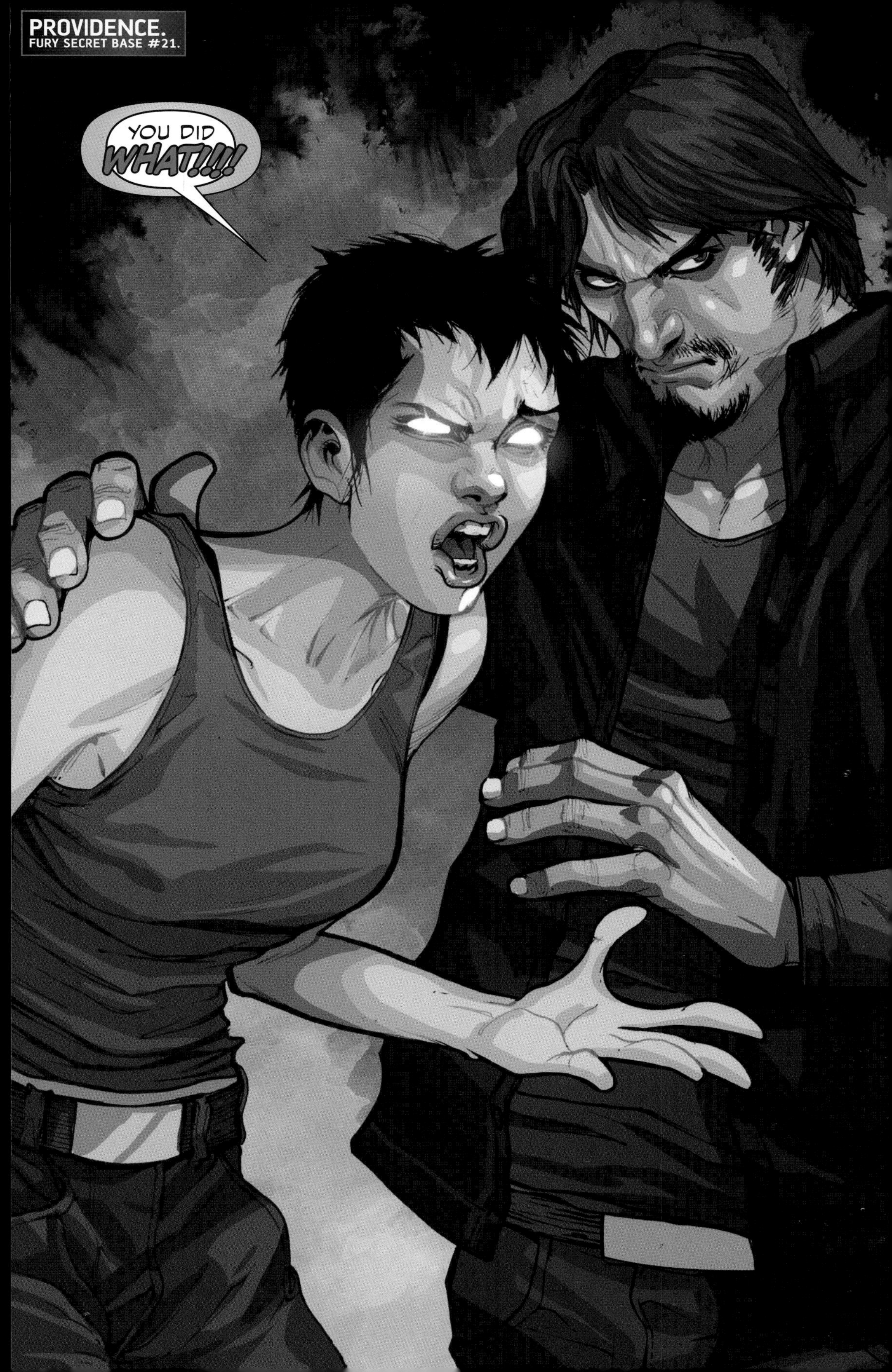
PROVIDENCE.
FURY SECRET BASE #21.
YOU DID WHAT!!!!

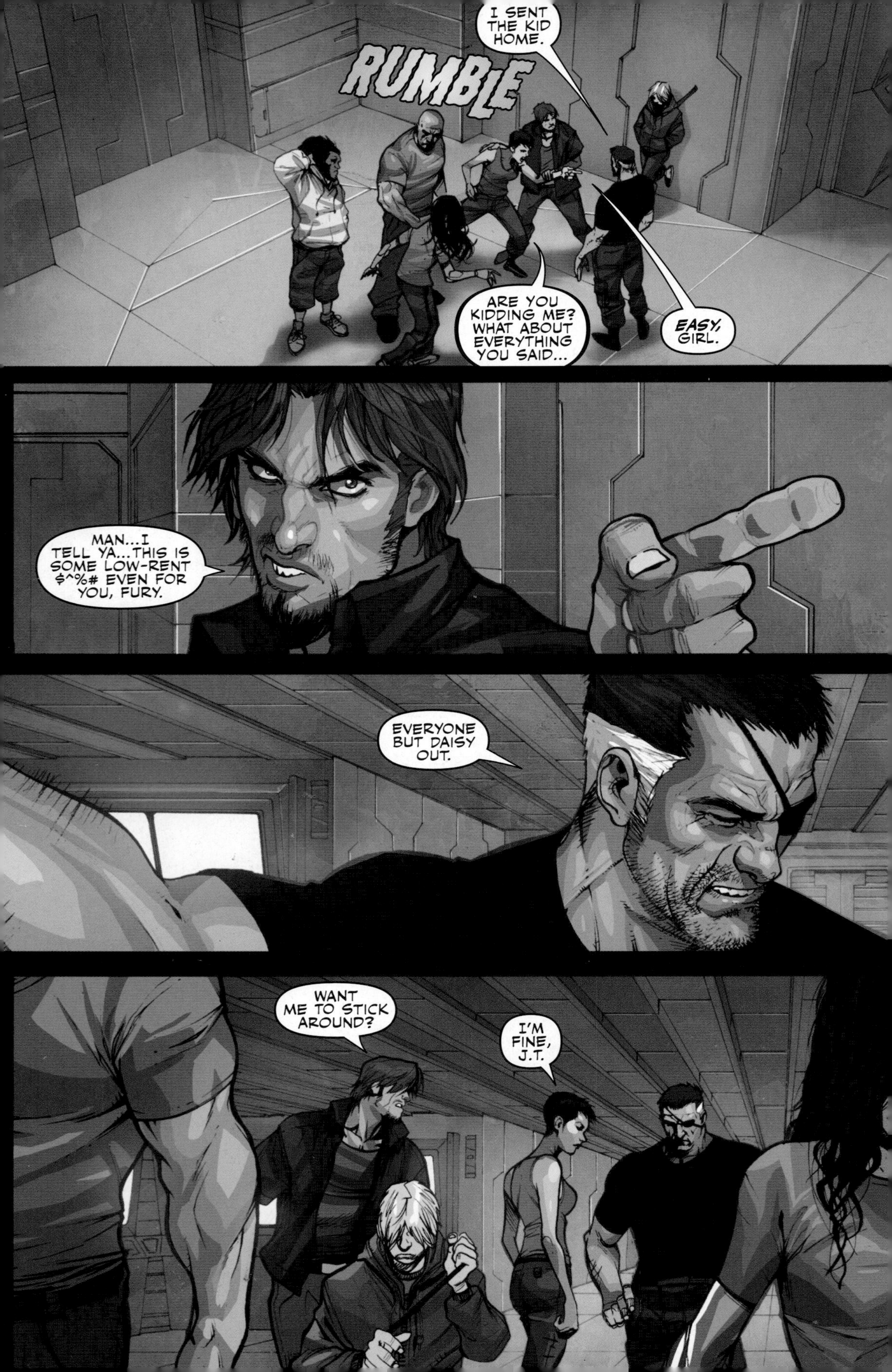

RUMBLE
I SENT THE KID HOME.
ARE YOU KIDDING ME? WHAT ABOUT EVERYTHING YOU SAID...
EASY, GIRL.
MAN...I TELL YA...THIS IS SOME LOW-RENT $^%# EVEN FOR YOU, FURY.
EVERYONE BUT DAISY OUT.
WANT ME TO STICK AROUND?
I'M FINE, J.T.

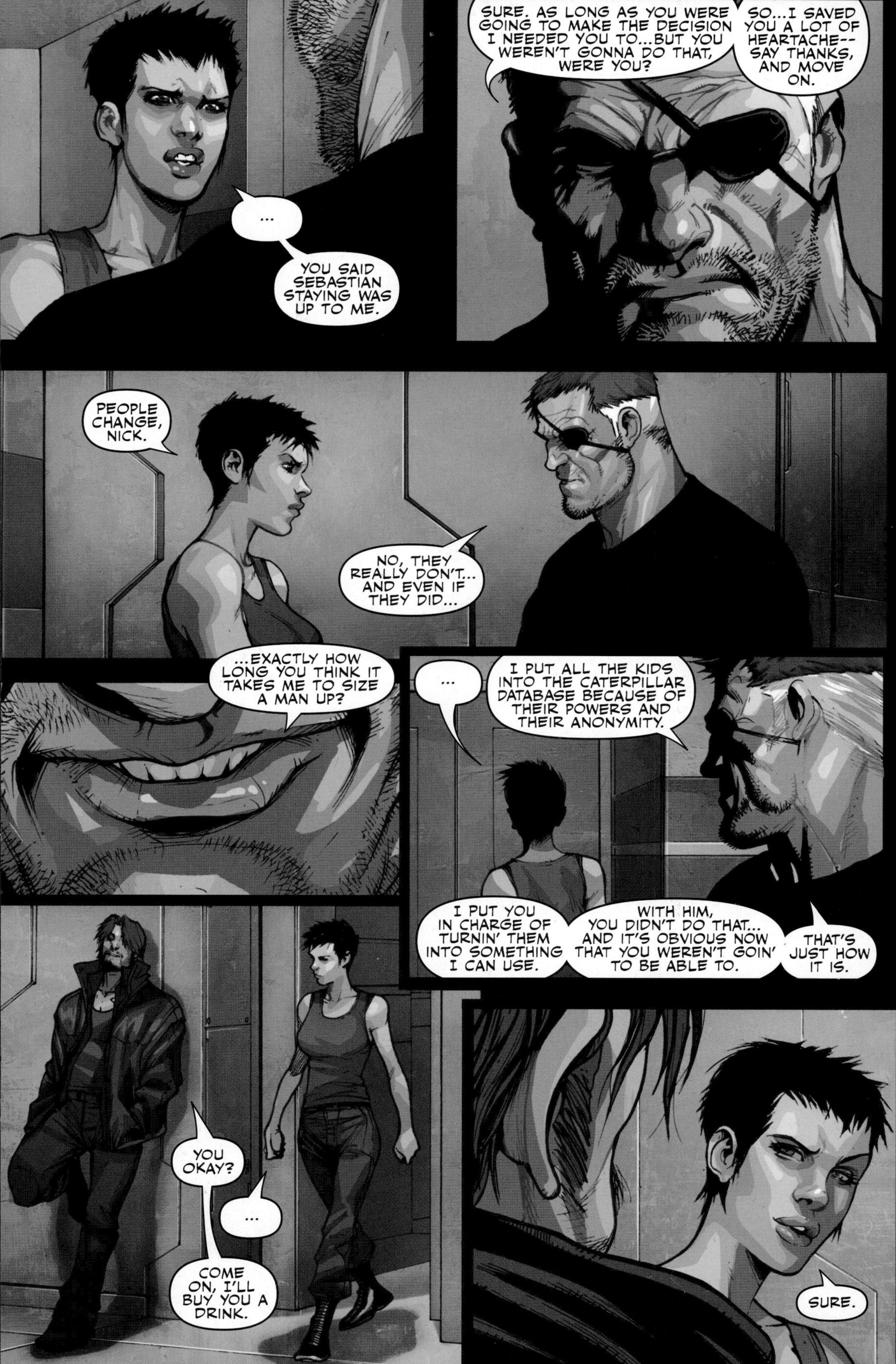
...
YOU SAID SEBASTIAN STAYING WAS UP TO ME.
SURE. AS LONG AS YOU WERE GOING TO MAKE THE DECISION I NEEDED YOU TO...BUT YOU WEREN'T GONNA DO THAT, WERE YOU?
SO...I SAVED YOU A LOT OF HEARTACHE-- SAY THANKS, AND MOVE ON.
PEOPLE CHANGE, NICK.
NO, THEY REALLY DON'T... AND EVEN IF THEY DID...
...EXACTLY HOW LONG YOU THINK IT TAKES ME TO SIZE A MAN UP?
...
I PUT ALL THE KIDS INTO THE CATERPILLAR DATABASE BECAUSE OF THEIR POWERS AND THEIR ANONYMITY.
I PUT YOU IN CHARGE OF TURNIN' THEM INTO SOMETHING I CAN USE.
WITH HIM, YOU DIDN'T DO THAT... AND IT'S OBVIOUS NOW THAT YOU WEREN'T GOIN' TO BE ABLE TO.
THAT'S JUST HOW IT IS.
YOU OKAY?
...
COME ON, I'LL BUY YOU A DRINK.
SURE.

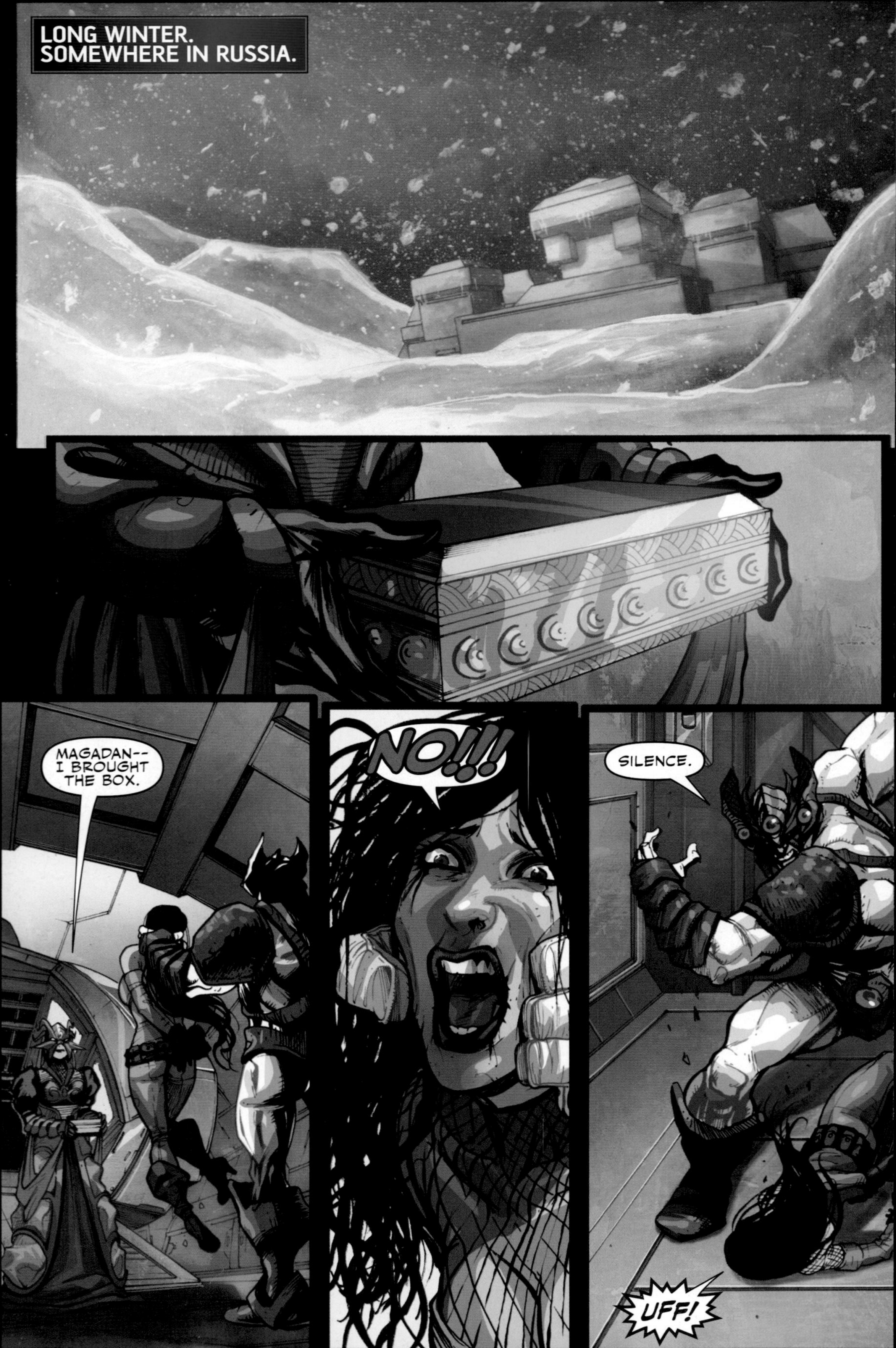
LONG WINTER.
SOMEWHERE IN RUSSIA.
MAGADAN-- I BROUGHT THE BOX.
NO!!!
SILENCE.
UFF!

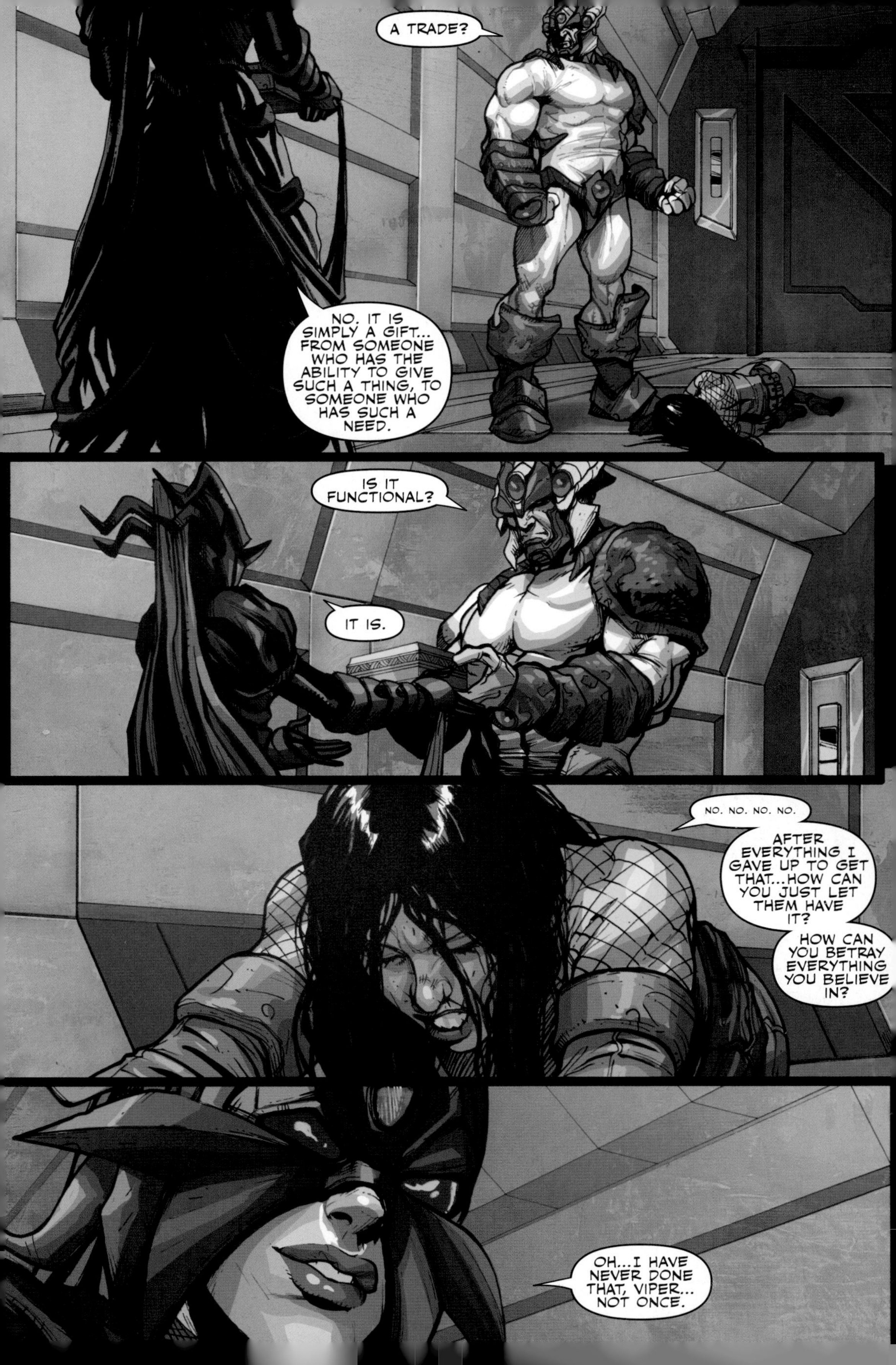
A TRADE?
NO. IT IS SIMPLY A GIFT... FROM SOMEONE WHO HAS THE ABILITY TO GIVE SUCH A THING, TO SOMEONE WHO HAS SUCH A NEED.
IS IT FUNCTIONAL?
IT IS.
NO. NO. NO. NO.
AFTER EVERYTHING I GAVE UP TO GET THAT...HOW CAN YOU JUST LET THEM HAVE IT?
HOW CAN YOU BETRAY EVERYTHING YOU BELIEVE IN?
OH...I HAVE NEVER DONE THAT, VIPER... NOT ONCE.

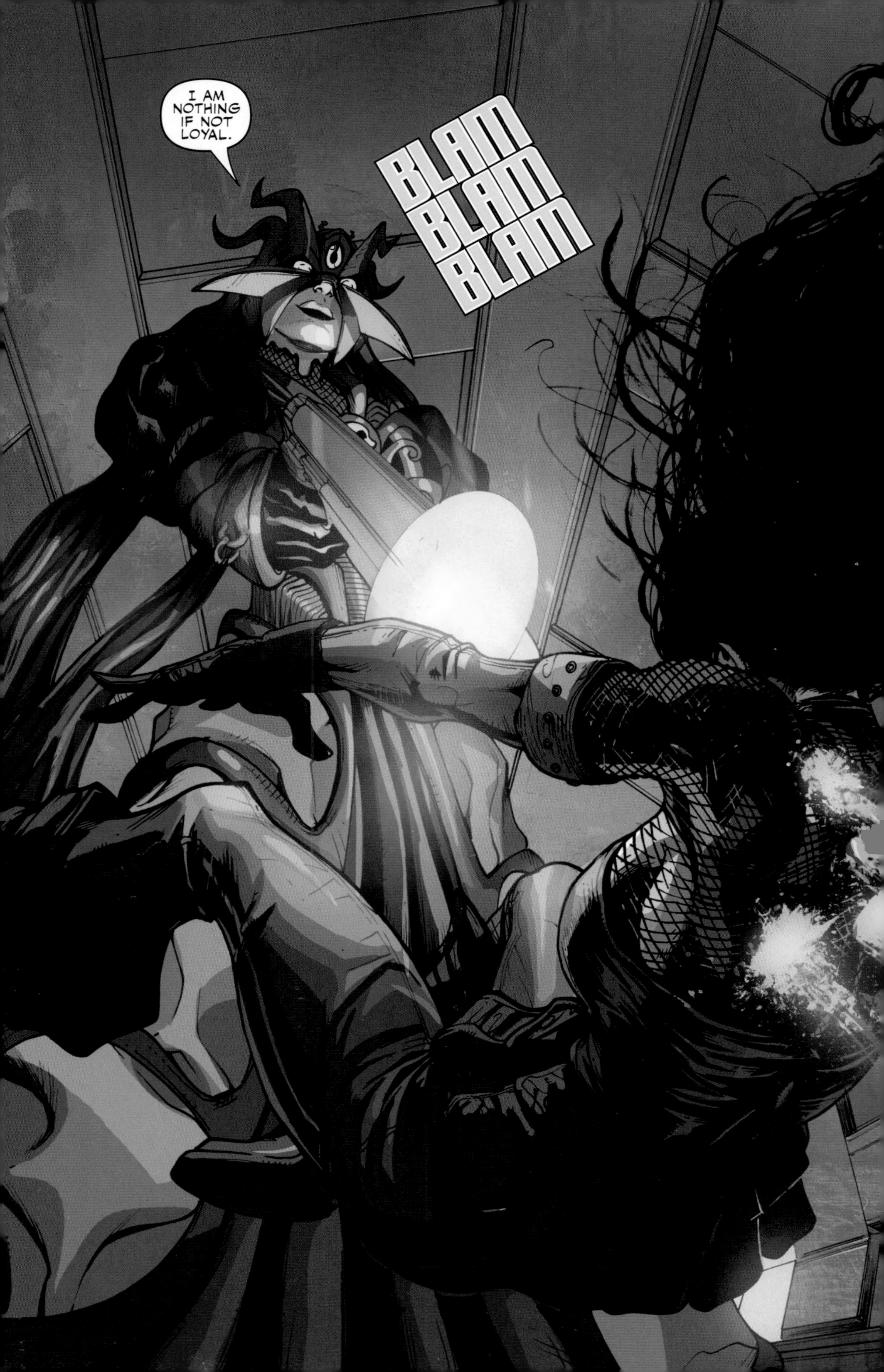
I AM NOTHING IF NOT LOYAL.
BLAM BLAM BLAM

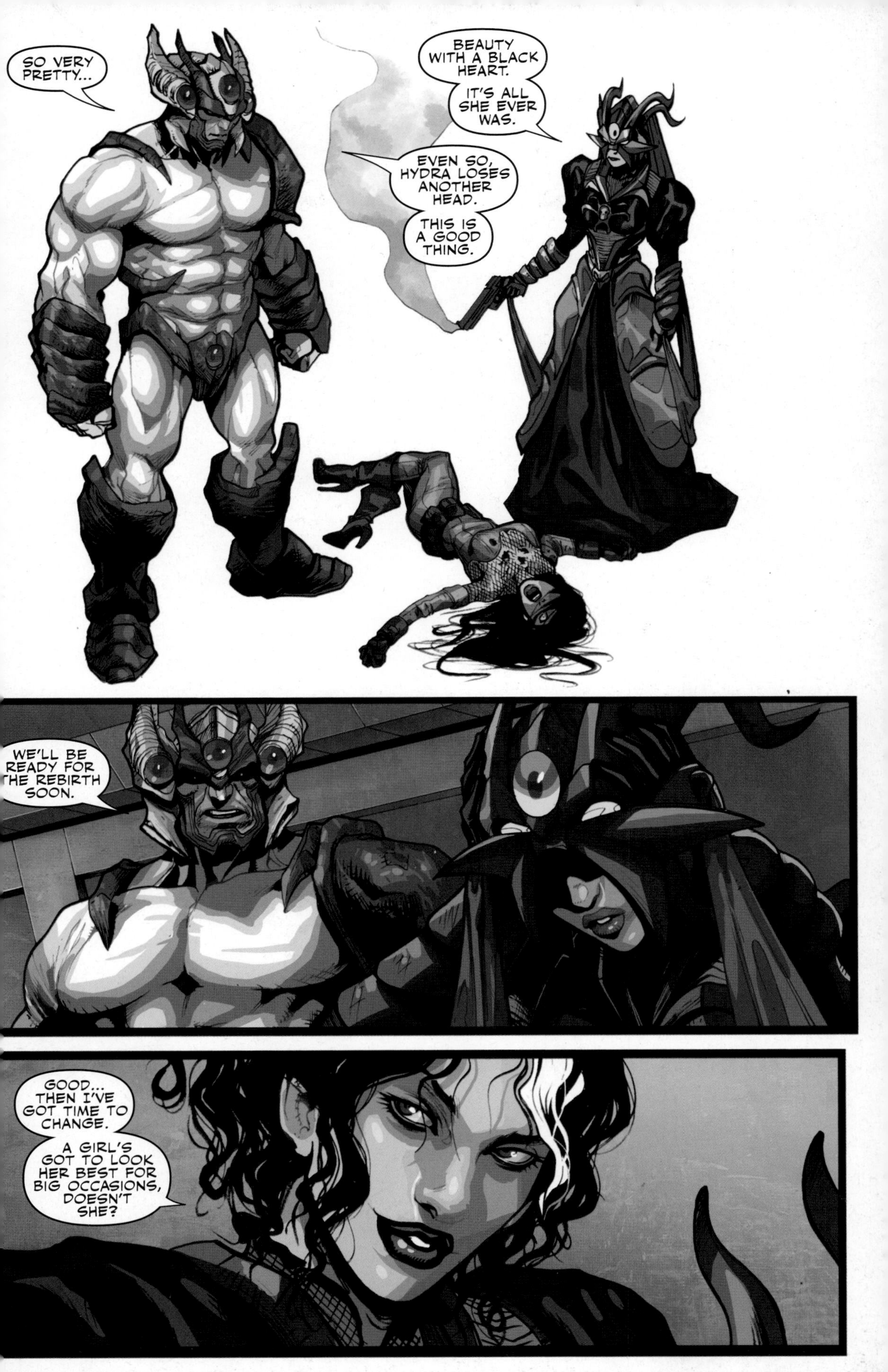
SO VERY PRETTY...
BEAUTY WITH A BLACK HEART.
IT'S ALL SHE EVER WAS.
EVEN SO, HYDRA LOSES ANOTHER HEAD.
THIS IS A GOOD THING.
WE'LL BE READY FOR THE REBIRTH SOON.
GOOD... THEN I'VE GOT TIME TO CHANGE.
A GIRL'S GOT TO LOOK HER BEST FOR BIG OCCASIONS, DOESN'T SHE?

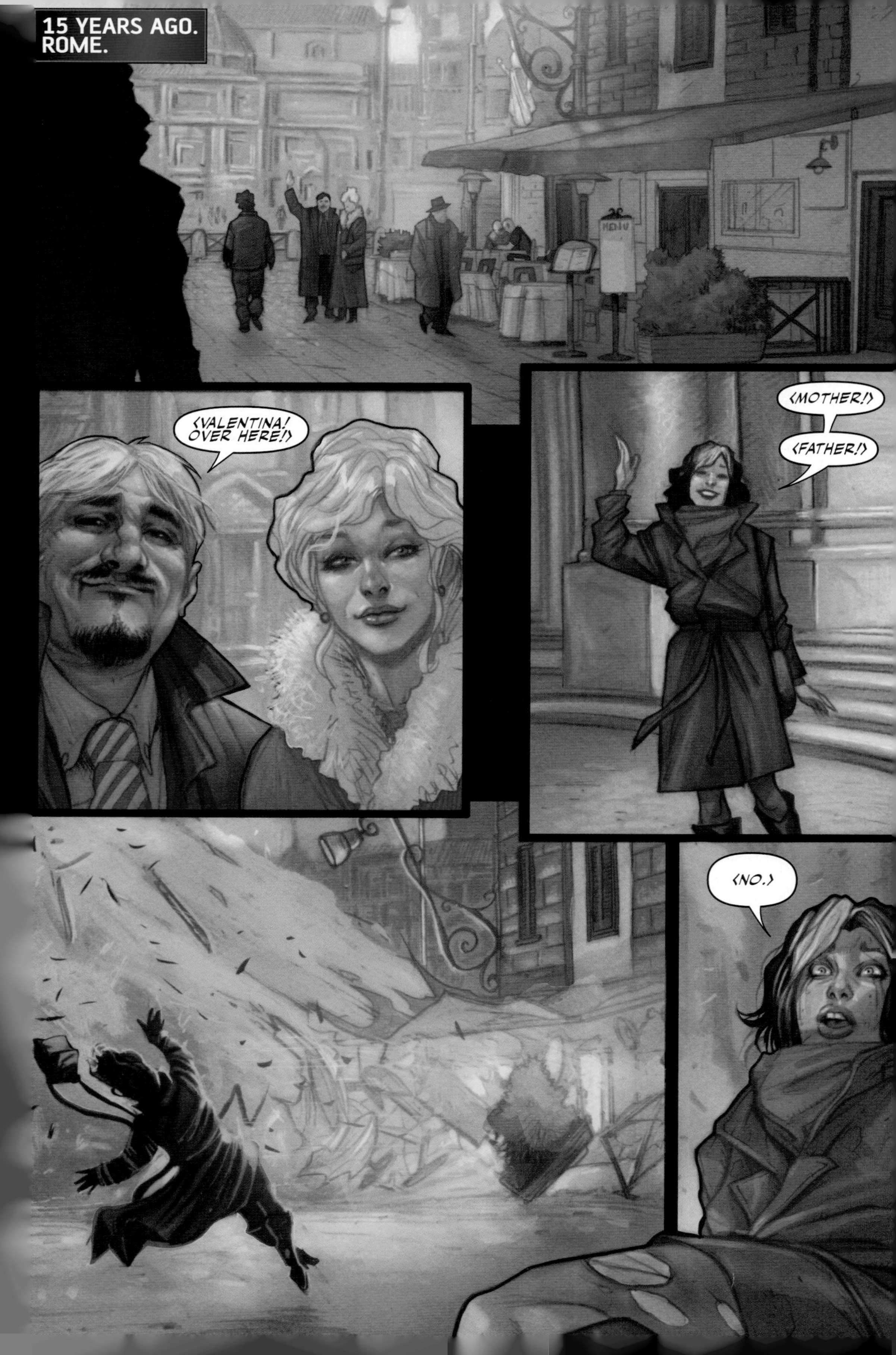
15 YEARS AGO.
ROME.
<VALENTINA! OVER HERE!>
<MOTHER!>
<FATHER!>
<NO.>

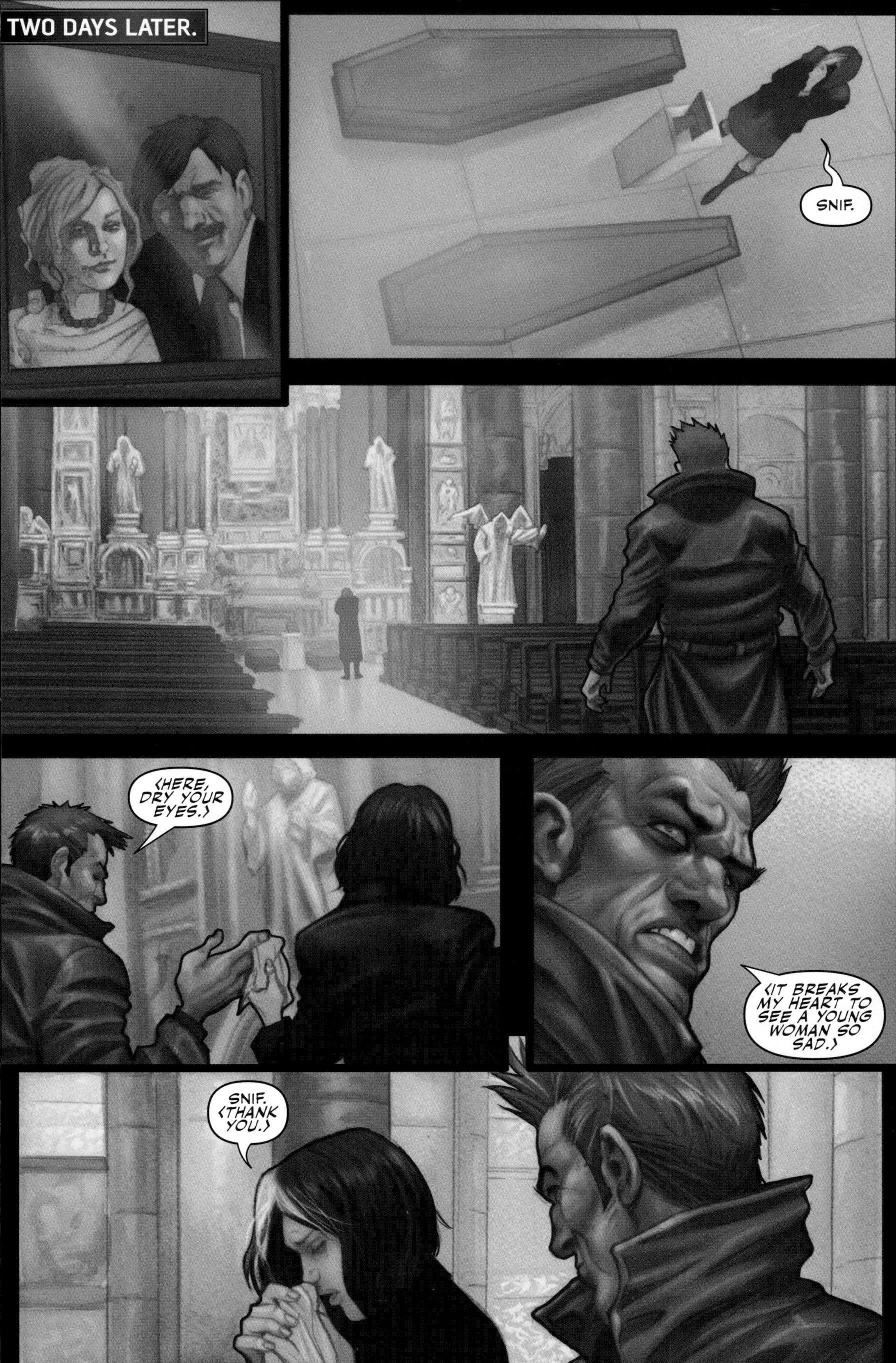
TWO DAYS LATER.
SNIF.
<HERE, DRY YOUR EYES.>
<IT BREAKS MY HEART TO SEE A YOUNG WOMAN SO SAD.>
SNIF. <THANK YOU.>

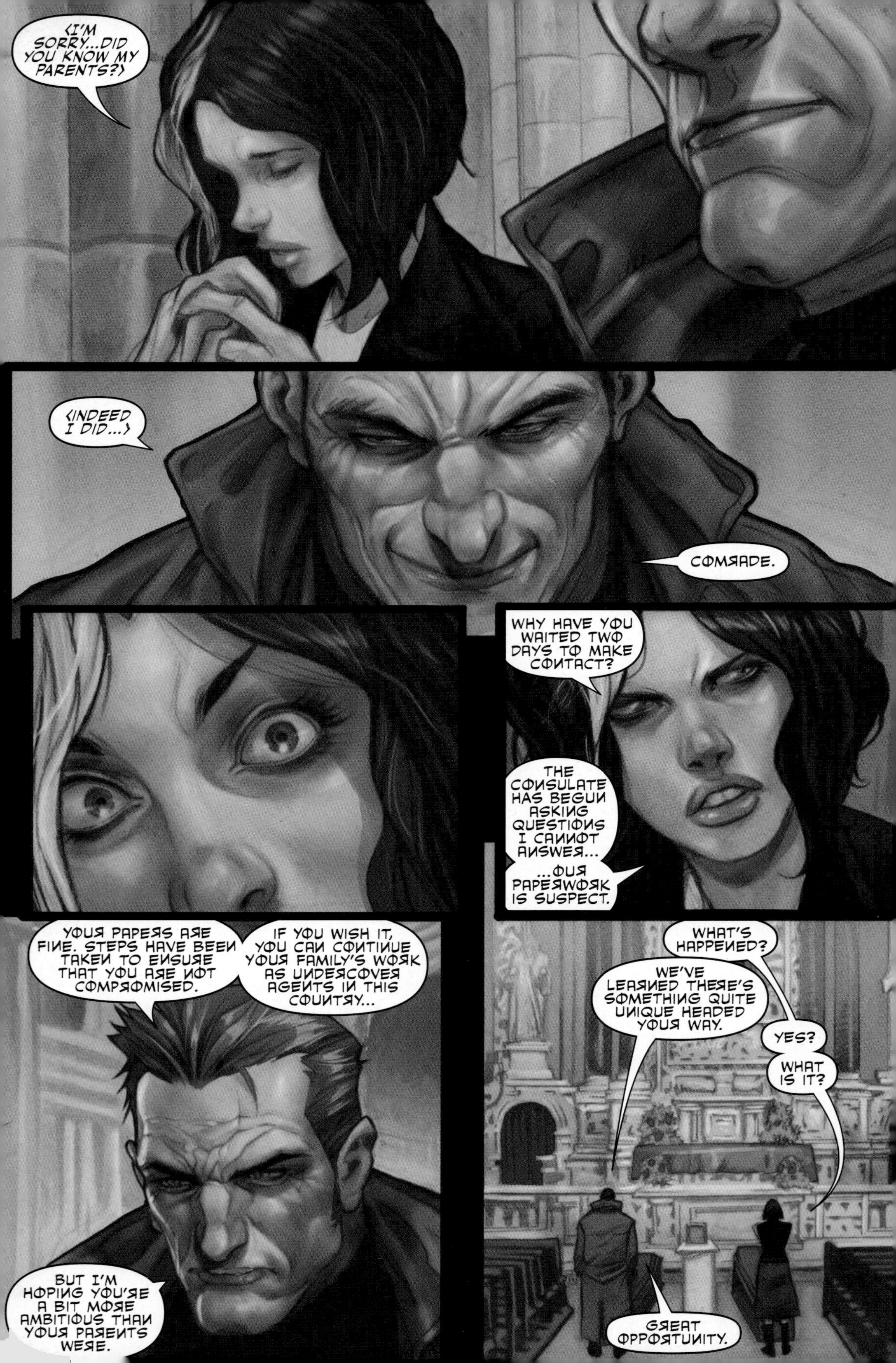

<I'M SORRY...DID YOU KNOW MY PARENTS?>
<INDEED I DID...>
COMRADE.
WHY HAVE YOU WAITED TWO DAYS TO MAKE CONTACT?
THE CONSULATE HAS BEGUN ASKING QUESTIONS I CANNOT ANSWER...
...OUR PAPERWORK IS SUSPECT.
YOUR PAPERS ARE FINE. STEPS HAVE BEEN TAKEN TO ENSURE THAT YOU ARE NOT COMPROMISED.
IF YOU WISH IT, YOU CAN CONTINUE YOUR FAMILY'S WORK AS UNDERCOVER AGENTS IN THIS COUNTRY...
BUT I'M HOPING YOU'RE A BIT MORE AMBITIOUS THAN YOUR PARENTS WERE.
WHAT'S HAPPENED?
WE'VE LEARNED THERE'S SOMETHING QUITE UNIQUE HEADED YOUR WAY.
YES?
WHAT IS IT?
GREAT OPPORTUNITY.

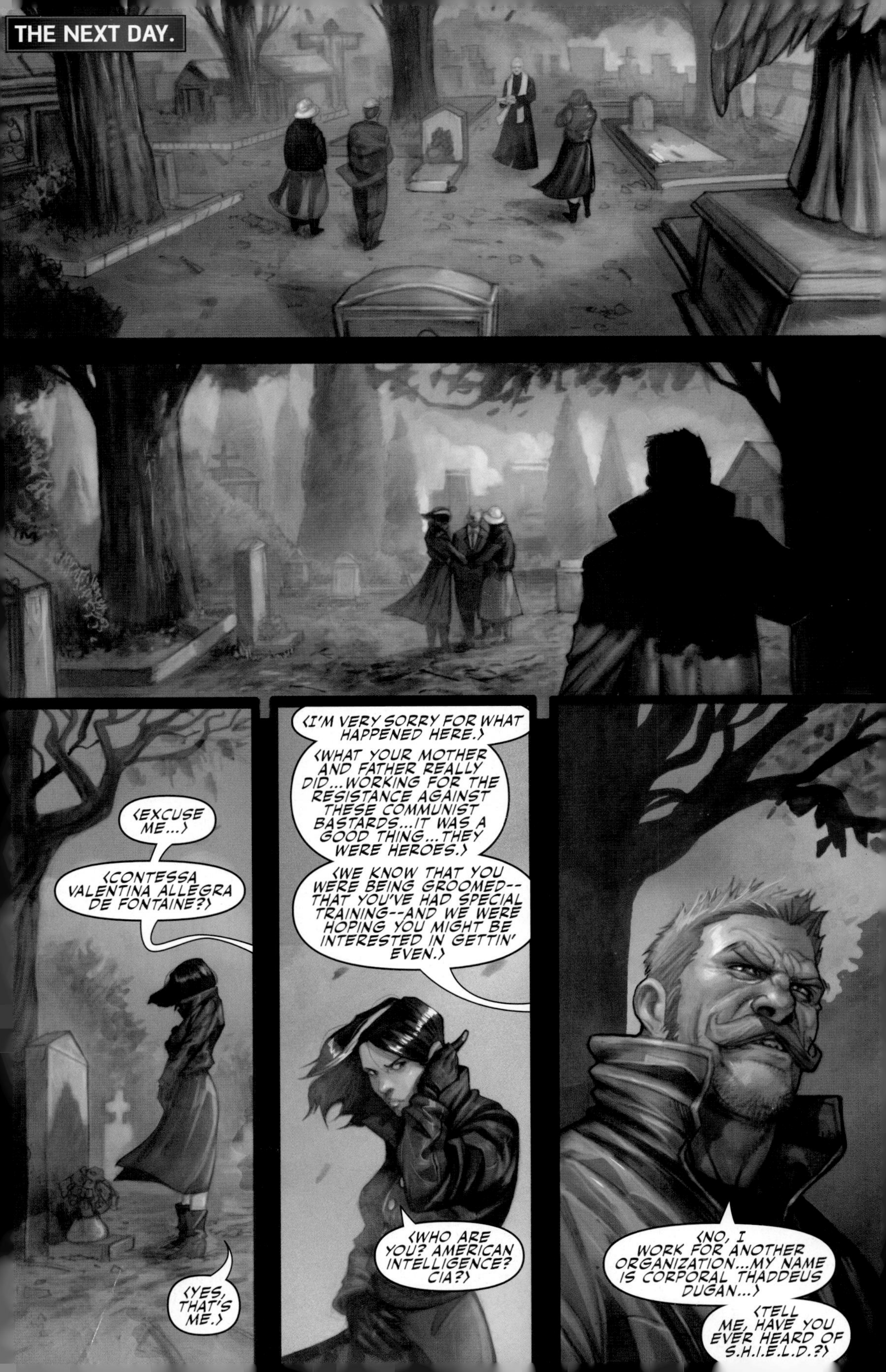
THE NEXT DAY.
<EXCUSE ME...>
<CONTESSA VALENTINA ALLEGRA DE FONTAINE?>
<YES, THAT'S ME.>
<I'M VERY SORRY FOR WHAT HAPPENED HERE.>
<WHAT YOUR MOTHER AND FATHER REALLY DID...WORKING FOR THE RESISTANCE AGAINST THESE COMMUNIST BASTARDS...IT WAS A GOOD THING...THEY WERE HEROES.>
<WE KNOW THAT YOU WERE BEING GROOMED--THAT YOU'VE HAD SPECIAL TRAINING--AND WE WERE HOPING YOU MIGHT BE INTERESTED IN GETTIN' EVEN.>
<WHO ARE YOU? AMERICAN INTELLIGENCE? CIA?>
<NO, I WORK FOR ANOTHER ORGANIZATION...MY NAME IS CORPORAL THADDEUS DUGAN...>
<TELL ME, HAVE YOU EVER HEARD OF S.H.I.E.L.D.?>

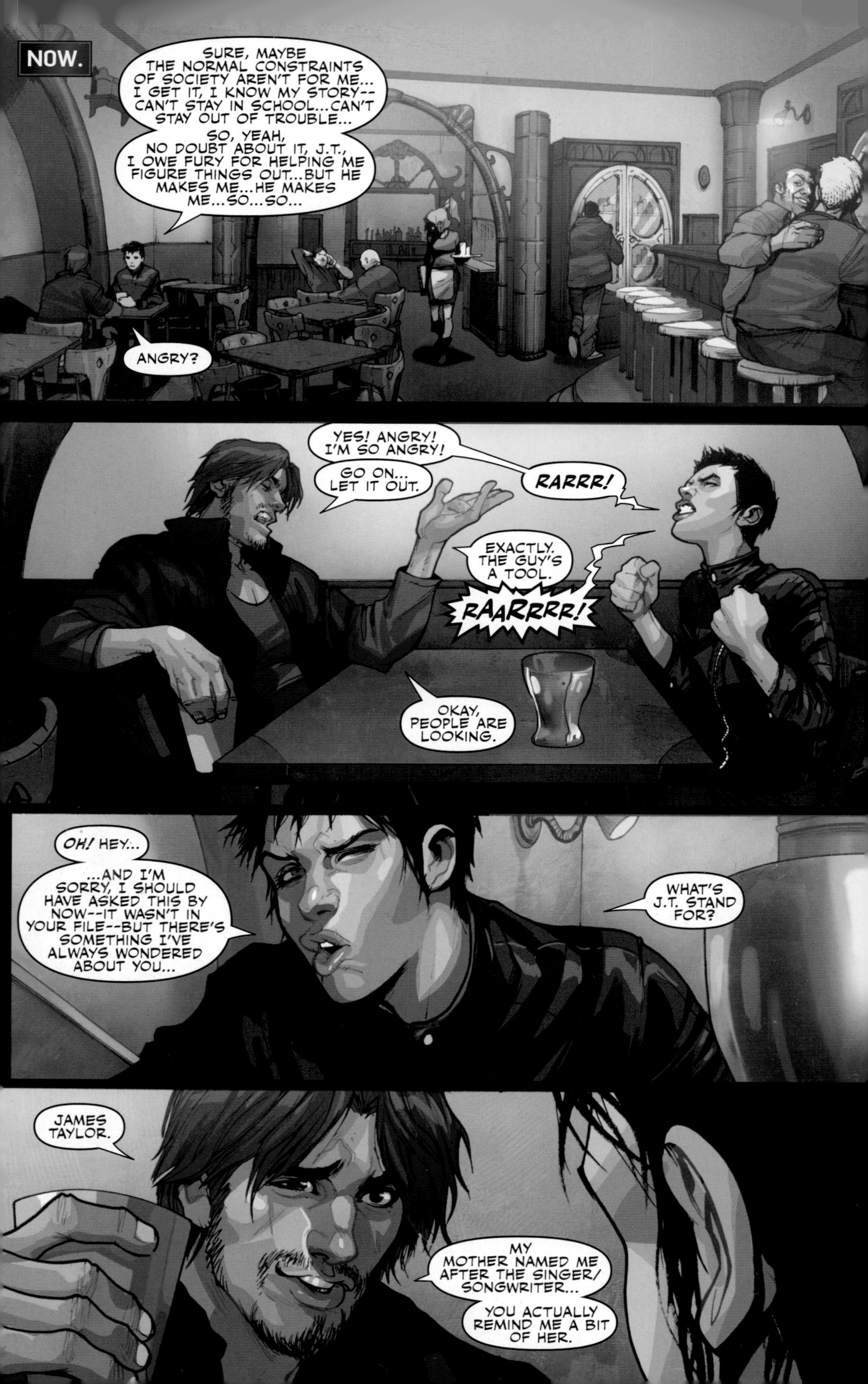
NOW.
SURE, MAYBE THE NORMAL CONSTRAINTS OF SOCIETY AREN'T FOR ME... I GET IT, I KNOW MY STORY--CAN'T STAY IN SCHOOL...CAN'T STAY OUT OF TROUBLE...
SO, YEAH, NO DOUBT ABOUT IT, J.T., I OWE FURY FOR HELPING ME FIGURE THINGS OUT...BUT HE MAKES ME...HE MAKES ME...SO...SO...
ANGRY?
YES! ANGRY! I'M SO ANGRY!
GO ON... LET IT OUT.
RARRR!
EXACTLY. THE GUY'S A TOOL.
RAARRRR!
OKAY, PEOPLE ARE LOOKING.
OH! HEY...
...AND I'M SORRY, I SHOULD HAVE ASKED THIS BY NOW--IT WASN'T IN YOUR FILE--BUT THERE'S SOMETHING I'VE ALWAYS WONDERED ABOUT YOU...
WHAT'S J.T. STAND FOR?
JAMES TAYLOR.
MY MOTHER NAMED ME AFTER THE SINGER/SONGWRITER...
YOU ACTUALLY REMIND ME A BIT OF HER.

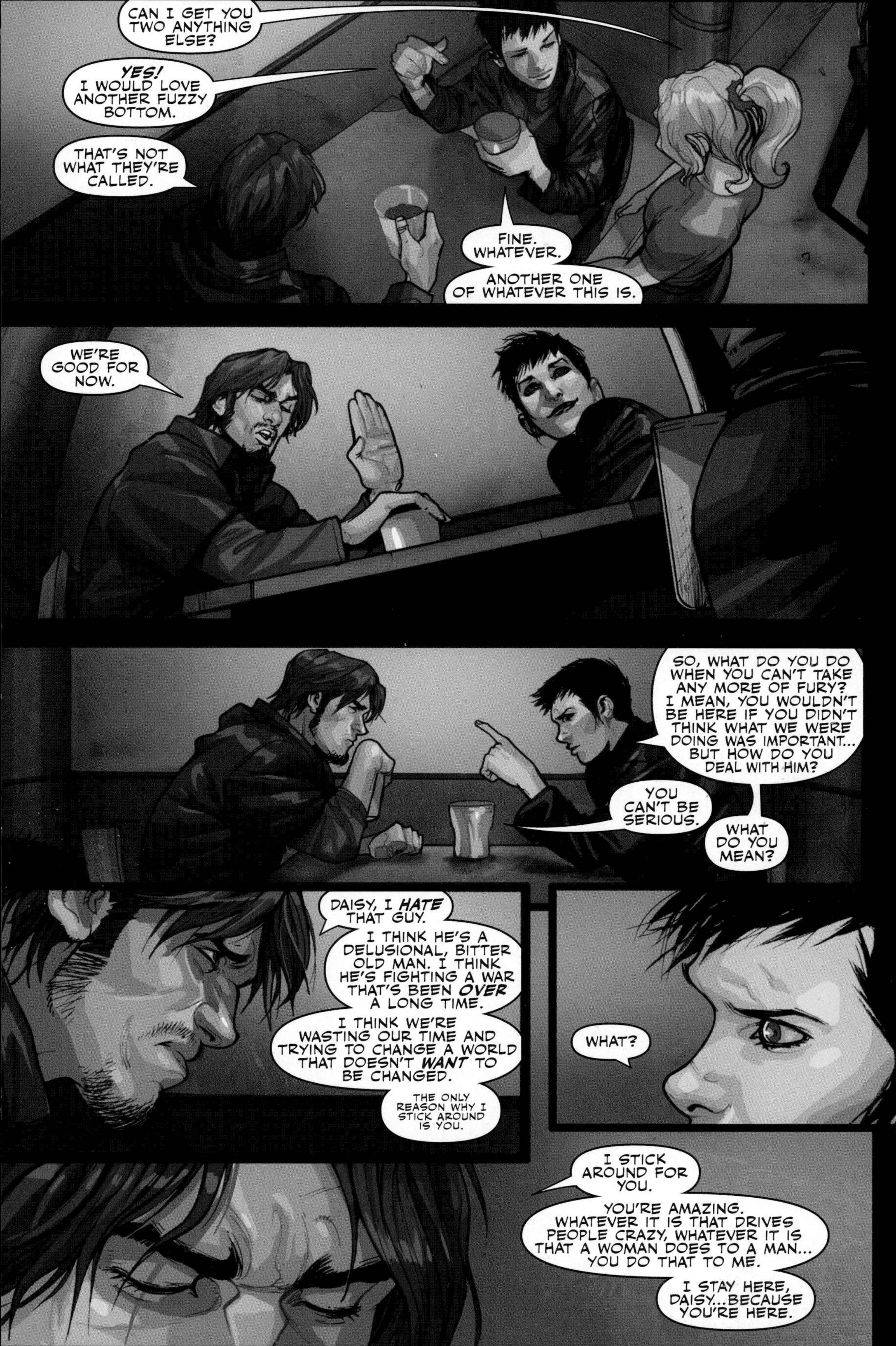
CAN I GET YOU TWO ANYTHING ELSE?
YES! I WOULD LOVE ANOTHER FUZZY BOTTOM.
THAT'S NOT WHAT THEY'RE CALLED.
FINE. WHATEVER.
ANOTHER ONE OF WHATEVER THIS IS.
WE'RE GOOD FOR NOW.
SO, WHAT DO YOU DO WHEN YOU CAN'T TAKE ANY MORE OF FURY? I MEAN, YOU WOULDN'T BE HERE IF YOU DIDN'T THINK WHAT WE WERE DOING WAS IMPORTANT... BUT HOW DO YOU DEAL WITH HIM?
YOU CAN'T BE SERIOUS.
WHAT DO YOU MEAN?
DAISY, I HATE THAT GUY.
I THINK HE'S A DELUSIONAL, BITTER OLD MAN. I THINK HE'S FIGHTING A WAR THAT'S BEEN OVER A LONG TIME.
I THINK WE'RE WASTING OUR TIME AND TRYING TO CHANGE A WORLD THAT DOESN'T WANT TO BE CHANGED.
THE ONLY REASON WHY I STICK AROUND IS YOU.
WHAT?
I STICK AROUND FOR YOU.
YOU'RE AMAZING. WHATEVER IT IS THAT DRIVES PEOPLE CRAZY, WHATEVER IT IS THAT A WOMAN DOES TO A MAN... YOU DO THAT TO ME.
I STAY HERE, DAISY...BECAUSE YOU'RE HERE.

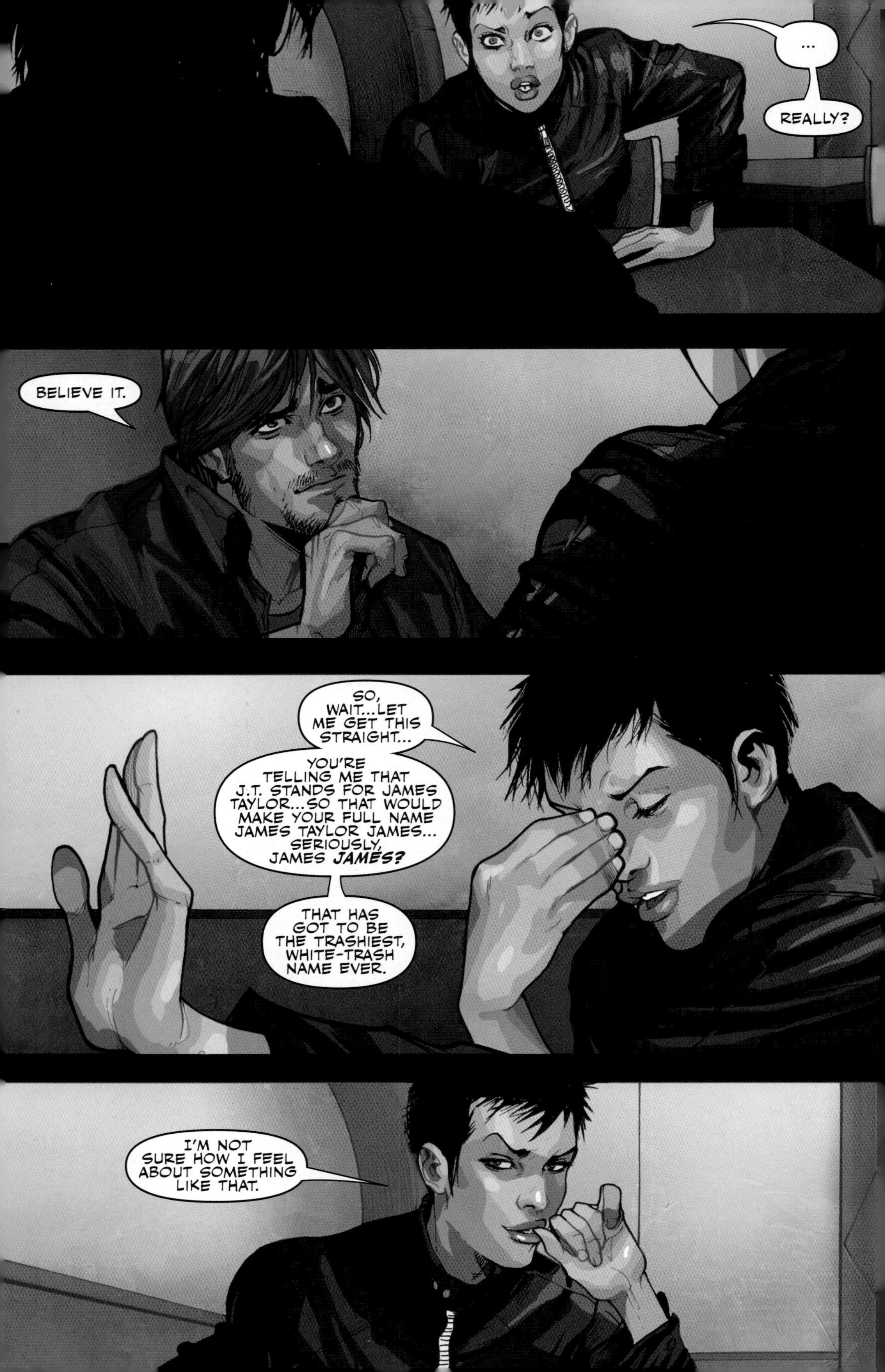
...
REALLY?
BELIEVE IT.
SO, WAIT...LET ME GET THIS STRAIGHT...
YOU'RE TELLING ME THAT J.T. STANDS FOR JAMES TAYLOR...SO THAT WOULD MAKE YOUR FULL NAME JAMES TAYLOR JAMES... SERIOUSLY, JAMES JAMES?
THAT HAS GOT TO BE THE TRASHIEST, WHITE-TRASH NAME EVER.
I'M NOT SURE HOW I FEEL ABOUT SOMETHING LIKE THAT.

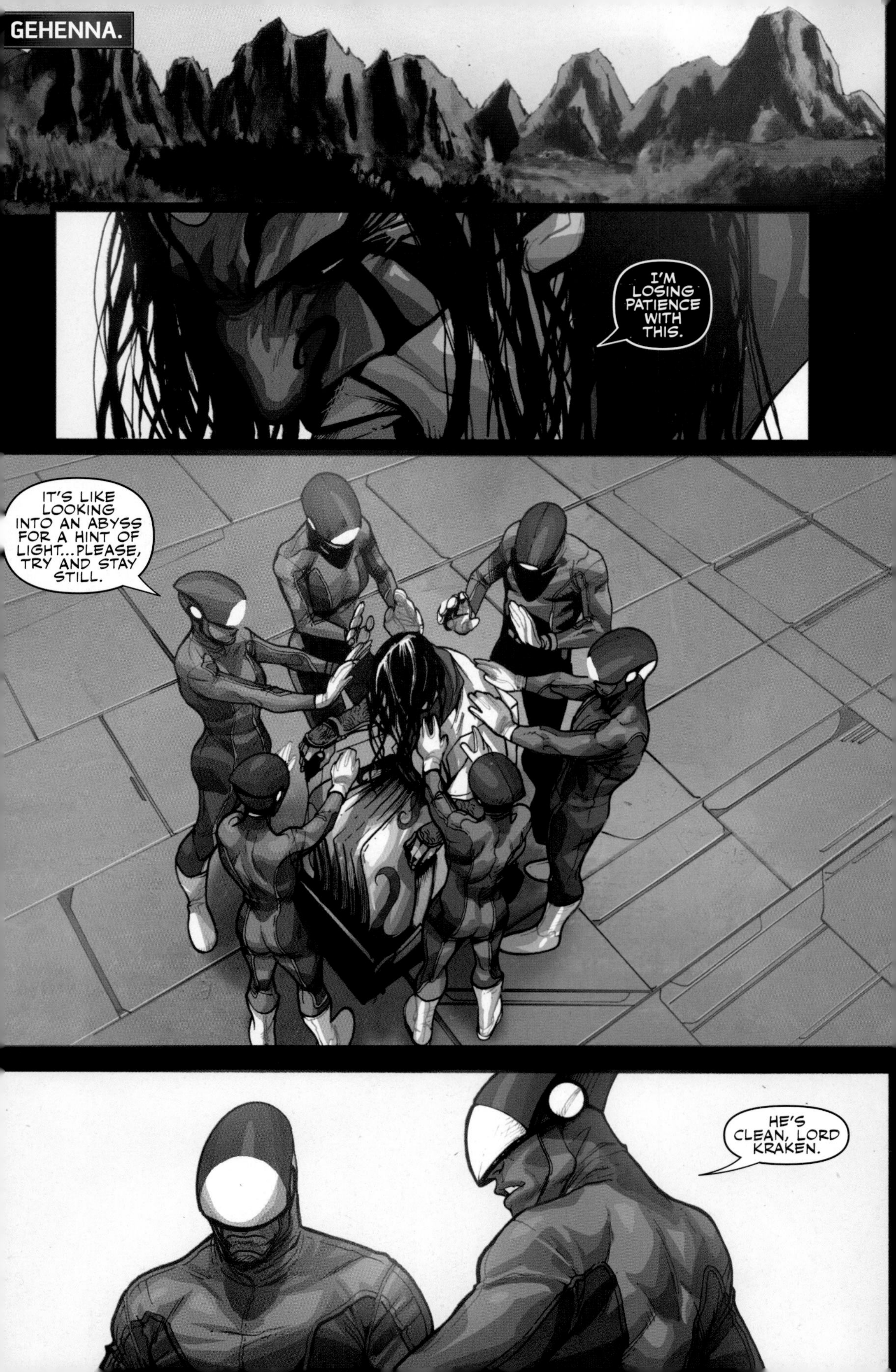
GEHENNA.
I'M LOSING PATIENCE WITH THIS.
IT'S LIKE LOOKING INTO AN ABYSS FOR A HINT OF LIGHT...PLEASE, TRY AND STAY STILL.
HE'S CLEAN, LORD KRAKEN.

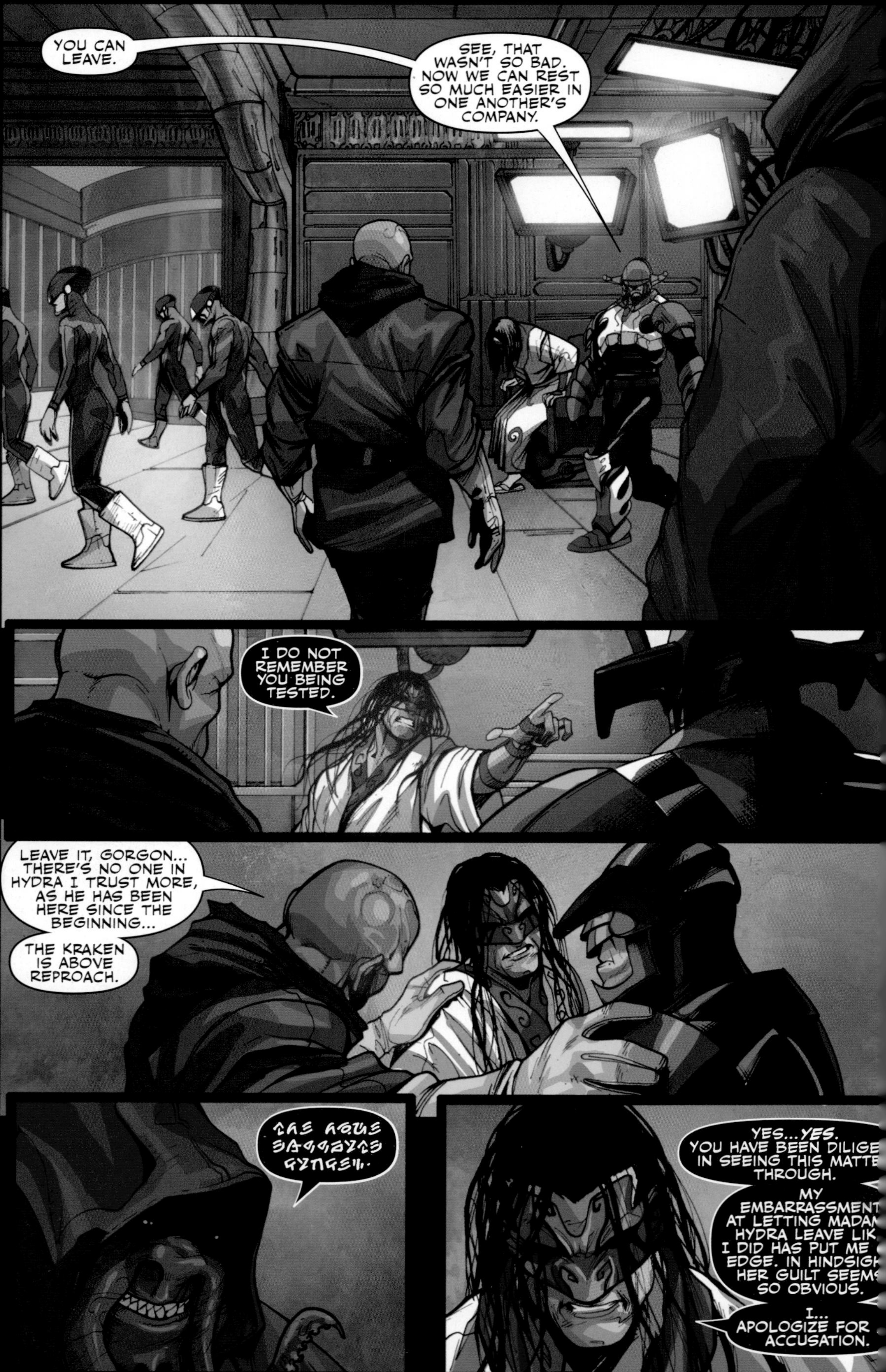
YOU CAN LEAVE.
SEE, THAT WASN'T SO BAD. NOW WE CAN REST SO MUCH EASIER IN ONE ANOTHER'S COMPANY.
I DO NOT REMEMBER YOU BEING TESTED.
LEAVE IT, GORGON... THERE'S NO ONE IN HYDRA I TRUST MORE, AS HE HAS BEEN HERE SINCE THE BEGINNING...
THE KRAKEN IS ABOVE REPROACH.
YES... YES. YOU HAVE BEEN DILIGE IN SEEING THIS MATTE THROUGH.
MY EMBARRASSMENT AT LETTING MADAM HYDRA LEAVE LIK I DID HAS PUT ME EDGE. IN HINDSIGH HER GUILT SEEM SO OBVIOUS.
I... APOLOGIZE FOR ACCUSATION.

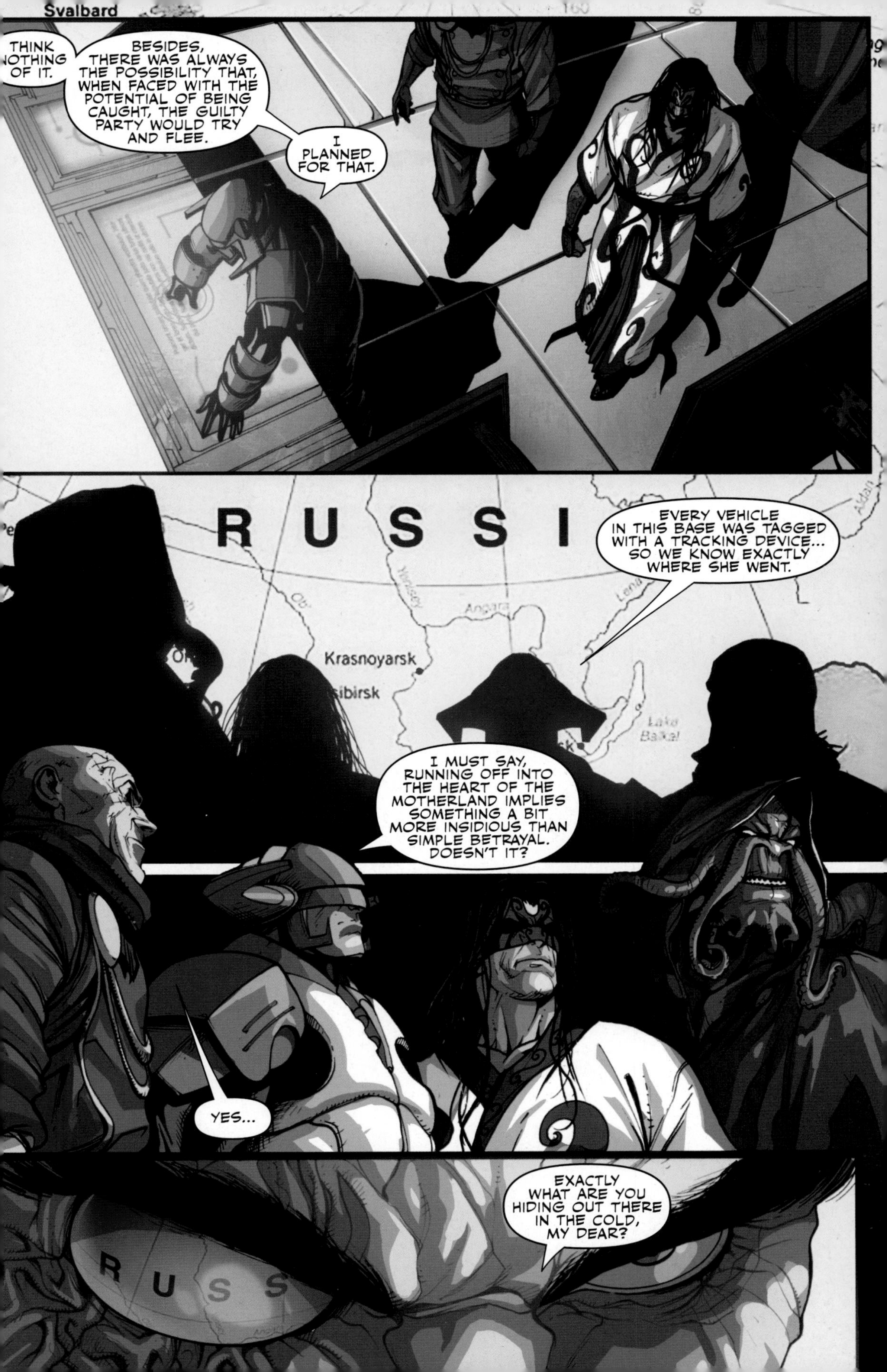

Svalbard
THINK NOTHING OF IT.
BESIDES, THERE WAS ALWAYS THE POSSIBILITY THAT, WHEN FACED WITH THE POTENTIAL OF BEING CAUGHT, THE GUILTY PARTY WOULD TRY AND FLEE.
I PLANNED FOR THAT.
RUSSI
EVERY VEHICLE IN THIS BASE WAS TAGGED WITH A TRACKING DEVICE... SO WE KNOW EXACTLY WHERE SHE WENT.
Angara
Krasnoyarsk
Lake Baikal
I MUST SAY, RUNNING OFF INTO THE HEART OF THE MOTHERLAND IMPLIES SOMETHING A BIT MORE INSIDIOUS THAN SIMPLE BETRAYAL. DOESN'T IT?
YES...
EXACTLY WHAT ARE YOU HIDING OUT THERE IN THE COLD, MY DEAR?
RUSS

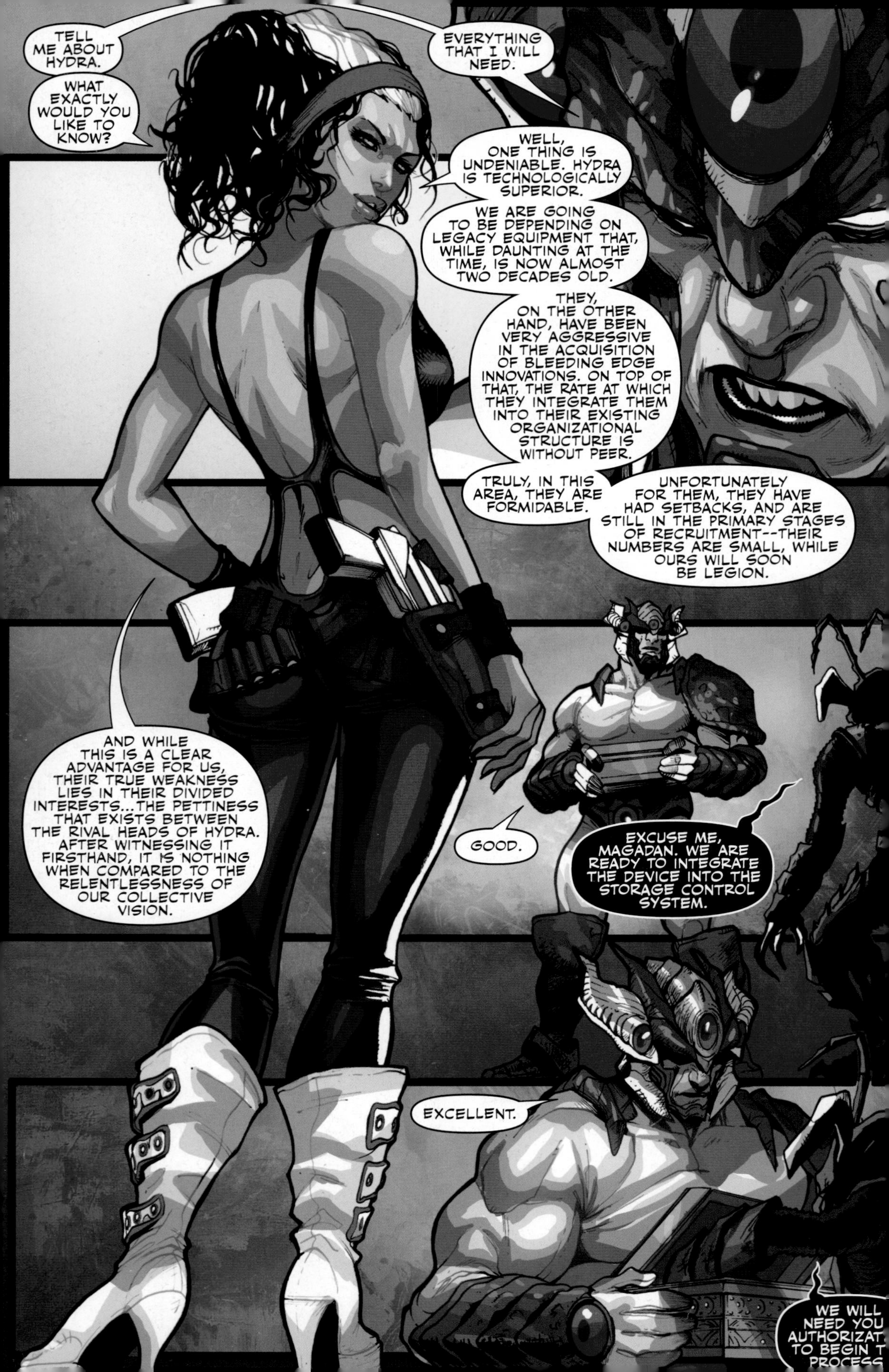

TELL ME ABOUT HYDRA.
EVERYTHING THAT I WILL NEED.
WHAT EXACTLY WOULD YOU LIKE TO KNOW?
WELL, ONE THING IS UNDENIABLE. HYDRA IS TECHNOLOGICALLY SUPERIOR.
WE ARE GOING TO BE DEPENDING ON LEGACY EQUIPMENT THAT, WHILE DAUNTING AT THE TIME, IS NOW ALMOST TWO DECADES OLD.
THEY, ON THE OTHER HAND, HAVE BEEN VERY AGGRESSIVE IN THE ACQUISITION OF BLEEDING EDGE INNOVATIONS. ON TOP OF THAT, THE RATE AT WHICH THEY INTEGRATE THEM INTO THEIR EXISTING ORGANIZATIONAL STRUCTURE IS WITHOUT PEER.
TRULY, IN THIS AREA, THEY ARE FORMIDABLE.
UNFORTUNATELY FOR THEM, THEY HAVE HAD SETBACKS, AND ARE STILL IN THE PRIMARY STAGES OF RECRUITMENT--THEIR NUMBERS ARE SMALL, WHILE OURS WILL SOON BE LEGION.
AND WHILE THIS IS A CLEAR ADVANTAGE FOR US, THEIR TRUE WEAKNESS LIES IN THEIR DIVIDED INTERESTS...THE PETTINESS THAT EXISTS BETWEEN THE RIVAL HEADS OF HYDRA. AFTER WITNESSING IT FIRSTHAND, IT IS NOTHING WHEN COMPARED TO THE RELENTLESSNESS OF OUR COLLECTIVE VISION.
GOOD.
EXCUSE ME, MAGADAN. WE ARE READY TO INTEGRATE THE DEVICE INTO THE STORAGE CONTROL SYSTEM.
EXCELLENT.
WE WILL NEED YOU AUTHORIZAT TO BEGIN T PROCESS

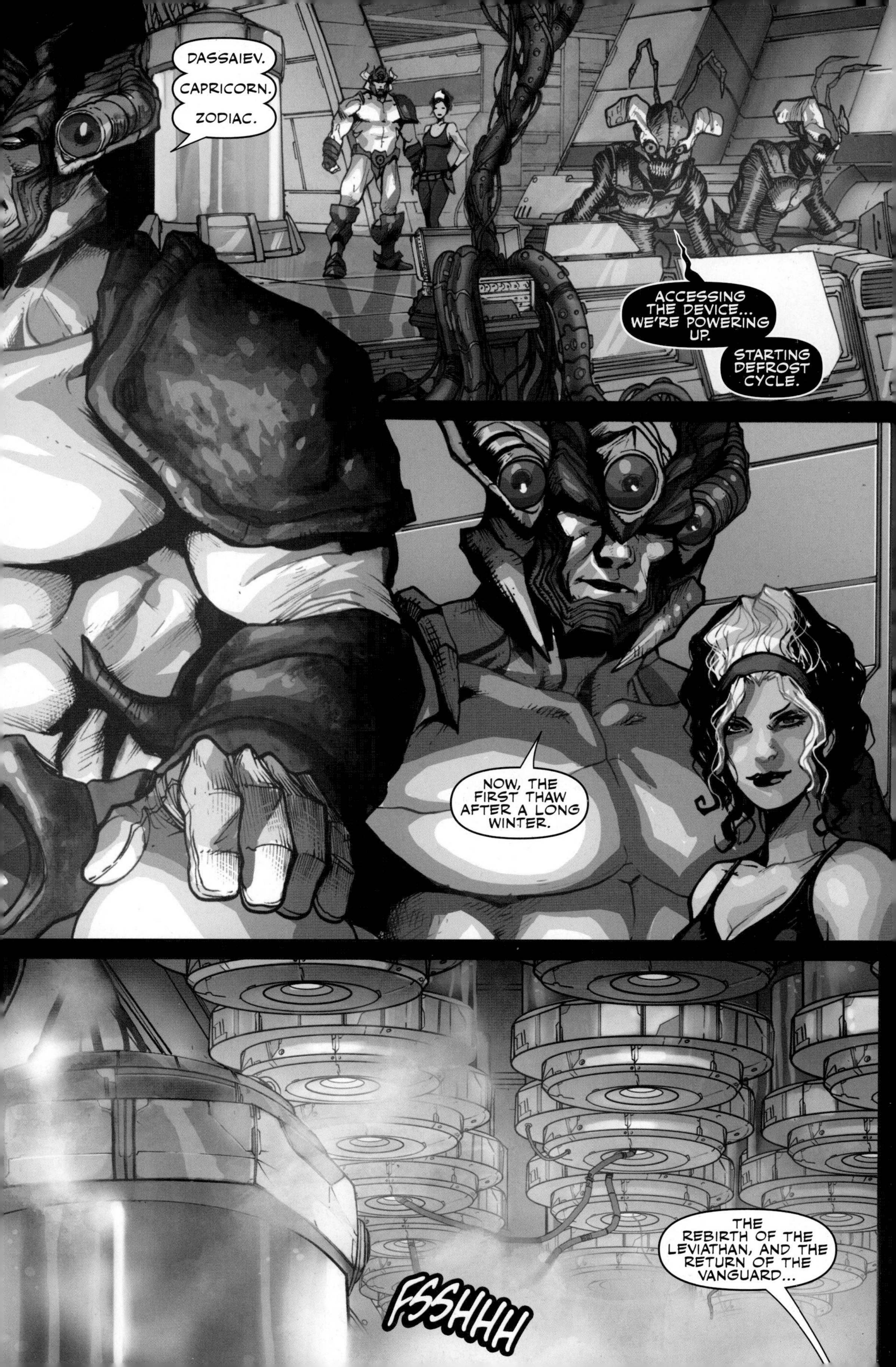
DASSAIEV.
CAPRICORN.
ZODIAC.
ACCESSING THE DEVICE... WE'RE POWERING UP.
STARTING DEFROST CYCLE.
NOW, THE FIRST THAW AFTER A LONG WINTER.
THE REBIRTH OF THE LEVIATHAN, AND THE RETURN OF THE VANGUARD...
FSSHHH

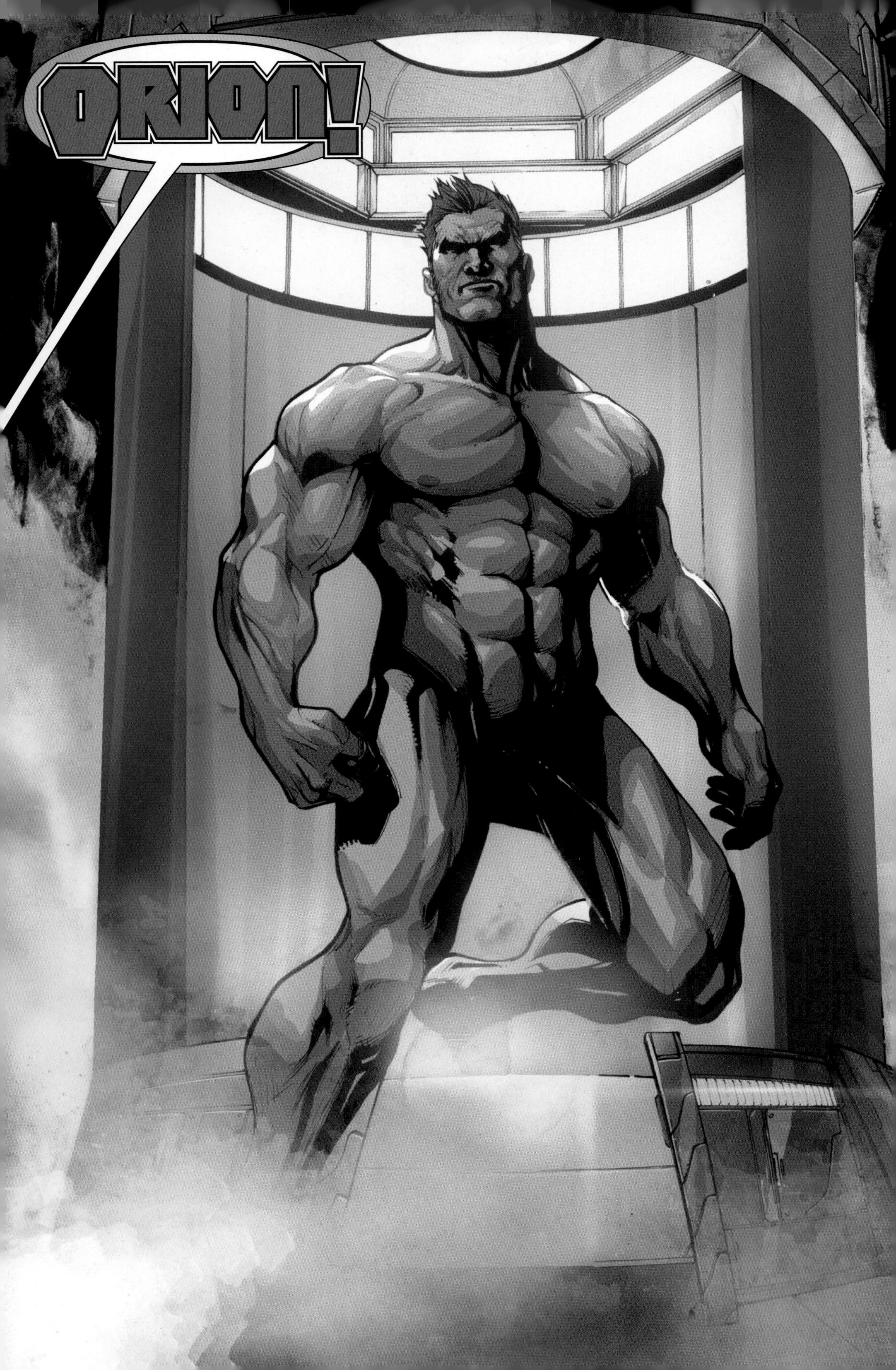
ORION!

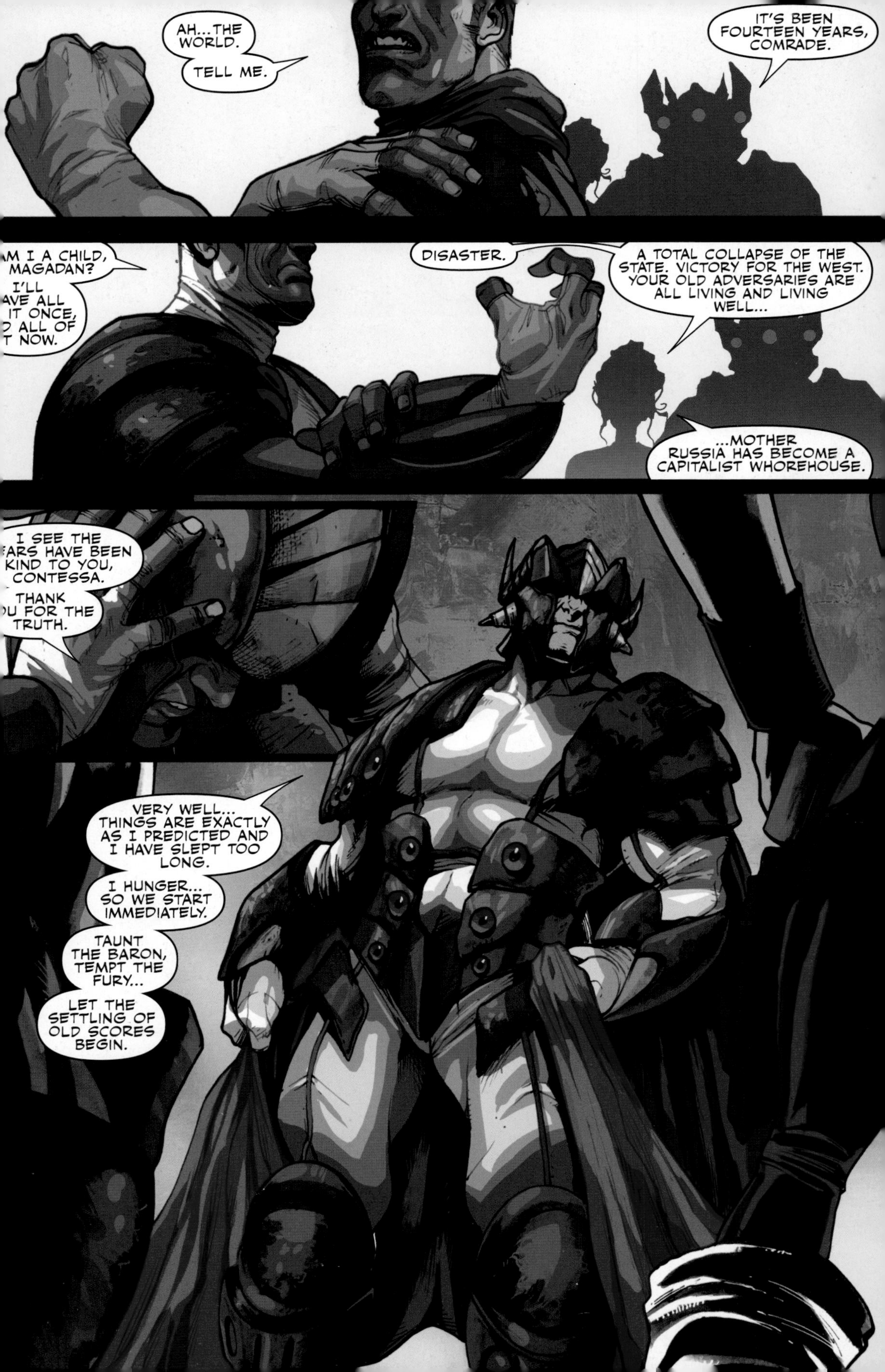
AH...THE WORLD.
TELL ME.
IT'S BEEN FOURTEEN YEARS, COMRADE.
M I A CHILD, MAGADAN?
I'LL AVE ALL IT ONCE, D ALL OF T NOW.
DISASTER.
A TOTAL COLLAPSE OF THE STATE. VICTORY FOR THE WEST. YOUR OLD ADVERSARIES ARE ALL LIVING AND LIVING WELL...
...MOTHER RUSSIA HAS BECOME A CAPITALIST WHOREHOUSE.
I SEE THE EARS HAVE BEEN KIND TO YOU, CONTESSA.
THANK OU FOR THE TRUTH.
VERY WELL... THINGS ARE EXACTLY AS I PREDICTED AND I HAVE SLEPT TOO LONG.
I HUNGER... SO WE START IMMEDIATELY.
TAUNT THE BARON, TEMPT THE FURY...
LET THE SETTLING OF OLD SCORES BEGIN.

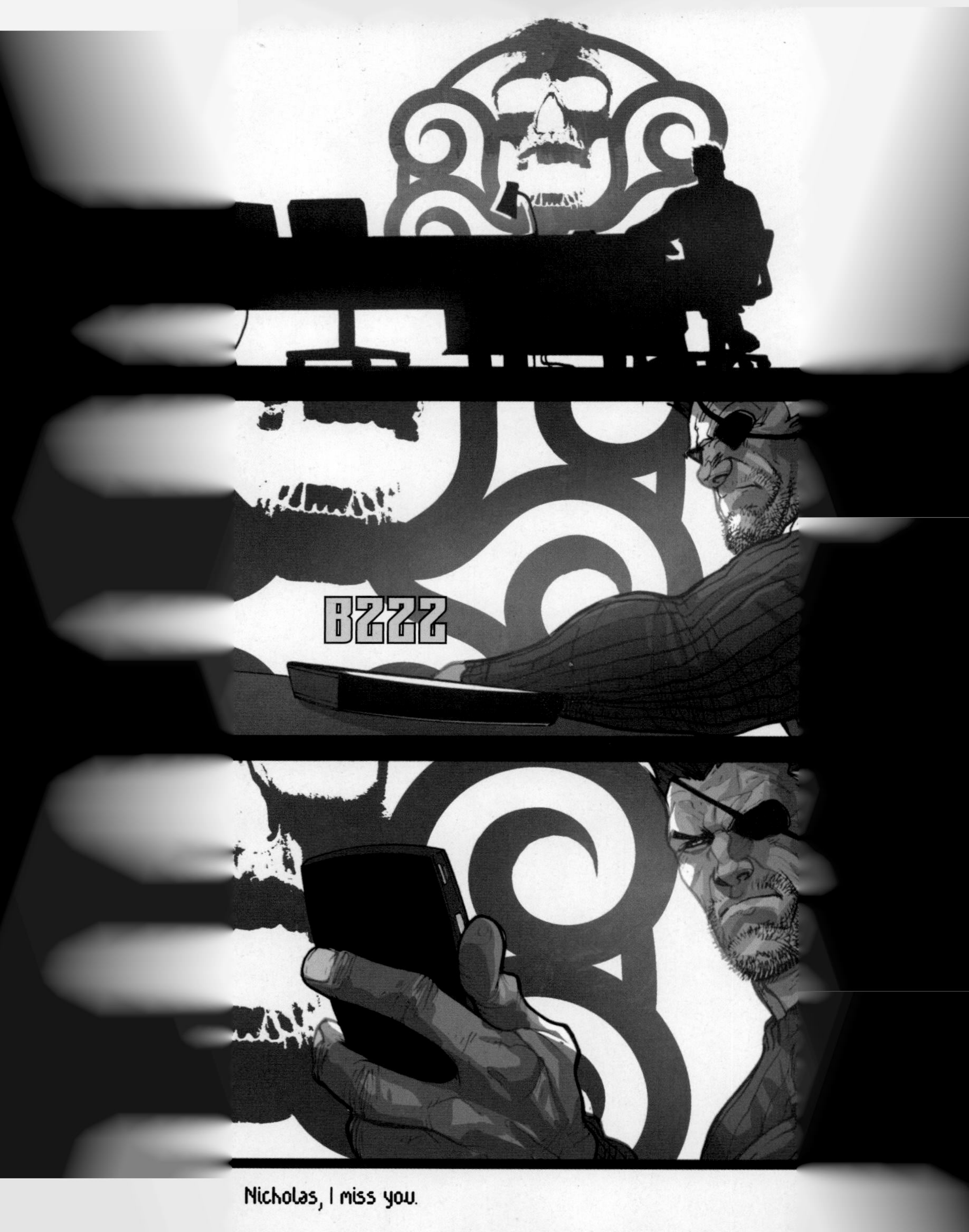
BZZZ

Nicholas, I miss you.

I woke up this morning and all I could think of was how things have become between us. How things should actually be.

So, maybe tomorrow evening? Dinner again?

At that place from that time with the stars and the open sky...

Ciao.
Contessa Valentina Allegra de Fontaine

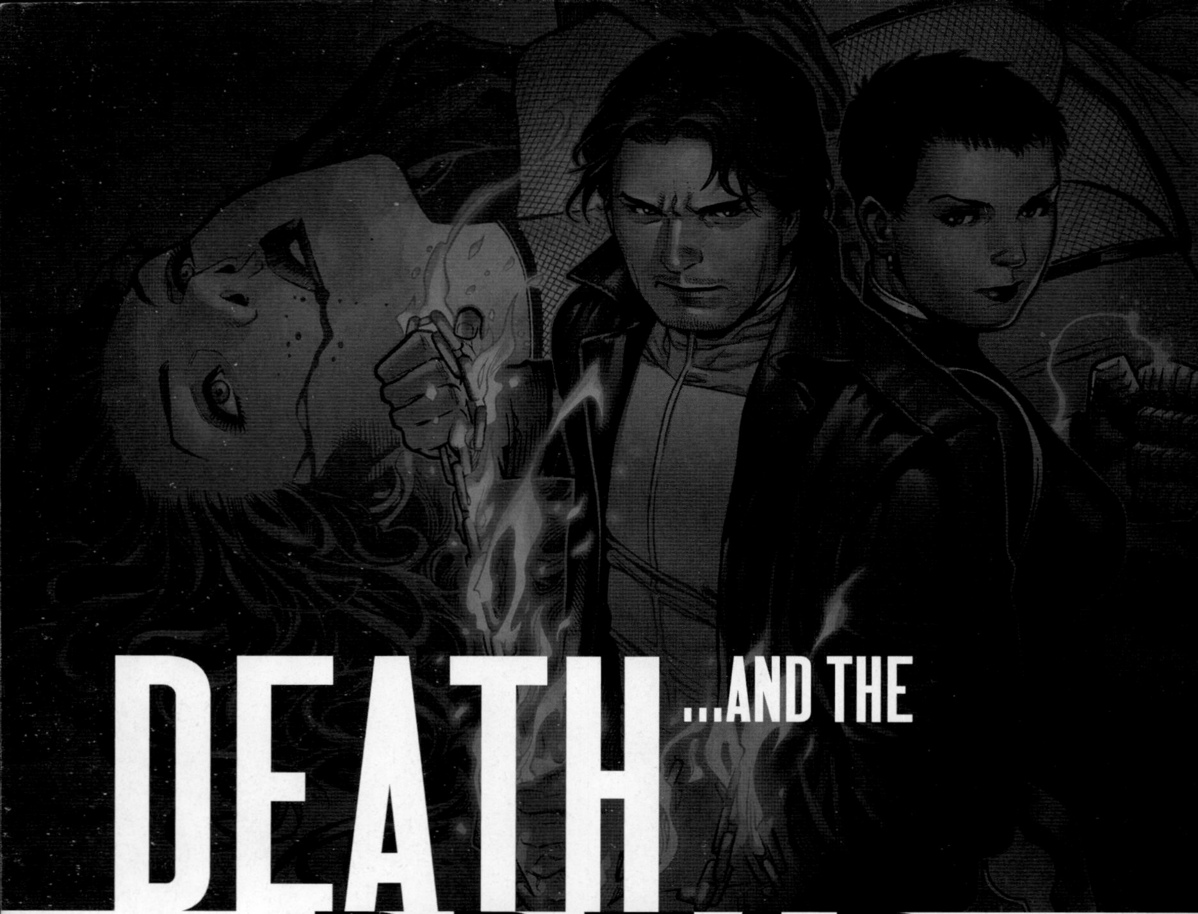

DEATH …AND THE DREAD THAT SURELY FOLLOWS

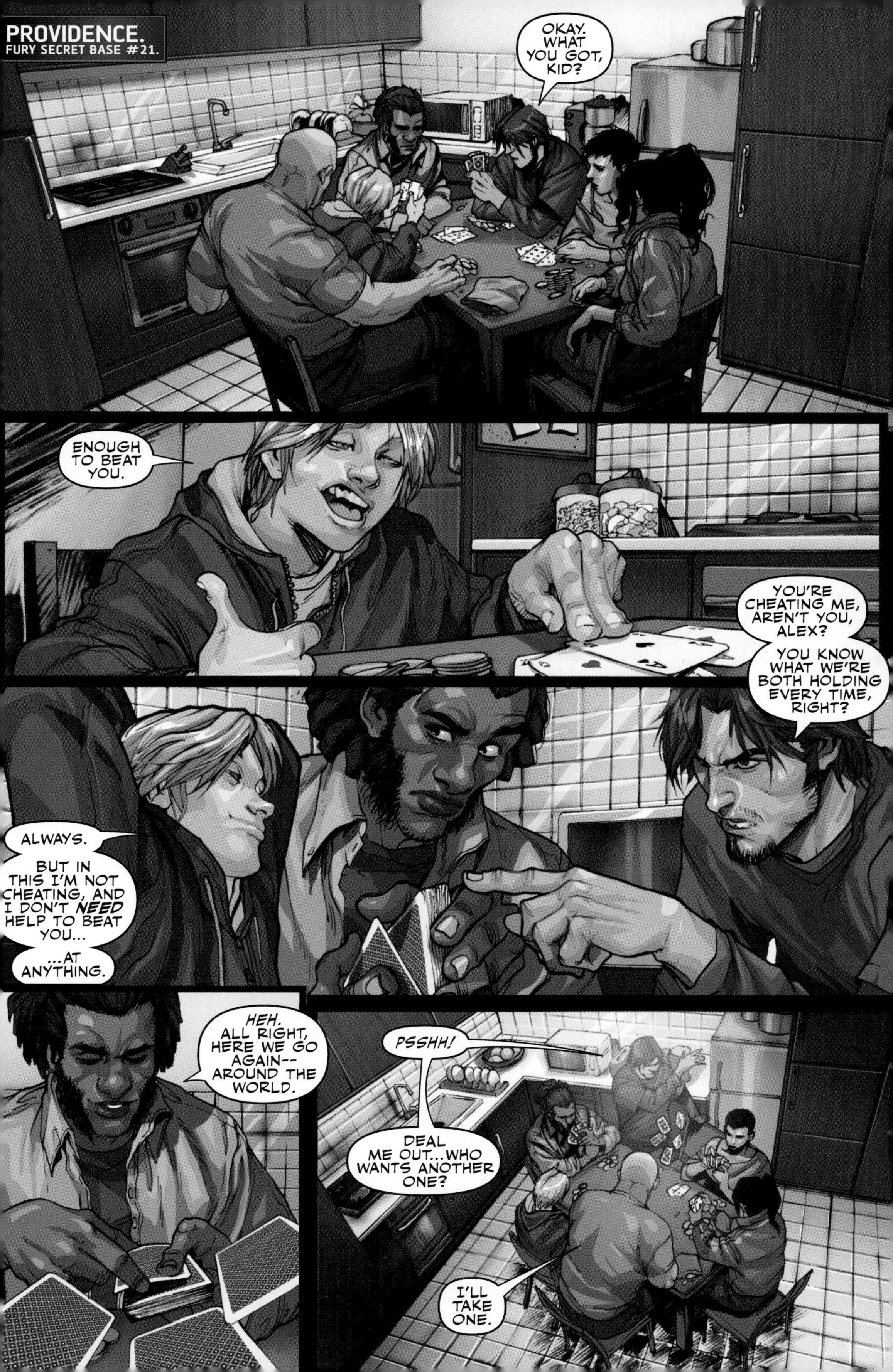
PROVIDENCE.
FURY SECRET BASE #21.
OKAY. WHAT YOU GOT, KID?
ENOUGH TO BEAT YOU.
YOU'RE CHEATING ME, AREN'T YOU, ALEX?
YOU KNOW WHAT WE'RE BOTH HOLDING EVERY TIME, RIGHT?
ALWAYS.
BUT IN THIS I'M NOT CHEATING, AND I DON'T *NEED* HELP TO BEAT YOU...
...AT ANYTHING.
HEH. ALL RIGHT, HERE WE GO AGAIN-- AROUND THE WORLD.
PSSHH!
DEAL ME OUT...WHO WANTS ANOTHER ONE?
I'LL TAKE ONE.

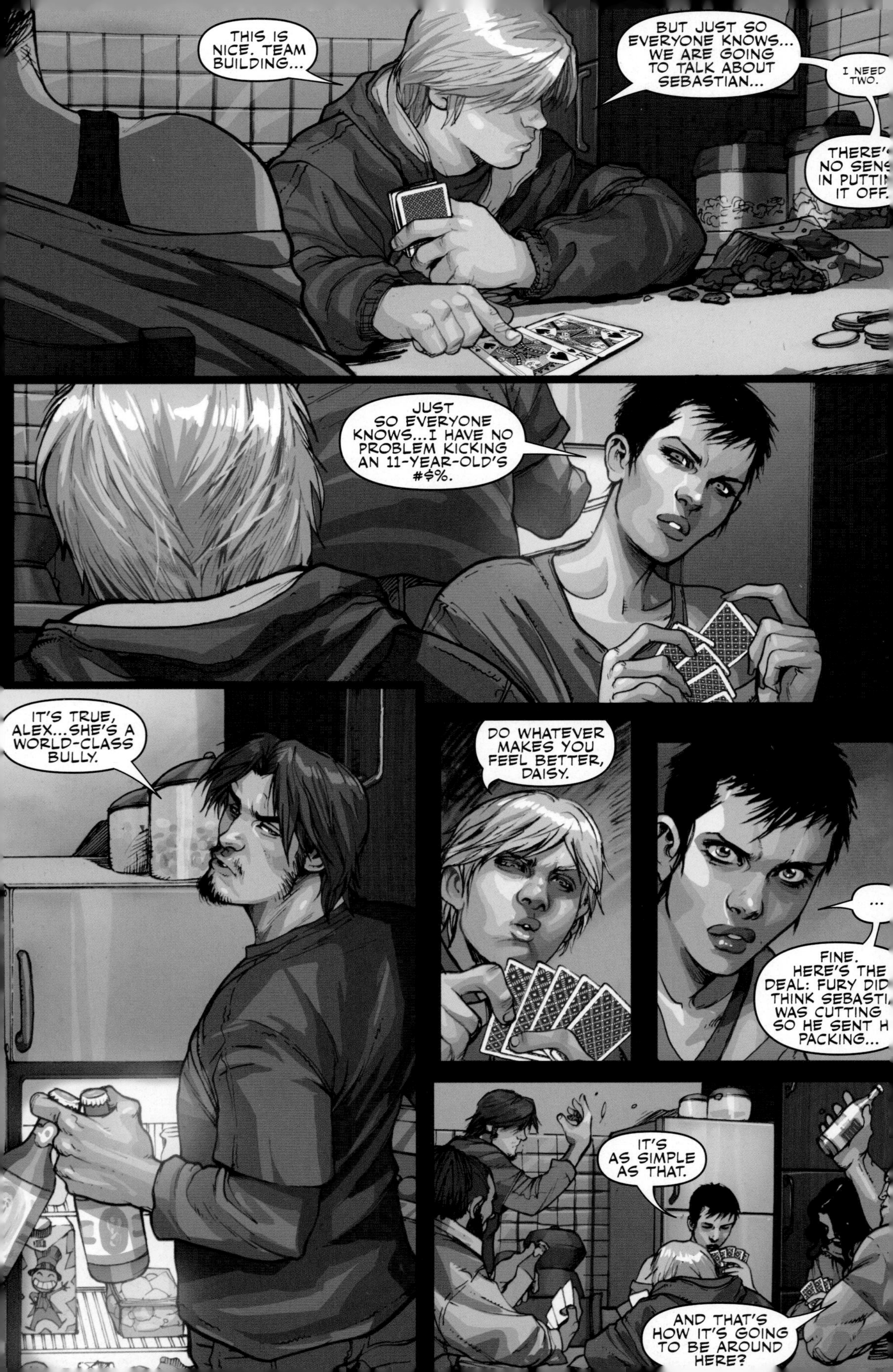
THIS IS NICE. TEAM BUILDING...
BUT JUST SO EVERYONE KNOWS... WE ARE GOING TO TALK ABOUT SEBASTIAN...
I NEED TWO.
JUST SO EVERYONE KNOWS...I HAVE NO PROBLEM KICKING AN 11-YEAR-OLD'S #$%.
IT'S TRUE, ALEX...SHE'S A WORLD-CLASS BULLY.
DO WHATEVER MAKES YOU FEEL BETTER, DAISY.
...
IT'S AS SIMPLE AS THAT.
AND THAT'S HOW IT'S GOING TO BE AROUND HERE?

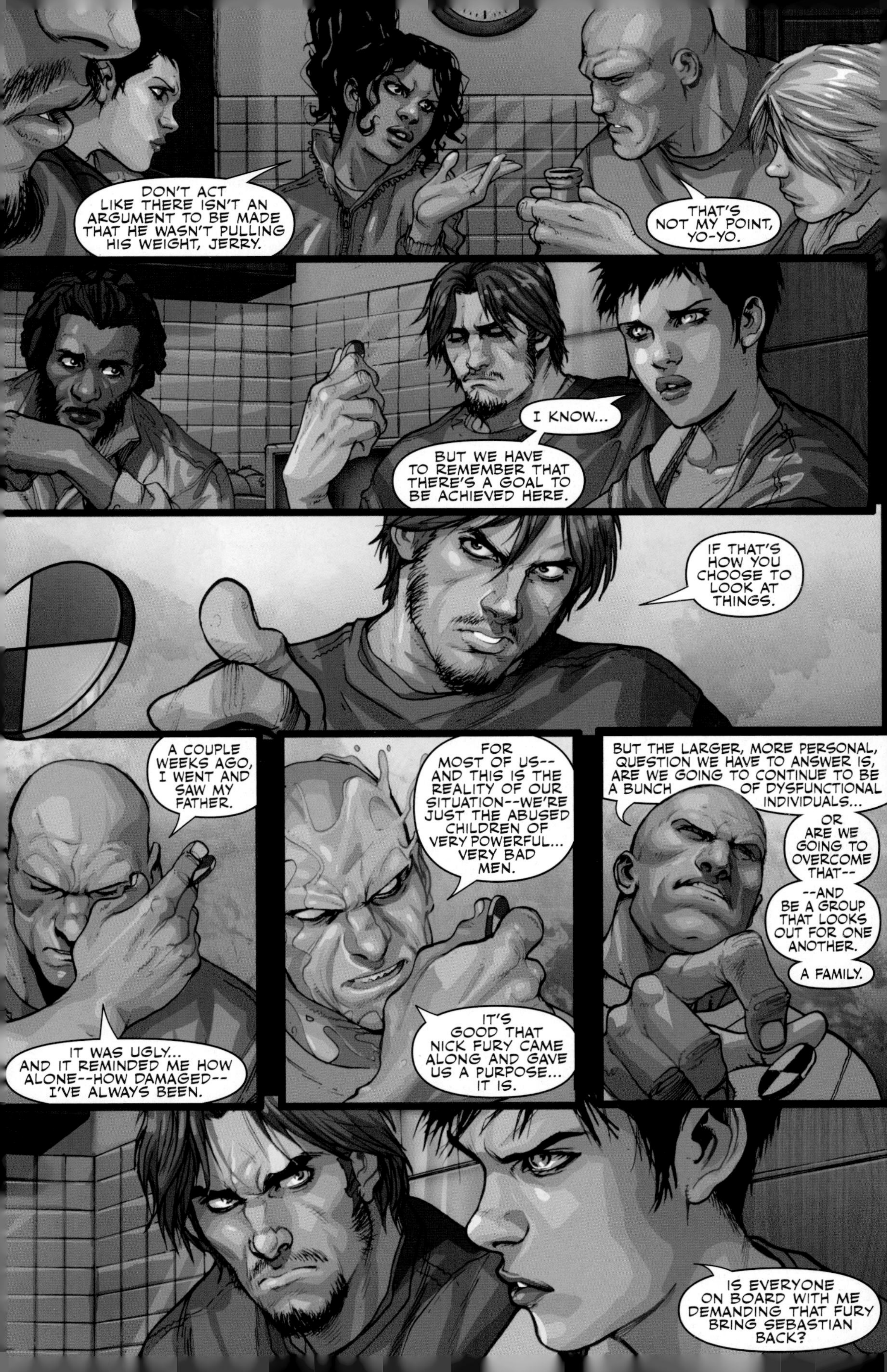
DON'T ACT LIKE THERE ISN'T AN ARGUMENT TO BE MADE THAT HE WASN'T PULLING HIS WEIGHT, JERRY.
THAT'S NOT MY POINT, YO-YO.
I KNOW...
BUT WE HAVE TO REMEMBER THAT THERE'S A GOAL TO BE ACHIEVED HERE.
IF THAT'S HOW YOU CHOOSE TO LOOK AT THINGS.
A COUPLE WEEKS AGO, I WENT AND SAW MY FATHER.
IT WAS UGLY... AND IT REMINDED ME HOW ALONE--HOW DAMAGED--I'VE ALWAYS BEEN.
FOR MOST OF US--AND THIS IS THE REALITY OF OUR SITUATION--WE'RE JUST THE ABUSED CHILDREN OF VERY POWERFUL... VERY BAD MEN.
IT'S GOOD THAT NICK FURY CAME ALONG AND GAVE US A PURPOSE... IT IS.
BUT THE LARGER, MORE PERSONAL, QUESTION WE HAVE TO ANSWER IS, ARE WE GOING TO CONTINUE TO BE A BUNCH OF DYSFUNCTIONAL INDIVIDUALS...
OR ARE WE GOING TO OVERCOME THAT--
--AND BE A GROUP THAT LOOKS OUT FOR ONE ANOTHER.
A FAMILY.
IS EVERYONE ON BOARD WITH ME DEMANDING THAT FURY BRING SEBASTIAN BACK?

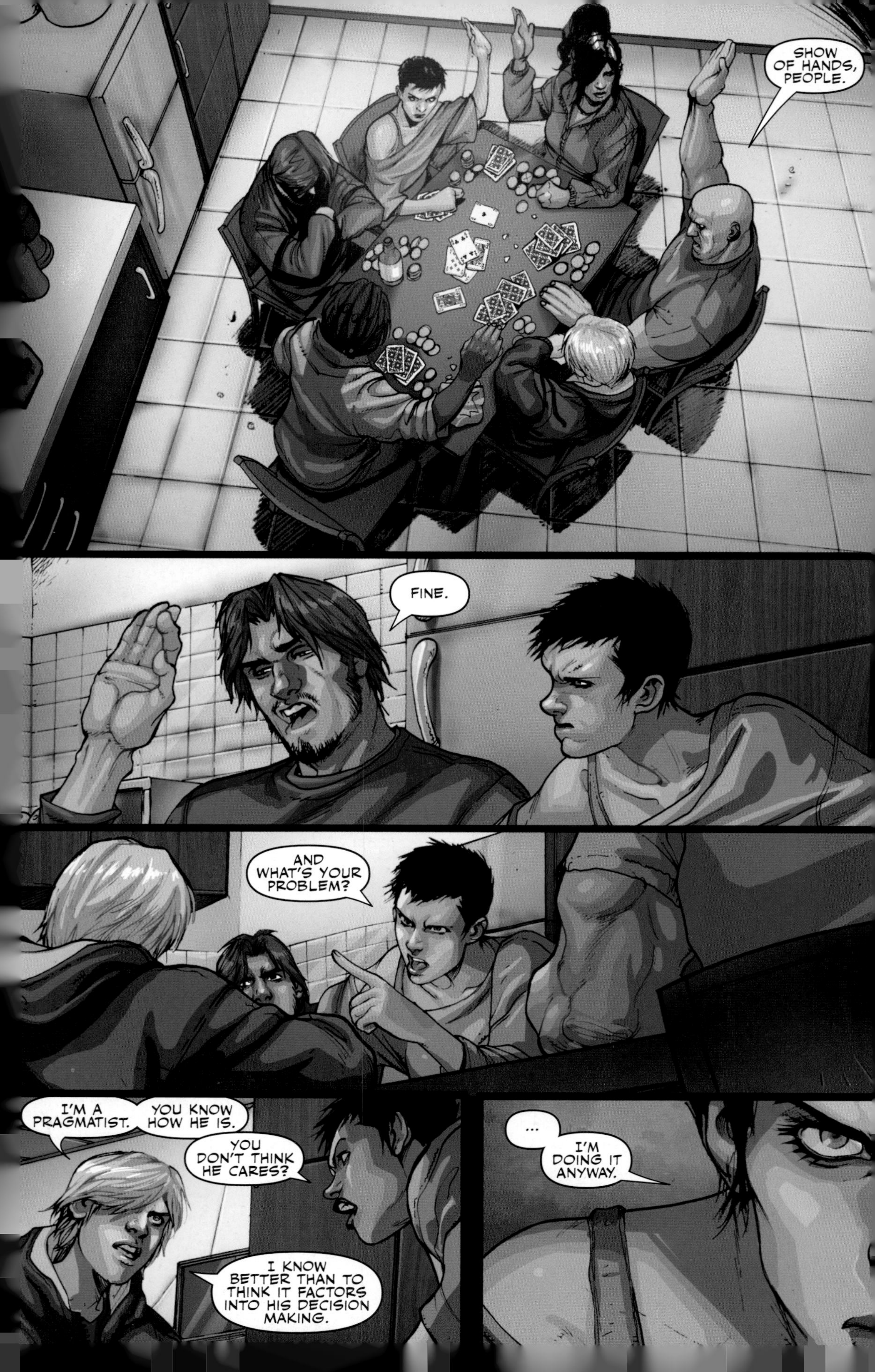
SHOW OF HANDS, PEOPLE.
FINE.
AND WHAT'S YOUR PROBLEM?
I'M A PRAGMATIST.
YOU KNOW HOW HE IS.
YOU DON'T THINK HE CARES?
I KNOW BETTER THAN TO THINK IT FACTORS INTO HIS DECISION MAKING.
...
I'M DOING IT ANYWAY.

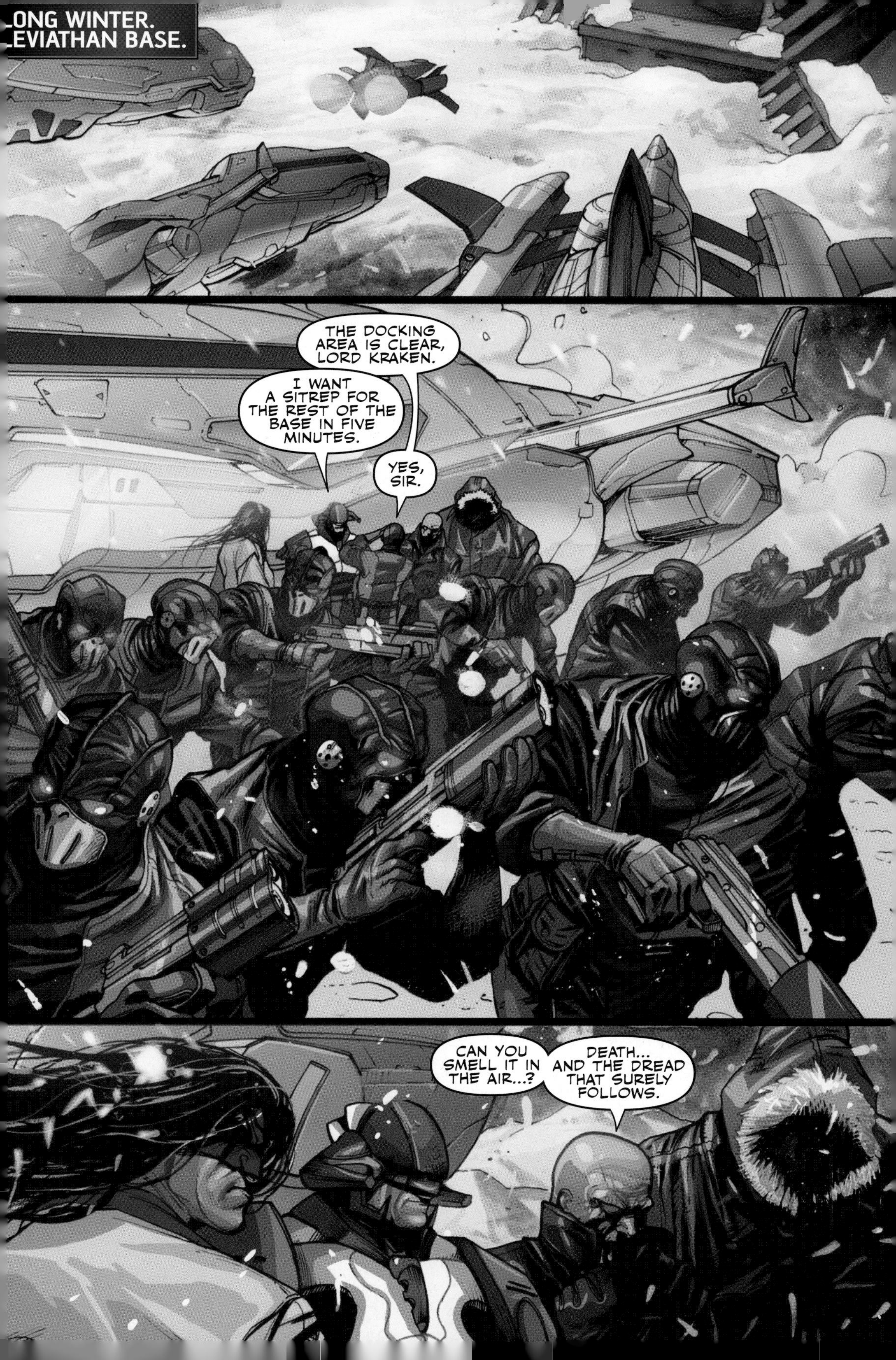
LONG WINTER.
LEVIATHAN BASE.
THE DOCKING AREA IS CLEAR, LORD KRAKEN.
I WANT A SITREP FOR THE REST OF THE BASE IN FIVE MINUTES.
YES, SIR.
CAN YOU SMELL IT IN THE AIR...?
DEATH... AND THE DREAD THAT SURELY FOLLOWS.

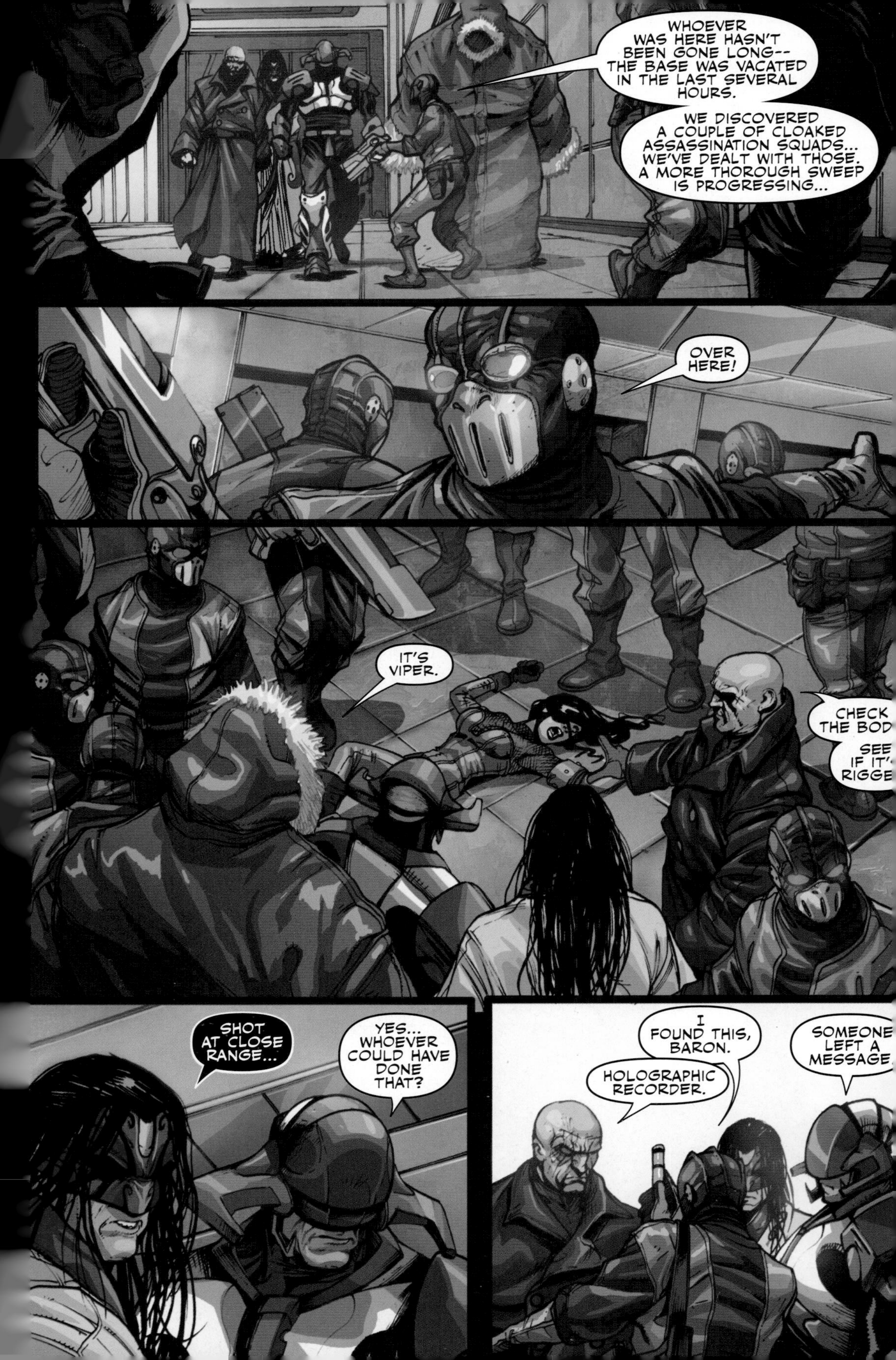
WHOEVER WAS HERE HASN'T BEEN GONE LONG-- THE BASE WAS VACATED IN THE LAST SEVERAL HOURS.
WE DISCOVERED A COUPLE OF CLOAKED ASSASSINATION SQUADS... WE'VE DEALT WITH THOSE. A MORE THOROUGH SWEEP IS PROGRESSING...
OVER HERE!
IT'S VIPER.
CHECK THE BOD
SEE IF IT' RIGGE
SHOT AT CLOSE RANGE...
YES... WHOEVER COULD HAVE DONE THAT?
I FOUND THIS, BARON.
HOLOGRAPHIC RECORDER.
SOMEONE LEFT A MESSAGE.

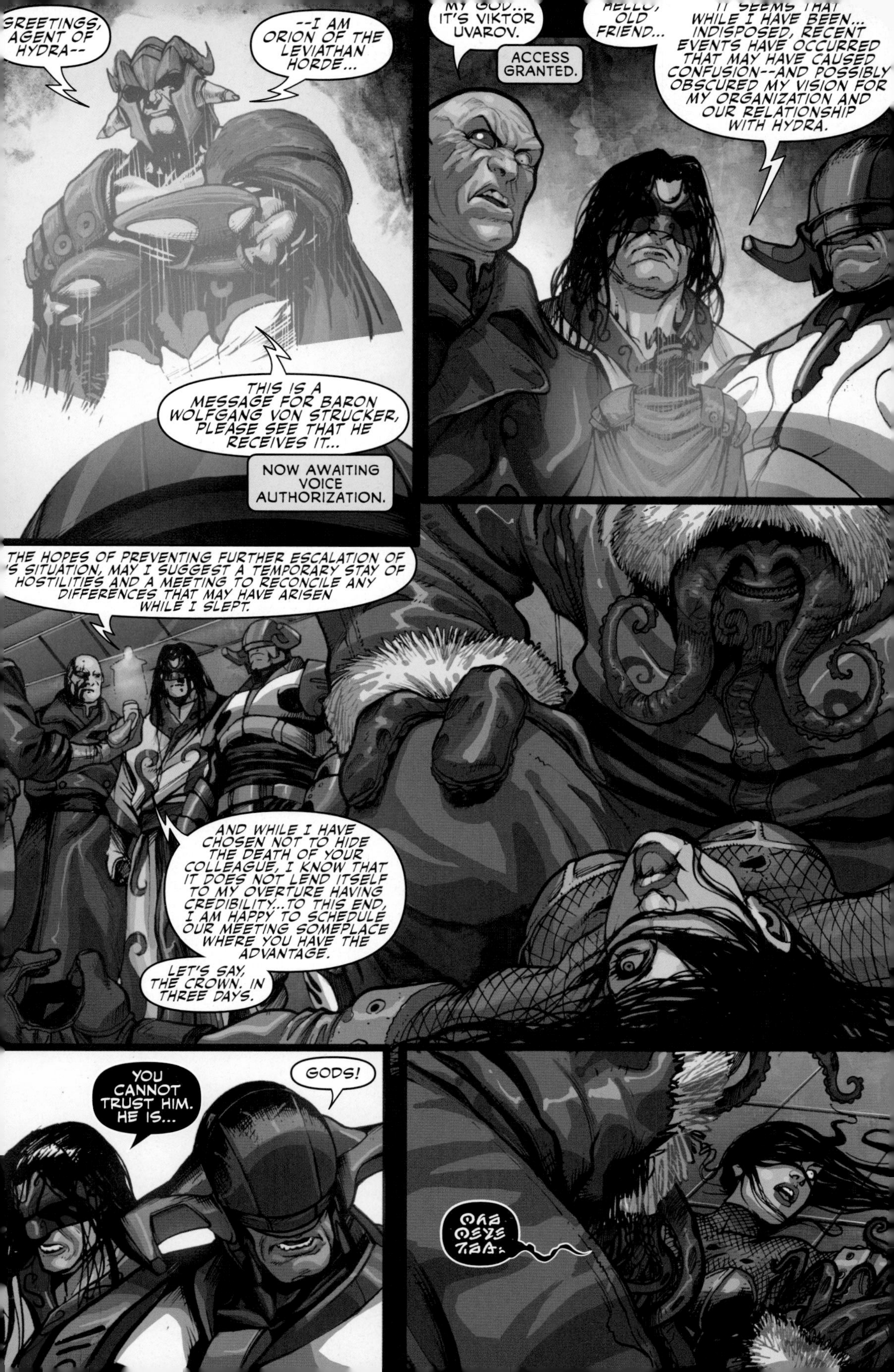
GREETINGS, AGENT OF HYDRA--
--I AM ORION OF THE LEVIATHAN HORDE...
THIS IS A MESSAGE FOR BARON WOLFGANG VON STRUCKER, PLEASE SEE THAT HE RECEIVES IT...
NOW AWAITING VOICE AUTHORIZATION.
MY GOD... IT'S VIKTOR UVAROV.
ACCESS GRANTED.
HELLO, OLD FRIEND...
IT SEEMS THAT WHILE I HAVE BEEN... INDISPOSED, RECENT EVENTS HAVE OCCURRED THAT MAY HAVE CAUSED CONFUSION--AND POSSIBLY OBSCURED MY VISION FOR MY ORGANIZATION AND OUR RELATIONSHIP WITH HYDRA.
THE HOPES OF PREVENTING FURTHER ESCALATION OF 'S SITUATION, MAY I SUGGEST A TEMPORARY STAY OF HOSTILITIES AND A MEETING TO RECONCILE ANY DIFFERENCES THAT MAY HAVE ARISEN WHILE I SLEPT.
AND WHILE I HAVE CHOSEN NOT TO HIDE THE DEATH OF YOUR COLLEAGUE, I KNOW THAT IT DOES NOT LEND ITSELF TO MY OVERTURE HAVING CREDIBILITY...TO THIS END, I AM HAPPY TO SCHEDULE OUR MEETING SOMEPLACE WHERE YOU HAVE THE ADVANTAGE.
LET'S SAY, THE CROWN. IN THREE DAYS.
YOU CANNOT TRUST HIM. HE IS...
GODS!

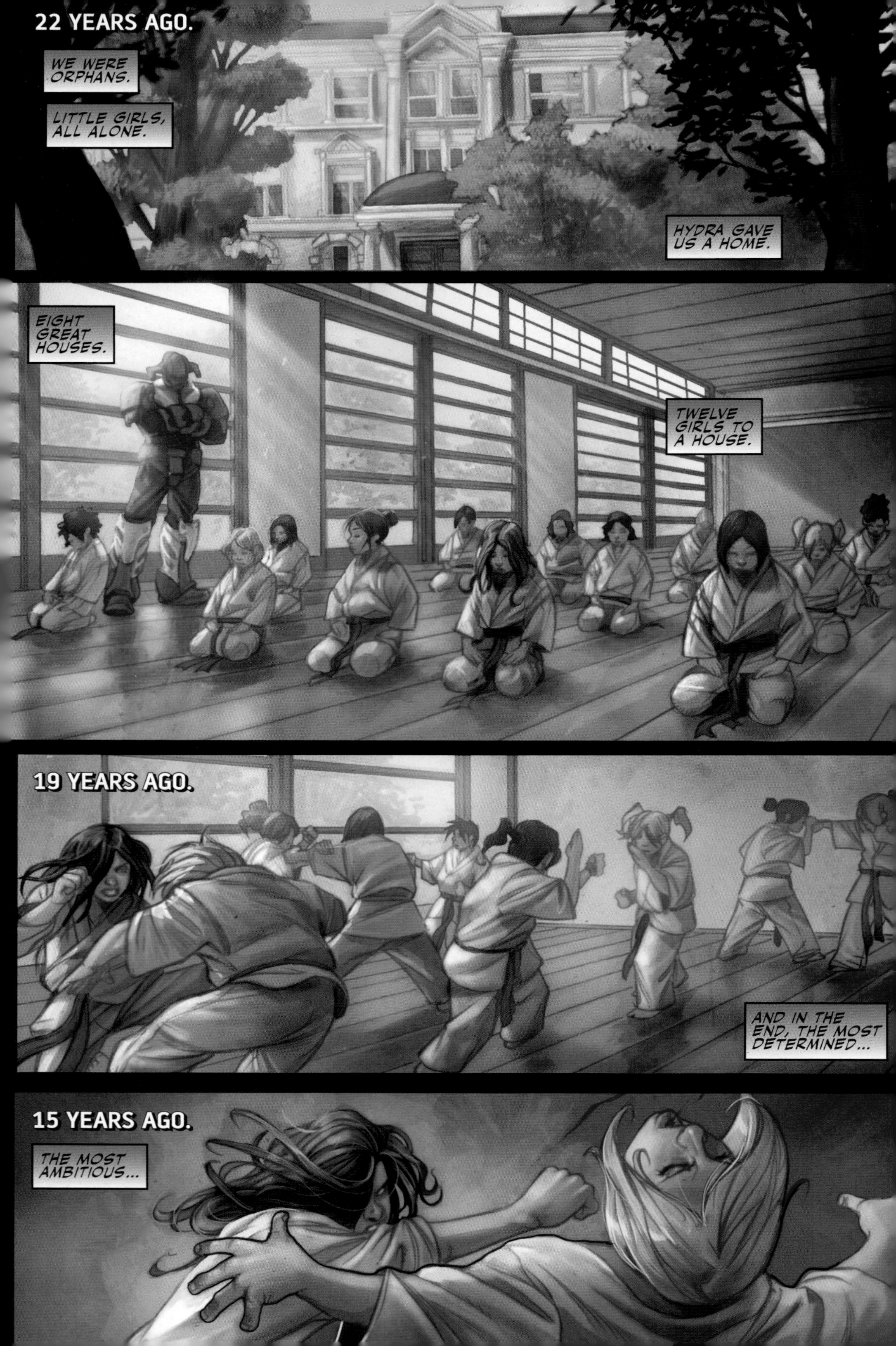
22 YEARS AGO.
WE WERE ORPHANS.
LITTLE GIRLS, ALL ALONE.
HYDRA GAVE US A HOME.
EIGHT GREAT HOUSES.
TWELVE GIRLS TO A HOUSE.
19 YEARS AGO.
AND IN THE END, THE MOST DETERMINED...
15 YEARS AGO.
THE MOST AMBITIOUS...

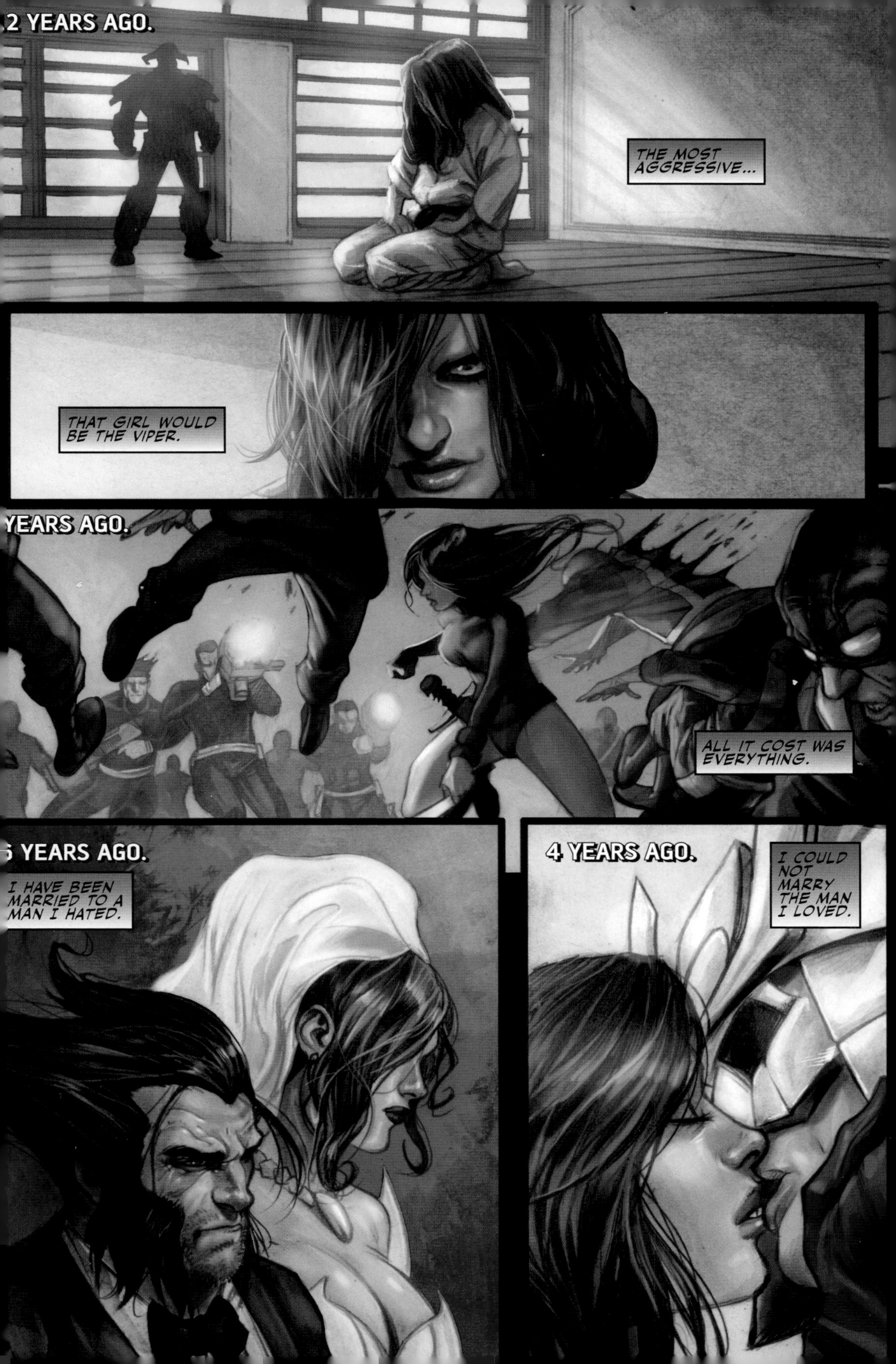
2 YEARS AGO.
THE MOST AGGRESSIVE...
THAT GIRL WOULD BE THE VIPER.
YEARS AGO.
ALL IT COST WAS EVERYTHING.
YEARS AGO.
I HAVE BEEN MARRIED TO A MAN I HATED.
4 YEARS AGO.
I COULD NOT MARRY THE MAN I LOVED.

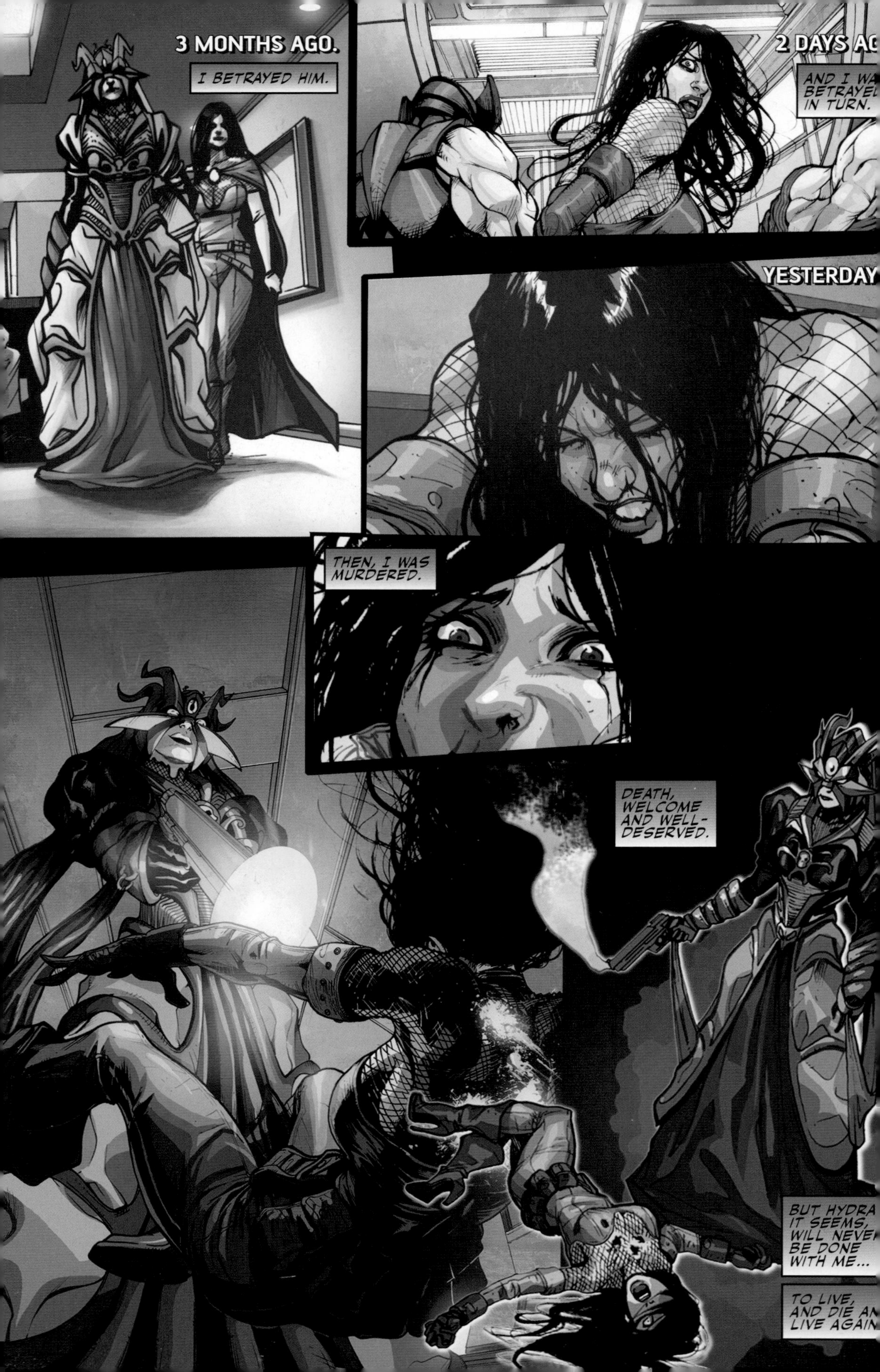
3 MONTHS AGO.
I BETRAYED HIM.
2 DAYS AG
AND I WA
BETRAYE
IN TURN.
YESTERDAY
THEN, I WAS MURDERED.
DEATH, WELCOME AND WELL-DESERVED.
BUT HYDRA IT SEEMS, WILL NEVE BE DONE WITH ME...
TO LIVE, AND DIE AN LIVE AGAIN

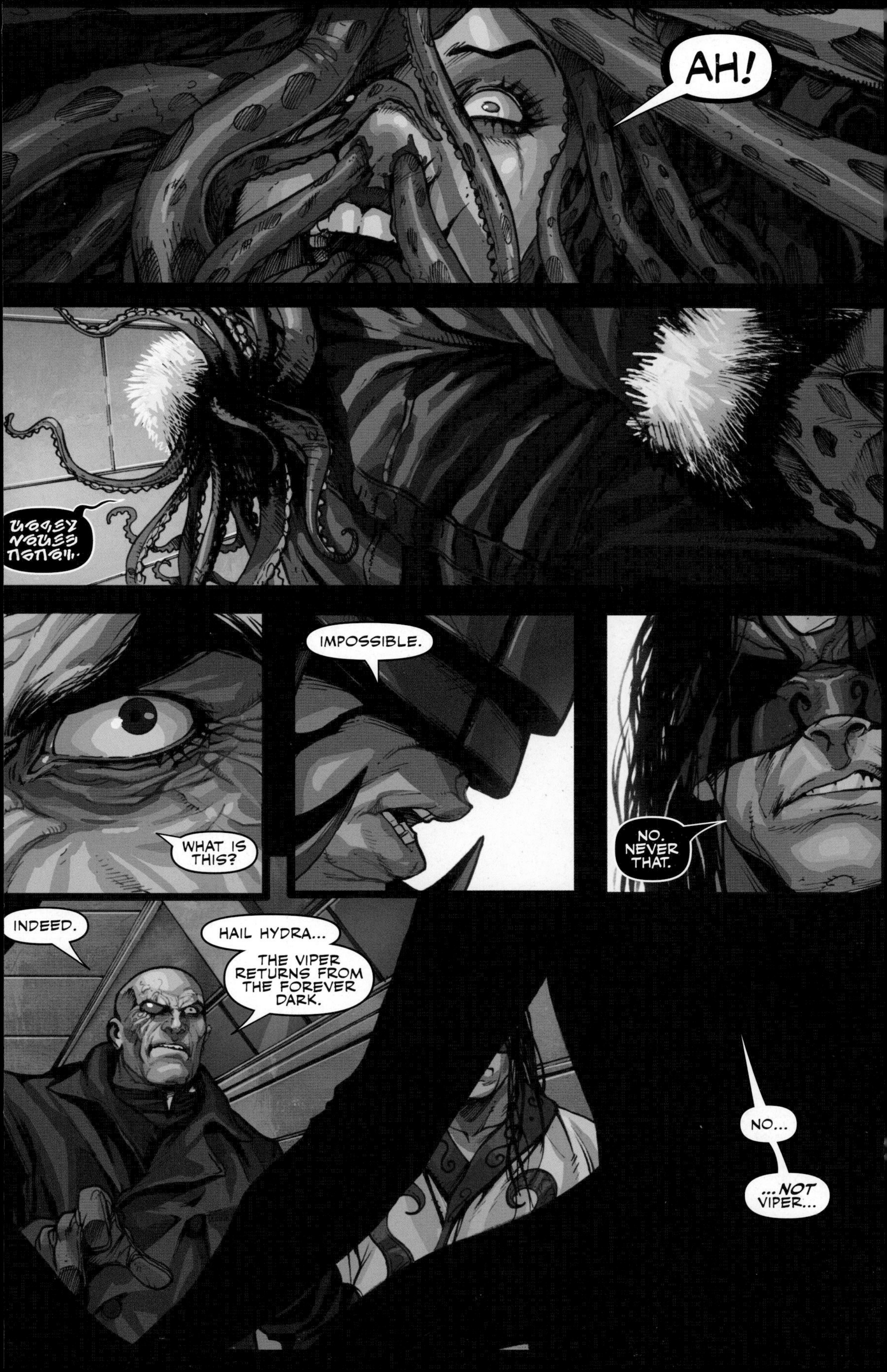

AH!
WHAT IS THIS?
IMPOSSIBLE.
NO. NEVER THAT.
INDEED.
HAIL HYDRA...
THE VIPER RETURNS FROM THE FOREVER DARK.
NO...
...NOT VIPER...

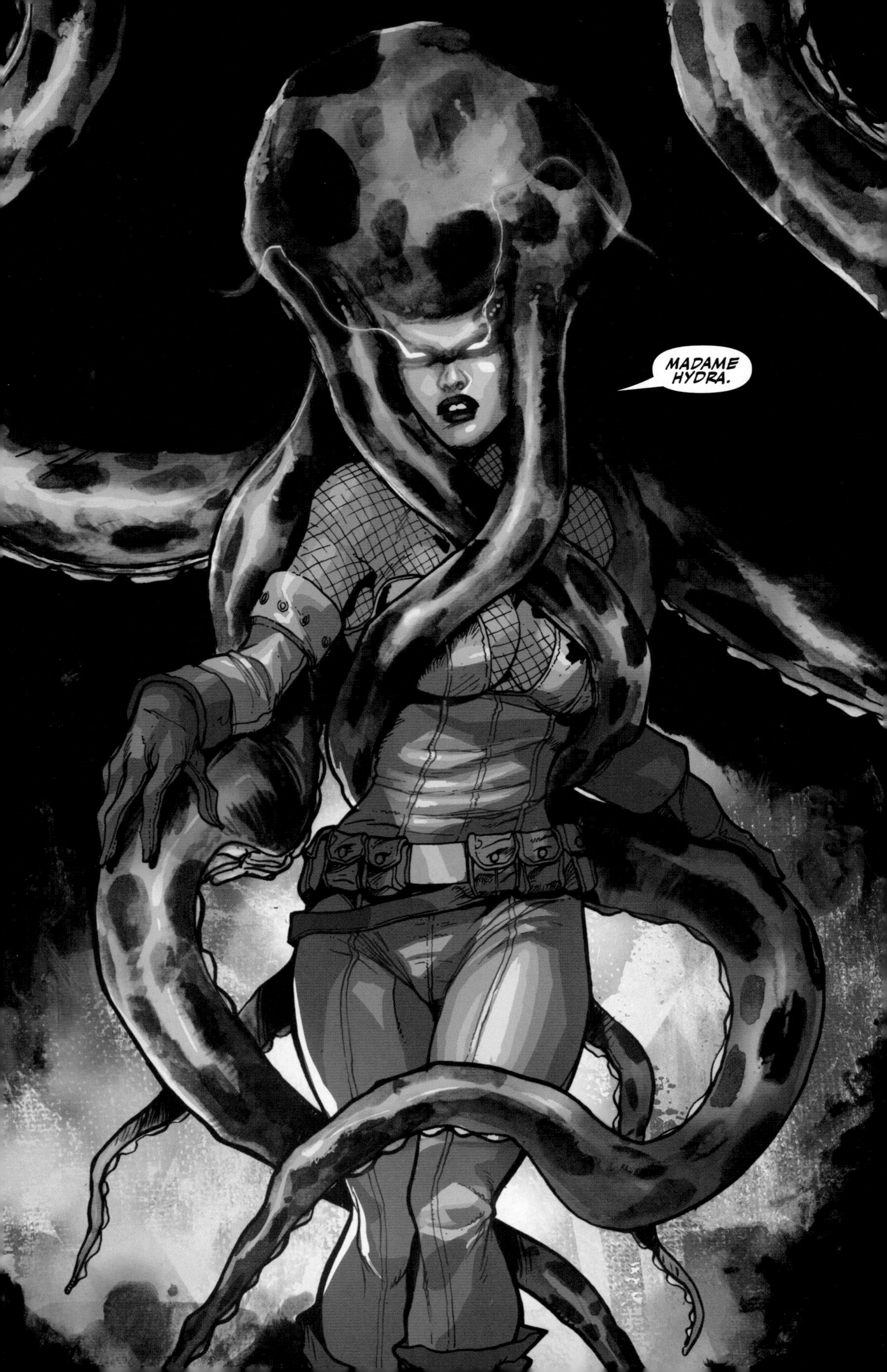
MADAME HYDRA.

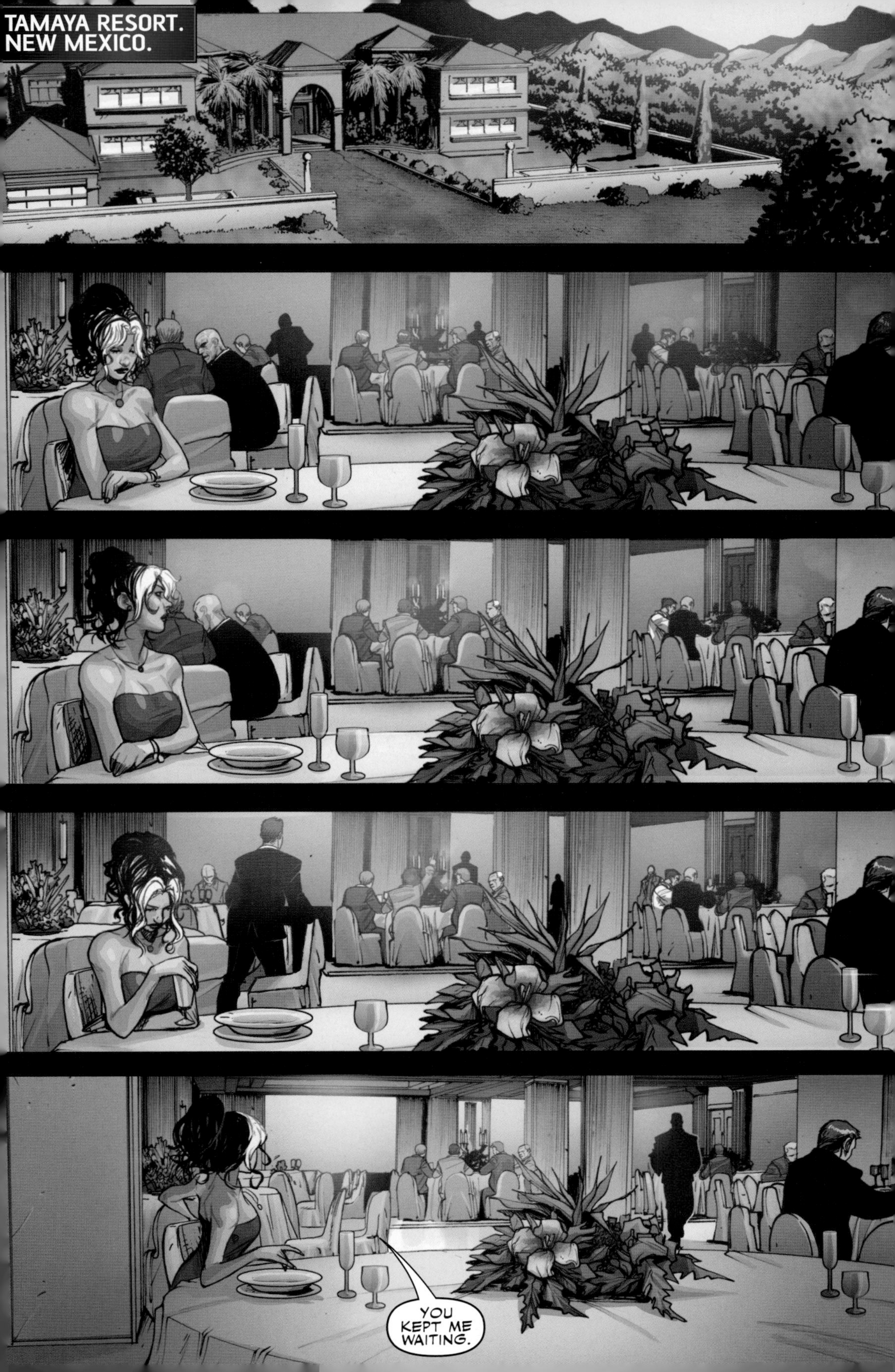
TAMAYA RESORT.
NEW MEXICO.
YOU KEPT ME WAITING.

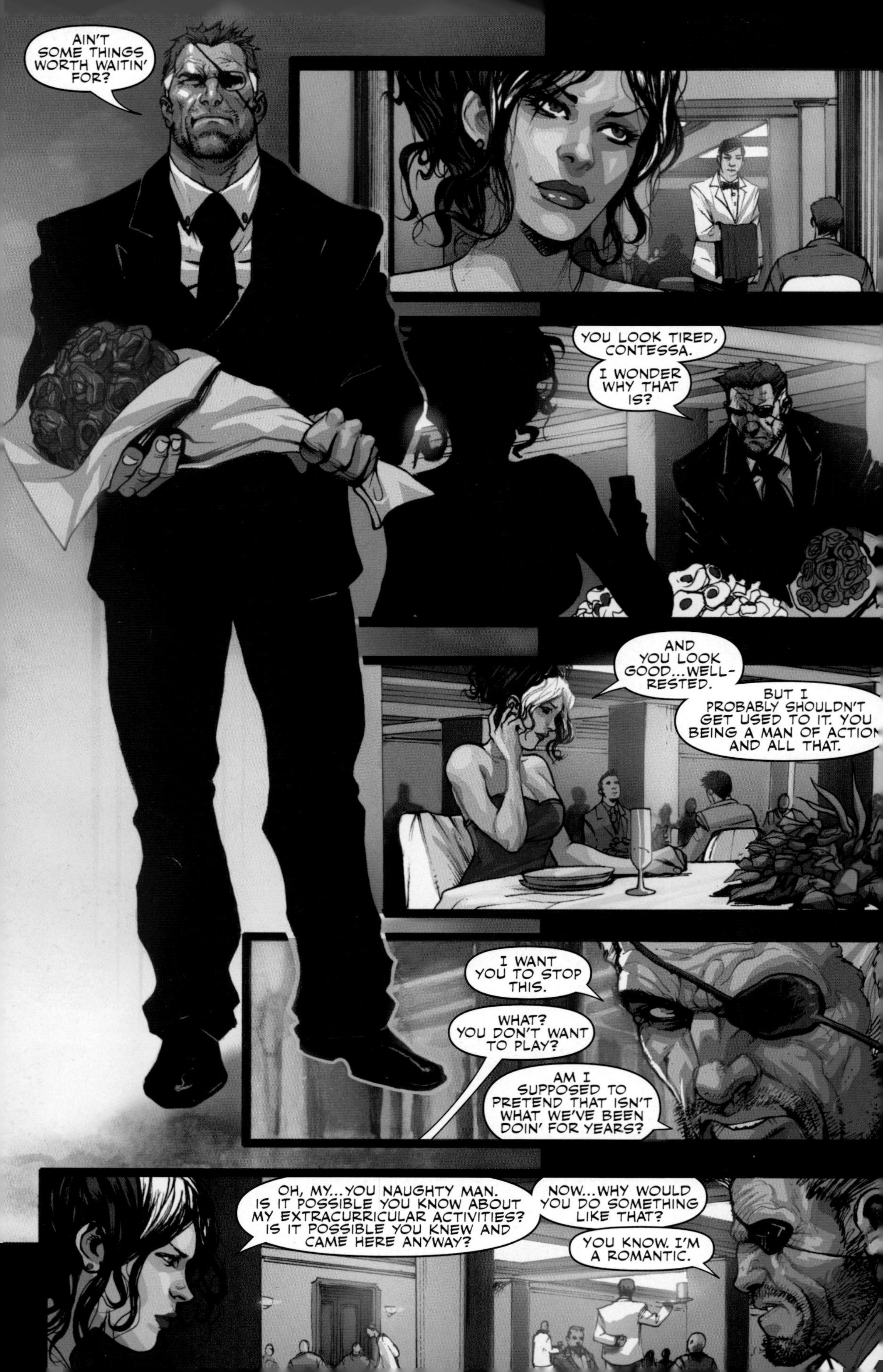
AIN'T SOME THINGS WORTH WAITIN' FOR?
YOU LOOK TIRED, CONTESSA.
I WONDER WHY THAT IS?
AND YOU LOOK GOOD...WELL-RESTED.
BUT I PROBABLY SHOULDN'T GET USED TO IT. YOU BEING A MAN OF ACTION AND ALL THAT.
I WANT YOU TO STOP THIS.
WHAT? YOU DON'T WANT TO PLAY?
AM I SUPPOSED TO PRETEND THAT ISN'T WHAT WE'VE BEEN DOIN' FOR YEARS?
OH, MY...YOU NAUGHTY MAN. IS IT POSSIBLE YOU KNOW ABOUT MY EXTRACURRICULAR ACTIVITIES? IS IT POSSIBLE YOU KNEW AND CAME HERE ANYWAY?
NOW...WHY WOULD YOU DO SOMETHING LIKE THAT?
YOU KNOW. I'M A ROMANTIC.

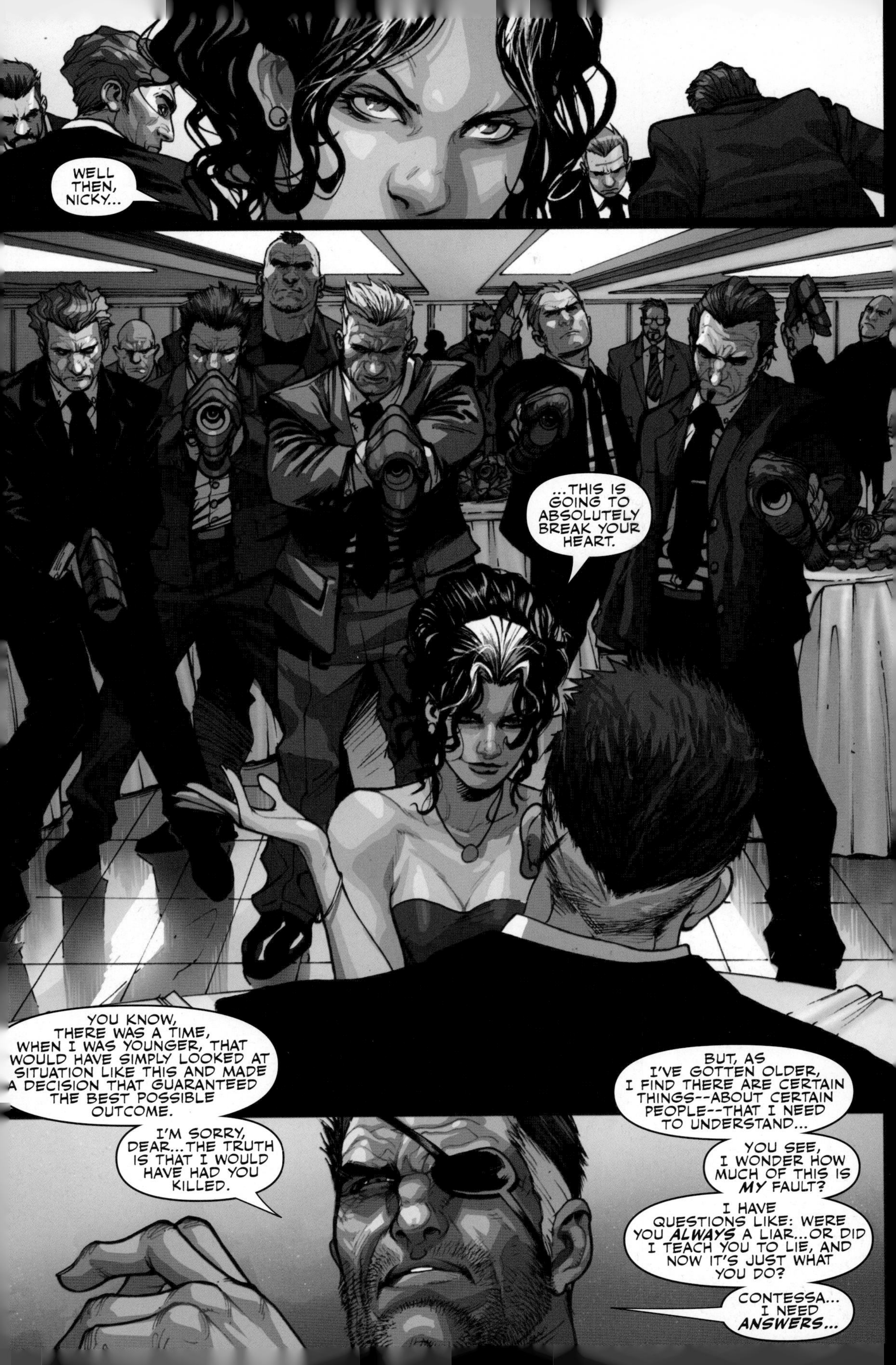
WELL THEN, NICKY...
...THIS IS GOING TO ABSOLUTELY BREAK YOUR HEART.
YOU KNOW, THERE WAS A TIME, WHEN I WAS YOUNGER, THAT WOULD HAVE SIMPLY LOOKED AT SITUATION LIKE THIS AND MADE A DECISION THAT GUARANTEED THE BEST POSSIBLE OUTCOME.
I'M SORRY, DEAR...THE TRUTH IS THAT I WOULD HAVE HAD YOU KILLED.
BUT, AS I'VE GOTTEN OLDER, I FIND THERE ARE CERTAIN THINGS--ABOUT CERTAIN PEOPLE--THAT I NEED TO UNDERSTAND...
YOU SEE, I WONDER HOW MUCH OF THIS IS *MY* FAULT?
I HAVE QUESTIONS LIKE: WERE YOU *ALWAYS* A LIAR...OR DID I TEACH YOU TO LIE, AND NOW IT'S JUST WHAT YOU DO?
CONTESSA... I NEED ***ANSWERS...***

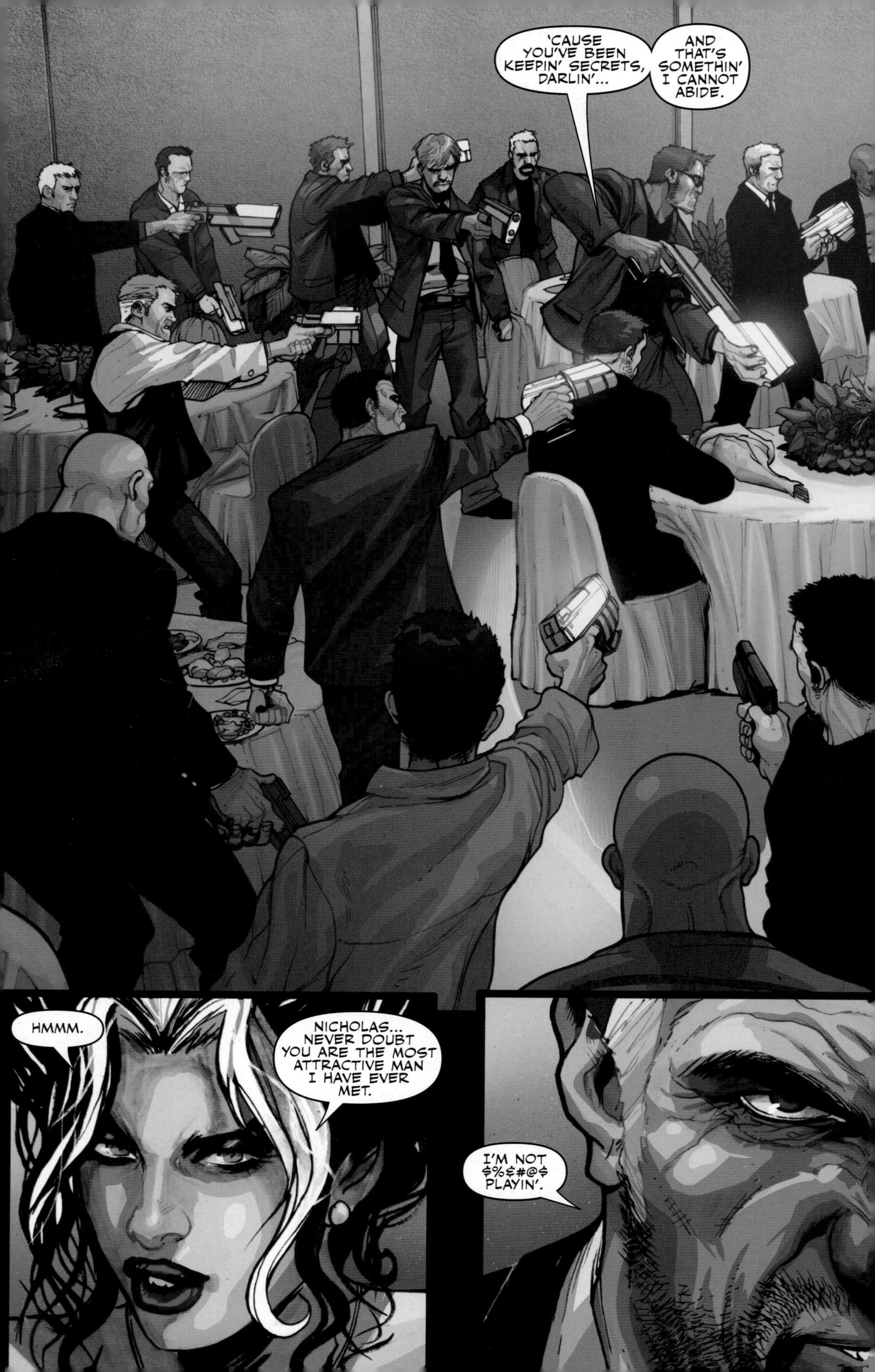
'CAUSE YOU'VE BEEN KEEPIN' SECRETS, DARLIN'...
AND THAT'S SOMETHIN' I CANNOT ABIDE.
HMMM.
NICHOLAS... NEVER DOUBT YOU ARE THE MOST ATTRACTIVE MAN I HAVE EVER MET.
I'M NOT $%¢#@$ PLAYIN'.

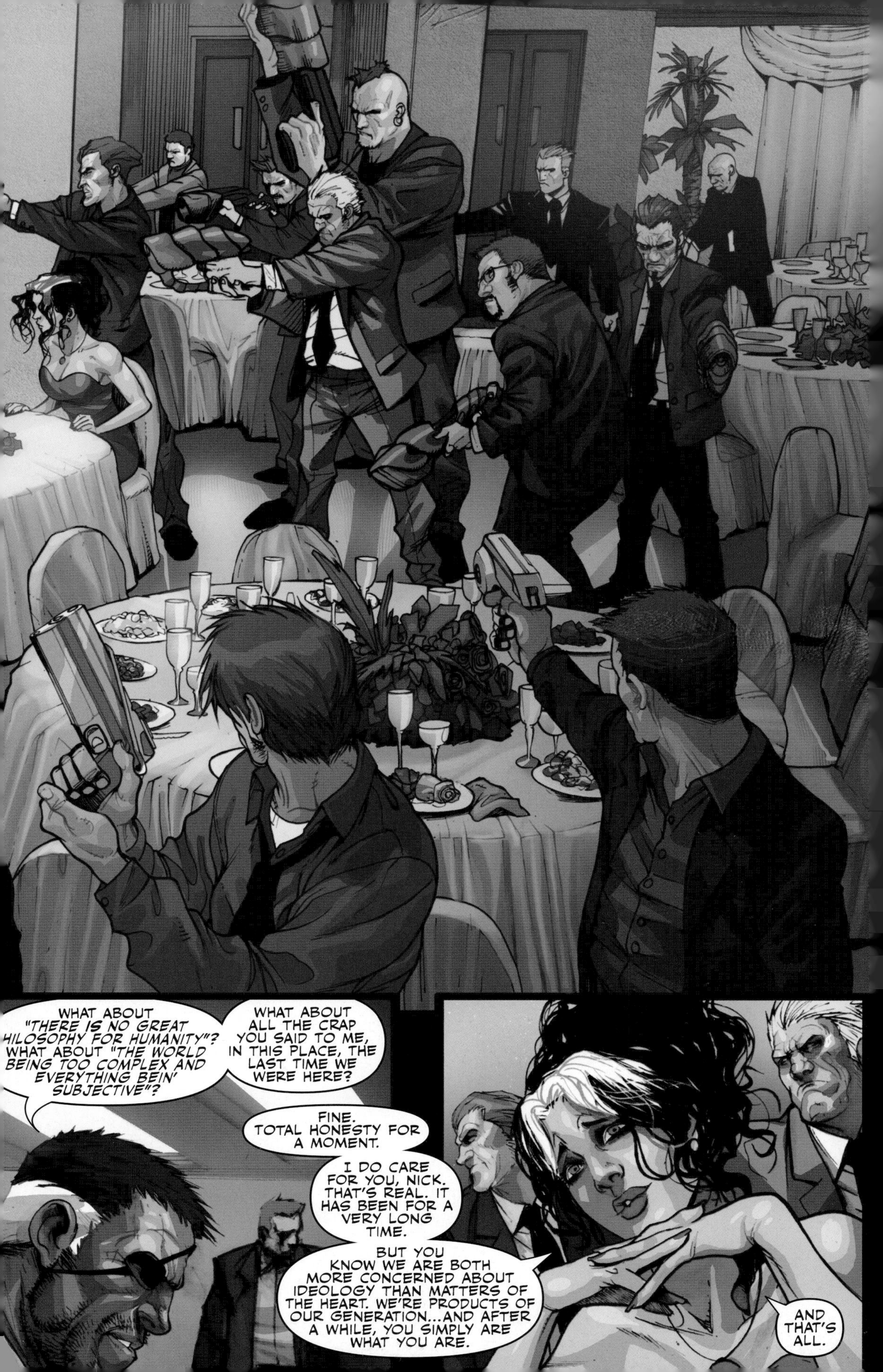

WHAT ABOUT "THERE IS NO GREAT HILOSOPHY FOR HUMANITY"? WHAT ABOUT "THE WORLD BEING TOO COMPLEX AND EVERYTHING BEIN' SUBJECTIVE"?
WHAT ABOUT ALL THE CRAP YOU SAID TO ME, IN THIS PLACE, THE LAST TIME WE WERE HERE?
FINE. TOTAL HONESTY FOR A MOMENT.
I DO CARE FOR YOU, NICK. THAT'S REAL. IT HAS BEEN FOR A VERY LONG TIME.
BUT YOU KNOW WE ARE BOTH MORE CONCERNED ABOUT IDEOLOGY THAN MATTERS OF THE HEART. WE'RE PRODUCTS OF OUR GENERATION...AND AFTER A WHILE, YOU SIMPLY ARE WHAT YOU ARE.
AND THAT'S ALL.

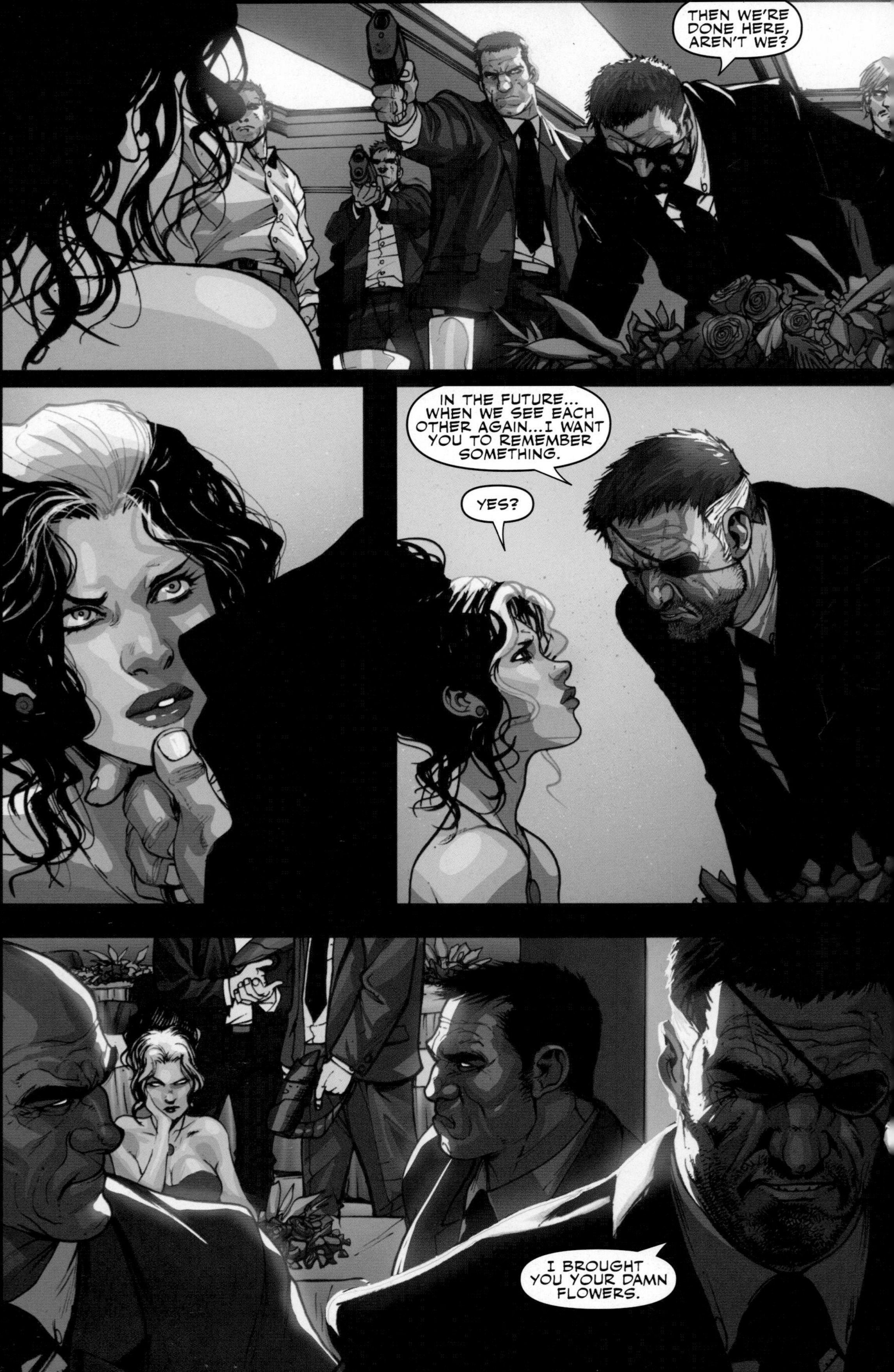
THEN WE'RE DONE HERE, AREN'T WE?
IN THE FUTURE... WHEN WE SEE EACH OTHER AGAIN...I WANT YOU TO REMEMBER SOMETHING.
YES?
I BROUGHT YOU YOUR DAMN FLOWERS.

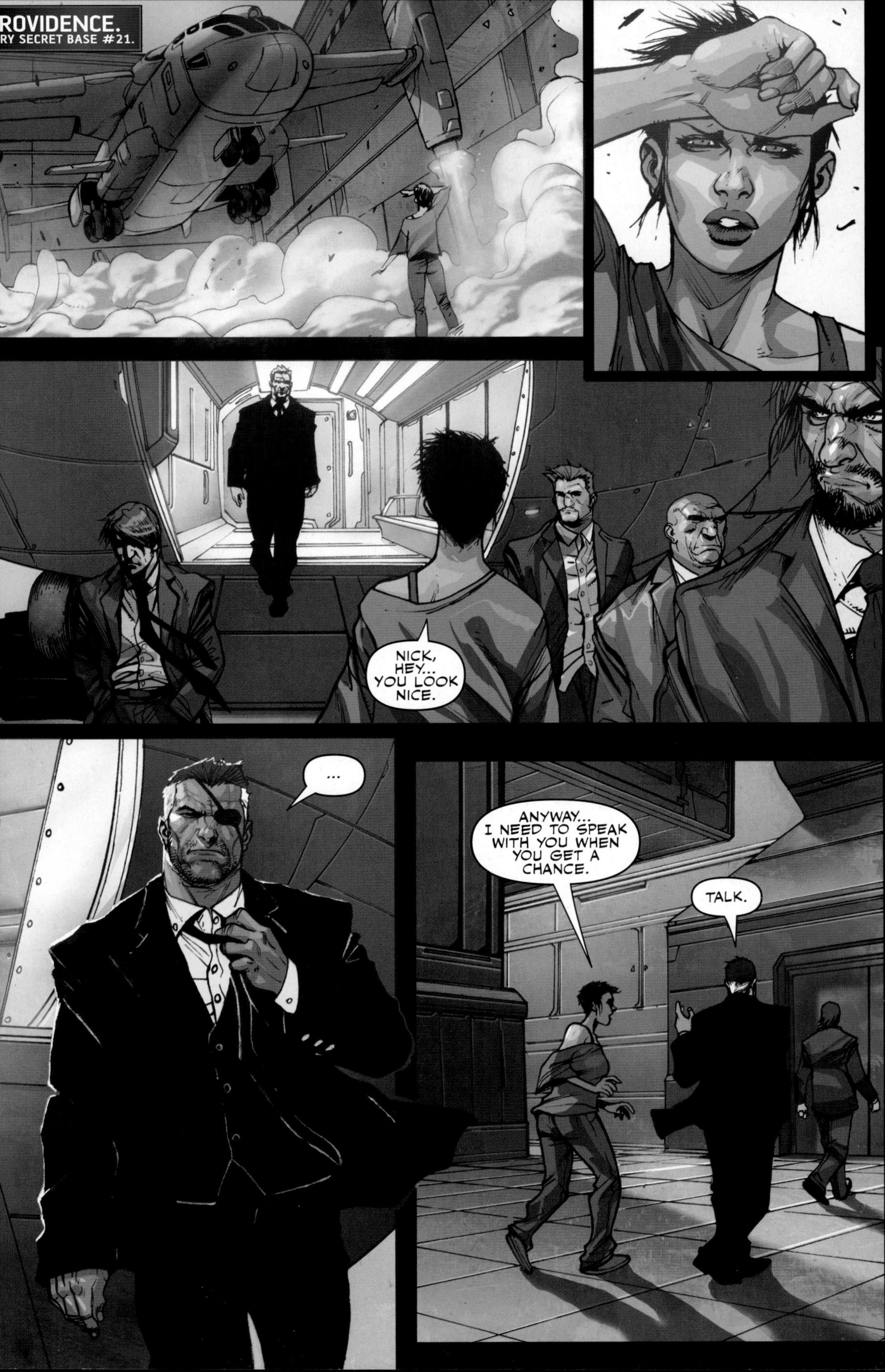
ROVIDENCE.
RY SECRET BASE #21.
NICK, HEY... YOU LOOK NICE.
...
ANYWAY... I NEED TO SPEAK WITH YOU WHEN YOU GET A CHANCE.
TALK.

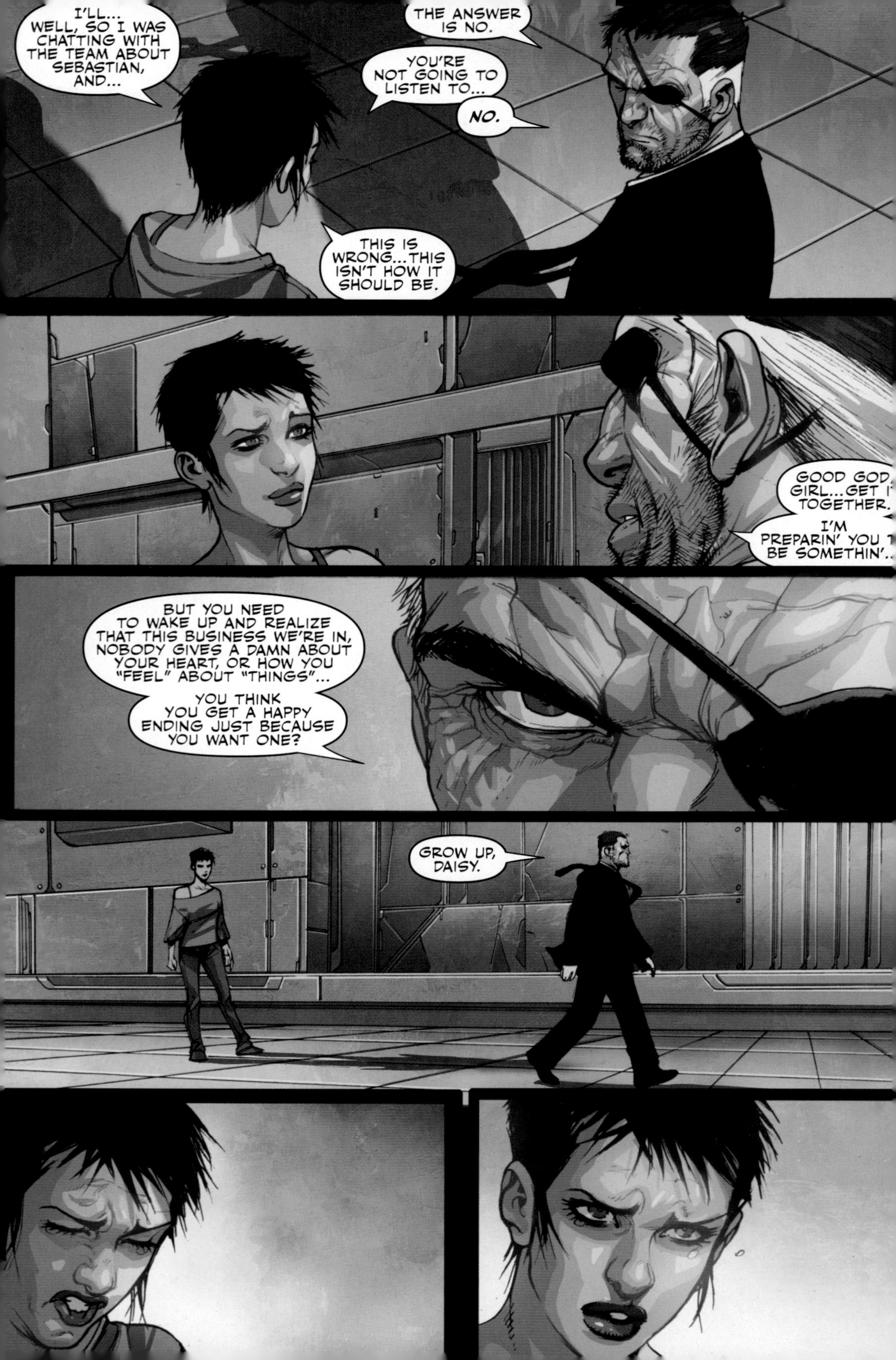
I'LL... WELL, SO I WAS CHATTING WITH THE TEAM ABOUT SEBASTIAN, AND...
THE ANSWER IS NO.
YOU'RE NOT GOING TO LISTEN TO...
NO.
THIS IS WRONG...THIS ISN'T HOW IT SHOULD BE.
GOOD GOD, GIRL...GET I TOGETHER.
I'M PREPARIN' YOU T BE SOMETHIN'..
BUT YOU NEED TO WAKE UP AND REALIZE THAT THIS BUSINESS WE'RE IN, NOBODY GIVES A DAMN ABOUT YOUR HEART, OR HOW YOU "FEEL" ABOUT "THINGS"...
YOU THINK YOU GET A HAPPY ENDING JUST BECAUSE YOU WANT ONE?
GROW UP, DAISY.

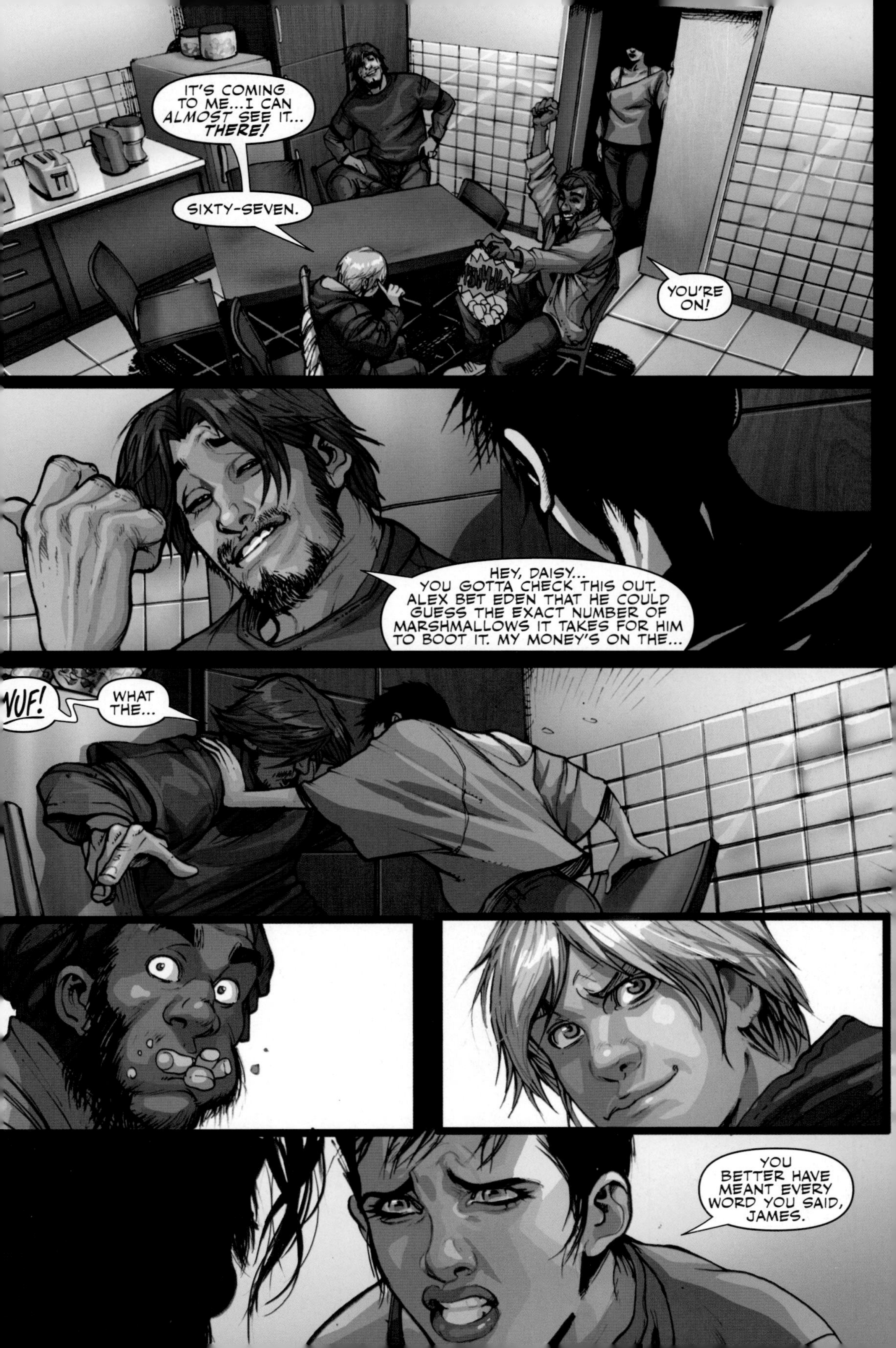
IT'S COMING TO ME...I CAN ALMOST SEE IT... THERE!
SIXTY-SEVEN.
YOU'RE ON!
HEY, DAISY... YOU GOTTA CHECK THIS OUT. ALEX BET EDEN THAT HE COULD GUESS THE EXACT NUMBER OF MARSHMALLOWS IT TAKES FOR HIM TO BOOT IT. MY MONEY'S ON THE...
WUF!
WHAT THE...
YOU BETTER HAVE MEANT EVERY WORD YOU SAID, JAMES.

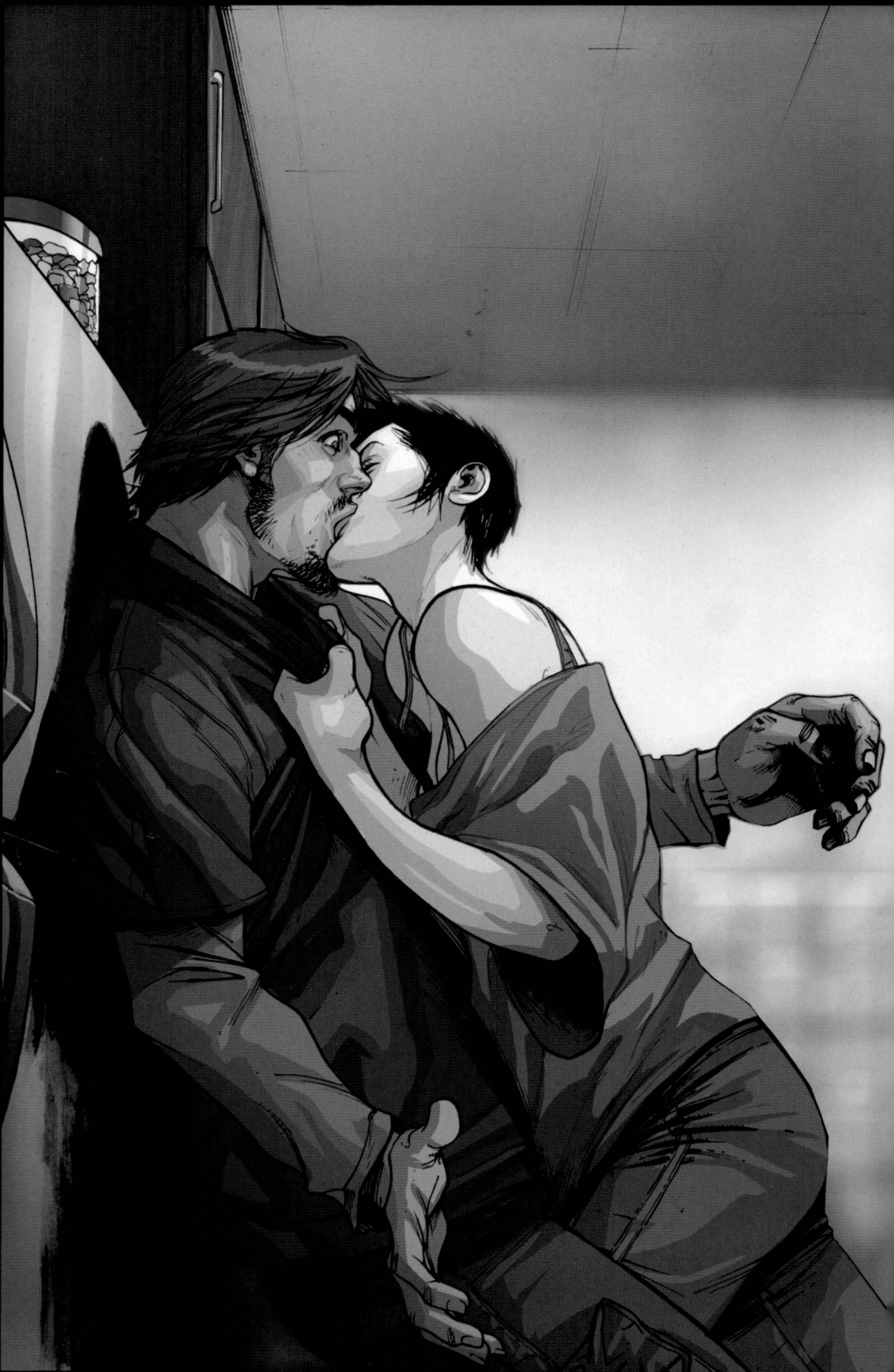

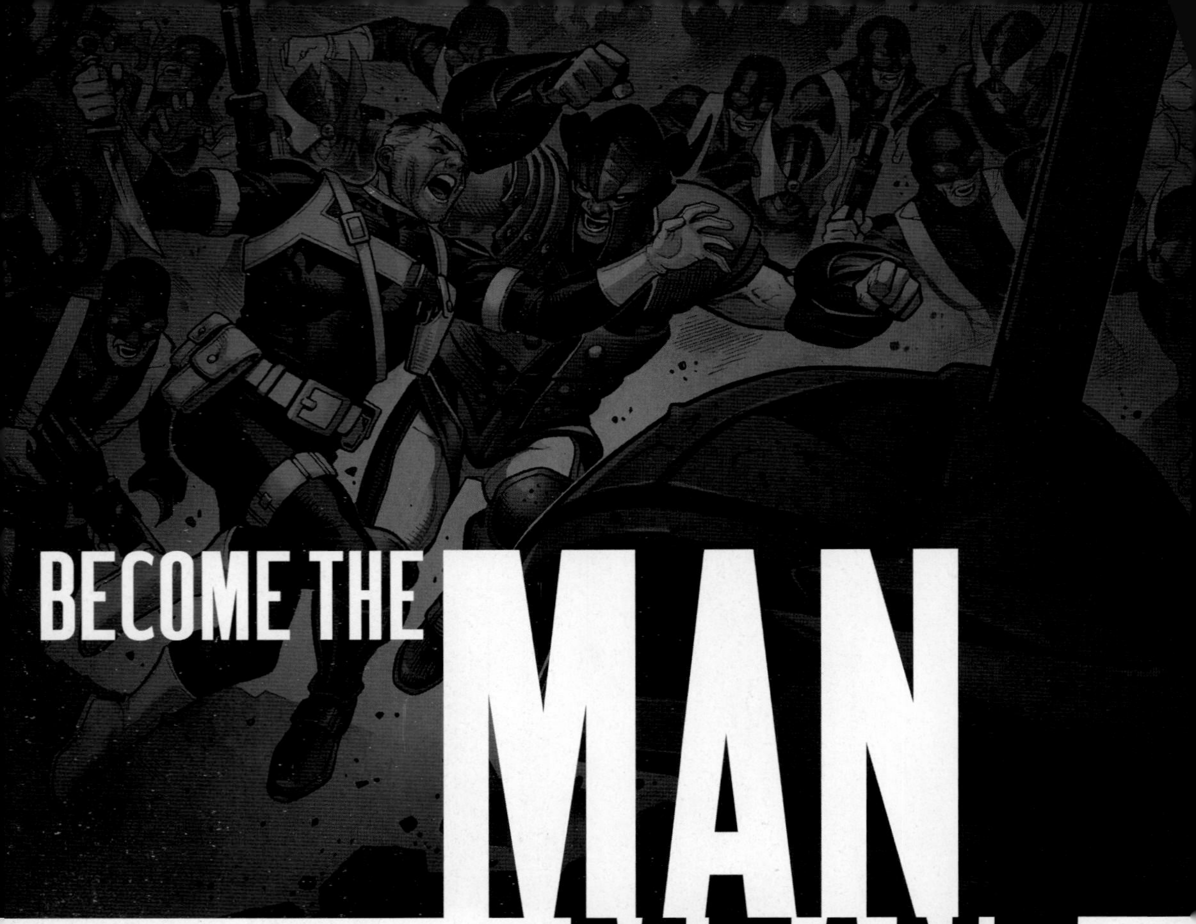

BECOME THE MAN YOU ARE MEANT TO BE

TWO WEEKS LATER.

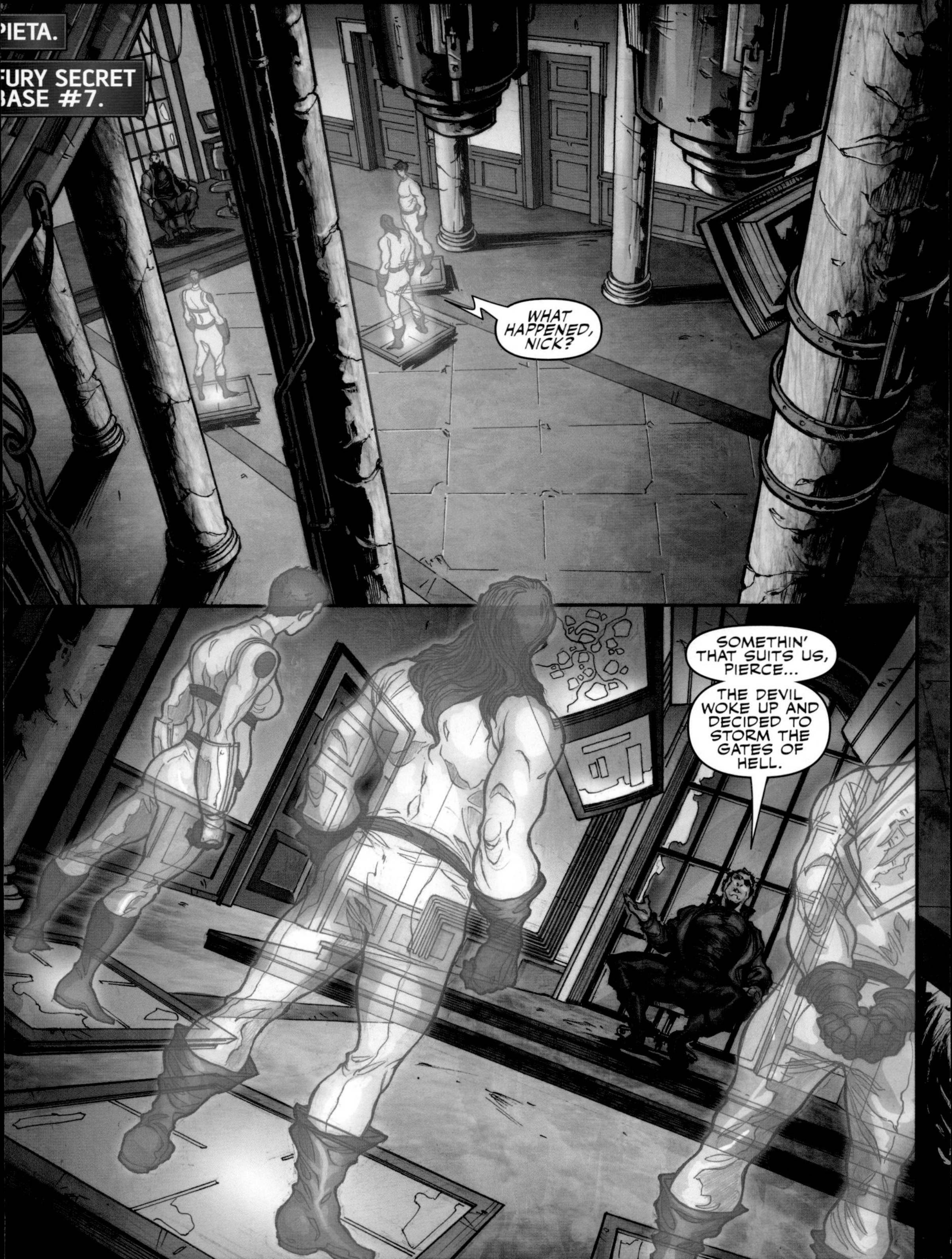
PIETA.
FURY SECRET BASE #7.
WHAT HAPPENED, NICK?
SOMETHIN' THAT SUITS US, PIERCE...
THE DEVIL WOKE UP AND DECIDED TO STORM THE GATES OF HELL.

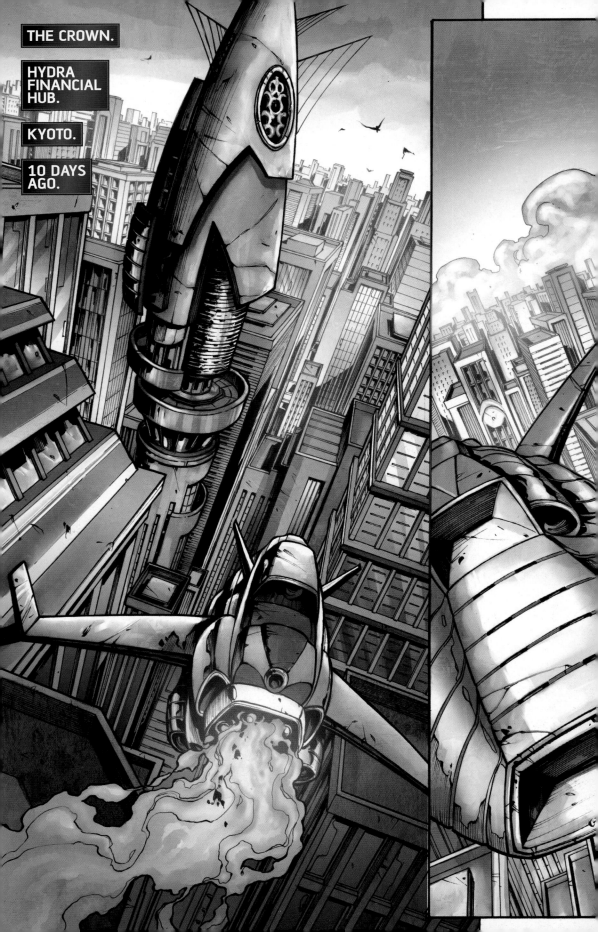

THE CROWN.

HYDRA
FINANCIAL
HUB.

KYOTO.

10 DAYS
AGO.

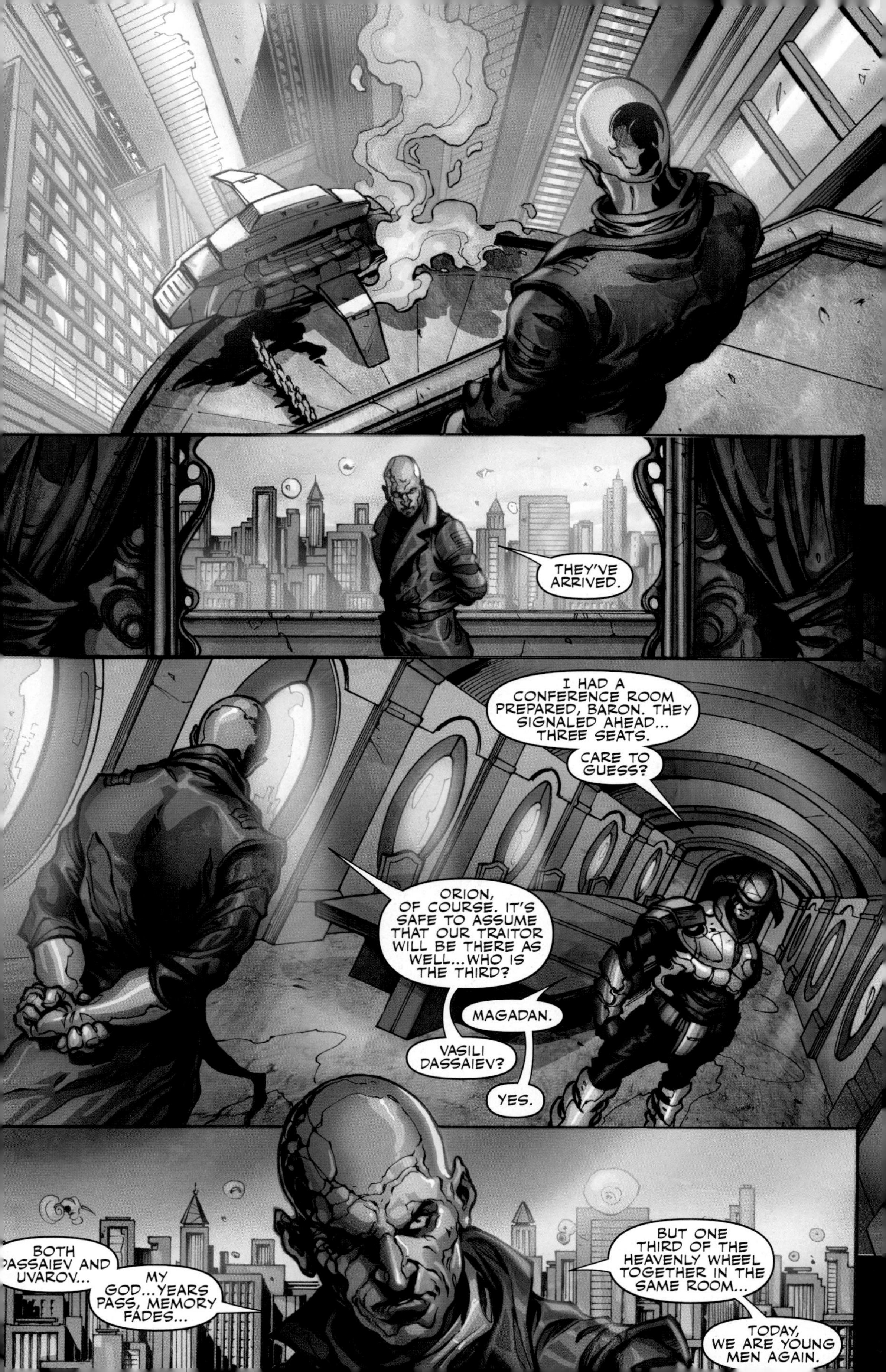
THEY'VE ARRIVED.
I HAD A CONFERENCE ROOM PREPARED, BARON. THEY SIGNALED AHEAD... THREE SEATS.
CARE TO GUESS?
ORION, OF COURSE. IT'S SAFE TO ASSUME THAT OUR TRAITOR WILL BE THERE AS WELL...WHO IS THE THIRD?
MAGADAN.
VASILI DASSAIEV?
YES.
BOTH DASSAIEV AND UVAROV...
MY GOD...YEARS PASS, MEMORY FADES...
BUT ONE THIRD OF THE HEAVENLY WHEEL TOGETHER IN THE SAME ROOM...
TODAY, WE ARE YOUNG MEN AGAIN.

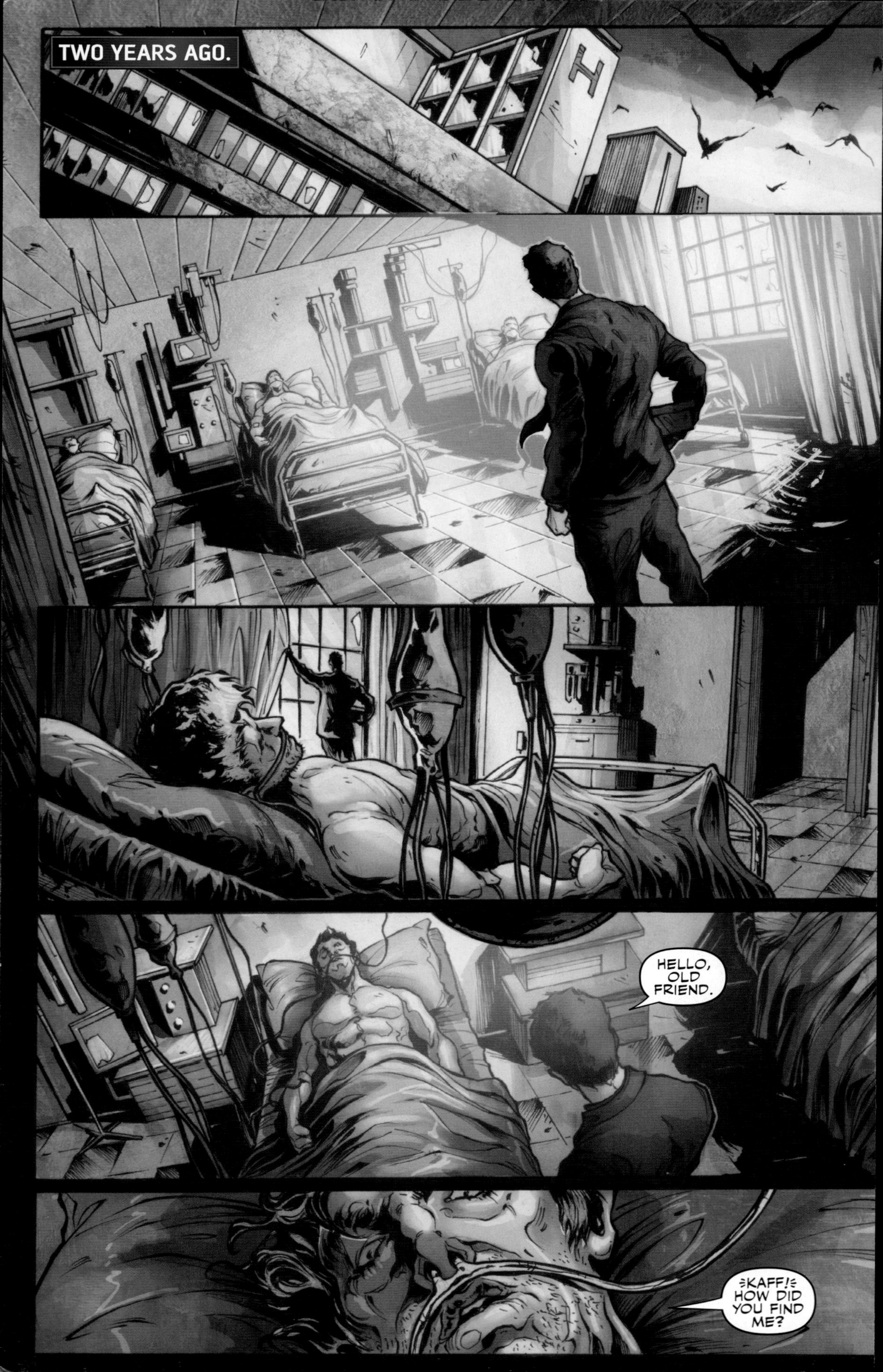
TWO YEARS AGO.
HELLO, OLD FRIEND.
KAFF! HOW DID YOU FIND ME?

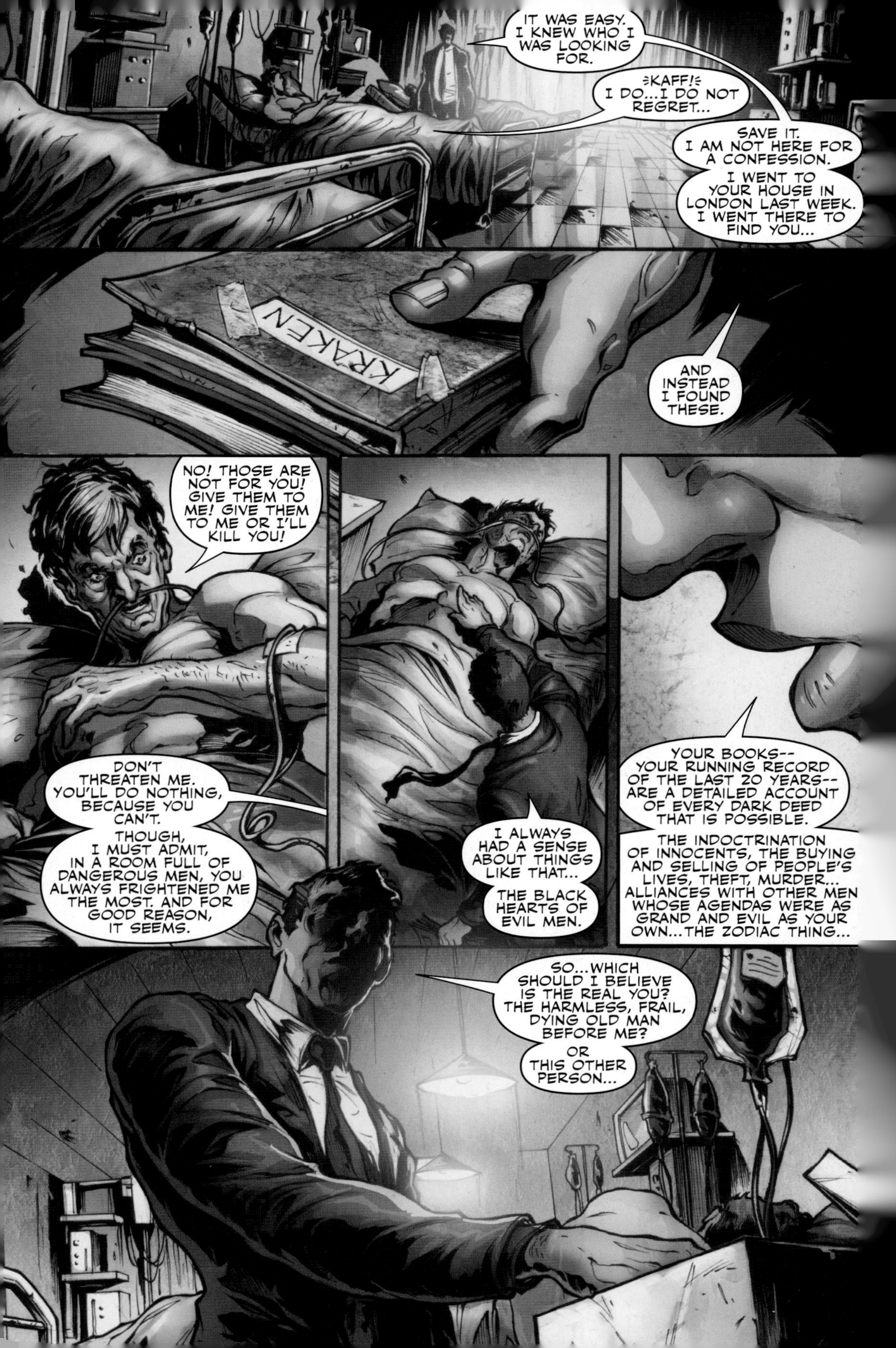
IT WAS EASY. I KNEW WHO I WAS LOOKING FOR.
KAFF! I DO...I DO NOT REGRET...
SAVE IT. I AM NOT HERE FOR A CONFESSION.
I WENT TO YOUR HOUSE IN LONDON LAST WEEK. I WENT THERE TO FIND YOU...
KRAKEN
AND INSTEAD I FOUND THESE.
NO! THOSE ARE NOT FOR YOU! GIVE THEM TO ME! GIVE THEM TO ME OR I'LL KILL YOU!
DON'T THREATEN ME. YOU'LL DO NOTHING, BECAUSE YOU CAN'T.
THOUGH, I MUST ADMIT, IN A ROOM FULL OF DANGEROUS MEN, YOU ALWAYS FRIGHTENED ME THE MOST. AND FOR GOOD REASON, IT SEEMS.
I ALWAYS HAD A SENSE ABOUT THINGS LIKE THAT...
THE BLACK HEARTS OF EVIL MEN.
YOUR BOOKS-- YOUR RUNNING RECORD OF THE LAST 20 YEARS-- ARE A DETAILED ACCOUNT OF EVERY DARK DEED THAT IS POSSIBLE.
THE INDOCTRINATION OF INNOCENTS, THE BUYING AND SELLING OF PEOPLE'S LIVES, THEFT, MURDER... ALLIANCES WITH OTHER MEN WHOSE AGENDAS WERE AS GRAND AND EVIL AS YOUR OWN...THE ZODIAC THING...
SO...WHICH SHOULD I BELIEVE IS THE REAL YOU? THE HARMLESS, FRAIL, DYING OLD MAN BEFORE ME?
OR THIS OTHER PERSON...

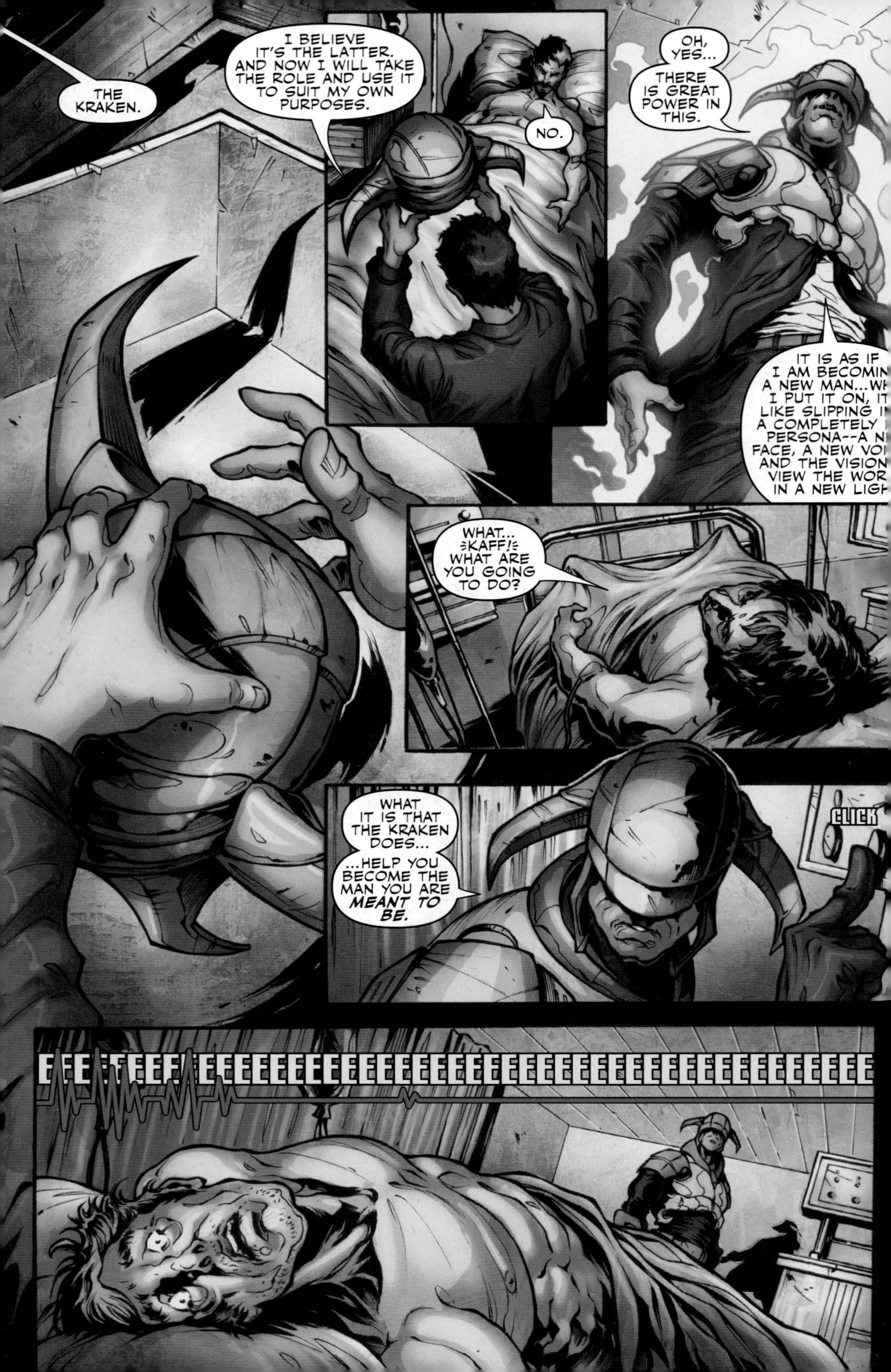
THE KRAKEN.
I BELIEVE IT'S THE LATTER. AND NOW I WILL TAKE THE ROLE AND USE IT TO SUIT MY OWN PURPOSES.
NO.
OH, YES...
THERE IS GREAT POWER IN THIS.
IT IS AS IF I AM BECOMIN A NEW MAN...WH I PUT IT ON, IT LIKE SLIPPING IN A COMPLETELY PERSONA--A N FACE, A NEW VOI AND THE VISION VIEW THE WOR IN A NEW LIGH
WHAT... =KAFF!= WHAT ARE YOU GOING TO DO?
WHAT IT IS THAT THE KRAKEN DOES...
...HELP YOU BECOME THE MAN YOU ARE *MEANT TO BE.*
CLICK
EEEEEEEEEEEEEEEEEEEEEEEEEEEEEEEEEEEEEEEEEEEEEEEEEEEEE

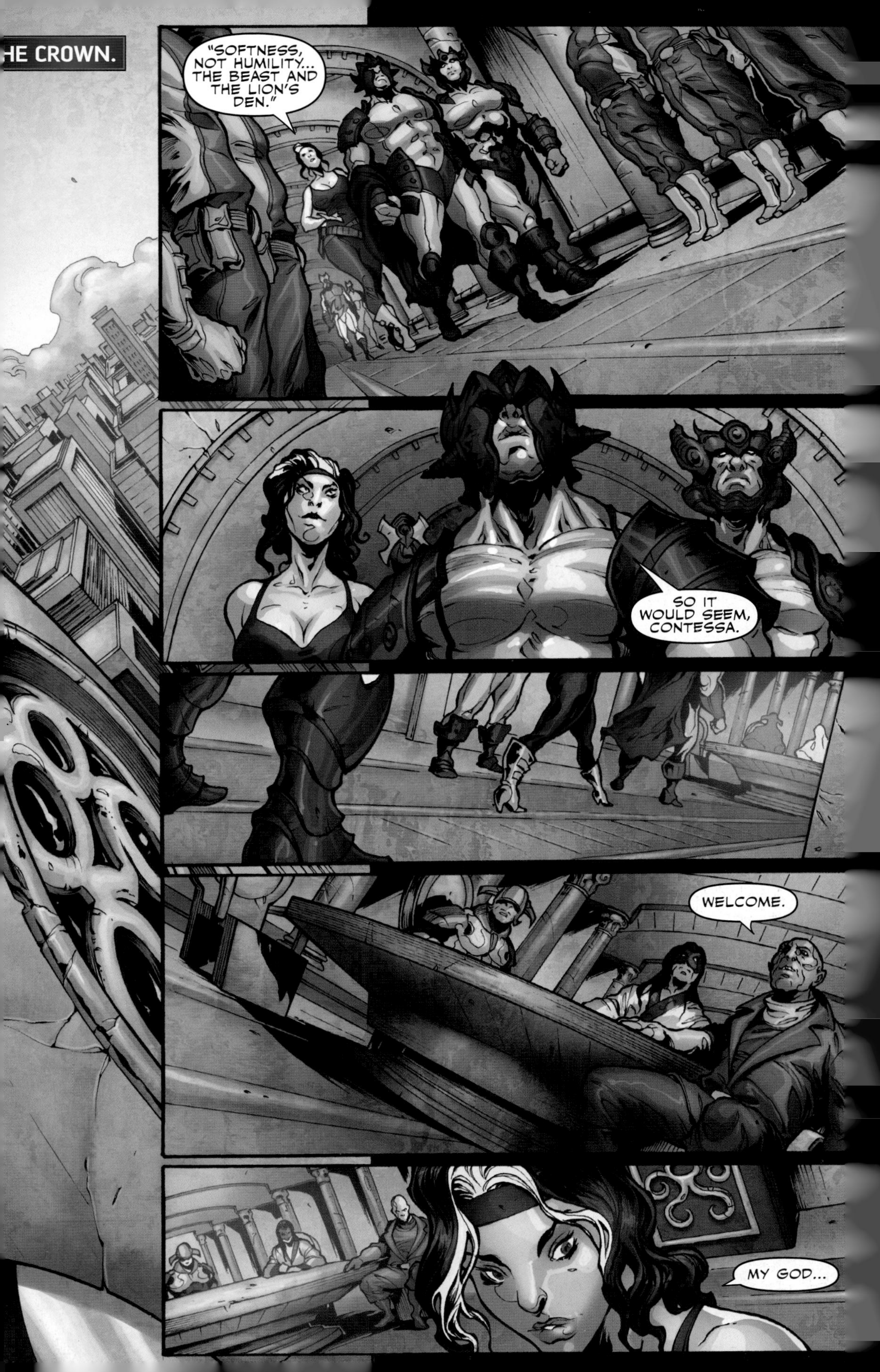
HE CROWN.
"SOFTNESS, NOT HUMILITY... THE BEAST AND THE LION'S DEN."
SO IT WOULD SEEM, CONTESSA.
WELCOME.
MY GOD...

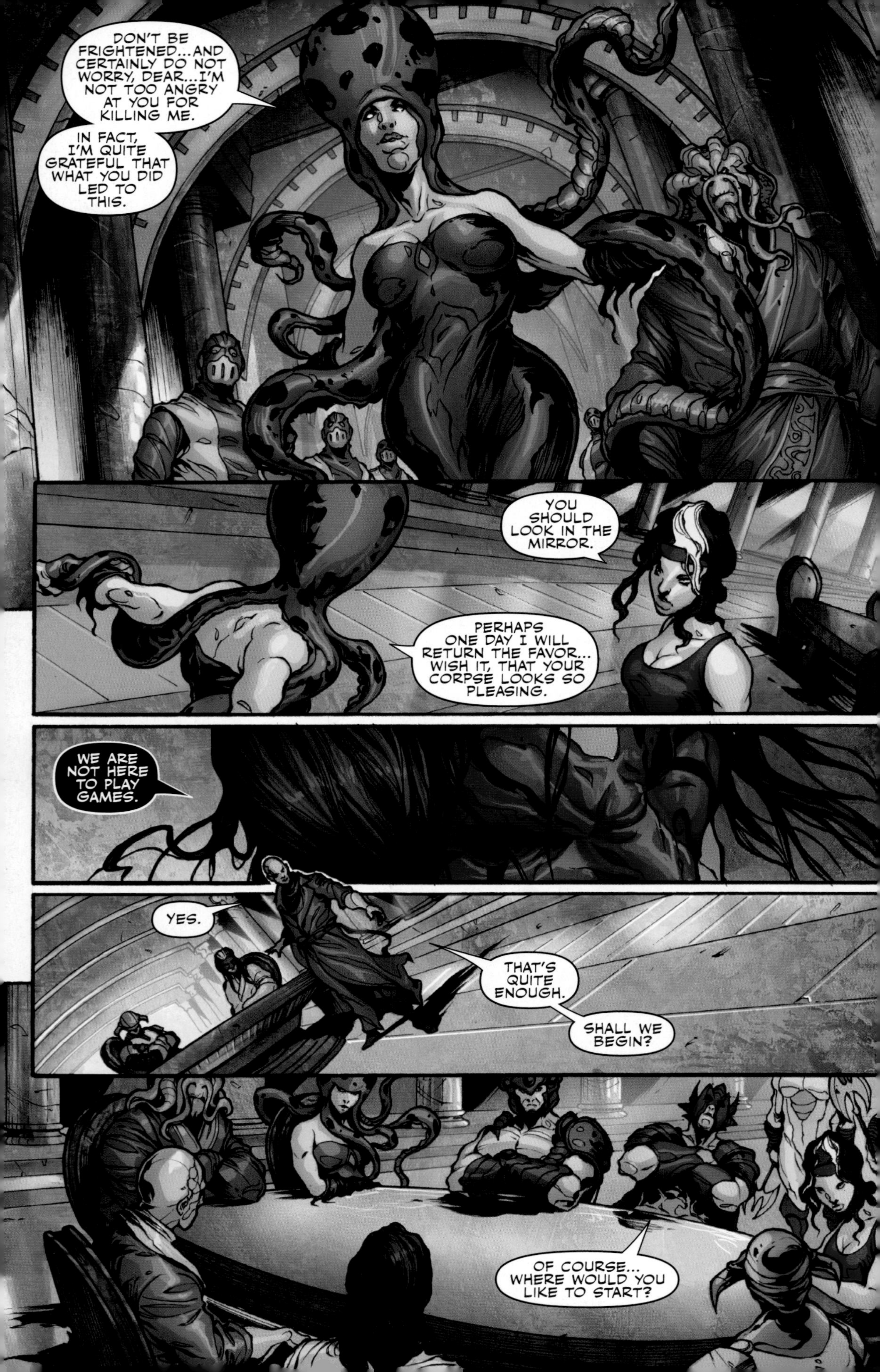
DON'T BE FRIGHTENED...AND CERTAINLY DO NOT WORRY, DEAR...I'M NOT TOO ANGRY AT YOU FOR KILLING ME.
IN FACT, I'M QUITE GRATEFUL THAT WHAT YOU DID LED TO THIS.
YOU SHOULD LOOK IN THE MIRROR.
PERHAPS ONE DAY I WILL RETURN THE FAVOR... WISH IT, THAT YOUR CORPSE LOOKS SO PLEASING.
WE ARE NOT HERE TO PLAY GAMES.
YES.
THAT'S QUITE ENOUGH.
SHALL WE BEGIN?
OF COURSE... WHERE WOULD YOU LIKE TO START?

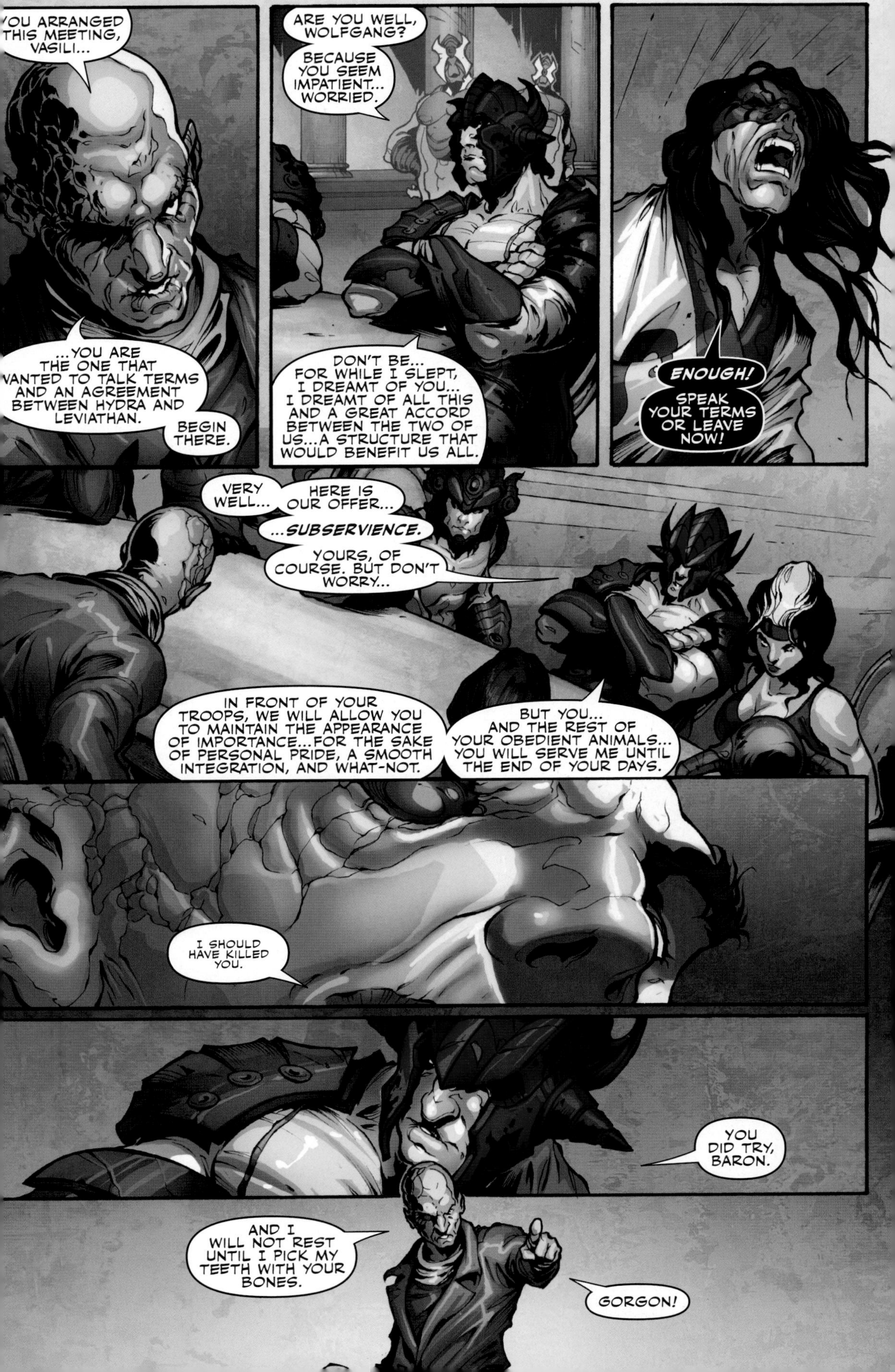
YOU ARRANGED THIS MEETING, VASILI...
...YOU ARE THE ONE THAT WANTED TO TALK TERMS AND AN AGREEMENT BETWEEN HYDRA AND LEVIATHAN.
BEGIN THERE.
ARE YOU WELL, WOLFGANG?
BECAUSE YOU SEEM IMPATIENT... WORRIED.
DON'T BE... FOR WHILE I SLEPT, I DREAMT OF YOU... I DREAMT OF ALL THIS AND A GREAT ACCORD BETWEEN THE TWO OF US...A STRUCTURE THAT WOULD BENEFIT US ALL.
ENOUGH!
SPEAK YOUR TERMS OR LEAVE NOW!
VERY WELL...
HERE IS OUR OFFER...
...SUBSERVIENCE.
YOURS, OF COURSE. BUT DON'T WORRY...
IN FRONT OF YOUR TROOPS, WE WILL ALLOW YOU TO MAINTAIN THE APPEARANCE OF IMPORTANCE...FOR THE SAKE OF PERSONAL PRIDE, A SMOOTH INTEGRATION, AND WHAT-NOT.
BUT YOU... AND THE REST OF YOUR OBEDIENT ANIMALS... YOU WILL SERVE ME UNTIL THE END OF YOUR DAYS.
I SHOULD HAVE KILLED YOU.
YOU DID TRY, BARON.
AND I WILL NOT REST UNTIL I PICK MY TEETH WITH YOUR BONES.
GORGON!

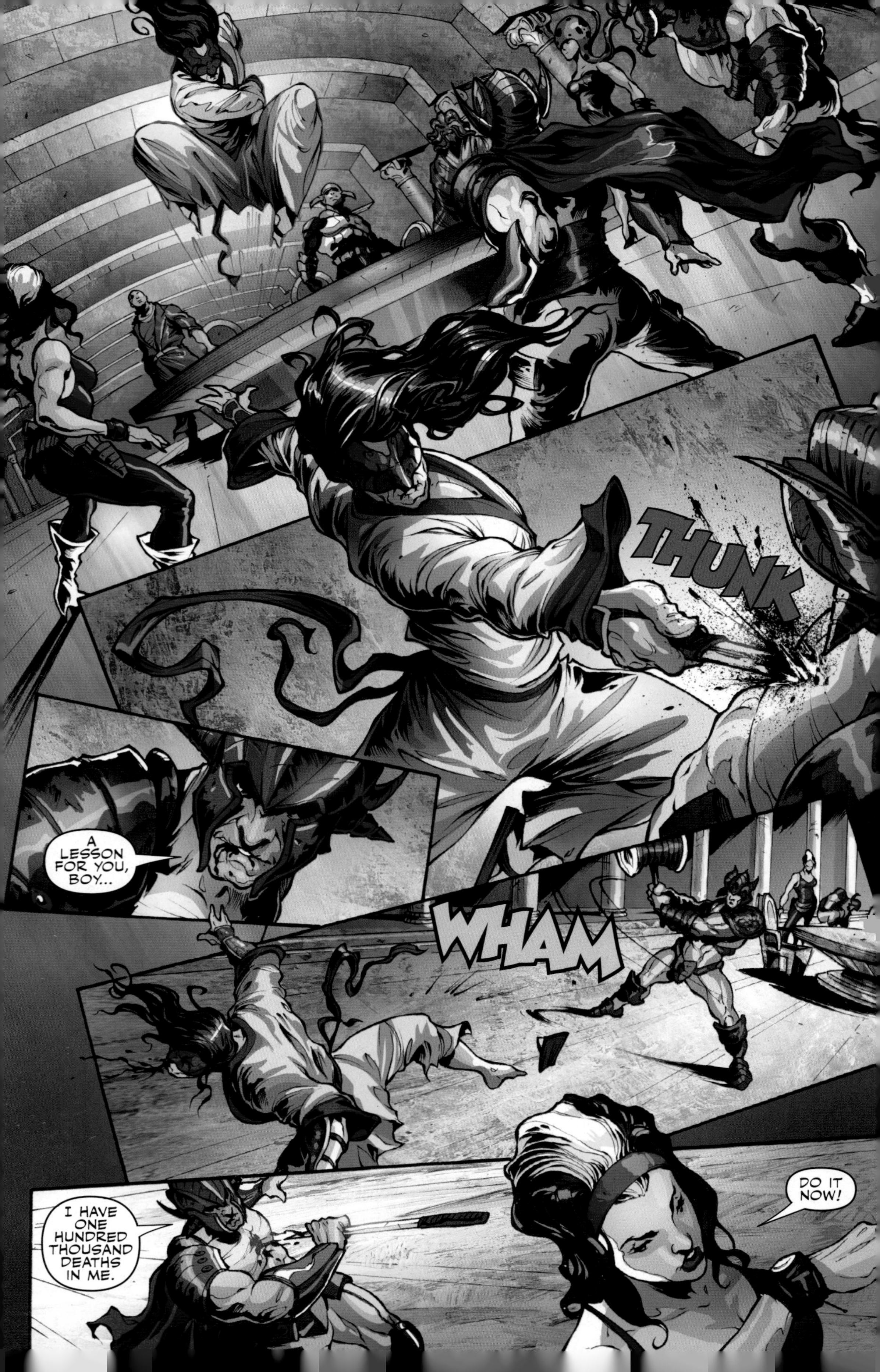
THUNK
A LESSON FOR YOU, BOY...
WHAM
I HAVE ONE HUNDRED THOUSAND DEATHS IN ME.
DO IT NOW!

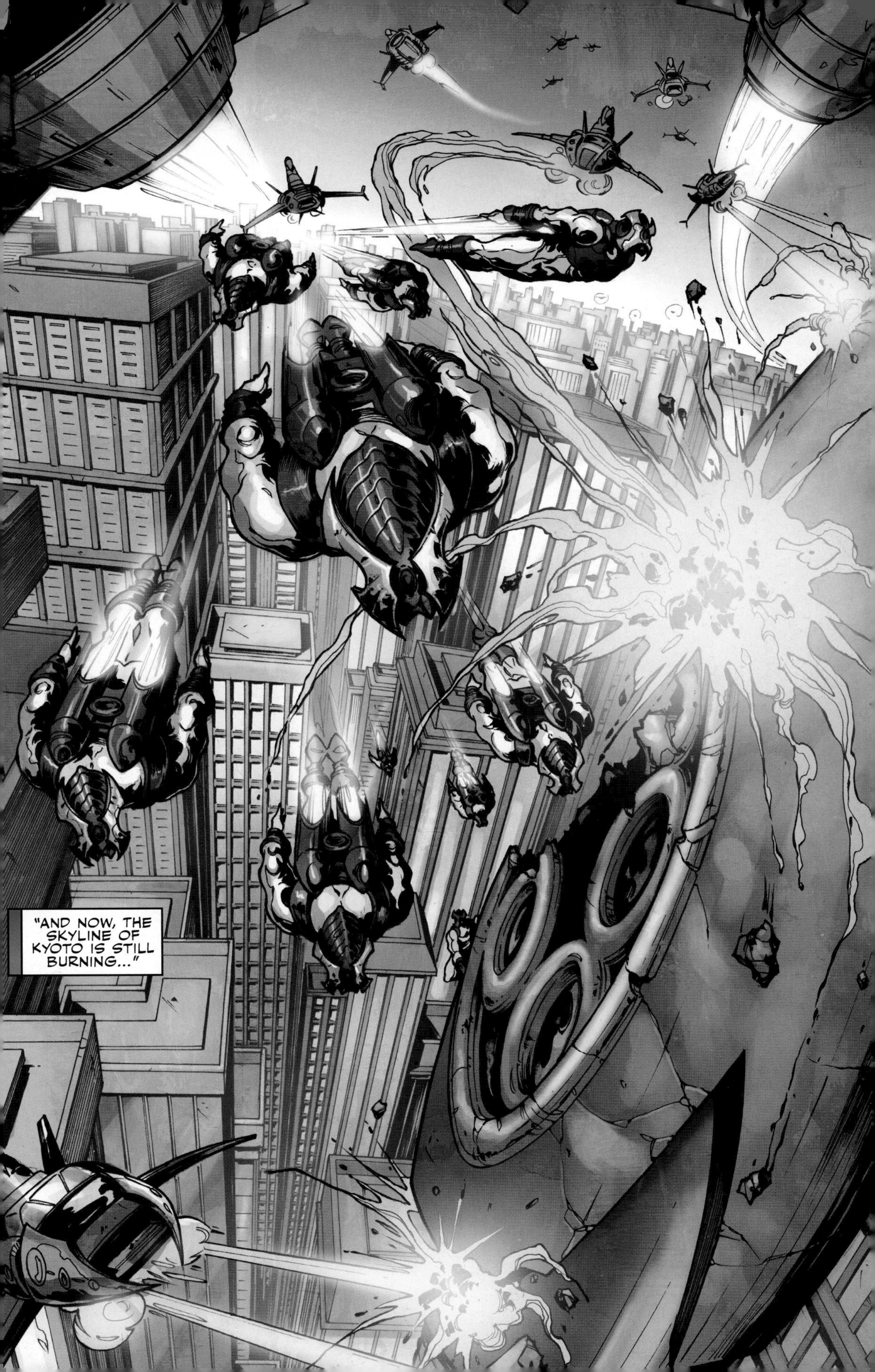
"AND NOW, THE SKYLINE OF KYOTO IS STILL BURNING..."

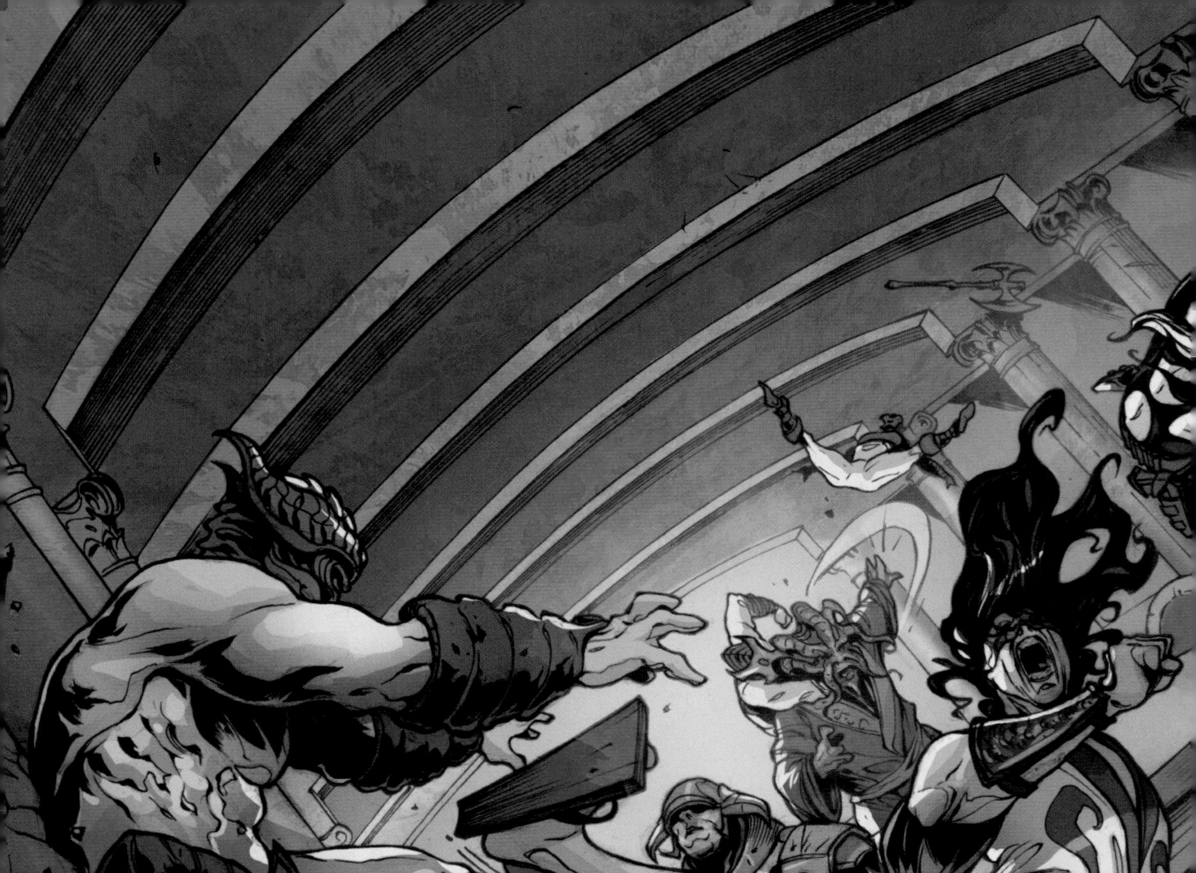
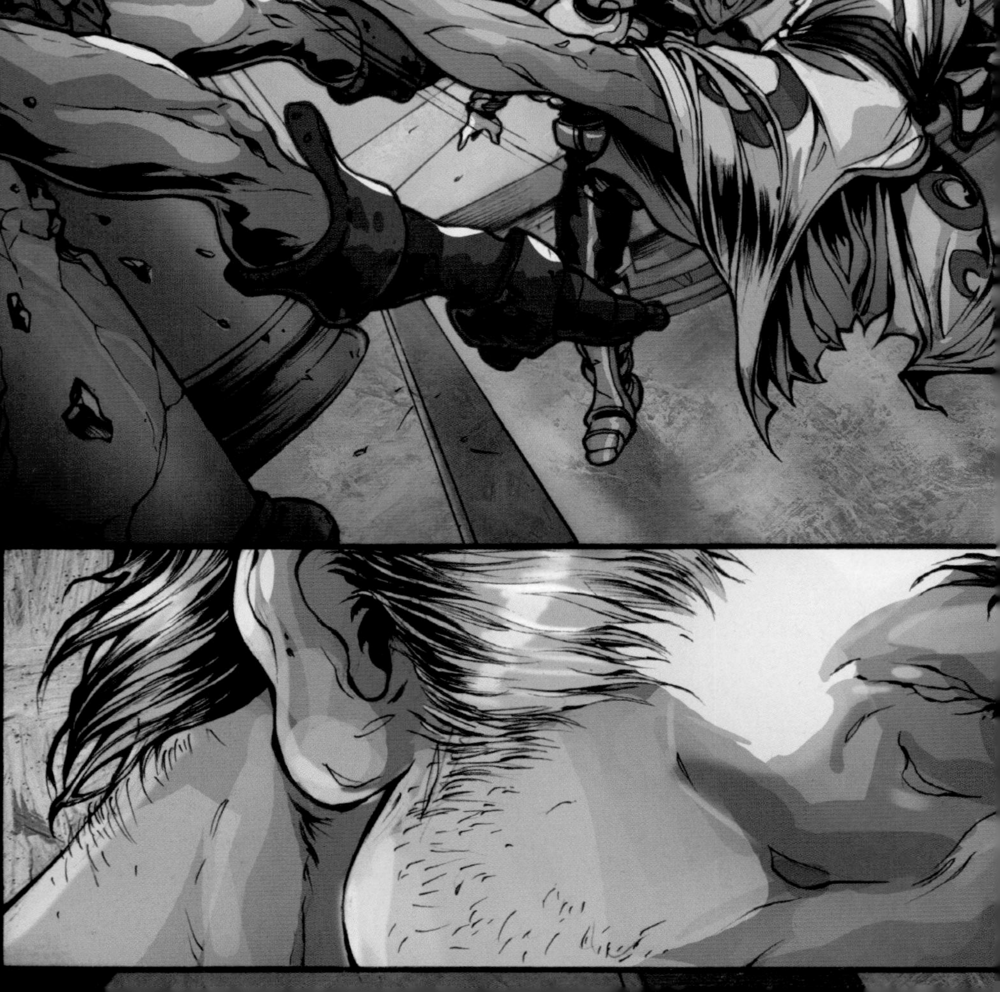

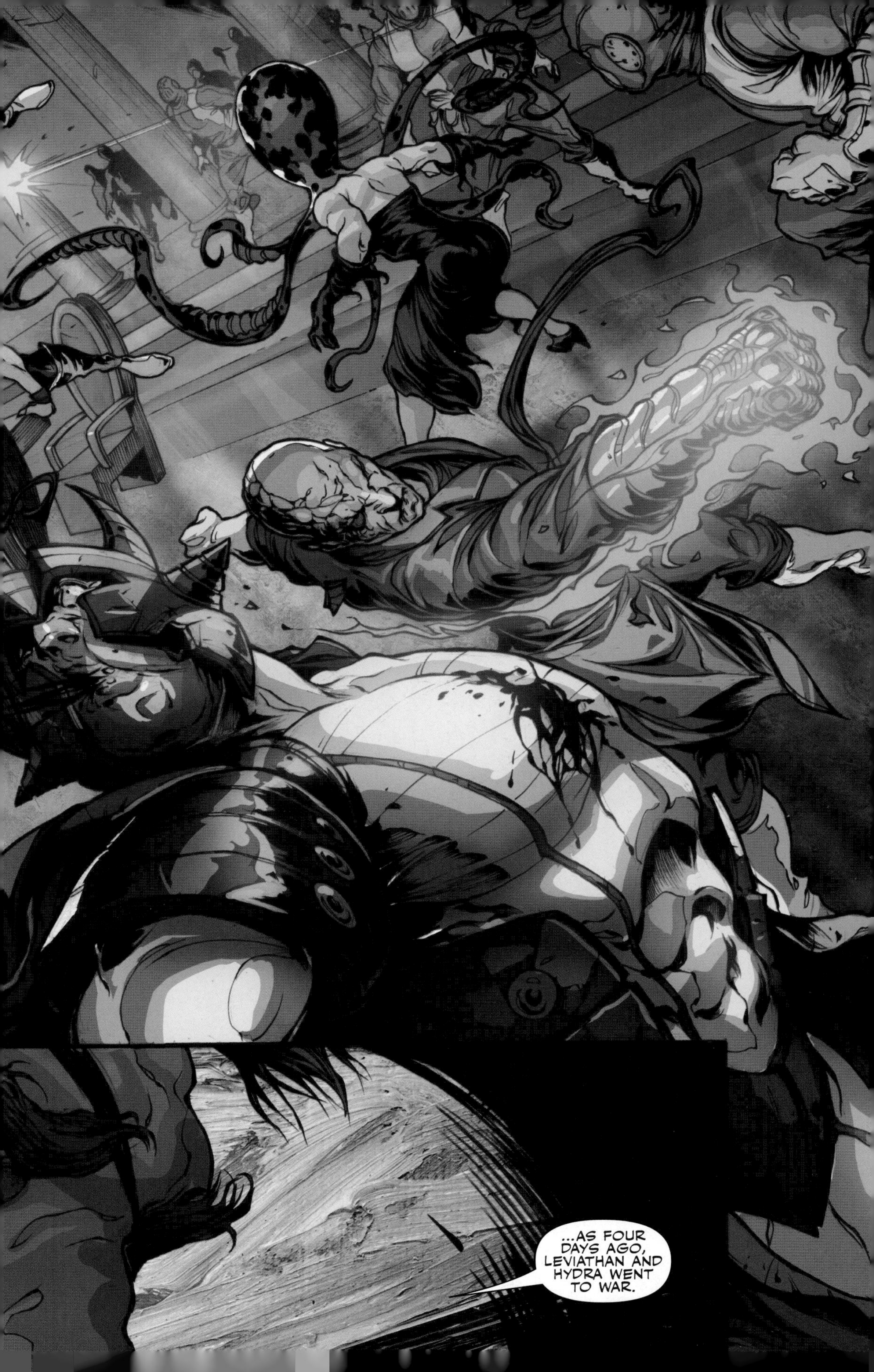
...AS FOUR DAYS AGO, LEVIATHAN AND HYDRA WENT TO WAR.

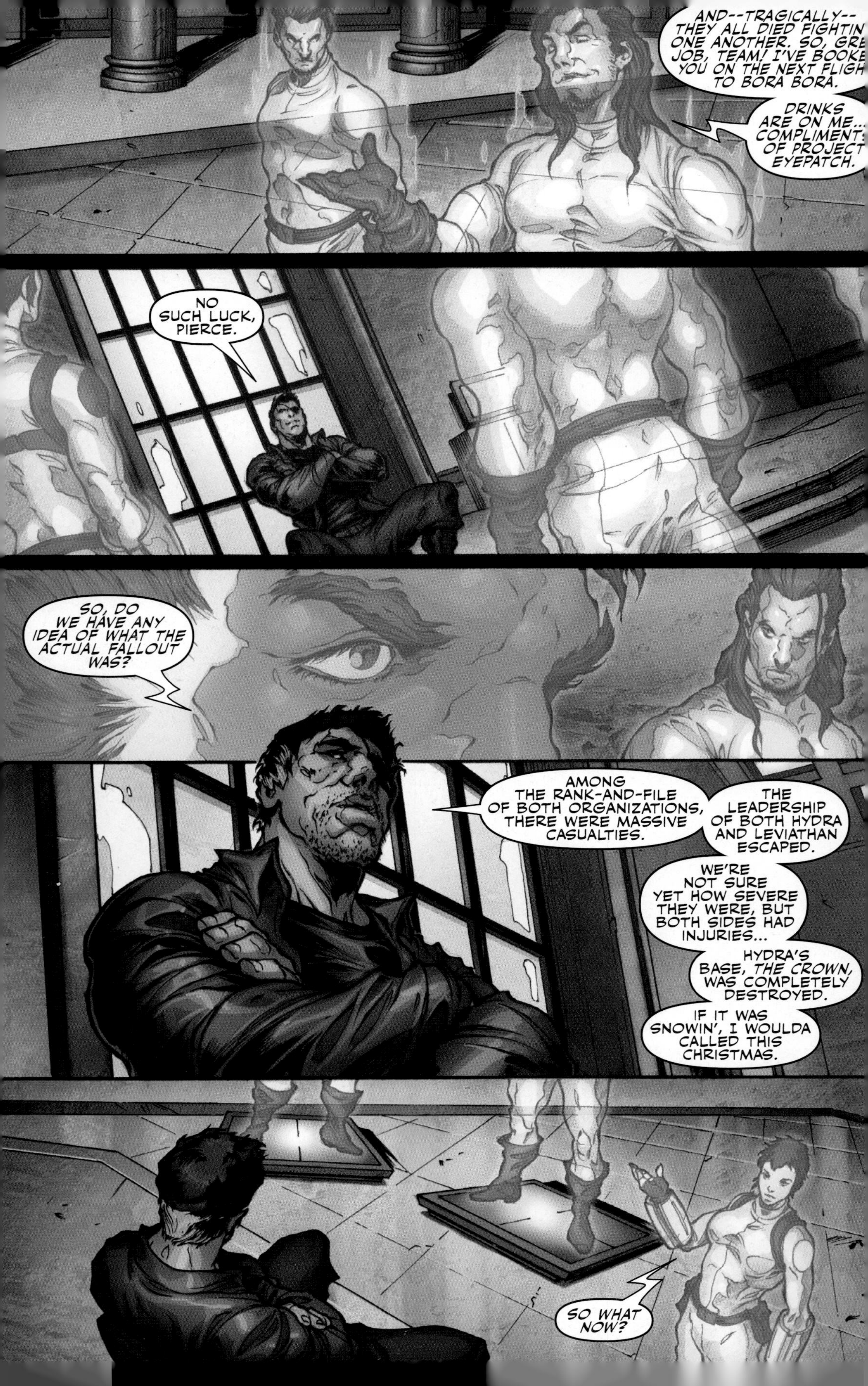
AND--TRAGICALLY-- THEY ALL DIED FIGHTIN ONE ANOTHER. SO, GRE JOB, TEAM! I'VE BOOKE YOU ON THE NEXT FLIGH TO BORA BORA.
DRINKS ARE ON ME... COMPLIMENT OF PROJECT EYEPATCH.
NO SUCH LUCK, PIERCE.
SO, DO WE HAVE ANY IDEA OF WHAT THE ACTUAL FALLOUT WAS?
AMONG THE RANK-AND-FILE OF BOTH ORGANIZATIONS, THERE WERE MASSIVE CASUALTIES.
THE LEADERSHIP OF BOTH HYDRA AND LEVIATHAN ESCAPED.
WE'RE NOT SURE YET HOW SEVERE THEY WERE, BUT BOTH SIDES HAD INJURIES...
HYDRA'S BASE, THE CROWN, WAS COMPLETELY DESTROYED.
IF IT WAS SNOWIN', I WOULDA CALLED THIS CHRISTMAS.
SO WHAT NOW?

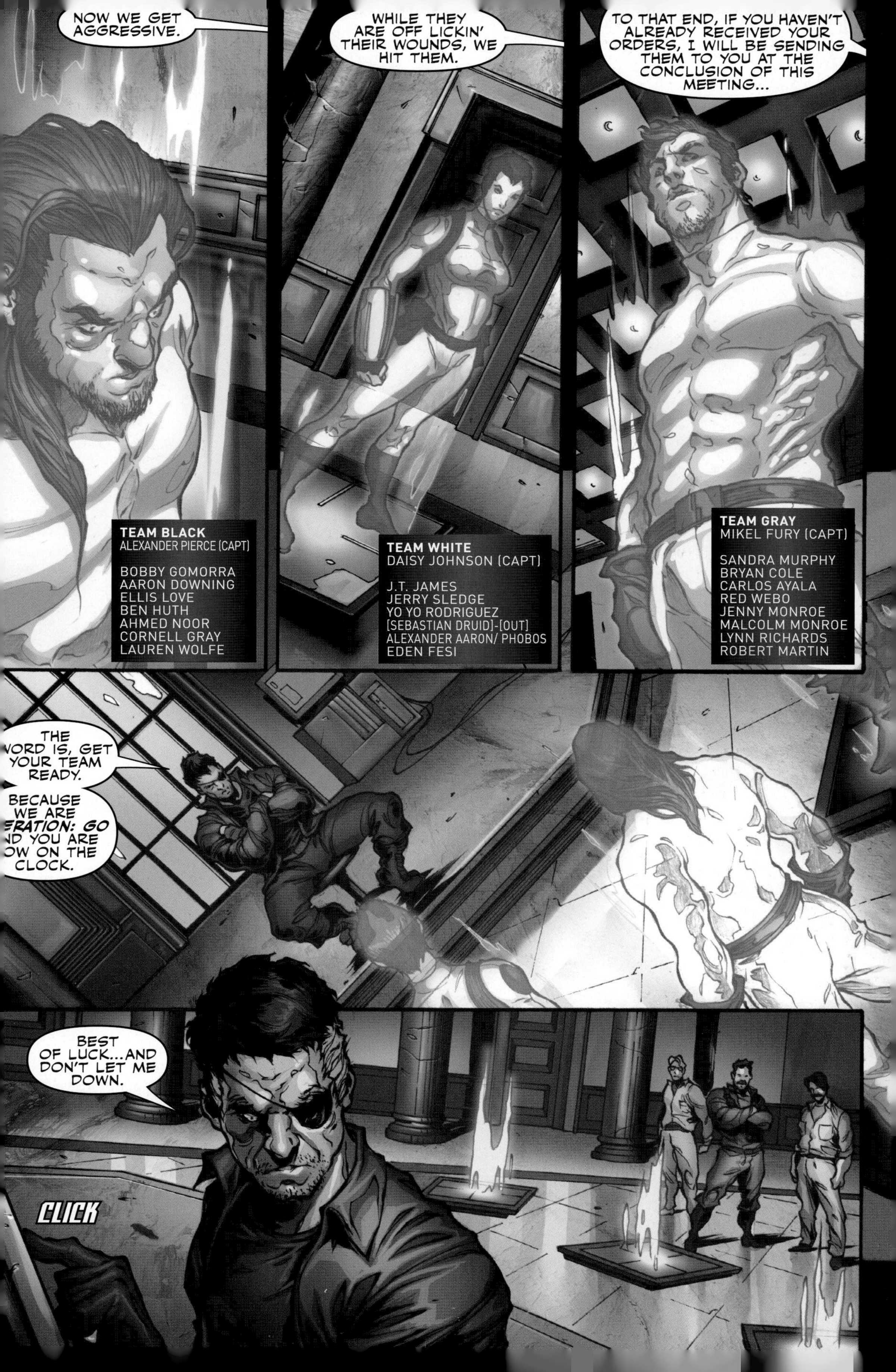
NOW WE GET AGGRESSIVE.
WHILE THEY ARE OFF LICKIN' THEIR WOUNDS, WE HIT THEM.
TO THAT END, IF YOU HAVEN'T ALREADY RECEIVED YOUR ORDERS, I WILL BE SENDING THEM TO YOU AT THE CONCLUSION OF THIS MEETING...
TEAM BLACK
ALEXANDER PIERCE (CAPT)
BOBBY GOMORRA
AARON DOWNING
ELLIS LOVE
BEN HUTH
AHMED NOOR
CORNELL GRAY
LAUREN WOLFE
TEAM WHITE
DAISY JOHNSON (CAPT)
J.T. JAMES
JERRY SLEDGE
YO YO RODRIGUEZ
[SEBASTIAN DRUID]-[OUT]
ALEXANDER AARON/ PHOBOS
EDEN FESI
TEAM GRAY
MIKEL FURY (CAPT)
SANDRA MURPHY
BRYAN COLE
CARLOS AYALA
RED WEBO
JENNY MONROE
MALCOLM MONROE
LYNN RICHARDS
ROBERT MARTIN
THE VORD IS, GET YOUR TEAM READY.
BECAUSE WE ARE ERATION: GO ND YOU ARE OW ON THE CLOCK.
BEST OF LUCK...AND DON'T LET ME DOWN.
CLICK

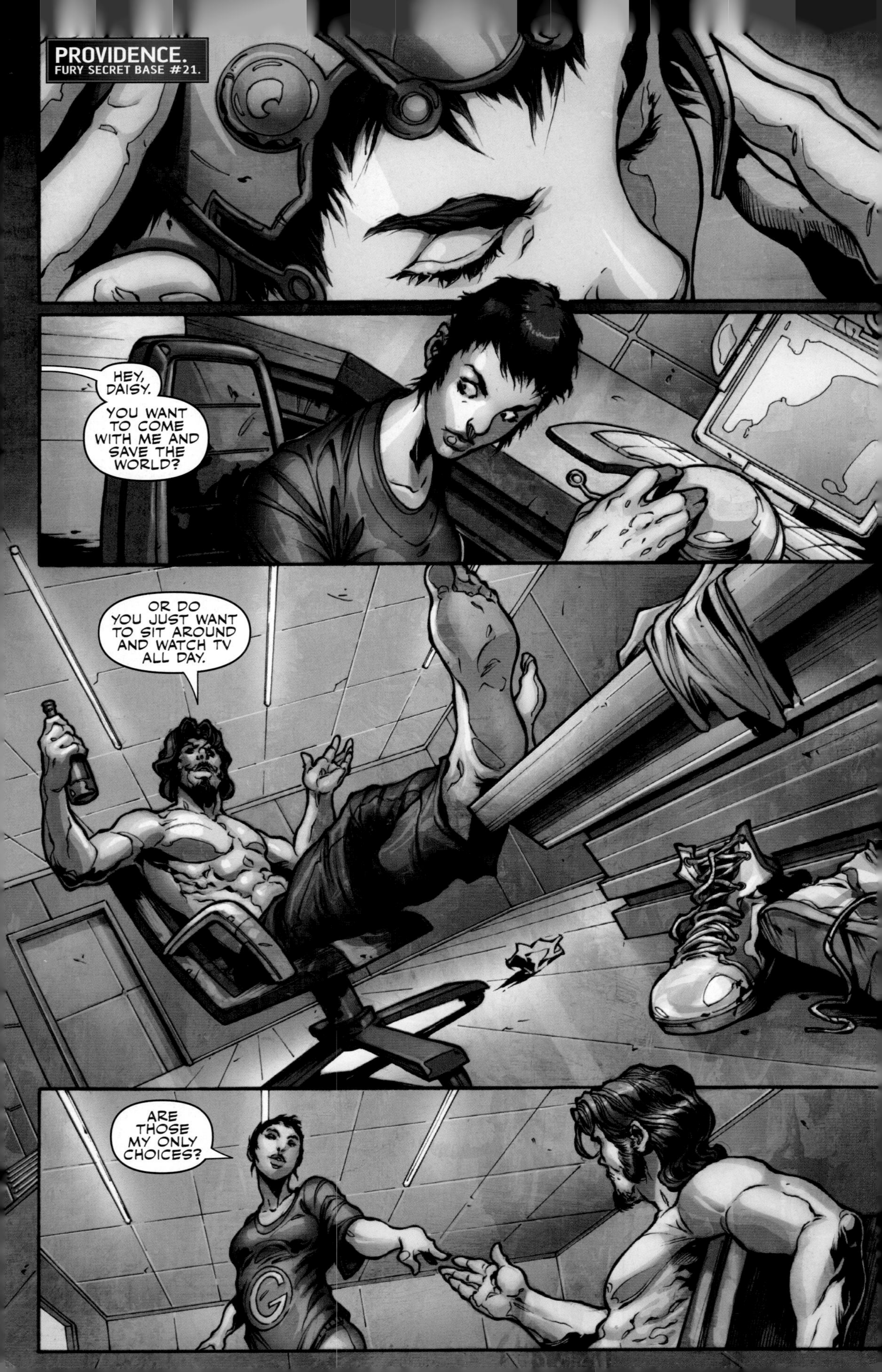
PROVIDENCE.
FURY SECRET BASE #21.
HEY, DAISY.
YOU WANT TO COME WITH ME AND SAVE THE WORLD?
OR DO YOU JUST WANT TO SIT AROUND AND WATCH TV ALL DAY.
ARE THOSE MY ONLY CHOICES?

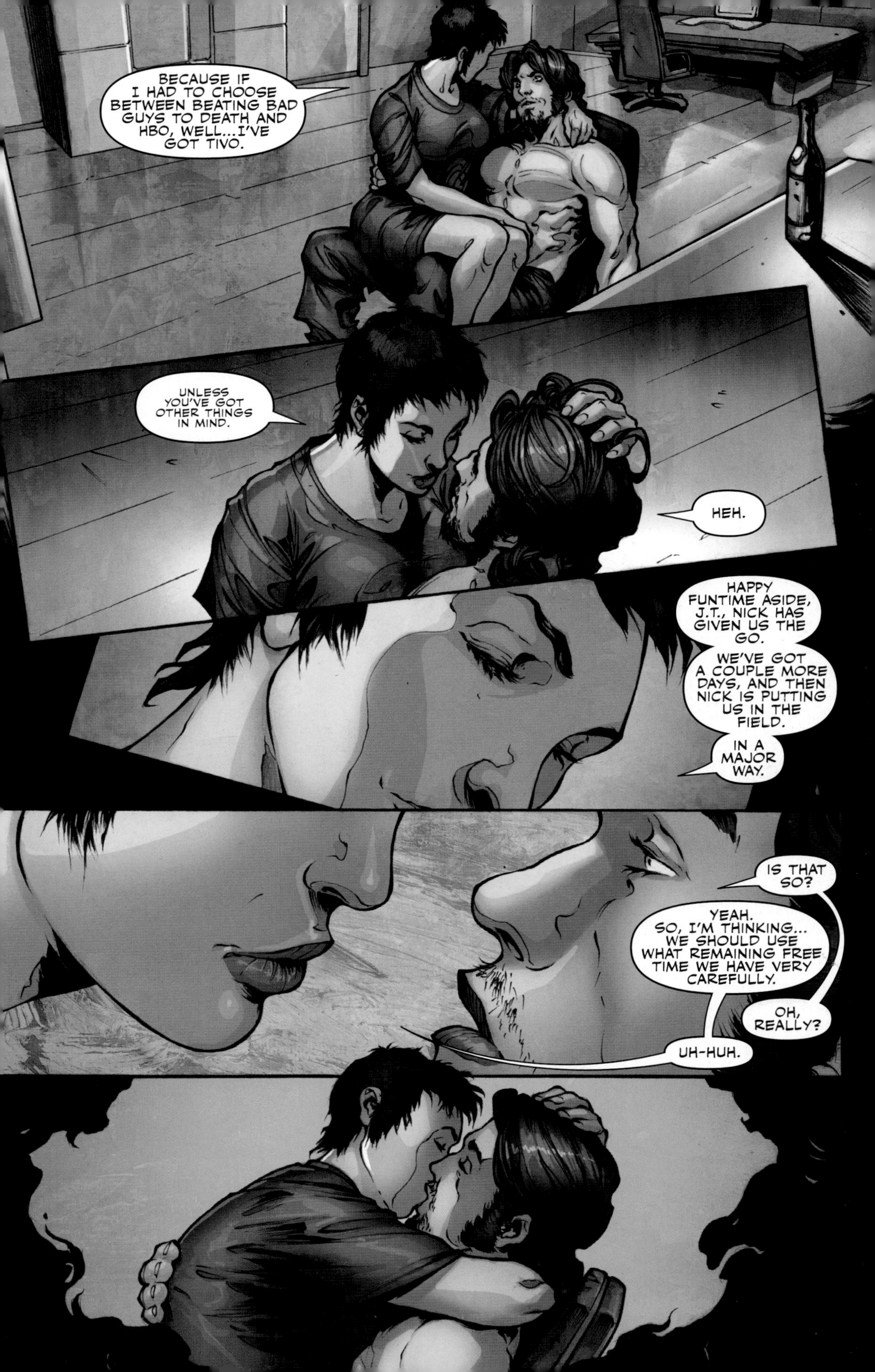
BECAUSE IF I HAD TO CHOOSE BETWEEN BEATING BAD GUYS TO DEATH AND HBO, WELL...I'VE GOT TIVO.
UNLESS YOU'VE GOT OTHER THINGS IN MIND.
HEH.
HAPPY FUNTIME ASIDE, J.T., NICK HAS GIVEN US THE GO.
WE'VE GOT A COUPLE MORE DAYS, AND THEN NICK IS PUTTING US IN THE FIELD.
IN A MAJOR WAY.
IS THAT SO?
YEAH. SO, I'M THINKING... WE SHOULD USE WHAT REMAINING FREE TIME WE HAVE VERY CAREFULLY.
OH, REALLY?
UH-HUH.

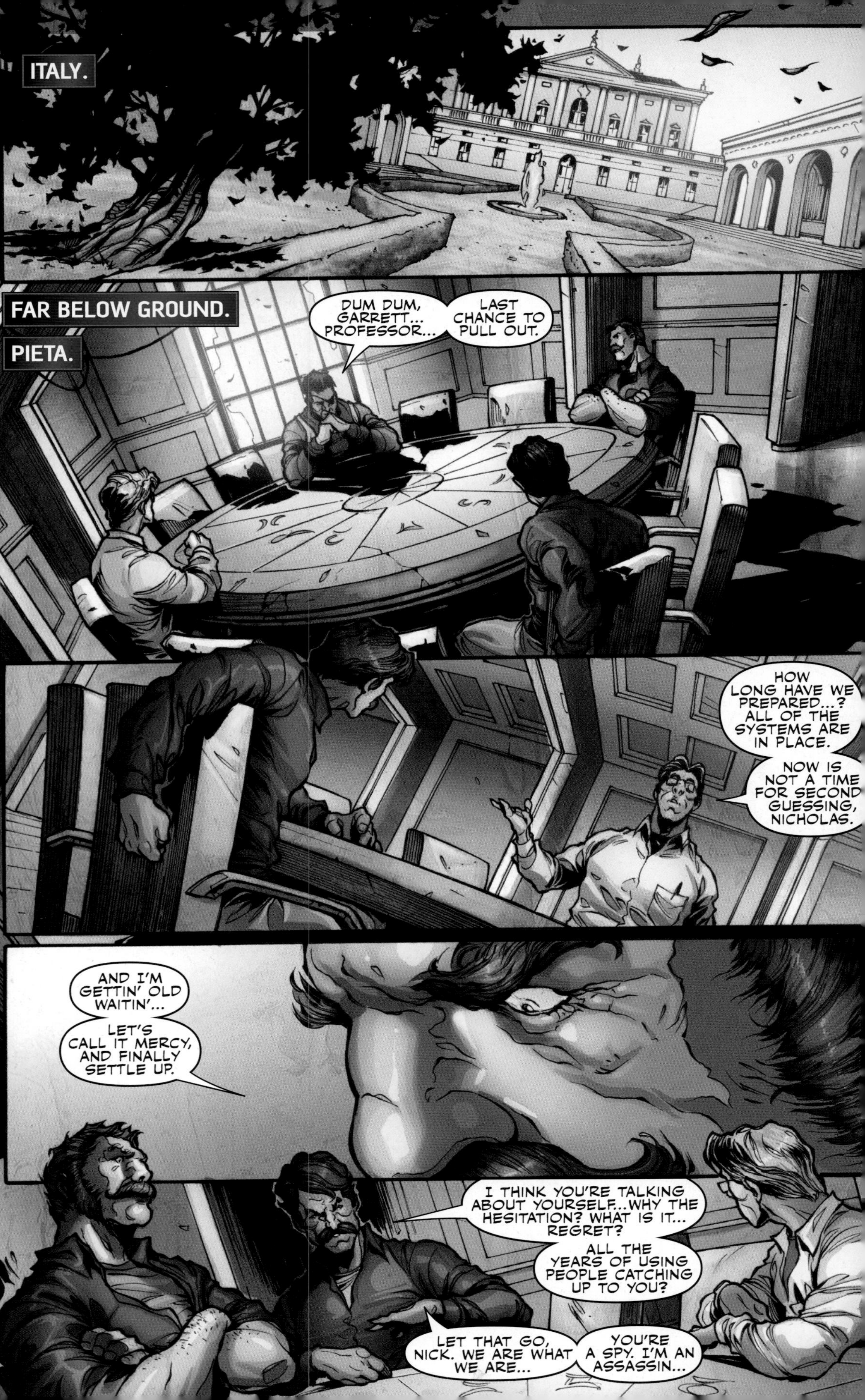

ITALY.
FAR BELOW GROUND.
PIETA.
DUM DUM, GARRETT... PROFESSOR...
LAST CHANCE TO PULL OUT.
HOW LONG HAVE WE PREPARED...? ALL OF THE SYSTEMS ARE IN PLACE.
NOW IS NOT A TIME FOR SECOND GUESSING, NICHOLAS.
AND I'M GETTIN' OLD WAITIN'...
LET'S CALL IT MERCY, AND FINALLY SETTLE UP.
I THINK YOU'RE TALKING ABOUT YOURSELF...WHY THE HESITATION? WHAT IS IT... REGRET?
ALL THE YEARS OF USING PEOPLE CATCHING UP TO YOU?
LET THAT GO, NICK. WE ARE WHAT WE ARE...
YOU'RE A SPY. I'M AN ASSASSIN...

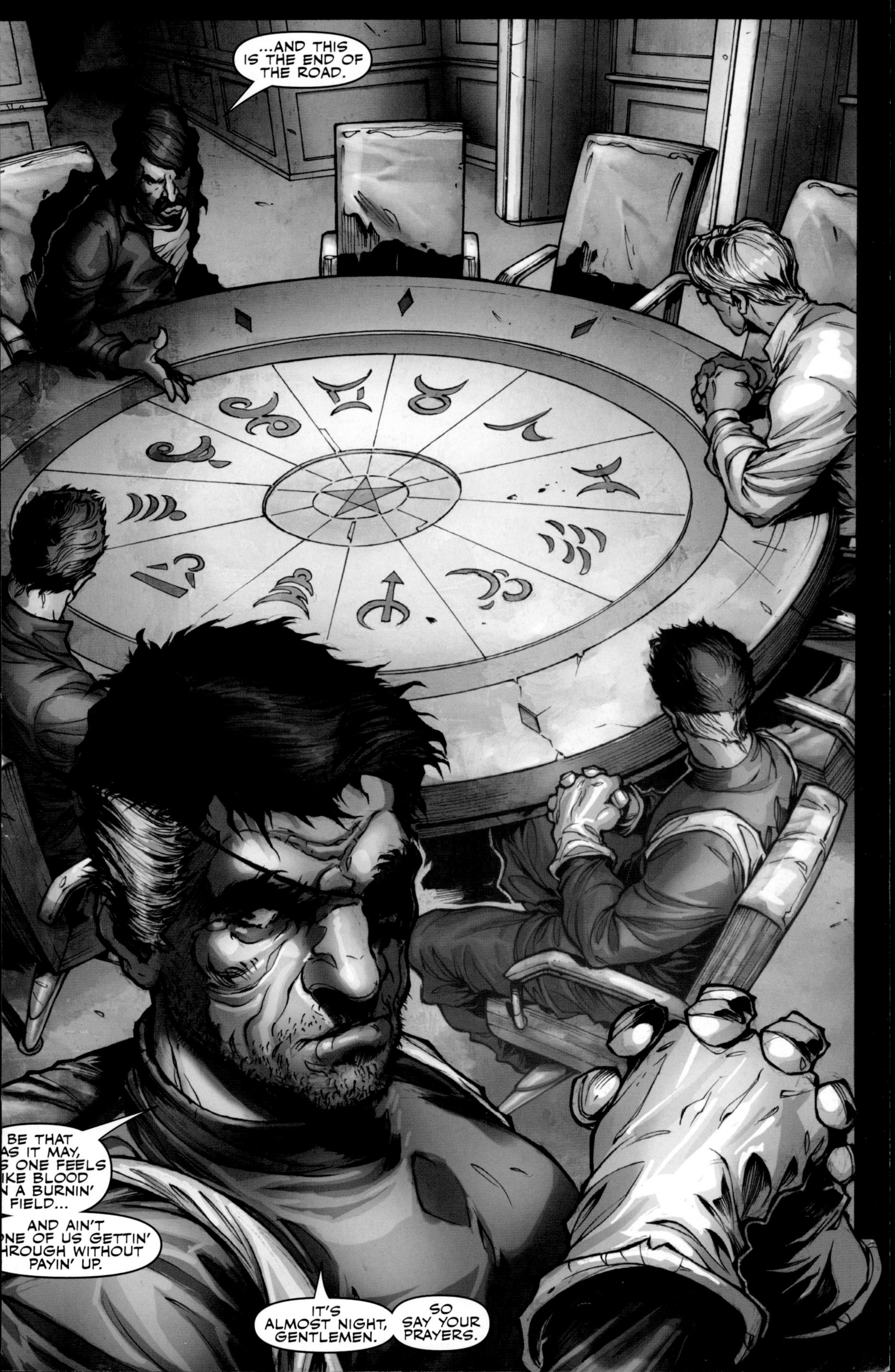
...AND THIS IS THE END OF THE ROAD.
BE THAT AS IT MAY, S ONE FEELS IKE BLOOD N A BURNIN' FIELD...
AND AIN'T NE OF US GETTIN' HROUGH WITHOUT PAYIN' UP.
IT'S ALMOST NIGHT, GENTLEMEN.
SO SAY YOUR PRAYERS.

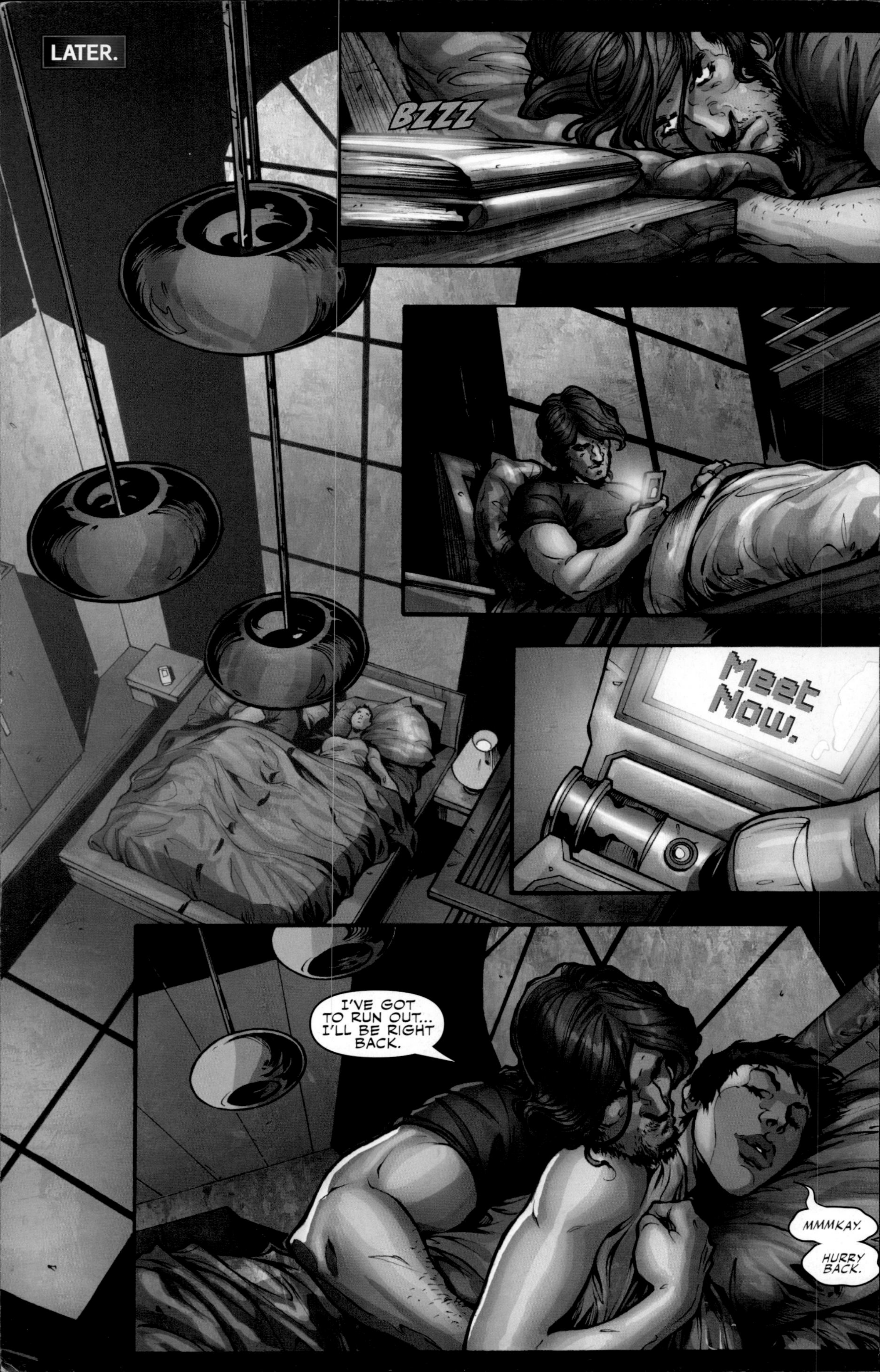
LATER.
BZZZ
Meet Now.
I'VE GOT TO RUN OUT... I'LL BE RIGHT BACK.
MMMKAY.
HURRY BACK.

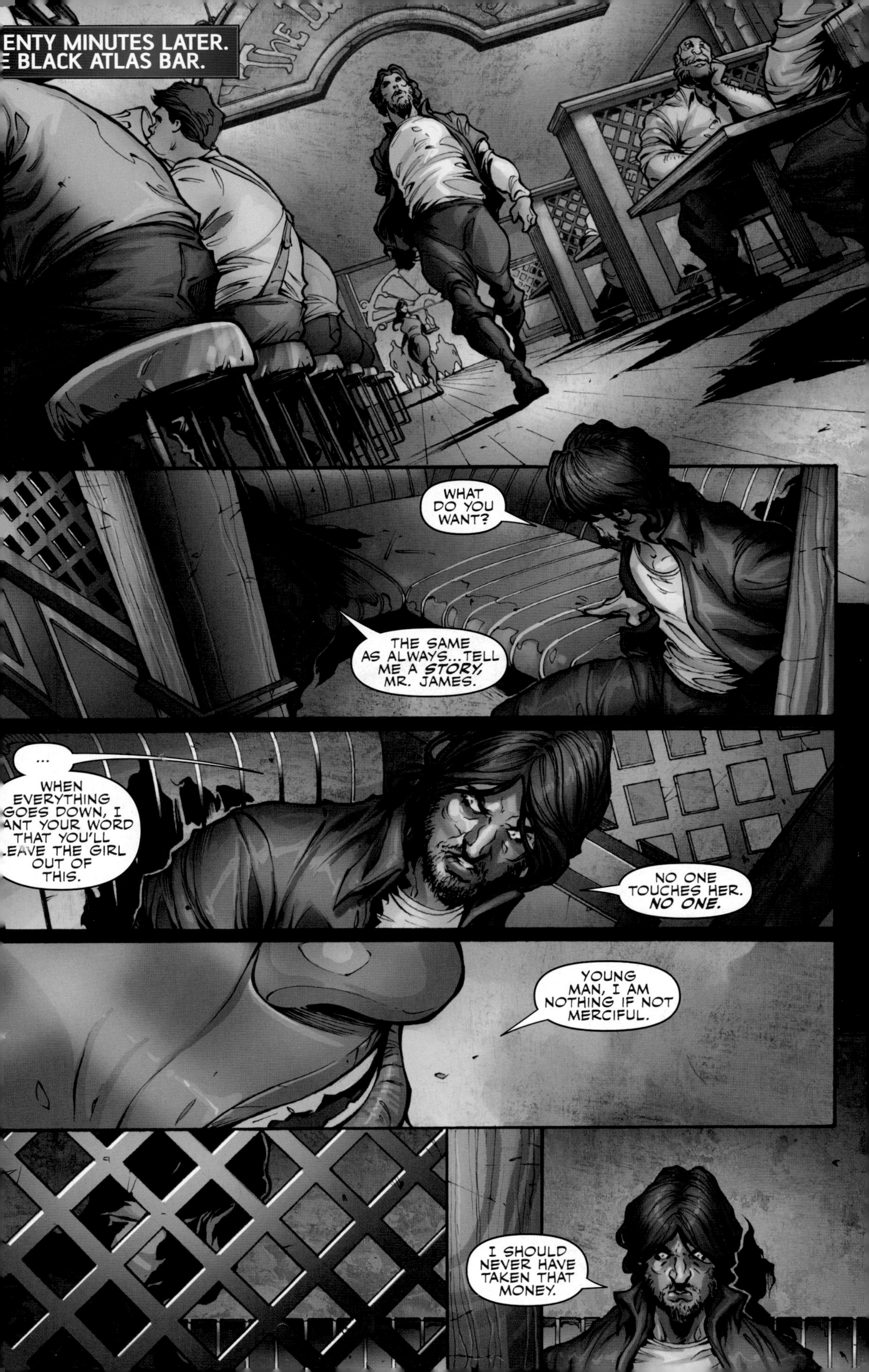
ENTY MINUTES LATER.
E BLACK ATLAS BAR.
WHAT DO YOU WANT?
THE SAME AS ALWAYS...TELL ME A *STORY,* MR. JAMES.
...
WHEN EVERYTHING GOES DOWN, I ANT YOUR WORD THAT YOU'LL EAVE THE GIRL OUT OF THIS.
NO ONE TOUCHES HER. *NO ONE.*
YOUNG MAN, I AM NOTHING IF NOT MERCIFUL.
I SHOULD NEVER HAVE TAKEN THAT MONEY.

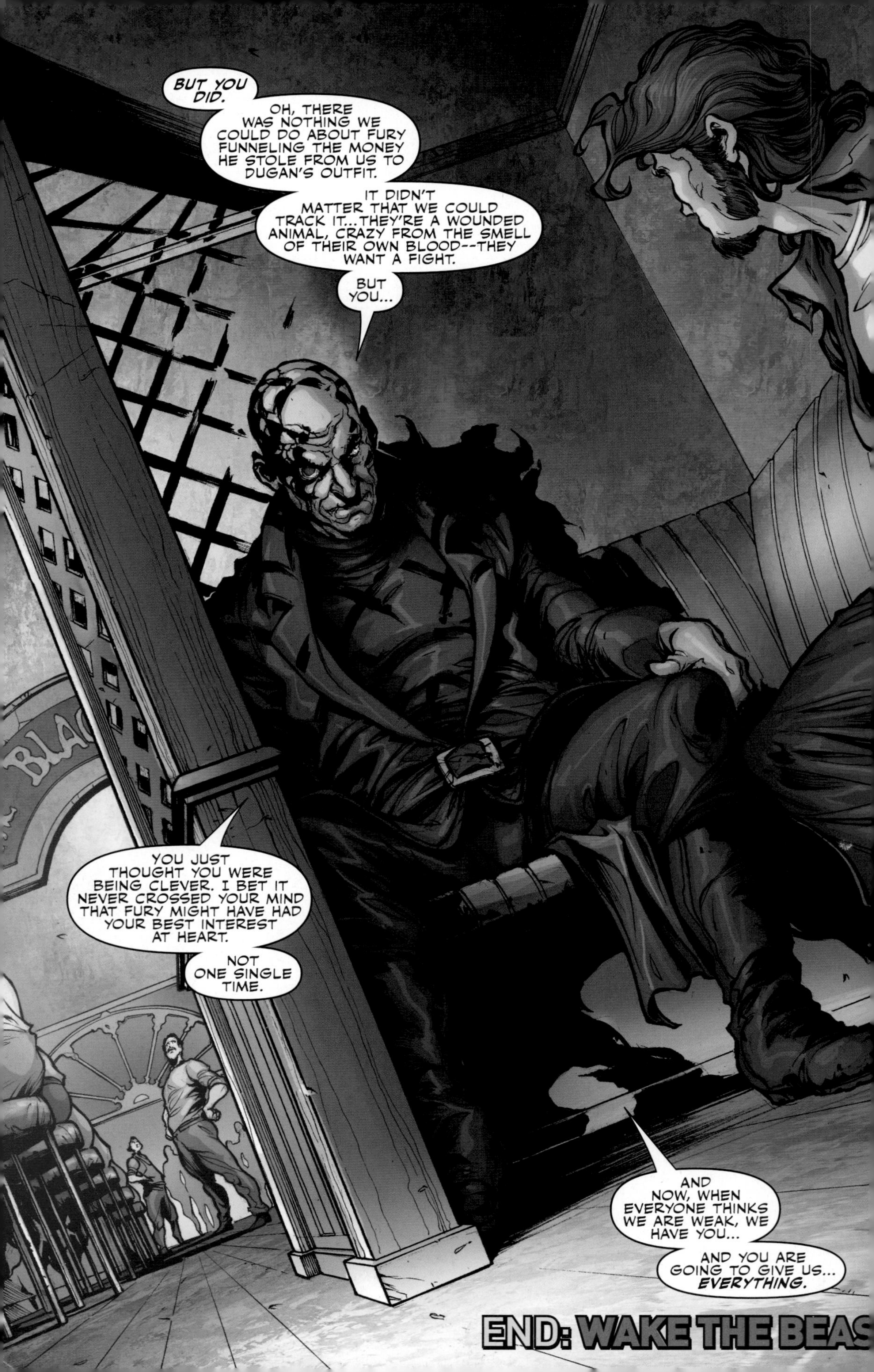
BUT YOU DID.
OH, THERE WAS NOTHING WE COULD DO ABOUT FURY FUNNELING THE MONEY HE STOLE FROM US TO DUGAN'S OUTFIT.
IT DIDN'T MATTER THAT WE COULD TRACK IT...THEY'RE A WOUNDED ANIMAL, CRAZY FROM THE SMELL OF THEIR OWN BLOOD--THEY WANT A FIGHT.
BUT YOU...
YOU JUST THOUGHT YOU WERE BEING CLEVER. I BET IT NEVER CROSSED YOUR MIND THAT FURY MIGHT HAVE HAD YOUR BEST INTEREST AT HEART.
NOT ONE SINGLE TIME.
AND NOW, WHEN EVERYONE THINKS WE ARE WEAK, WE HAVE YOU...
AND YOU ARE GOING TO GIVE US... *EVERYTHING.*
END: WAKE THE BEAS

COVER GALLERY
JIM CHEUNG

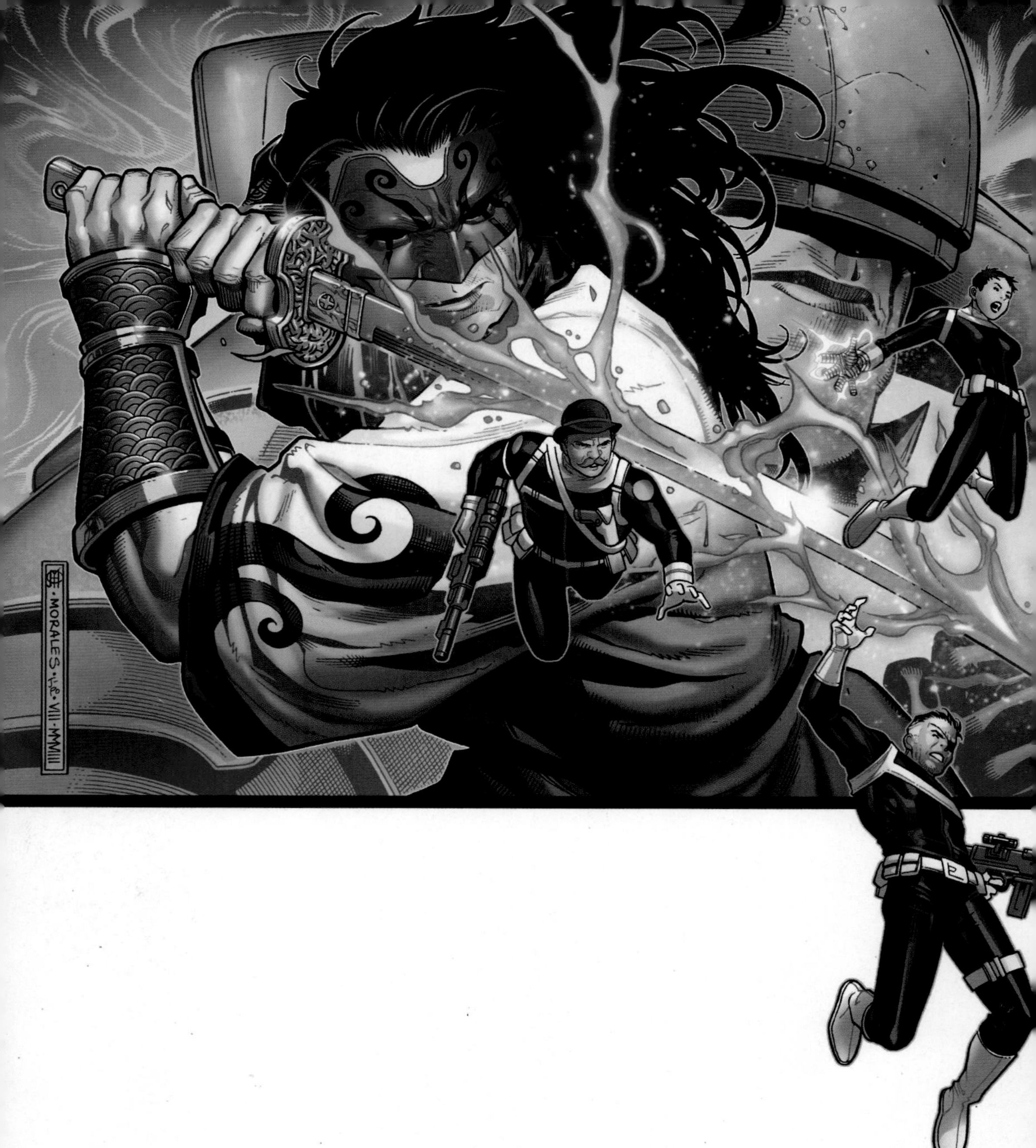
MORALES VIII·MMIII

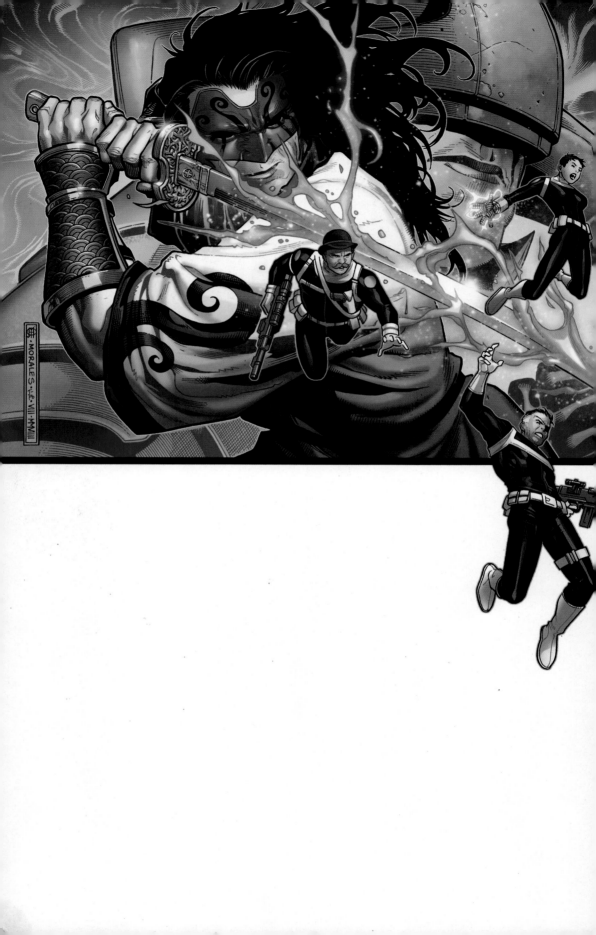

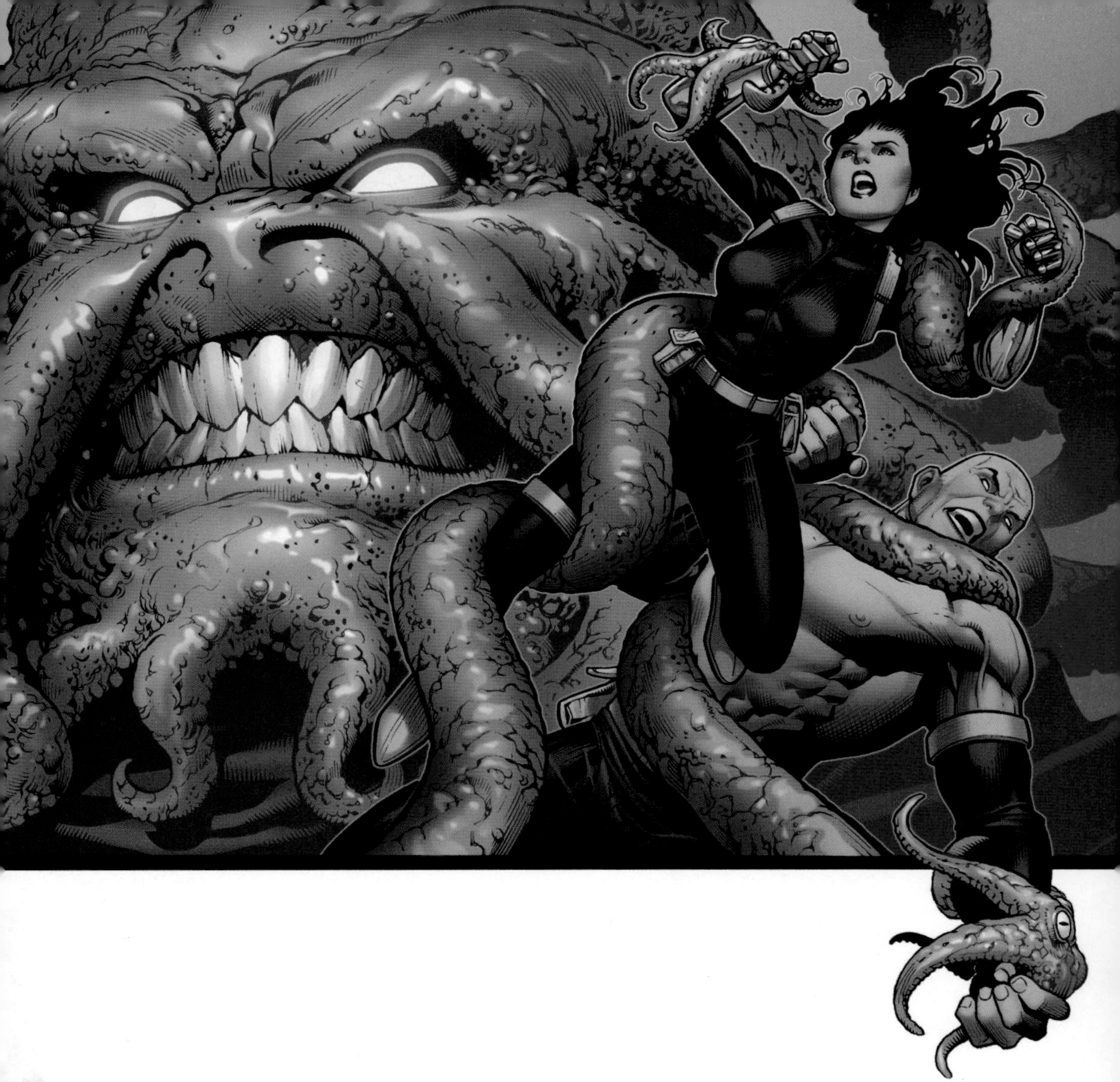

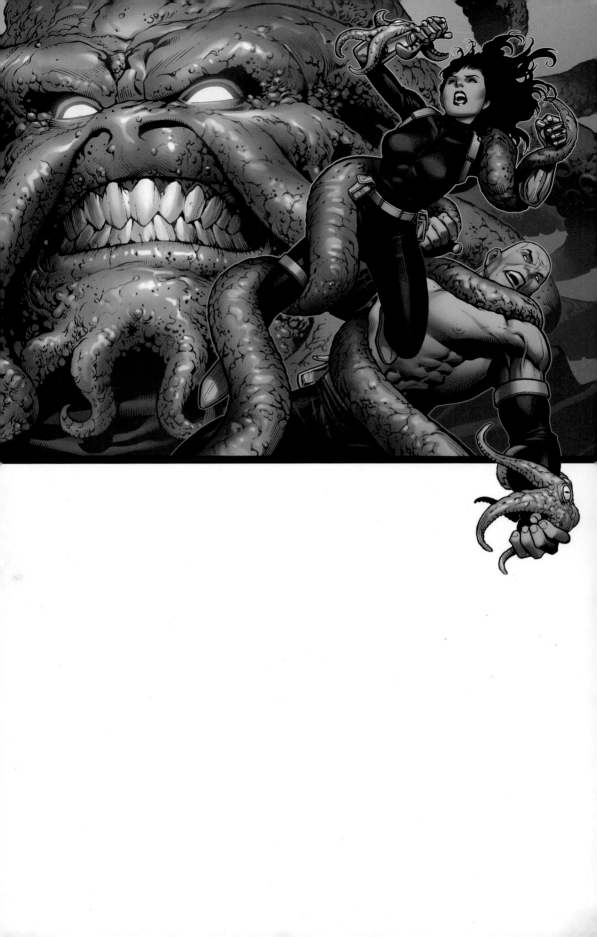

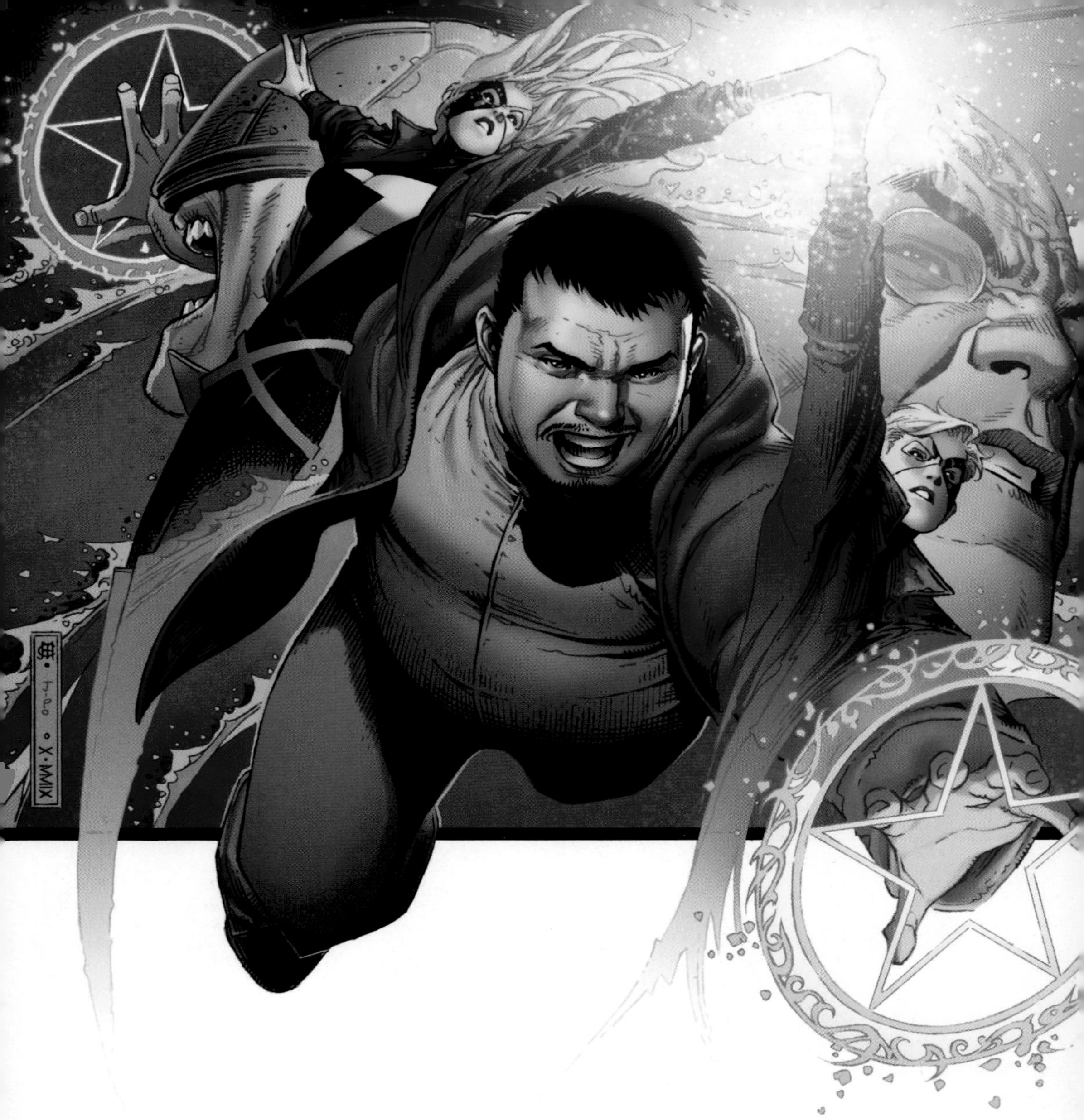

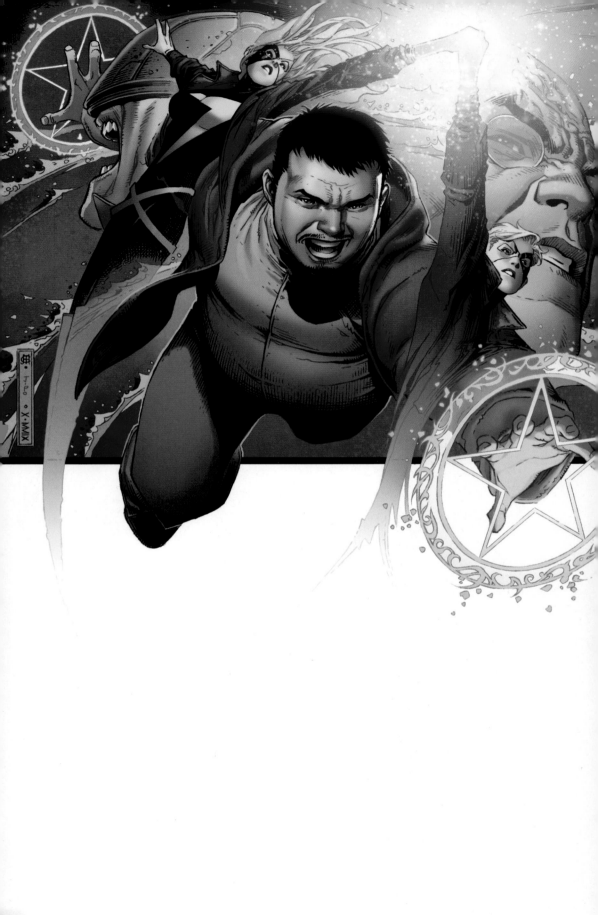

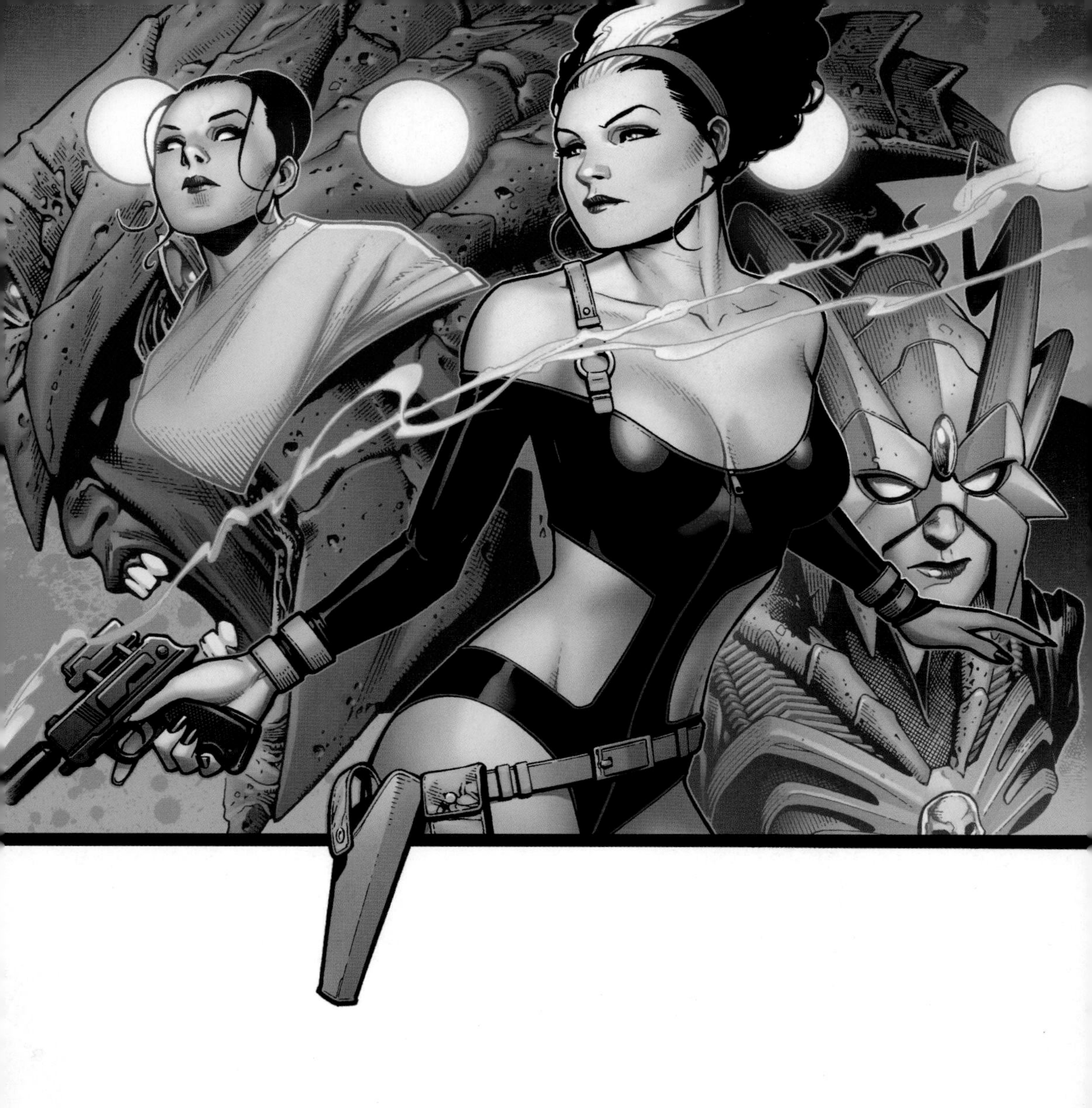

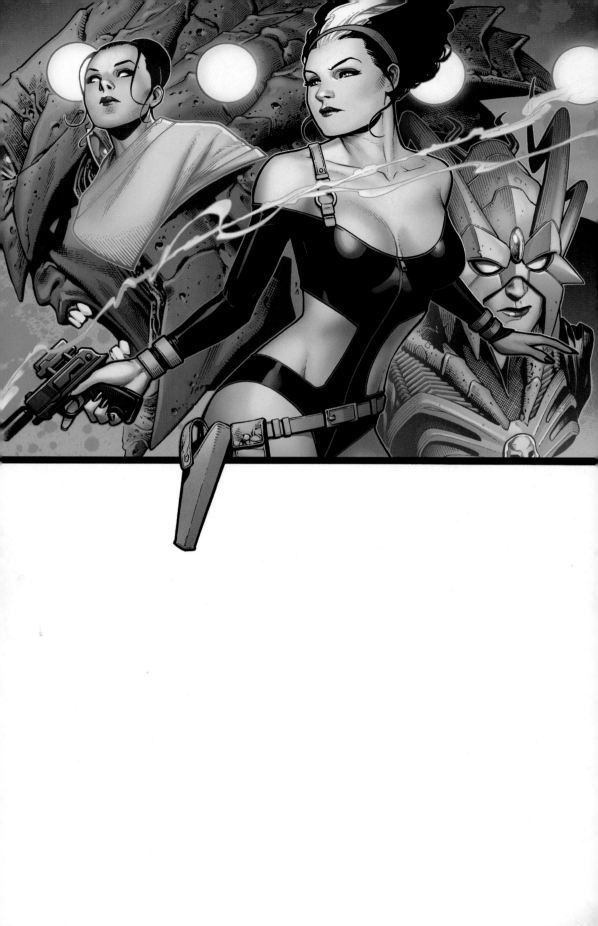

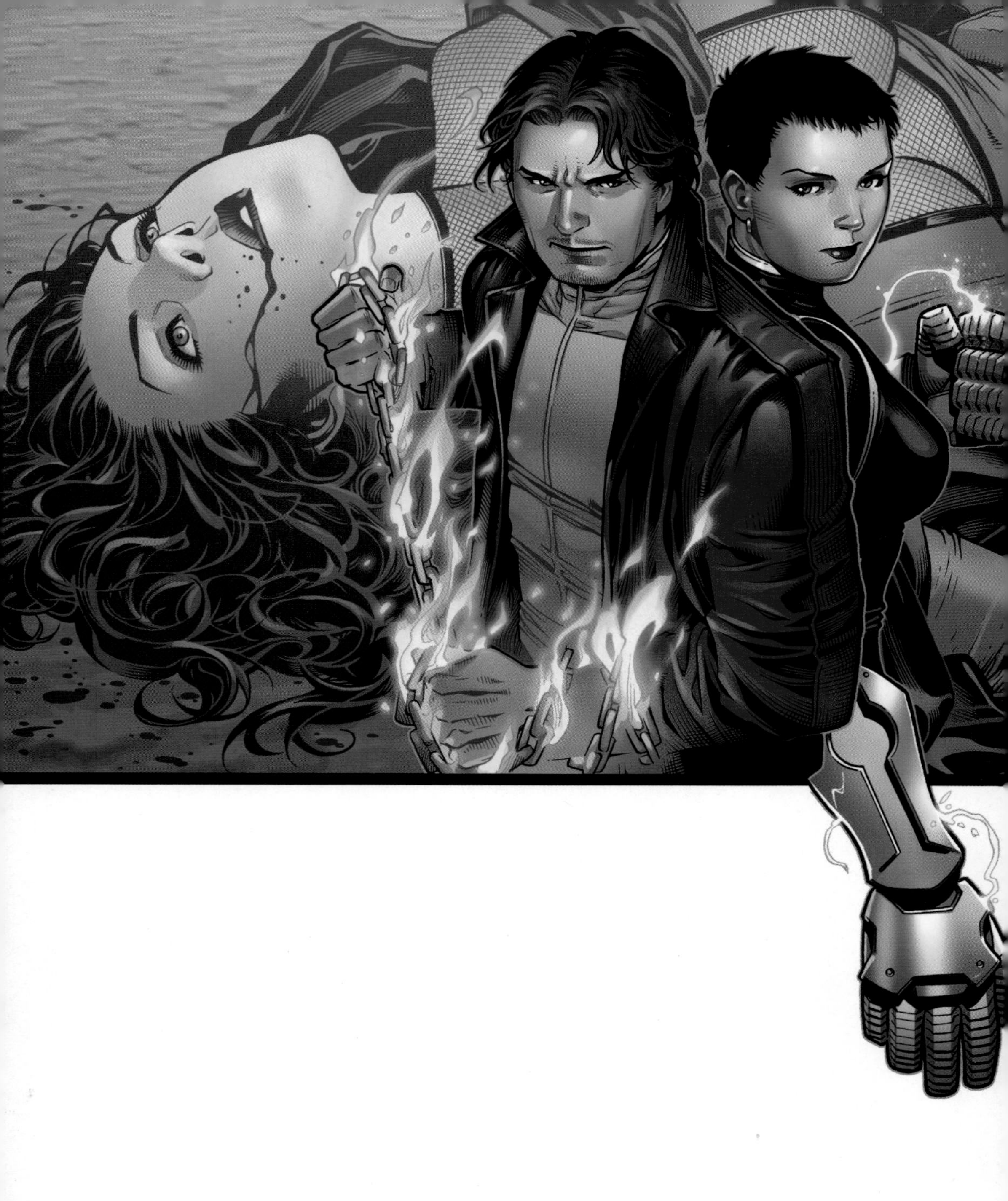

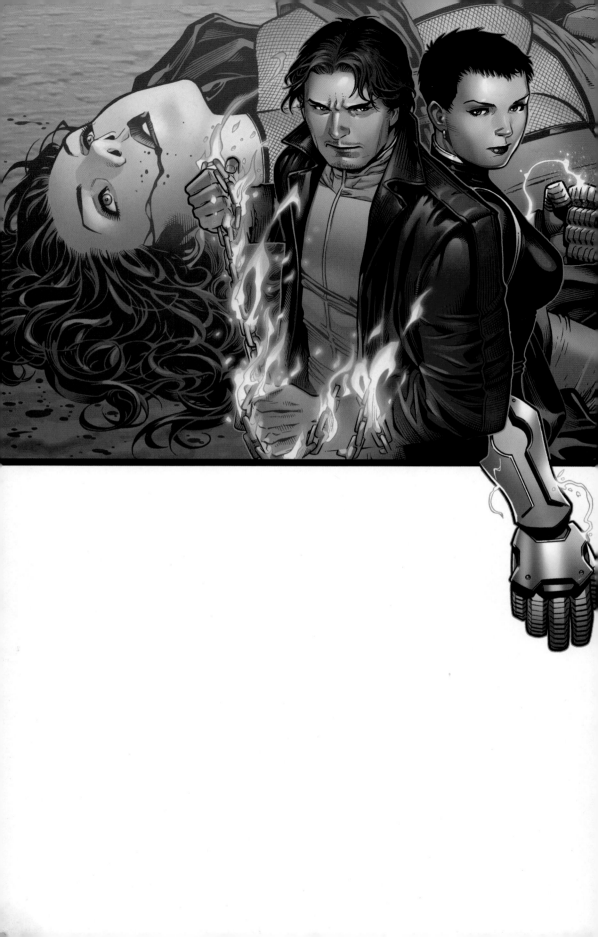

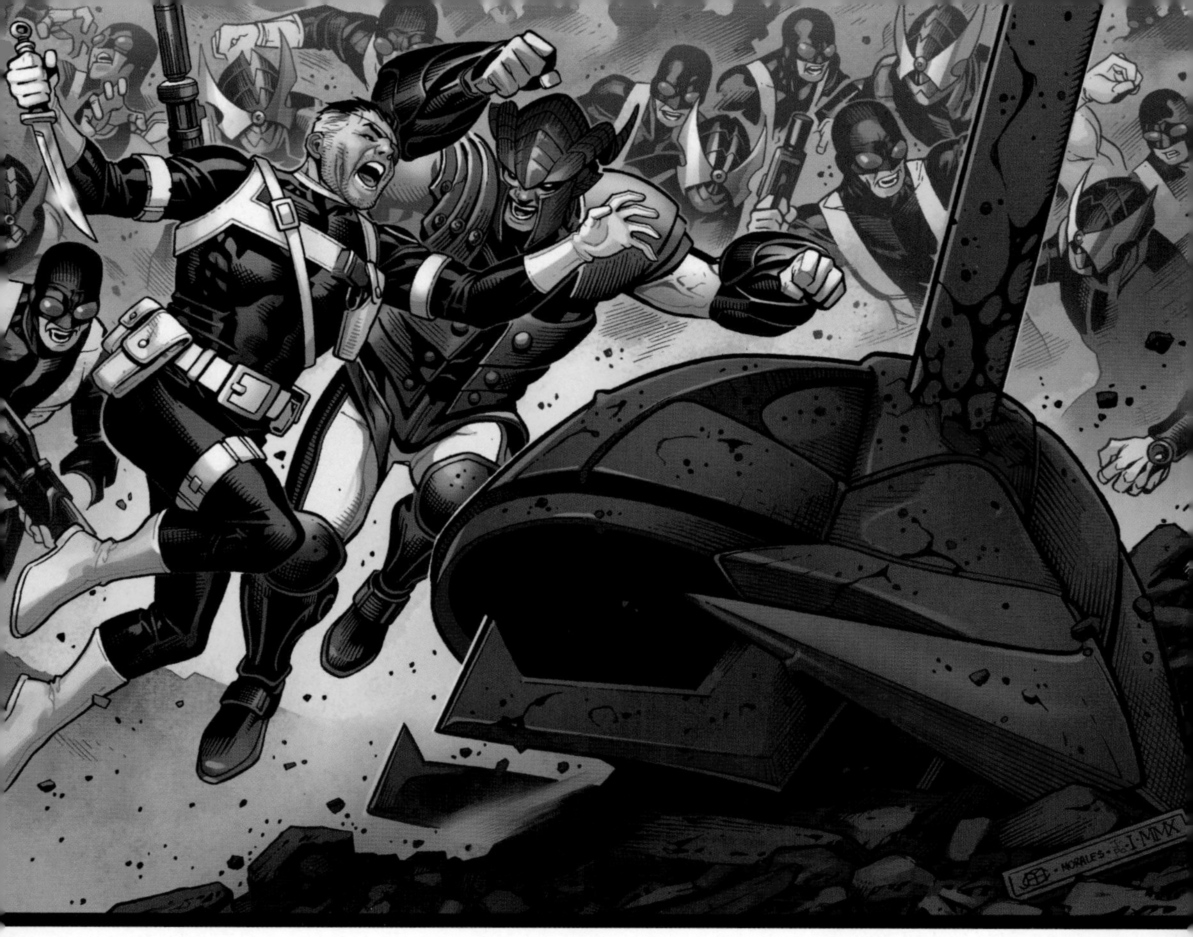
MORALES · I·MMX

ISSUE #16 HEROIC AGE VARIANT BY **MIKE PERKINS** & **MORRY HOLLOWELL**

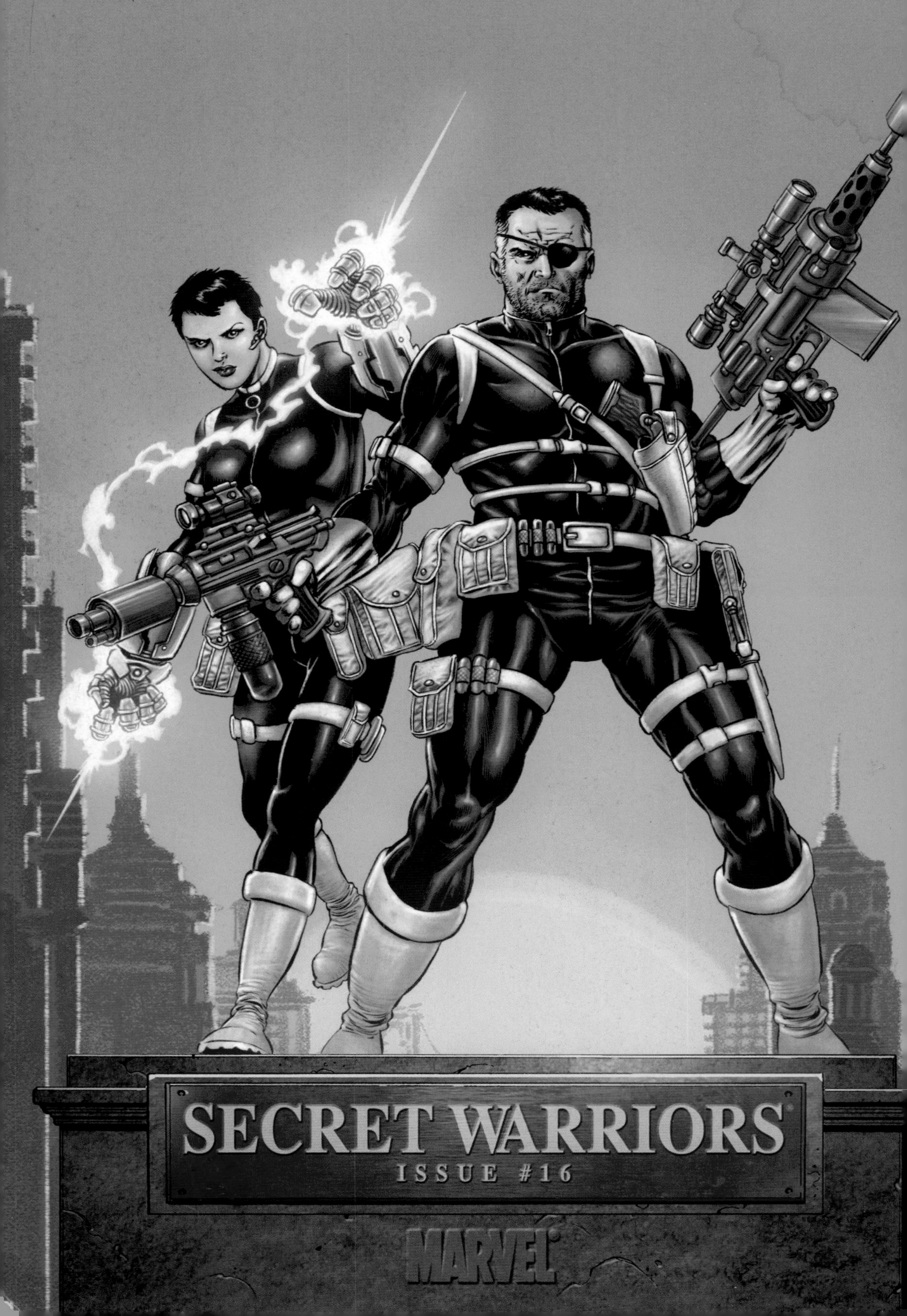
SECRET WARRIORS
ISSUE #16
MARVEL

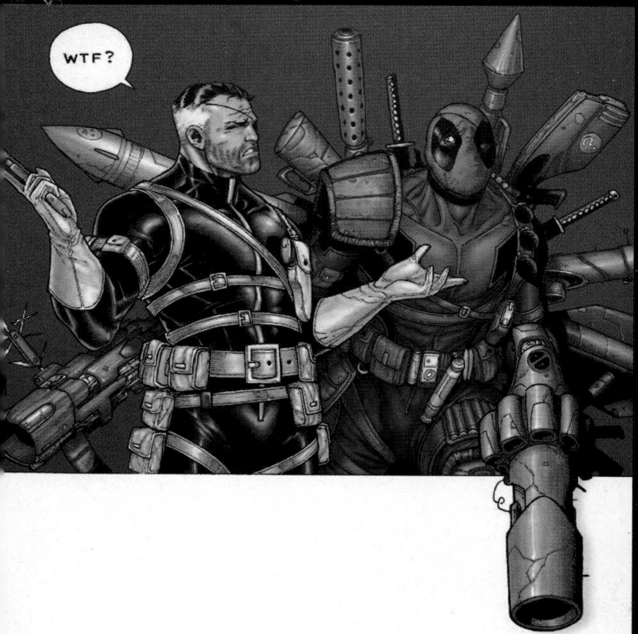
WTF?

ISSUE #15 IRON MAN BY DESIGN VARIANT BY **NIC KLEIN**

SUE #13 DEADPOOL VARIANT BY **KHOI PHAM & MORRY HOLLOWELL**

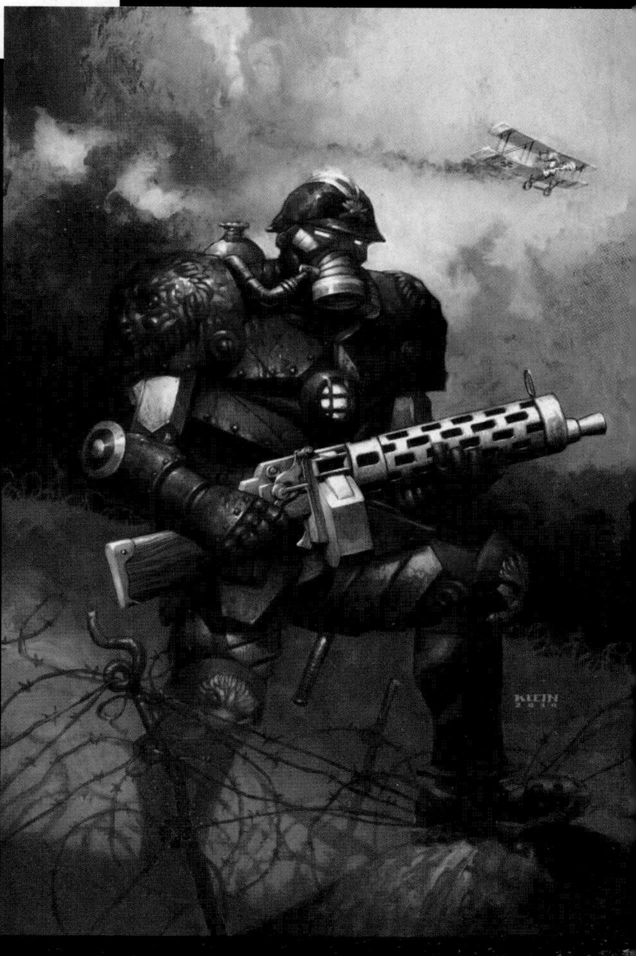